D0207756

systems programming

RICHARD W. HAMMING
Bell Telephone Laboratories

EDWARD A. FEIGENBAUM
Stanford University

systems programming
JOHN J. DONOVAN

Project MAC,
Massachusetts Institute of Technology

McGraw-Hill Book Company
New York   St. Louis   San Francisco   Düsseldorf   Johannesburg
Kuala Lumpur   London   Mexico   Montreal   New Delhi
Panama   Rio de Janeiro   Singapore   Sydney   Toronto

SYSTEMS PROGRAMMING

Library of Congress Catalog Card Number 79-172263

07-017603-5

10 DODO 7987

This book was set in Press Roman by Allen-Wayne,
and printed and bound by R. R. Donnelley & Sons.
The designer was Allen-Wayne.
The editor was Richard F. Dojny.
Alice Cohen supervised production.

To
6.251
Teaching Assistants

contents

preface

SCOPE

In this book we address ourselves to the full spectrum of systems programming endeavors, including the use and implementation of assemblers, macros, loaders, compilers, and operating systems. We present each of these components in detail, exposing the pertinent design issues. The issues are discussed within the context of modern computer languages and advanced operating systems; it is recognized that in addition to the traditional compiler problem of syntax and semantics, we now have storage allocation and accessing methods to contend with, and that file systems, multiprocessing, and multiprogramming are now commonplace in operating systems. To introduce the more formal aspects of computer science, we have included a presentation of formal systems and their application to programming languages.

The book is written as a text, with problems and exercises, with particular emphasis on the problems and examples. We have assumed that the reader has had experience in some high level language.

An attempt has been made to keep the book as machine-independent as possible; the text has, in fact, been used in conjunction with several different types of machines. However, to add substance to the book, we have taken specific examples from an IBM 360/370 type machine and, in our discussion of compilers, from languages with features like those exhibited in PL/I.

The book covers material contained in six courses of Curriculum 68 as described by the Association of Computing Machinery (ACM) Curriculum Committee in Computer Science.[1] The basic course, Computer Organization and

---

[1] As documented in the Communications of the Association of Computing Machinery (CACM), vol. 11, no. 3, p. 151 (March 1968).

Programming (B2), is covered in Chapters 1 through 5; Programming Languages (12) and Compiler Construction (15), are covered in Chapters 6, 7, and 8; Systems Programming (14); Advanced Computer Organization (A2); and Large Scale Information Systems (A8) are covered in Chapter 9.

MAIN USES

We feel that the book has three major uses: (1) as an undergraduate text in a one- or two-semester course on systems programming; (2) as a book for professionals; and (3) as a reference for graduate students.

More specifically, the book has been used to meet the needs of the following types of courses:

1. A first course in the undergraduate computer science curriculum (following an introductory programming course, e.g., FORTRAN, PL/I).
2. A general Institute service course for non-computer scientists.
3. An advanced course in software.
4. A software engineering course emphasizing practical issues.
5. An extensive review or introductory course for graduate students in computer science.

At M.I.T. the book is used in the undergraduate course 6.251, Digital Computer Programming Systems. There is a tradition and excitement associated with the course, and it is one of the most highly subscribed elective courses, having as many as 350 students per semester. I am also told that it is one of the most challenging. At M.I.T. the course is used to meet all of the above needs.

We have also used the material as a two-semester graduate course. In the first semester we dealt with the topics of machine organization, assemblers, macros, loaders, I/O programming, and operating systems (Chapter 1, 2, 3, 4, 5, and parts of 9). In the second we discussed programming languages, design of compilers, formal systems, and other aspects of operating systems not covered in the first semester (Chapters 6, 7, 8, 9).

The course has been given at several industrial firms: Honeywell, U. S. Underwater Systems Center, Martin Marietta, and others, where it focused mainly on the design issues of these system components, and omitted the formal systems aspects (Chapter 7).

This text was used to give an intensive course in programming at SESA in France, and also for the sequence of computer courses included in a two-year technical program at the Lowell School in Boston.

At Texas Tech University in Lubbock, Texas the programming course was first taught by using the video tapes of the lectures at M.I.T., which were sent to Texas for replay in the subsequent week. This method of transferring the course proved to be effective, since the undergraduates in Texas took the same quizzes and exams as did the M.I.T. students, and there was no appreciable difference in grades. Video tapes of the course are available, and may be obtained by writing the author at M.I.T.

At M.I.T. the machine used in conjunction with this course was the IBM 360/370 type computer. At U. S. Underwater Sound Laboratories a UNIVAC 1108 was employed, while at Honeywell various Honeywell machines were used.

It is helpful for students to have had experience with assembly language and PL/I, though we have found that in many cases they have had neither. Some students have been able to use Chapters 2 and 6 as an introduction to assembly language and PL/I, especially in conjunction with reference manuals and lectures.

If used by professionals or graduate students, the book is self-sufficient in that there are enough details for 370 and PL/I to support the rest of the material.

In addition to discussing the traditional system components of assemblers and macros, the book gives special emphasis to important features of systems programming presently not covered in many texts—compilers, the advanced problems of storage allocation, recursion, operating systems, and I/O programming.

The problems are designed to be expository and solutions are available in the Teacher's Manual. Also included in the Teacher's Manual are sample syllabuses, quizzes, and helpful hints in presenting material.

acknowledgments

This book itself is an acknowledgment to the intensity, drive, and technical competence of the many individuals who have contributed to it. I list here only a few of the contributors.

One individual, Mr. Stuart Madnick, stands apart from all other contributors to this book. Mr. Madnick is the most competent systems programmer I know. He worked with me for five years, both as a teaching assistant and lecturer, on the M.I.T. course (Digital Computer Programming Systems) that uses this book. He is responsible for the presentation of the material file systems and the view of operating systems, and he has read and contributed to every chapter. I wish to thank him for both his technical contributions and his loyalty.

The M.I.T. course on Digital Computer Programming Systems has evolved from the contributions that every lecturer associated with it has made. We list these lecturers here.

1959	Professor F. Verzuh
1960	Professor F. J. Corbató
1961	Professor W. Poduska, N. Haller
1962	Professor J. Saltzer
1963	Professors C. L. Liu, D. Kuck, F. J. Corbató, D. Thornhill
1964	Professors J. Saltzer, D. Kuck, R. Fabry, T. Stockham
1965	Professors W. Poduska, L. Hatfield, R. Baecker, R. M. Graham
1966	Professor R. M. Graham
1967 – Present	Professor J. J. Donovan

It is difficult to state the exact contributions of each lecturer, as course content has evolved from assemblers to include loaders, compilers, searching techniques, debugging techniques, and recently, operating systems. Professor Corbató set the philosophy and introduced the case study method, and my immediate predecessor, Professor Graham, greatly influenced my thinking, as he taught me many of the fundamentals.

During the past five years, with the help of many teaching assistants, we reconstructed the course around the IBM 360, introducing the direct-linking loading schemes, PL/I, advanced compiling techniques, memory, processor management, and most recently, I/O programming.

Each year an excellent group of teaching assistants has worked with me on the course, which has enrollments as high as 350 students a semester. We owe much to these assistants both for their administrative help and for their ingenuity in handling the diverse needs of the students. The head teaching assistants in the past few years were Stuart Madnick, Steven Zilles, Richard Mulhern, William Michels, and Glen Brunk, but many others helped and contributed in countless ways, especially in problem sets. To name a few: David Quimby, Jerry Johnson, Michael Hammer, Benjamin Ashton, Orville Dodson, Steven Halfich, Norman Kohn, Martin Jack, Al Moulton, Chander Ramchandani, and Harris Berman. Mrs. Muriel Webber did the diagrams, and Max Byer contributed in the administration of the course at M.I.T.

A tremendous team effort by the following individuals has given this book its quality: William Michels contributed greatly to the compiler chapter; Norman Kohn to the macro and formal systems chapters and to the compilation of the references; Sterling Eanes proofread the formal systems and compilers chapters, and David Quimby assisted in assembling the problems and commenting on early drafts of the book. Leonard Goodman proofread the entire book—I thank him for the errors that are not here. Mr. David M. Jones edited the manuscript. Ellen Nangle supervised the typing and preparation of the manuscript—she cared. She further edited the manuscript, problems, solutions and teacher's manual.

Work reported herein was supported in part by Project MAC, an M.I.T. research project sponsored by the Advanced Research Projects Agency, Department of Defense, under Office of Naval Research Contract Nonr-4102(01), and in part by the Electrical Engineering Department of M.I.T.

Finally—and I hesitate to say this because it seems like a formality when I read it, which it is not—I simply and sincerely thank my wife and five children. I thank them for their patience, support, and endurance of my working essentially twenty-four hours a day, seven days a week for the past two years and for the long hours previous to that in preparation of this manuscript.

John J. Donovan

note to the student

This book does not presuppose extensive knowledge of assembly language although students with some experience in this language will find the material easier to approach. Chapter 2 contains basic information on assembly-language programming, Chapter 6 on high level languages, PL/I in particular. Students may wish to refer to additional sources on assembly language programming and PL/I.

Chapters 8 and 9 (Compilers and Operating Systems) are long and dense. (Entire courses have been built around the material in these chapters.) While both these chapters, like all the others in the book, are logical entities, we have divided them, for your convenience, into parts that are more manageable.

To be competent in any technical field, and particularly in one developing as rapidly as that of computer science, it is important to be familiar with the current literature. Chapter 10 contains references. Use them.

The book does presuppose familiarity with programming. The inexperienced reader should not therefore be discouraged if he finds the material difficult because of its depth and density.

This material is basic to computer science, and we believe that the student who explores it in depth will find it both relevant and exciting. I know of no other formal way of acquiring this material.

systems programming

1

background

This book has two major objectives: to teach procedures for the design of software systems and to provide a basis for judgement in the design of software. To facilitate our task, we have taken specific examples from systems programs. We discuss the design and implementation of the major system components.

What is systems programming? You may visualize a computer as some sort of beast that obeys all commands. It has been said that computers are basically people made out of metal or, conversely, people are computers made out of flesh and blood. However, once we get close to computers, we see that they are basically machines that follow very specific and primitive instructions.

In the early days of computers, people communicated with them by *on* and *off* switches denoting primitive instructions. Soon people wanted to give more complex instructions. For example, they wanted to be able to say $X = 30 * Y$; given that $Y = 10$, what is X? Present day computers cannot understand such language without the aid of systems programs. Systems programs (e.g., compilers, loaders, macro processors, operating systems) were developed to make computers better adapted to the needs of their users. Further, people wanted more assistance in the mechanics of preparing their programs.

Compilers are systems programs that accept people-like languages and translate them into machine language. Loaders are systems programs that prepare machine language programs for execution. Macro processors allow programmers to use abbreviations. Operating systems and file systems allow flexible storing and retrieval of information (Fig. 1.1).

There are over 100,000 computers in use now in virtually every application. The productivity of each computer is heavily dependent upon the effectiveness, efficiency, and sophistication of the systems programs.

In this chapter we introduce some terminology and outline machine structure and the basic tasks of an operating system.

1

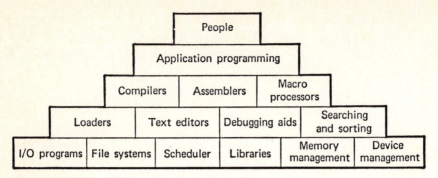

FIGURE 1.1 Foundations of systems programming

1.1 MACHINE STRUCTURE

We begin by sketching the general hardware organization of a computer system (Fig. 1.2).

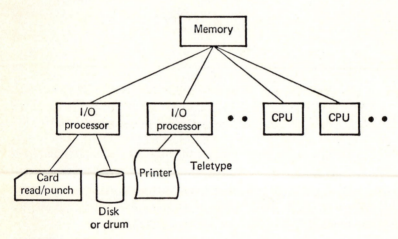

FIGURE 1.2 General hardware organization of a computer system

Memory is the device where information is stored. *Processors* are the devices that operate on this information. One may view information as being stored in the form of ones and zeros. Each one or zero is a separate binary digit called a *bit*. Bits are typically grouped in units that are called words, characters, or *bytes*. Memory locations are specified by *addresses*, where each address identifies a specific byte, word, or character.

The contents of a word may be interpreted as *data* (values to be operated on) or *instructions* (operations to be performed). A processor is a device that performs a sequence of operations specified by instructions in memory. A *program* (or procedure) is a sequence of instructions.

Memory may be thought of as mailboxes containing groups of ones and zeros. Below we depict a series of memory locations whose addresses are 10,000 through 10,002.

Address	Contents
10,000	0000 0000 0000 0001
10,001	0011 0000 0000 0000
10,002	0000 0000 0000 0100

An IBM 1130 processor treating location 10,001 as an instruction would interpret its contents as a "halt" instruction. Treating the same location as numerical data, the processor would interpret its contents as the binary number 0011 0000 0000 0000 (decimal 12,288). Thus instructions and data share the same storage medium.

Information in memory is coded into groups of bits that may be interpreted as characters, instructions, or numbers. A *code* is a set of rules for interpreting groups of bits, e.g., codes for representation of decimal digits (BCD), for characters (EBCDIC, or ASCII), or for instructions (specific processor operation codes). We have depicted two types of processors: *Input/Output* (I/O) processors and *Central Processing Units* (CPUs). The I/O processors are concerned with the transfer of data between memory and peripheral devices such as disks, drums, printers, and typewriters. The CPUs are concerned with manipulations of data stored in memory. The I/O processors execute I/O instructions that are stored in memory; they are generally activated by a command from the CPU. Typically, this consists of an "execute I/O" instruction whose argument is the address of the start of the I/O program. The CPU interprets this instruction and passes the argument to the I/O processor (commonly called I/O channels).

The I/O instruction set may be entirely different from that of the CPU and may be executed *asynchronously* (simultaneously) with CPU operation. Asynchronous operation of I/O channels and CPUs was one of the earliest forms of *multiprocessing*. Multiprocessing means having more than one processor operating on the same memory simultaneously.

Since instructions, like data, are stored in memory and can be treated as data, by changing the bit configuration of an instruction — adding a number to it — we may change it to a different instruction. Procedures that modify themselves are called *impure* procedures. Writing such procedures is poor programming practice. Other programmers find them difficult to read, and moreover they cannot be shared by multiple processors. Each processor executing an impure procedure modifies its contents. Another processor attempting to execute the same procedure may encounter different instructions or data. Thus, impure procedures are not readily reusable. A *pure* procedure does not modify itself. To ensure that the instructions are the same each time a program is used, pure procedures (*re-entrant code*) are employed.

1.2　EVOLUTION OF THE COMPONENTS OF A PROGRAMMING SYSTEM

1.2.1　Assemblers

Let us review some aspects of the development of the components of a programming system.

At one time, the computer programmer had at his disposal a basic machine that interpreted, through hardware, certain fundamental instructions. He would program this computer by writing a series of ones and zeros (machine language), place them into the memory of the machine, and press a button, whereupon the computer would start to interpret them as instructions.

Programmers found it difficult to write or read programs in machine language. In their quest for a more convenient language they began to use a *mnemonic* (symbol) for each machine instruction, which they would subsequently translate into machine language. Such a mnemonic machine language is now called an *assembly language*. Programs known as *assemblers* were written to automate the translation of assembly language into machine language. The input to an assembler program is called the *source program*; the output is a machine language translation (*object program*).

1.2.2　Loaders

Once the assembler produces an object program, that program must be placed into memory and executed. It is the purpose of the loader to assure that object programs are placed in memory in an executable form.

The assembler could place the object program directly in memory and transfer control to it, thereby causing the machine language program to be executed.

However, this would waste core[1] by leaving the assembler in memory while the user's program was being executed. Also the programmer would have to retranslate his program with each execution, thus wasting translation time. To overcome the problems of wasted translation time and wasted memory, systems programmers developed another component, called the loader.

A *loader* is a program that places programs into memory and prepares them for execution. In a simple loading scheme, the assembler outputs the machine language translation of a program on a secondary storage device and a loader is placed in core. The loader places into memory the machine language version of the user's program and transfers control to it. Since the loader program is much smaller than the assembler, this makes more core available to the user's program.

The realization that many users were writing virtually the same programs led to the development of "ready-made" programs (packages). These packages were written by the computer manufacturers or the users. As the programmer became more sophisticated, he wanted to mix and combine ready-made programs with his own. In response to this demand, a facility was provided whereby the user could write a main program that used several other programs or subroutines. A *subroutine* is a body of computer instructions designed to be used by other routines to accomplish a task. There are two types of subroutines: closed and open subroutines. An *open subroutine* or *macro definition* is one whose code is inserted into the main program (flow continues). Thus if the same open subroutine were called four times, it would appear in four different places in the calling program. A *closed subroutine* can be stored outside the main routine, and control transfers to the subroutine. Associated with the closed subroutine are two tasks the main program must perform: transfer of control and transfer of data.

Initially, closed subroutines had to be loaded into memory at a specific address. For example, if a user wished to employ a square root subroutine, he would have to write his main program so that it would transfer to the location assigned to the square root routine (SQRT). His program and the subroutine would be assembled together. If a second user wished to use the same subroutine, he also would assemble it along with his own program, and the complete machine language translation would be loaded into memory. An example of core allocation under this inflexible loading scheme is depicted in Figure 1.3, where core is depicted as a linear array of locations with the program areas shaded.

---

[1]Main memory is typically implemented as magnetic cores; hence *memory* and *core* are used synonymously.

Locations

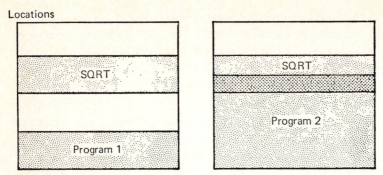

FIGURE 1.3 Example core allocation for absolute loading

Note that program 1 has "holes" in core. Program 2 *overlays* and thereby destroys part of the SQRT subroutine.

Programmers wished to use subroutines that referred to each other symbolically and did not want to be concerned with the address of parts of their programs. They expected the computer system to assign locations to their subroutines and to substitute addresses for their symbolic references.

Systems programmers noted that it would be more efficient if subroutines could be translated into an object form that the loader could "relocate" directly behind the user's program. The task of adjusting programs so they may be placed in arbitrary core locations is called *relocation. Relocating* loaders perform four functions:

1. Allocate space in memory for the programs (*allocation*)
2. Resolve symbolic references between object decks (*linking*)
3. Adjust all address-dependent locations, such as address constants, to correspond to the allocated space (*relocation*)
4. Physically place the machine instructions and data into memory (*loading*).

The various types of loaders that we will discuss ("compile-and-go," absolute, relocating, direct-linking, dynamic-loading, and dynamic-linking) differ primarily in the manner in which these four basic functions are accomplished.

The period of execution of a user's program is called *execution time*. The period of translating a user's source program is called *assembly* or *compile time*. *Load time* refers to the period of loading and preparing an object program for execution.

1.2.3 Macros

To relieve programmers of the need to repeat identical parts of their program, operating systems provide a macro processing facility, which permits the programmer to define an abbreviation for a part of his program and to use the abbreviation in his program. The macro processor treats the identical parts of the program defined by the abbreviation as a *macro definition* and saves the definition. The macro processor substitutes the definition for all occurrences of the abbreviation (macro call) in the program.

In addition to helping programmers abbreviate their programs, macro facilities have been used as general text handlers and for specializing operating systems to individual computer installations. In specializing operating systems (systems generation), the entire operating system is written as a series of macro definitions. To specialize the operating system, a series of macro calls are written. These are processed by the macro processor by substituting the appropriate definitions, thereby producing all the programs for an operating system.

1.2.4 Compilers

As the user's problems became more categorized into areas such as scientific, business, and statistical problems, specialized languages (*high level languages*) were developed that allowed the user to express certain problems concisely and easily. These high level languages — examples are FORTRAN, COBOL, ALGOL, and PL/I — are processed by compilers and interpreters. A *compiler* is a program that accepts a program written in a high level language and produces an object program. An *interpreter* is a program that appears to execute a source program as if it were machine language. The same name (FORTRAN, COBOL, etc.) is often used to designate both a compiler and its associated language.

Modern compilers must be able to provide the complex facilities that programmers are now demanding. The compiler must furnish complex accessing methods for pointer variables and data structures used in languages like PL/I, COBOL, and ALGOL 68. Modern compilers must interact closely with the operating system to handle statements concerning the hardware interrupts of a computer (e.g. conditional statements in PL/I).

1.2.5 Formal Systems

A formal system is an uninterpreted calculus. It consists of an alphabet, a set of words called axioms, and a finite set of relations called rules of inference. Examples of formal systems are: set theory, boolean algebra, Post systems, and Backus Normal Form. Formal systems are becoming important in the design, implementation, and study of programming languages. Specifically, they can be used to specify the *syntax* (form) and the semantics (meaning) of programming languages. They have been used in syntax-directed compilation, compiler verification, and complexity studies of languages.

1.3 EVOLUTION OF OPERATING SYSTEMS

Just a few years ago a FORTRAN programmer would approach the computer with his source deck in his left hand and a green deck of cards that would be a FORTRAN compiler in his right hand. He would:

1. Place the FORTRAN compiler (green deck) in the card hopper and press the load button. The computer would load the FORTRAN compiler.
2. Place his source language deck into the card hopper. The FORTRAN compiler would proceed to translate it into a machine language deck, which was punched onto red cards.
3. Reach into the card library for a pink deck of cards marked "loader," and place them in the card hopper. The computer would load the loader into its memory.
4. Place his newly translated object deck in the card hopper. The loader would load it into the machine.
5. Place in the card hopper the decks of any subroutines which his program called. The loader would load these subroutines.
6. Finally, the loader would transfer execution to the user's program, which might require the reading of data cards.

This system of multicolored decks was somewhat unsatisfactory, and there was strong motivation for moving to a more flexible system. One reason was that valuable computer time was being wasted as the machine stood idle during card-handling activities and between jobs. (A *job* is a unit of specified work, e.g., an assembly of a program.) To eliminate this waste, the facility to *batch* jobs was provided, permitting a number of jobs to be placed together into the card hopper to be read. A *batch operating system* performed the task of batching jobs. For example the batch system would perform steps 1 through 6 above retrieving the FORTRAN compiler and loader from secondary storage.

As the demands for computer time, memory, devices, and files increased, the efficient management of these resources became more critical. In Chapter 9 we discuss various methods of managing them. These resources are valuable, and inefficient management of them can be costly. The management of each resource has evolved as the cost and sophistication of its use increased.

In simple batched systems, the memory resource was allocated totally to a single program. Thus, if a program did not need the entire memory, a portion of that resource was wasted. Multiprogramming operating systems with *partitioned core memory* were developed to circumvent this problem. *Multiprogramming* allows multiple programs to reside in separate areas of core at the same time. Programs were given a fixed portion of core (*Multiprogramming with Fixed Tasks* (MFT)) or a varying-size portion of core (*Multiprogramming with Variable Tasks* (MVT)).

Often in such partitioned memory systems some portion could not be used since it was too small to contain a program. The problem of "holes" or unused portions of core is called *fragmentation*. Fragmentation has been minimized by the technique of relocatable partitions (Burroughs 6500) and by paging (XDS 940, HIS 645). *Relocatable partitioned core* allows the unused portions to be condensed into one continuous part of core.

Paging is a method of memory allocation by which the program is subdivided into equal portions or pages, and core is subdivided into equal portions or *blocks*. The pages are loaded into blocks.

There are two paging techniques: simple and demand. In *simple paging* all the pages of a program must be in core for execution. In *demand paging* a program can be executed without all pages being in core, i.e., pages are fetched into core as they are needed (demanded).

The reader will recall from section 1.1 that a system with several processors is termed a multiprocessing system. The *traffic controller* coordinates the processors and the processes. The resource of processor time is allocated by a program known as the *scheduler*. The processor concerned with I/O is referred to as the *I/O processor*, and programming this processor is called *I/O programming*.

The resource of files of information is allocated by the *file system*. A *segment* is a group of information that a user wishes to treat as an entity. *Files* are segments. There are two types of files: (1) directories and (2) data or programs. *Directories* contain the locations of other files. In a hierarchical file system, directories may point to other directories, which in turn may point to directories or files.

Time-sharing is one method of allocating processor time. It is typically characterized by interactive processing and time-slicing of the CPU's time to allow quick response to each user.

A *virtual memory* (*name space, address space*) consists of those addresses that may be generated by a processor during execution of a computation. The *memory space* consists of the set of addresses that correspond to physical memory locations. The technique of *segmentation* provides a large name space and a good protection mechanism. Protection and sharing are methods of allowing controlled access to segments.

1.4 OPERATING SYSTEM USER VIEWPOINT: FUNCTIONS

From the user's point of view, the purpose of an operating system (monitor) is to assist him in the *mechanics* of solving problems. Specifically, the following functions are performed by the system:

1. Job sequencing, scheduling, and traffic controller operation
2. Input/output programming
3. Protecting itself from the user; protecting the user from other users
4. Secondary storage management
5. Error handling

Consider the situation in which one user has a job that takes four hours, and another user has a job that takes four seconds. If both jobs were submitted simultaneously, it would seem to be more appropriate for the four-second user to have his run go first. Based on considerations such as this, job scheduling is automatically performed by the operating system. If it is possible to do input and output while simultaneously executing a program, as is the case with many computer systems, all these functions are scheduled by the traffic controller.

As we have said, the I/O channel may be thought of as a separate computer with its own specialized set of instructions. Most users do not want to learn how to program it (in many cases quite a complicated task). The user would like to simply say in his program, "Read," causing the monitor system to supply a program to the I/O channel for execution. Such a facility is provided by operating systems. In many cases the program supplied to the I/O channel consists of a sequence of closely interwoven interrupt routines that handle the situation in this way: "Hey, Mr. I/O Channel, did you receive that character?" "Yes, I received it." "Are you sure you received it?" "Yes, I'm sure." "Okay, I'll send another one." "Fine, send it." "You're sure you want me to send another one?" "*Send* it!"

An extremely important function of an operating system is to protect the user from being hurt, either maliciously or accidentally, by other users; that is, protect him when other users are executing or changing their programs, files, or data bases. The operating system must insure inviolability. As well as protecting users from each other, the operating system must also protect itself from users who, whether maliciously or accidentally, might "crash" the system.

Students are great challengers of protection mechanisms. When the systems programming course is given at M.I.T., we find that due to the large number of students participating it is very difficult to personally grade every program run on the machine problems. So for the very simple problems — certainly the first problem which may be to count the number of A's in a register and leave the answer in another register — we have written a grading program that is included as part of the operating system. The grading program calls the student's program and transfers control to it. In this simple problem the student's program processes the contents of the register, leaves his answer in another register, and returns to the grading program. The latter checks to find out if the correct number has been left in the answer register. Afterwards, the grading program prints out a listing of all the students in the class and their grades. For example:

VITA KOHN	—	CORRECT
RACHEL BUXBAUM	—	CORRECT
JOE LEVIN	—	INCORRECT
LOFTI ZADEH	—	CORRECT

On last year's run, the computer listing began as follows:

JAMES ARCHER	—	CORRECT
ED MCCARTHY	—	CORRECT
ELLEN NANGLE	—	INCORRECT
JOHN SCHWARTZ	—	MAYBE

(We are not sure how John Schwartz did this; we gave him an A in the course.)

Secondary storage management is a task performed by an operating system in conjunction with the use of disks, tapes, and other secondary storage for a user's programs and data.

An operating system must respond to errors. For example, if the programmer should overflow a register, it is not economical for the computer to simply stop and wait for an operator to intervene. When an error occurs, the operating system must take appropriate action.

1.5 OPERATING SYSTEM USER VIEWPOINT: BATCH CONTROL LANGUAGE

Many users view an operating system only through the batch system control cards by which they must preface their programs. In this section we will discuss a simple monitor system and the control cards associated with it. Other more complex monitors are discussed in Chapter 9.

Monitor is a term that refers to the control programs of an operating system. Typically, in a batch system the jobs are stacked in a card reader, and the monitor system sequentially processes each job. A job may consist of several separate programs to be executed sequentially, each individual program being called a *job step*. In a *batch monitor system* the user communicates with the system by way of a control language. In a simple batch monitor system we have two classes of control cards: execution cards and definition cards. For example, an execution card may be in the following format:

    // step name   EXEC   name of program to be executed, Argument 1, Argument 2

The job control card, a definition card, may take on the following format:

    // job name   JOB   (User name, identification, expected time use, lines to
                             be printed out, expected number of cards to be printed
                             out.

Usually there is an end-of-file card, whose format might consist of /*, signifying the termination of a collection of data. Let us take the following example of a FORTRAN job.

```
//EXAMPLE    JOB      DONOVAN,    T168,1,100,0
//STEP1          EXEC    FORTRAN, NOPUNCH
             READ 9100,N
             DO 100 I = 1,N
             I2 = I*I
             I3 = I*I*I
        100  PRINT 9100, I, I2, I3
       9100  FORMAT (3I10)
             END
/*
//STEP2          EXEC LOAD
/*
//STEP3          EXEC OBJECT
          10
/*
```

The first control card is an example of a definition card. We have defined the user to be Donovan. The system must set up an accounting file for the user, noting that he expects to use one minute of time, to output a hundred lines of output, and to punch no cards. The next control card, EXEC FORTRAN, NOPUNCH, is an example of an execution card; that is, the system is to execute the program FORTRAN, given one argument — NOPUNCH. This argument allows the monitor system to perform more efficiently; since no cards are to be punched, it need not utilize the punch routines. The data to the compiler is the FORTRAN program shown, terminated by an end-of-file card /*.

The next control card is another example of an execution card and in this case causes the execution of the loader. The program that has just been compiled will be loaded, together with all the routines necessary for its execution, whereupon the loader will "bind" the subroutines to the main program. This job step is terminated by an end-of-file card. The EXEC OBJECT card is another execution card, causing the monitor system to execute the object program just compiled. The data card, 10, is input to the program and is followed by the end-of-file card.

The simple loop shown in Figure 1.4 presents an overview of an implementation of a batch monitor system. The monitor system must read in the first card, presumably a job card. In processing a job card, the monitor saves the user's name, account number, allotted time, card punch limit, and line print limit. If the next control card happens to be an execution card, then the monitor will load the corresponding program from secondary storage and process the job step by transferring control to the executable program. If there is an error during processing, the system notes the error and goes back to process the next job step.

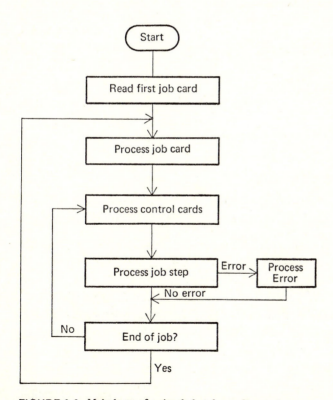

FIGURE 1.4 Main loop of a simple batch monitor system

1.6 OPERATING SYSTEM USER VIEWPOINT: FACILITIES

For the applications-oriented user, the function of the operating system is to provide facilities to help solve problems. The questions of scheduling or protection are of no interest to him; what he is concerned with is the available software. The following facilities are typically provided by modern operating systems:

1. Assemblers
2. Compilers, such as FORTRAN, COBOL, and PL/I
3. Subroutine libraries, such as SINE, COSINE, SQUARE ROOT
4. Linkage editors and program loaders that bind subroutines together and prepare programs for execution
5. Utility routines, such as SORT/MERGE and TAPE COPY
6. Application packages, such as circuit analysis or simulation
7. Debugging facilities, such as program tracing and "core dumps"
8. Data management and file processing
9. Management of system hardware

Although this "facilities" aspect of an operating system may be of great interest to the user, we feel that the answer to the question, "How many compilers does that operating system have?" may tell more about the orientation of the manufacturer's marketing force than it does about the structure and effectiveness of the operating system.

1.7 SUMMARY

The major components of a programming system are:

1. Assembler

Input to an assembler is an *assembly language program*. Output is an object program plus information that enables the loader to prepare the object program for execution.

2. Macro Processor

A *macro call* is an abbreviation (or name) for some code. A *macro definition* is a sequence of code that has a name (macro call). A *macro processor* is a program that substitutes and specializes macro definitions for macro calls.

3. Loader

A loader is a routine that loads an object program and prepares it for execution.

There are various loading schemes: absolute, relocating, and direct-linking. In general, the loader must *load, relocate,* and *link* the object program.

4. Compilers

A compiler is a program that accepts a source program "in a high-level language" and produces a corresponding object program.

5. Operating Systems

An operating system is concerned with the allocation of resources and services, such as memory, processors, devices, and information. The operating system correspondingly includes programs to manage these resources, such as a *traffic controller*, a *scheduler*, *memory management module*, *I/O programs*, and a *file system*.

QUESTIONS

1. What is the difference between (processor, procedure); (procedure, program); (processor, I/O channel); (multiprocessing, multiprogramming); and (open subroutine, closed subroutine)?

2. Bits in memory may represent data or instructions. How does the processor "know" whether a given location represents an instruction or a piece of data?

3. Assume that you have available to you a 360-type computer and the following available input decks:

   Deck A: A Basic Assembly Language (BAL) assembler written in *binary* code (machine language)
   Deck B: A FORTRAN to BAL translator, written in BAL
   Deck C: A FORTRAN program that will read data cards and print the square roots of the data
   Deck D: A data deck for the square root program of deck C

   In order to compute the square roots you will have to make four computer runs. The runs are described schematically below. Each run involves (reading from left to right) an input deck that will be operated on by a program to produce an output deck. Of course, the output deck produced by one run may be used as either the input deck or the program of a subsequent run.

   In the figure below identify the unlabelled decks with the letters A, B, C, D, E, F, G.

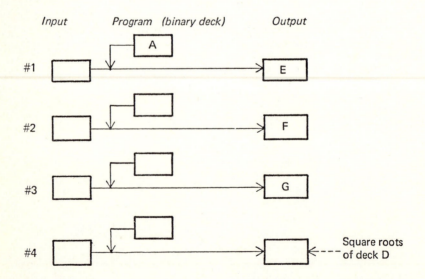

4. There is a distinction between hardware (physical devices made of nuts, bolts, transistors, etc.) and software (information stored as a binary pat-

tern on cards, tape, disc, with the ultimate purpose of being loaded into core memory to be used as a program or data). Label each of the following as hardware or software:

a. Compiler
b. Processor
c. Operating system
d. Loader
e. I/O channel
f. Core memory
g. Assembler
h. File
i. Monitor
j. Disk drive

5. A simple batch monitor was discussed in section 1.5. In this problem, we will increase its flexibility and look more closely at its structure. To give the user more control over resource allocation, we introduce the concept of a *data set*; a data set is simply a source or repository for data, which can take the physical form of a disk, printer, card reader, etc. The user defines his data sets by means of a new control card:

```
//  Logical data set name   DD      parameter list
```

For instance, in the FORTRAN compilation of section 1.5, SYSPRINT is the logical name for the source language listing data set, and

```
//  SYSPRINT   DD    UNIT = 00E
```

says that the listing is to be made on the device numbered 00E (printer). Other data sets used by the compiler are:

```
SYSIN       (Source language input; usually card reader)
SYSLIN      (Object code output; usually disk)
```

The loader would use:

```
SYSLIN      (Output of translator)
SYSPRINT    (Messages—usually printer)
SYSLIB      (Library subroutines; usually on disk)
```

And the user program:

```
SYSIN       (Data, usually from card reader)
SYSPRINT    (Printer, Same as above)
```

To include data cards in the same deck as control cards, an asterisk (*) is put in the parameter field of the DD card, meaning "follows in input stream." The data cards must be ended with a /* (end of data set) card, and a DD * data set must be the last data set in a job step.

On a system with a disk numbered 141 and printer numbered 00E, the job from section 1.5 with all data sets defined would be:

```
// EXAMPLE        JOB          DONOVAN, T168, 1, 100, 0
// STEP1          EXEC         FORTRAN, NO PUNCH
// SYSPRINT       DD           UNIT = 00E
// SYSLIN         DD           UNIT = 141
// SYSIN          DD           *
            READ          9100,N
            DO      100   I=1,N
            I2 = I*I
            I3 = I*I*I
   100      PRINT         9100, I, I2, I3
   9100     FORMAT        (3I10)
            END
/*
// STEP2          EXEC         LOADER
// SYSPRINT       DD           UNIT = 00E
// SYSLIB         DD           DSNAME = FORTLIB
// SYSLIN         DD           FROM STEP1.SYSLIN
// STEP3          EXEC         OBJECT
// SYSPRINT       DD           UNIT = 00E
// SYSIN          DD           *
            10
/*
```

The monitor must read the user's control cards, allocate resources as requested, and initiate execution of the requested job steps. Consider it to be broken down into two sections:

1) The reader/interpreter (RDR/INT) reads control cards, interprets them, and builds data bases from the information on the control cards.
2) The initiator/terminator (INIT/TERM) schedules resources and initiates and terminates job steps, using the data bases created by the RDR/INT.

   a. Why is it useful to have logical names that can be assigned by the user to any physical unit he chooses?
   b. What data base(s) must the RDR/INT build for the INIT/TERM to support the DD control card feature?
   c. What other data base(s) are needed?
   d. As the RDR/INT reads cards sequentially, at what point does it transfer control to the INIT/TERM to actually perform the job step? (Remember that data cards in a DD * data set are not read by the RDR/INT, but as data by the program being executed.)
   e. What would happen to each data base of the RDR/INT at the end of each job step?
   f. What would happen to each data base at the end of each job?
   g. What errors might be recognized by RDR/INT? By INIT/TERM? What action could be taken?

6. To increase the flexibility of our batch monitor system even more, we want to add a new parameter called PRIORITY to the JOB card. This would be a number from 0 to 9, with higher numbers being run first and, of course, charged more. Obviously, we can no longer read in one job at a time, so we add a facility called a *queue.*

The data bases created by the RDR/INT for each job will be placed on the queue until there are no more jobs to be read, and then INIT/TERM will be allowed to run the highest priority job. A check will be made afterwards to see whether any new jobs must be added to the queue, and then the remaining job with the highest priority will be run:

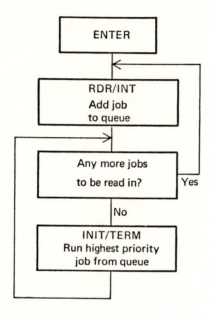

a. What addition(s) must be made to the data bases created by the RDR/INT?
b. In the model of section 1.5 we could ignore data cards in DD * data sets. What, if anything, is done about them now?
c. Why is the PRIORITY parameter useful?

2

machine structure, machine language, and assembly language

The purpose of this chapter is to discuss machine structure, machine language, and assembly language.

We have taken examples from the IBM Systems/360 and 370.[1] Our purpose is not to teach specific assembly languages, and we present only enough material to illustrate the design of assemblers (and later the design of compilers). The introduction to 370 assembly language afforded by our discussion should be supplemented by further reading (see Chapter 10 (References) — machine structure). We have written this section primarily for two classes of people: those who know assembly language programming well and want to become somewhat familiar with the 370; and those who have not programmed in any assembly language and who may use this chapter as an introduction to the manuals. The approach and examples can be easily translated to other machines.

2.1 GENERAL MACHINE STRUCTURE

Almost all conventional modern computers are based upon the "stored program computer" concept, generally credited to the mathematician John von Neumann (1903-1957). Figure 2.1 illustrates the structure of the CPU for a typical von Neumann machine, such as the IBM System/360.

The CPU consists of an instruction interpreter, a location counter, an instruction register and various working registers and general registers. The *instruction interpreter* is a group of electrical circuits (*hardware*), that performs the intent of instructions fetched from memory. The *Location Counter* (LC), also called

---

[1]The IBM System/360 (or just 360) is the name of a series of IBM computers in production since 1964, all of which have compatible instruction sets and manuals. The IBM 370, a revised version of the 360, was introduced in 1970. The *370 is compatible with the 360.*

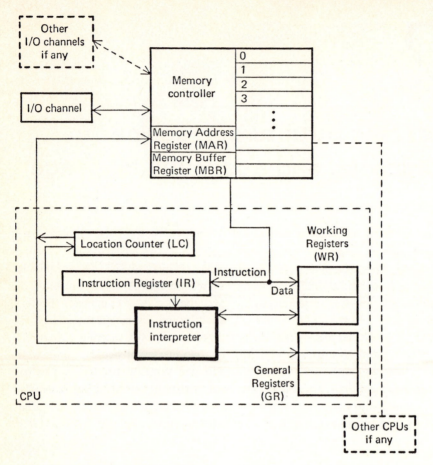

FIGURE 2.1 General machine structure

Program Counter (PC) or *Instruction Counter* (IC), is a hardware memory device which denotes the location of the current instruction being executed. A copy of the current instruction is stored in the *Instruction Register* (IR). The *working registers* are memory devices that serve as "scratch pads" for the instruction interpreter, while the *general registers* are used by the programmer as storage locations and for special functions.

The primary interface between the memory and the CPU is via the memory address register and the memory buffer register. The *Memory Address Register* (MAR) contains the address of the memory location that is to be read from or stored into. The *Memory Buffer Register* (MBR) contains a copy of the designated memory location specified by the MAR after a "read," or the new contents of the memory location prior to a "write." The *memory controller* is hardware that transfers data between the MBR and the core memory location the address of which is in the MAR.

The *I/O channels* may be thought of as separate computers which interpret special instructions for inputting and outputting information from the memory.

To illustrate how these components of the machine structure interact, let us consider a simple computer (SC-6251). The SC-6251 has four general registers, designated 00, 01, 10, and 11 in binary rotation. The basic instruction format is as follows:

Operation code	Register number	Memory location
(op)	(reg)	(addr)

For example, the instruction

ADD   2,176

would cause the data stored in memory location 176 to be added to the current contents of general register 2. The resulting sum would be left as the new contents of register 2. The micro-flowchart in Figure 2.2 illustrates the sequence of hardware operations performed within the instruction interpreter to execute an instruction.

Although the specific details vary from computer to computer, this example of machine structure is representative of all conventional machines.

2.1.1 General Approach to a New Machine

Outlined in this section is an approach that may be taken to become familiar with a new machine. It consists of finding answers to a series of questions that we ask if we wish to program the machine.

We first list these questions and then answer them for the IBM 360 and 370. In section 9.1 we will ask these same questions regarding I/O channels (which may be considered as separate computers).

1. MEMORY
What is the memory's basic unit, size, and addressing scheme?

2. REGISTERS
How many registers are there? What are their size, function, and interrelationship?

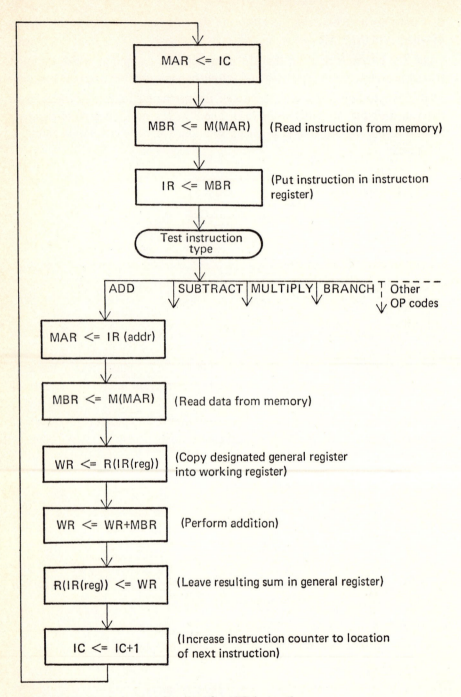

FIGURE 2.2 Example micro flowchart for ADD instruction

3. DATA

What types of data can be handled by the computer? Can it handle characters, numbers, logical data? How is this data stored?

4. INSTRUCTIONS

What are the classes of instructions on the machine? Are there arithmetic instructions, logical instructions, symbol-manipulation instructions? What are their formats? How are they stored in memory?

5. SPECIAL FEATURES

What is the interrupt structure of the machine? What sort of protection mechanism is available to the user?

2.1.2   Machine Structure — 360 and 370

In this section we will answer these questions in the context of the IBM 360. The material is equally applicable to the 370.

1. MEMORY

The basic unit of memory in the 360 is a byte — eight bits of information. That is, each addressable position in memory can contain eight bits of information. There are facilities to operate on contiguous bytes in basic units. The basic units are as follows:

Unit of memory	Bytes	Length in bits
Byte	1	8
Halfword	2	16
Word	4	32
Doubleword	8	64

A unit of memory consisting of four bits is sometimes referred to as a *nibble*. The size of the 360 memory is up to 2^{24} bytes (about sixteen million).

The addressing on the 360 memory may consist of three components. Specifically, the value of an address equals the value of an offset, plus the contents of a base register, plus the contents of an index register. We will give examples of this addressing later.

In general, operations on units of memory are specified by the low-order byte address. For example, when addressing a word (four bytes) the address of the word is that of the low order byte.

2. REGISTERS

The 360 has 16 general-purpose registers consisting of 32 bits each. In addition there are 4 floating-point registers consisting of 64 bits each. It has a 64-bit

Program Status Word (PSW) that contains the value of the location counter, protection information, and interrupt status.

The general-purpose registers may be used for various arithmetic and logical operations and as base registers. When the programmer uses them in arithmetic or logical operations, he thinks of these registers as scratch pads to which numbers are added, subtracted, compared, and so forth. When used as base registers, they aid in the formation of the address. Take for example the instruction

<pre>
                      Index register
                           ↘
    A   1,901 (2, 15)
                    ↗   ↗
                 Offset Base
                         register
</pre>

It is interpreted as an add instruction. A number is to be added to the contents of register 1.

The location of the number is 901 (*offset*) plus the contents of register 2 (*index*) plus the contents of register 15 (*base*). That is, if those three numbers were added together, the result would be the address of the memory location whose contents we wish to add to the contents of register 1.

One may ask why such complexity in the formation of addressing is necessary. The motivation is twofold. First, a base register aids in the process of relocation of a program. As we will see, an entire program may be moved from one series of locations to another by changing the contents of a base register.[2] A major motivation for employing base registers, however, is to promote efficient addressing of core. For example, in order to address all possible core locations (16 million) in the 360 without the use of a base register, we would need 24 bits for every address. By way of illustration, if the preceding add instruction were formed in core as depicted in the following diagram, we would need a total of 40 bits to store it: 8 bits for the op code, 4 bits to specify one of 16 possible registers to which the number is added, an additional 4 bits to specify one of 16 possible index registers, and lastly, 24 bits to specify the address of the number we wish to add

---

[2]Base registers do not completely solve the problem of relocation. The difficult problem of *address constants* must also be resolved. An address constant is a feature by which a programmer may specify that a certain location in memory contains an address of a specified memory location.

Op code	Arg reg	Index reg	Address
8 bits	4 bits	4 bits	24 bits

Total: 40

If we use a base register, we can store the instruction in the following format. We could specify any one of 16 possible registers as the base register, using 4 bits, and employ an additional 12 for an offset. The total number of bits for an add instruction would be 32, a savings of 8 bits per address reference.

Op code	Arg reg	Index reg	Base	Offset
8 bits	4 bits	4 bits	4 bits	12 bits

Total: 32

The disadvantages of this shorter form are the overhead associated with the formation of the address during execution and the fact that the offset, which is 12 bits long, can only specify a number from 0 to 4,095. Thus, it may be difficult to "reach" the data. That is, without using an index register and without changing the contents of the base register, the core location we wish to address cannot be any further than 4,095 locations away from the core location to which the base register is pointing.

3. DATA

The 360 may store several different types of data as is depicted in Figure 2.3. That is, groups of bits stored in memory are interpreted by a 360 processor in several ways. If a 360 interprets the contents of two bytes as an integer (Fig. 2.3a), it interprets the first bit as a sign and the remaining 15 as a binary number (e.g., 0000 0010 0001 1101 is interpreted as the binary number equivalent to the decimal number +541).[3] If a 360 interprets the contents of two bytes as a packed decimal (Fig. 2.3c), it would interpret the first byte as two BCD coded digits, the first four bits of the second byte as a BCD digit, and the last four as a sign (e.g., 0000 0010 0001 1101 is interpreted as the decimal number -021).

0   2   1   Sign

All data and instructions are physically stored as sequences of binary ones and zeros. Thus, a 16-bit fixed-point halfword with decimal value +300 would be

---

[3]See Appendix A for binary to decimal conversions.

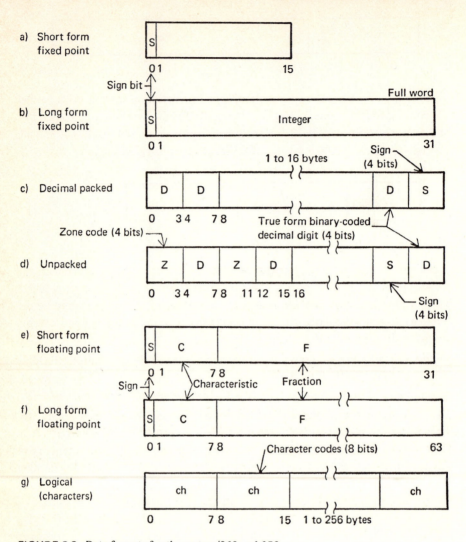

FIGURE 2.3 Data formats for the system/360 and 370

stored in binary as '0000 0001 0010 1100'. For convenience, binary numbers are usually written in the hexadecimal (base 16) number system rather than the binary (base 2) number system. The *hexadecimal* digits are shown in Figure 2.4. Note that every hexadecimal digit can be replaced by exactly four binary digits and vice versa. Thus when we have the number +300 in decimal, which equals

B'0000 0001 0010 1100} in binary
X' 0   1   2   C } in hexadecimal

Hexadecimal	Binary	Decimal
0	0000	0
1	0001	1
2	0010	2
3	0011	3
4	0100	4
5	0101	5
6	0110	6
7	0111	7
8	1000	8
9	1001	9
A	1010	10
B	1011	11
C	1100	12
D	1101	13
E	1110	14
F	1111	15

FIGURE 2.4   Hexadecimal-binary-decimal conversion

The prefixes X and B indicate mode of representation (hexadecimal, binary).

Fixed-point numbers may be stored in either a halfword or a fullword (Figs. 2.3a and 2.3b).

The 360 allows the storage of numbers in decimal form (Figs. 2.3c and 2.3d). That is, numbers may be stored not as binary numbers but in a format closely approximating the decimal representation. For example, the number 12 could appear in one byte where the first four bits would contain a decimal 1 (0001) and the second four bits would contain a decimal 2 (0010). Decimal forms are useful in business data processing.

The 360 allows floating-point numbers, logical data, and character strings (Fig. 2.3g) to be represented in memory as depicted in Figure 2.3.

There are instructions to operate on all these types of data.

4. INSTRUCTIONS

The 360 has arithmetic, logical, control or transfer, and special interrupt instructions.

The formats of the 360 instructions are depicted in Figure 2.5.

These five types of instructions differ basically in the types of operands they use.

Register operands refer to data stored in one of the 16 general registers (32 bits long), which are addressed by a four-bit field in the instruction. Since registers are usually constructed of high-speed circuitry, they provide faster access to data than does core storage.

For example, the instruction *Add register   3, 4*

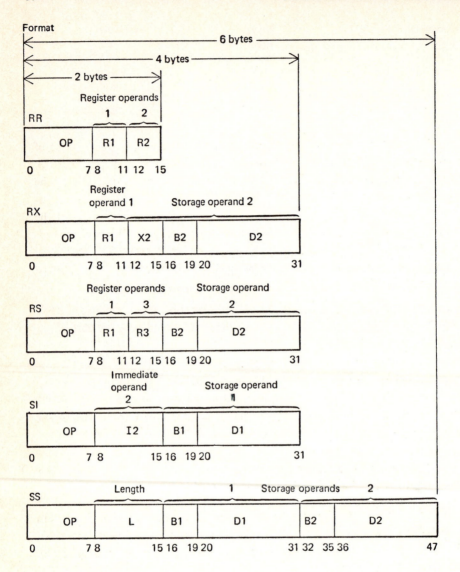

FIGURE 2.5 Basic 360 instruction formats

Mnemonics used:

OP ~ operation code
Ri ~ contents of general register used as operand
Xi ~ contents of general register used as index
Bi ~ contents of general register used as base
Di ~ displacement
Ii ~ immediate data
L ~ operand length

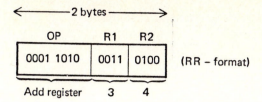

causes the contents of general register 4 (32 bits) to be added to the contents of general register 3 (32 bits) and the resulting sum to be left in general register 3.

Storage operands refer to data stored in core memory. The length of the operand depends upon the specific data type (as illustrated in Figure 2.3). Operand data fields that are longer than one byte are specified by the address of the lowest-address byte (logically leftmost). For example, the 32-bit binary fixed-point full word with value +267 (in hexadecimal X'00 00 01 0B'), stored in locations 1016, 1017, 1018, and 1019 as depicted below is said to be "located at address 1016."

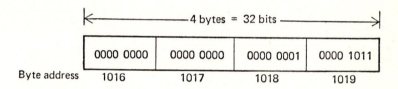

The address of the ith storage operand is computed from the instruction in the following way:

Address = c(Bi) + c(Xi) + Di   (RX format)
   or   c(Bi) + Di   (RS, SI, SS format)

where c(Bi) and c(Xi) denote the contents of general registers Bi and Xi respectively. Exception: if Xi=0, then c(Xi) are treated as 0; likewise for Bi=0.

For example, if we assume that general register 5 contains the number 1000, the following instruction:

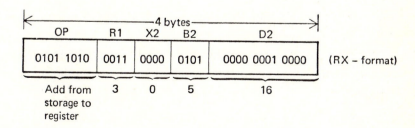

causes the contents of the word (32 bits) located at address

```
= c(B2) + c(X2) + D2
= c(5)  + c(0)  + 16
= 1000 + 0      + 16
= 1016
```

to be added to the contents of general register 3 (32 bits), with the resulting sum left in general register 3.

Another example, assuming again that general register 5 contains 1000, is the following instruction: (Note: in SS instructions the length is always one less than the data moved, e.g., length = 0 means move one byte.)

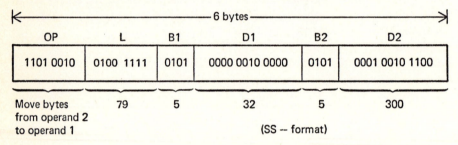

			6 bytes		
OP	L	B1	D1	B2	D2
1101 0010	0100 1111	0101	0000 0010 0000	0101	0001 0010 1100

Move bytes   79   5   32   5   300
from operand 2
to operand 1   (SS -- format)

This instruction involves two storage operands:

```
Storage operand 1 address = c(B1) + D1  = c(5) + 32
                          = 1000 + 32   = 1032
Storage operand 2 address = c(B2) + D2  = c(5) + 300
                          = 1000 + 300  = 1300
```

This instruction copies (moves) the 80 bytes from locations 1032 - 1111 to locations 1300 - 1379. Since a character is stored as a byte (see Fig. 2.3g), this instruction could be viewed as copying an 80-character "card image" from one area to another.

Immediate operands are a single byte of data and are stored as part of the instruction.

Again assuming register 5 to contain 1000, the following SS instruction, causes the byte 0100 0000 (bits 8 through 15 of instruction) to be stored at location 1004.

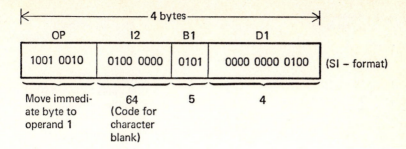

Representative 360/370 instructions

Various 360 instructions will be used throughout this book in examples and as needed in problem sets and machine problem assignments. The following subset is particularly relevant to our purpose and should be studied in the appropriate reference manual. (See Appendix A for complete set of instructions.)

	Hexadecimal op code	Mnemonic	Meaning (format)
		Load group	
Load-store-register	58	L	Load (RX)
	48	LH	Load halfword (RX)
	98	LM	Load multiple (RS)
	18	LR	Load (RR)
	12	LTR	Load and test (RR)
		Store group	
	50	ST	Store (RX)
	40	STH	Store halfword (RX)
	90	STM	Store multiple (RS)
		Add-group	
Fixed-point arithmetic	5A	A	Add (RX)
	4A	AH	Add halfword (RX)
	1A	AR	Add (RR)
		Compare-group	
	59	C	Compare (RX)
	49	CH	Compare halfword (RX)
	19	CR	Compare (RR)
		Divide-group	
	5D	D	Divide (RX)
	1D	DR	Divide (RR)

	Hexadecimal op code	Mnemonic	Meaning (format)
	Multiply-group		
	5C	M	Multiply (RX)
	4C	MH	Multiply halfword (RX)
	1C	MR	Multiply (RR)
	Subtract-group		
	5B	S	Subtract (RX)
	4B	SH	Subtract halfword (RX)
	1B	SR	Subtract (RR)
	Compare-group		
	55	CL	Compare logical (RX)
	D5	CLC	Compare logical (SS)
	95	CLI	Compare logical (SI)
	15	CLR	Compare logical (RR)
	Move-group		
	D2	MVC	Move (SS)
	92	MVI	Move (SI)
	And-group		
	54	N	Boolean AND (RX)
	D4	NC	Boolean AND (SS)
	94	NI	Boolean AND (SI)
	14	NR	Boolean AND (RR)
	Or-group		
	56	O	Boolean OR (RX)
	D6	OC	Boolean OR (SS)
	96	OI	Boolean OR (SI)
	16	OR	Boolean OR (RR)
	Exclusive-or group		
	57	X	Exclusive-or (RX)
	D7	XC	Exclusive-or (SS)
	97	XI	Exclusive-or (SI)
	17	XR	Exclusive-or (RR)
	Shift		
	8D	SLDL	Shift left (double logical) (RS)
	89	SLL	Shift left (single logical) (RS)
	8C	SRDL	Shift right (double logical) (RS)
	88	SRL	Shift right (single logical) (RS)

Fixed-point arithmetic (groups: Multiply-group, Subtract-group)

Logical (groups: Compare-group, Move-group, And-group, Or-group, Exclusive-or group, Shift)

Hexadecimal op code	Mnemonic	Meaning (format)
	Linkage group	
45	BAL	Branch and link (RX)
05	BALR	Branch and link (RR)
	Branch group	
47	BC	Branch on condition (RX)
07	BCR	Branch on condition (RR)
46	BCT	Branch on count (RX)
06	BCTR	Branch on count (RR)
	Miscellaneous	
9E	HIO	Halt I/O (RX)
41	LA	Load address (RX)
9C	SIO	Start I/O (RX)
0A	SVC	Supervisor call (SI)
9D	TIO	Test I/O (RX)
43	IC	Insert character (RX)
91	TM	Test under mask (SI)
42	STC	Store character (RX)

Transfer brackets the Linkage group and Branch group.
Miscellaneous brackets the Miscellaneous group.

5. SPECIAL FEATURES

The 360 has hardware protection in blocks of 2,048 bytes and has an elaborate interrupt structure discussed in Chapter 9.

2.2 MACHINE LANGUAGE

In this section we will discuss machine language (the actual code executed by a computer). Again, our examples are taken from a 360-type computer. However, they are easily applied to other machines.

In this section we will start the reader on his way to learning machine language. After reading this section, the reader is referred to one of the many books or manuals that discuss the machine language of the particular machine that he will be using.

We will not write machine language in ones and zeros, nor will we use hexa-decimal numbers. Rather, we will use a mnemonic form of machine language.

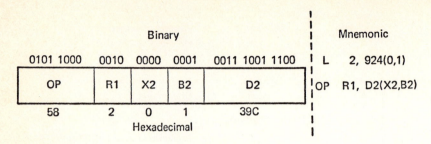

FIGURE 2.6 Mnemonic form of machine language

Figure 2.6 depicts a series of ones and zeros that may be interpreted by the CPU as a load instruction, and the mnemonic form that we shall employ to represent this instruction.

The following simple example will be used several times in this chapter to demonstrate features of machine language:

Write a program that will add the number 49 to the contents of 10 adjacent fullwords in memory, under the following set of assumptions:

Assumption 1.	The 10 numbers that are to be added to are in contiguous fullwords beginning at absolute core location 952.
Assumption 2.	The program is in core starting at absolute location 48.
Assumption 3.	The number 49 is a fullword at absolute location 948.
Assumption 4.	Register 1 contains a 48.

Core may be thought of as shown in Figure 2.7.

2.2.1 Long Way, No Looping

Figure 2.8 illustrates a program to accomplish this addition.

The first instruction L 2,904(0,1) loads the first number into register 2. Register 2 will be used as the accumulator. As was explained in section 2.1.3, the 360 addresses are made up of an offset plus the contents of an index register, plus the contents of a base register. In this instruction we have denoted the index register as being 0. There is a zero register. However, when it is used as an index, base, or branch register, it is assumed to have zero contents. Therefore, the address specified in the first load instruction above is equal to 904 plus the contents of register 1 (which contains a 48), i.e., 952. This is the absolute address of the first data element, DATA1.

The next instruction in the program adds the contents of absolute location 948 to register 2. Absolute location 948 contains a 49. Next comes a store instruction that stores the contents of register 2 back into absolute location 952,

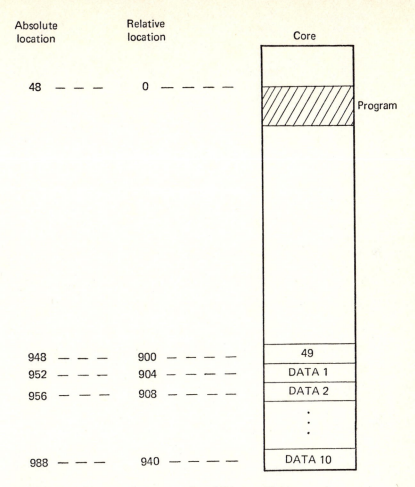

FIGURE 2.7 Diagram of core setup for addition problem

destroying the original first data item and replacing it by a new one that is equal to DATA1 plus 49. Similarly, the next three instructions add 49 to DATA2. An identical set of three instructions is used for each data item.

The preceding program will work; however, there are some potential problems. For example, if we wanted to process 300 data items rather than just 10, the storage needed for the instructions would be (3 instructions) x (length of each instruction) x (number of data items) = 3,600 bytes. Thus the instructions would overlay our data in core. Furthermore, the distance from the first instruction to the last piece of data would be 4,800 bytes, since the data itself occupies 4 x 300 = 1,200 bytes. Using register 1 as a base register, it would be impossible to

Absolute address	Relative address	Hexadecimal	Instructions	Comments
48	0	58201388	L 2,904(0,1)	Load reg 2 from loc 904+C(reg 1) = 952
52	4	5A201384	A 2,900(0,1)	Add 49 (loc=900+ c(reg 1)) = 948
56	8	50201388	ST 2,904(0,1)	Store back
60	12	5820138C	L 2,908(0,1)	Load next data
64	16	5A201384	A 2,900(0,1)	Add 49
68	20	5020138C	ST 2,908(0,1)	Store back
⋮	⋮	⋮	⋮	
948	900	00000031	49	
952	904	⋮	⋮	

FIGURE 2.8   Program for addition problem – straightforward approach

access both the first data item and the last. The programmer must be aware of this type of problem if he is writing in machine language, and should bear in mind the fact that the largest possible value of an offset is 2^{12}-1 or 4,095, which may not reach all his data. (It is, of course, possible to use more than one base register.)

Note that if the preceding program were loaded into location 336 instead of location 48, it would still execute correctly if the content of register 1 was 336. Moving the program to a different location is a process called *relocation*. The use of base registers facilitates this process.

2.2.2   Address Modification Using Instructions As Data

Our example may be analogous to the "program" depicted in Figure 2.9. If an M.I.T. student had a date with a girl, he might write a program to do the following.

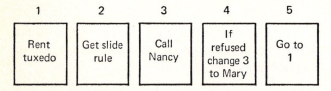

FIGURE 2.9   Situation

The preceding boxes represent locations, and the words in those boxes represent instructions to the processor, in this case, the M.I.T. student. The program would have the student rent a tuxedo, get a slide rule (this is M.I.T.), and call Nancy. But if Nancy refuses, the M.I.T. student does not want to write a new program, so he writes an instruction that simply changes the contents of location 3 from Nancy to Mary and then repeats 1 through 4. The execution of the instruction in location 4 changes the instruction in location 3. Of course, in the preceding program he could end up renting many tuxedos, and if Mary refuses, she will receive an awful lot of telephone calls.

This M.I.T. student, however, has grasped two basic programming techniques. The first is that the instruction in location 3 may be treated as data. The second is looping, which he accomplished with the transfer rule in step 5. In this section and the next we will see how these two techniques can simplify our previous program.

Observe that in the program in Figure 2.8 we were merely using three instructions over and over again. The only element that changed was the offset of the load and store commands. In the first set of three instructions, the offset was 904. In the next set it was 908, then 912. An alternate technique is to write a machine language program consisting only of those three instructions, followed by a sequence of commands that would change the offset of the load and store instructions by adding 4 to them. The computer would execute the three instructions, change two of them so that the offset was increased by 4, and loop back to re-execute the set of three instructions. Of course, they would now have a different offset and therefore would refer to a different address.

The program in Figure 2.10 depicts a sequence of instructions that will perform the operation of adding the number 49 to 10 locations in core by modifying the instructions themselves.

Absolute address	Relative address	Instructions	Comments
48	0	L 2,904(0,1)	
52	4	A 2,900(0,1)	Add 49 to a number
56	8	ST 2,904(0,1)	
60	12	L 2,0(0,1)	
64	16	A 2,896(0,1)	Increase displacement of load instruction by 4
68	20	ST 2,0(0,1)	
72	24	L 2,8(0,1)	
76	28	A 2,896(0,1)	Increase displacement of store instruction by 4
80	32	ST 2,8(0,1)	
		Branch to relative location 0 nine times	
⋮	⋮		
944	896	4	
948	900	49	
952	904	Numbers	
⋮	⋮		

FIGURE 2.10 Program for addition problem using instruction modification

ADDITIONAL ASSUMPTIONS:

Assumption 5.   Relative location 896 contains a 4.

To see how the program operates we must keep in mind that the contents of location 48 (Fig. 2.11) are not L 2,904(0,1), but rather

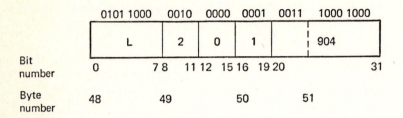

FIGURE 2.11   Contents of location 48

The offset of the instruction is the last and rightmost part of the number stored in that location. This instruction may be interpreted as a piece of data, and adding the number 4 to it updates the offset.

Treating instructions as data is not a good programming technique because in maintaining the program over a period of time, it may become difficult to understand what the original programmer was doing. In the case of multiprocessing systems it would violate all the rules of pure procedures (*re-entrant code*), which are procedures that do not modify themselves. We are including this example merely to exemplify instruction formats and explicitly demonstrate that instructions are stored as a type of data.

2.2.3 Address Modification Using Index Registers

Perhaps the most elegant way to solve this example is to use the index registers for address modification. Recall that an address equals the offset plus the contents of the base register plus the contents of an index register. We use the same three main instructions: the load instruction, add 49, and the store instruction. We simply loop through those three instructions, updating the contents of an index register by 4 during each pass and so updating the value of the address specified in the load and store instructions. The following program section uses this technique:

Absolute address	Relative address	Instructions	Comments
48	0	SR 4,4	Clear register 4
50	2	L 2,904(4,1)	Load data element of array
54	6	A 2,900(0,1)	Add 49
58	10	ST 2,904(4,1)	Replace data element
62	14	A 4,896(0,1)	Add 4 to index register
		Branch back to relative location 2, nine times	

The first instruction in this program is a subtract instruction. It is a register-to-register instruction, subtracting register 4 from register 4, thereby initializing its contents to 0. Note that this instruction is only two bytes long. As we discussed in the previous section, the 360/370 has different length instructions. The SR instruction starts at absolute location 48. The next instruction starts at location 50. Notice also that the load and store instructions now specify register 4 as an index register. The first time through the loop, register 4 will contain 0, the next time, 4, etc. This will point the load and store instructions at a different data item each time.

Now that we have seen how to modify instruction addresses, we will proceed to add the instructions that will carry out the actual looping.

2.2.4 Looping

In this section we will discuss two looping methods using machine language. We will make the additional assumptions:

Assumption 6.   Relative location 892 contains a 10
Assumption 7.   Relative location 888 contains a 1 (first method only)

Figure 2.12 depicts one looping scheme.

After the first four basic instructions are executed, there is a sequence of instructions that subtracts one from the temporary location and detects whether or not the result is positive. If positive, control loops back to the main program at relative location 2.

There is one instruction, Branch on Count (BCT, shown in Fig. 2.13) that accomplishes the work of the last four instructions in Figure 2.12.

The reader is referred to the manuals for the explanation of the BCT instruction. Essentially, register 3 is decremented by 1 until a 0 is reached. While the content of register 3 is positive, we transfer to the address specified in the address field, in this case, 6 plus the contents of register 1. When zero is reached, no branch occurs. Most computers have a similar branching instruction.

Absolute address	Relative address	Instructions		
48	0	SR	4,4	
50	2	L	2,904(4,1)⎫	
54	6	A	2,900(0,1)⎬	Add 49 to a number
58	10	ST	2,904(4,1)⎭	
62	14	A	4,896(0,1)	Add 4 to index register
66	18	L	3,892(0,1)	Load temp into register 3
70	22	S	3,888(0,1)	Subtract 1
74	26	ST	3,892(0,1)	Store temp
78	30	BC	2,2(0,1)	Branch if result is positive (2 denotes a condition code)
—	—	—		
≡	—	—		
936	888	1		
940	892	(Initially 10 - decremented by 1 after each loop)		
944	896	4		
948	900	49		
952	904	Numbers		

FIGURE 2.12 Program for addition problem showing looping

Absolute address	Relative address	Instructions		
48	0	L	3,892(0,1)	Load register 3 with 10
52	4	SR	4,4	Clear register 4
54	6	L	2,904(4,1)	
58	10	A	2,900(0,1)	Add 49 to a number
62	14	ST	2,904(4,1)	
66	18	A	4,896(0,1)	Add 4 to index register
70	22	BCT	3,6(0,1)	Subtract one from register 3 and branch to relative location 6 when positive
⋮	⋮	⋮		
940	892	10		
944	896	4		
948	900	49		
952	904	Numbers		
⋮	⋮			
992	unused			
⋮				

FIGURE 2.13 Final version of example

We now have reduced the program to 26 bytes of instructions and 52 bytes of data, in contrast to the 120 bytes of instructions and 44 of data utilized in our first attempt. This is a savings of 86 bytes. Note: all of the preceding programs could be placed elsewhere in core, at location 400 rather than 48, for example, and only register 1 need be changed.

2.3 ASSEMBLY LANGUAGE

When the user wishes to communicate with the computer, he has available to him a spectrum of languages:

English	Best for programmer
PL/I, FORTRAN	↑
⋮	
Assembly language	
Mnemonic machine language	↓
Machine language	Best for machine

So far we have discussed the two lowest members of this spectrum. We will now go into assembly language, which is the most machine-dependent language used by programmers today.

There are four main advantages to using assembly language rather than machine language.

1. It is mnemonic; e.g., we write ST instead of the bit configuration 01010000 for the store instruction
2. Addresses are symbolic, not absolute
3. Reading is easier
4. Introduction of data to program is easier

A disadvantage of assembly language is that it requires the use of an assembler to translate a source program into object code. Many of the features of 360 or 370 assembly language exist in assembly languages for other machines (if the reader is using another machine). These examples may be easily translated into the machine he is using.

2.3.1 An Assembly Language Program

Let us rewrite the program discussed in the previous section in assembly language (shown in Fig. 2.14). In doing so, the assumptions that were made when written in machine language are eliminated. One of the assumptions is that the program's starting address was absolute core location 48. We, as programmers, cannot presume to know into what location our program will be loaded in core. Thus there must be a way for us to load the base register with the address of the program in core just prior to execution time. That is, execution time is the only time in which the program, the programmer, or anyone else can be certain as to where in core the loader will load the user's program. The BALR instruction is one mechanism for loading the base register.

If the assembler is to automatically compute the displacement field of instructions, it must know what register can be used as a base register and what that register will contain. The USING instruction tells both of these things to the assembler and thus makes it possible for it to produce correct code. The USING instruction is a *pseudo-op*. A pseudo-op is an assembly language instruction that specifies an operation of the assembler; it is distinguished from a *machine-op* which represents to the assembler a machine instruction. The Define Constant (DC) and Define Storage (DS) instructions are pseudo-ops that instruct the assembler to place a 10, a 4, and a 49 in 3 consecutive fullwords ("F") in memory and leave 10 more for data. A number before the F would cause multiple allocations, e.g. DS 100F causes the assembler to set aside a 100 full word area.

	Program		Comments
TEST	START		Identifies name of program
BEGIN	BALR	15,0	Set register 15 to the address of the next instruction
	USING	BEGIN+2,15	Pseudo-op indicating to assembler register 15 is base register and its content is address of next instruction
	SR	4,4	Clear register 4 (set index=0)
	L	3,TEN	Load the number 10 into register 3
LOOP	L	2,DATA(4)	Load data (index) into register 2
	A	2,FORTY9	Add 49
	ST	2,DATA(4)	Store updated value of data (index)
	A	4,FOUR	Add 4 to register 4 (set index = index+4)
	BCT	3,LOOP	Decrement register 3 by 1, if result non-zero, branch back to loop
	BR	14	Branch back to caller
TEN	DC	F'10'	Constant 10
FOUR	DC	F'4'	Constant 4
FORTY9	DC	F'49'	Constant 49
DATA	DC	F'1,3,3,3,3, 4,5,8,9,0'	Words to be processed
	END		

FIGURE 2.14 An assembly language program

CLARIFICATION

1. *USING* is a pseudo-op that indicates to the assembler which general register to use as a base and what its contents will be. This is necessary because no special registers are set aside for addressing, thus the programmer must inform the assembler which register(s) to use and how to use them. Since addresses are relative, he can indicate to the assembler the address contained in the base register. The assembler is thus able to produce the machine code with the correct base register and offset.

2. *BALR* is an instruction to the computer to load a register with the next address and branch to the address in the second field. When the second operand is register 0, as it is here, execution proceeds with the next instruction. It is important to see the distinction between the BALR, which loads the base register, and the USING, which informs the assembler what is in the base register. The distinction will be clearer after we study the assembler, but for now, note that a USING only provides information to the assembler but does not load the register. Therefore, if the register does not contain the address that the USING says it should contain, a program error may result.

3. *START* is a pseudo-op that tells the assembler where the beginning of the program is and allows the user to give a name to the program. In this case the name is TEST.

4. *END* is a pseudo-op that tells the assembler that the last card of the program has been reached.

5. Note that instead of addresses in the operand fields of the instructions as in the example of Figure 2.8, there are symbolic names. The main reason for assemblers coming into existence was to shift the burdens of calculating specific addresses from the programmer to the computer.

6. BR 14, the last machine-op instruction, is a branch to the location whose address is in general register 14. By convention, calling programs leave their return address in register 14.

2.3.2 Example Using Literals

Here we will repeat the same example using *literals*, which are mechanisms whereby the assembler creates data areas for the programmer, containing constants he requests.

In the program of Figure 2.15 the arguments =F'10', =F'49', =F'4' are literals which will result in the creation of a data area containing 10,49,4 and replacement of the literal operand with the address of the data it describes.

The assembler translates the instruction L 3, = F'10' so that its address portion points to a full word that contains a 10. Normally, the assembler will construct

```
TEST        START     0
BEGIN       BALR      BASE,0
            USING     BEGIN+2,BASE
            SR        4,4
            L         3, = F'10'
LOOP        L         2,DATA (4)
            A         2, = F'49'
            ST        2,DATA (4)
            A         4, = F'4'
            BCT       3, *-16
            BR        14
            LTORG
DATA        DC        F'1,3,3,3,3,4,5,8,9,0'
BASE        EQU       15
            END
```

FIGURE 2.15 Assembly language program using literals

a "literal table" at the end of the program. This table will contain all the constants that have been requested through the use of literals. However, the pseudo-op LTORG can tell the assembler to place the encountered literals at an earlier location. This pseudo-op is used in the case where we have a very long program. For example, if our DC instruction contained 10,000 pieces of data, it would have been impossible for the offset of the load instruction to reach the literals at the end of our program. In this case, we would want to force the literals into the program before the DC instruction.

In the BCT instruction in the same program we have used as an address *-16. The star is a mnemonic that means "here." The expression *-16 refers to the address of the present instruction minus 16 locations, which is LOOP. (This type of addressing is not usually good practice: should it become necessary for the programmer to insert other statements in-between LOOP and BCT, he would have to remember to change the 16.)

The statement BASE EQU 15 assigns this value 15 to the symbol BASE; BASE will be everywhere evaluated as 15. The EQU pseudo-op allows the programmer to define variables. Here, for example, if he wished to use a different base register, he would need only to change the EQU statement. Any sort of valid arithmetic expression may appear as the operand of the EQU statement.

Depicted in Figure 2.16 is the assembled version (that is, the output of the assembler) of the preceding program.

Observe that some pseudo-ops (e.g., START and USING) do not generate machine code. Note also that the BR 14 instruction has been translated to BCR 15,14. This is because BR is a member of the assembler mnemonic group of instructions that allow the programmer to use a more mnemonic op code in place of BC followed by a particular mask value (see Appendix A).

2.4 SUMMARY

We have presented a general approach to understanding a new machine, and applied this approach in the context of the IBM 360 and 370. We have evolved a machine language example illustrating base register use, storage of instructions and data, indexing and looping. Some features of 360 Basic Assembly Language (BAL) were introduced, e.g., symbolic addressing, literals and pseudo-ops.

Assembly language program			Relative location	Assembled mnemonic program	
TEST	START				
BEGIN	BALR	15,0	0	BALR	15,0
	USING	BEGIN+2,15			
	SR	4,4	2	SR	4,4
	L	3, =F'10'	4	L	3,30(0,15)
LOOP	L	2, DATA (4)	8	L	2,42(4,15)
	A	2, =F'49'	12	A	2,34(0,15)
	ST	2, DATA (4)	16	ST	2,42(4,15)
	A	4, =F'4'	20	A	4,38(0,15)
	BCT	3, *-16	24	BCT	3,6(0,15)
	BR	14	28	BCR	15,14
	LTORG				
			32	10	
			36	49	
			40	4	
DATA	DC	F'1,3,3,3,3,4,5,9,0'	44	1	
			48	3	
			52	3	
			.		
			.		
	END				

FIGURE 2.16 Assembled version of example program

QUESTIONS[4]

1. All data is stored as ones and zeros, taking on meaning only when interpreted according to some rule. Order the following sets of strings according to the specified conditions:

   a. OP1   1001   0111   1001   1100

   OP2   0110   1001   0010   1100

   OP3   1000   0011   0110   1101

   1) Halfword integers
   2) Packed decimals

   b. OP1   0100   1110   1111   0110

   OP2   0110   0000   1111   0001

   OP3   1111   0101   1111   0010

   1) Halfword integers
   2) Characters (EBCDIC)

2. Below are several hexadecimal strings representing fullwords and halfwords from core.

   (1)   052C   (2)   452C
   (3)   4528367D   (4)   5914973C

   For each of the above,

   a. Write the binary equivalent.
   b. Assume each to be a halfword/fullword integer, and write its value in decimal.
   c. Assume each to be a packed decimal number, and write its value in decimal.
   d. If it represents a legitimate 360 machine instruction, give the mnemonic representation; if not, tell why not.

3. This problem will investigate basic properties of machine architecture. The simple machine in our example consists of a location-addressed memory where instructions and data are stored, and a Central Processing Unit (CPU) that interprets instructions and performs the specified operations. The CPU contains an Instruction Register (IR) which holds the present instruction being interpreted.

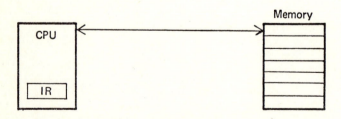

----

[4]An * denotes that the question may require the use of IBM 360 manuals. A † denotes that the question is a machine problem.

An instruction on this machine has the form

Op code	Operand 1	Operand 2	Result	Next

In questions a - d you are to redesign this basic machine with the objective of shortening the instruction length. For these questions consider the following instruction

ADD	A	B	C	NEXT

which adds the number at location A to that at location B and stores the result at C. The next instruction fetched for interpretation is located at NEXT.

a. Give a method by which the NEXT field of the instruction could be eliminated. What additional instruction would be required in this new machine that was not required in the original? What additional register must be added to the CPU?

b. Give a method by which the RESULT field of the instruction would be eliminated. (Do not add any registers to the CPU.) What additional instruction would be required for this new machine that was not required in the original?

c. Another way to eliminate the RESULT field is to add a single register to the CPU that is the same size as a memory word. Such a register is usually referred to as an accumulator (AC). The additional instruction that is required in this case is a store instruction which stores the contents of the accumulator into a specified word in memory. All other instructions take two operands and place their result into the accumulator. In addition to the RESULT field, one of the operand fields can also be eliminated. Describe how this can be done. What additional instruction is required?

d. The IBM 360 and many other computers use the two-address instruction format that you obtained from questions 2 and 3, rather than the four-address format of our basic machine. What advantages are to be found by shortening the instruction length? What are the disadvantages of this scheme?

4. a. What are the advantages of the 360's multiple register scheme over machines with fewer or specialized registers?

  *b. On the 360, register 0 operates differently in three contexts from the other registers. Give an example of each and explain how register 0 is being used in each case.

5. *a. What is the difference in function between the BALR and USING

instructions? What happens to each at assembly time? At execution time?

b. For each of the following program segments show the equivalent mnemonic machine language and determine the value placed in register 1 by the instruction LH 1,DATA2.

OCT15	START	0	OCT15	START	0
	BALR	15,0		USING	*,15
	USING	*,15		BALR	15,0
	LR	10,15		LA	10,DATA2
	USING	*,10		USING	DATA2,10
	LH	1,DATA2		DROP	15
	BR	14		LH	1,DATA2
DATA1	DC	H'1'	DATA1	DC	F'1'
DATA2	DC	H'2'	DATA2	DC	F'2'
DATA3	DC	H'3'	DATA3	DC	F'3'
	END			END	

6. *a. The following program is supposed to multiply 3 times 2 and store the result into location 1000. Will it? (Note: The address of 1000 refers to location 1000 in core; no base or index register is used.)

```
L       3, = F'2'
M       3, = F'3'
ST      3, 1000
```

b. Will the following divide 10 by 2? Justify.

```
L       3, = F'10'
D       2, = F'2'
ST      3, 1000
```

7. *a. What is the difference between

```
INDEX   EQU     5
INDEX   DC      F'5'
```

b. What is the difference between the CR instruction and the CLR instruction?

8. *a. What will be in register 3 after each instruction in the following sequence of instructions:

```
        LA      3, = A(XYZ)
        LR      3, 3
        L       3, = F'5'
XYZ     LCR     3, 3
        LNR     3, 3
```

b. Which instruction will be executed after the BE SAME. Why?

```
        CLI     =F'3',3
        BE      SAME
        LR      3,5
SAME    AR      5,5
```

9. *a. When do 'SRDA 0,5' and 'SRDL 0,5' execute differently?
   b. When do 'SLL 1,1' and 'LA 1,0(1,1)' execute differently?
   c. When do 'MVC TEMP(0), DATA' and 'MVC TEMP(1), DATA' execute differently?
   d. Is 'LA 1,0(1)' equivalent to a no-operation? Is 'SRA 1,0'? If not, explain.
   e. Assume STOMP is defined by:

   STOMP   DC   C' ERASURE'

   How will the following instructions execute individually?

   ```
   MVC     STOMP+1(8), STOMP
   MVC     STOMP(8), STOMP+1
   ```

10. *Do all the 360's instructions set or check the CC (Condition Code)? What is the role of the CC in the 360's instruction set?

11. Draw micro-flowcharts for the following IBM 360 instructions (see Fig. 2.2).

   a. S   (Subtract, RX form)
   b. BCR (Branch on Condition, RR form)
   c. BXLE   (Branch on Index Less than or Equal, RS form).

12. Consider the following computer system organization, referred to as a "stack" computer.

   There are two memories: one memory is directly addressable, that is, it is possible to load from or store into any location at any time. The other memory has an associated register, called the "stack pointer;" it is only possible to load from or store into the location currently specified by the "stack pointer." We will refer to the "Stack Pointer" as SP.

   There are three types of instructions: (1) instructions that transfer data between the two memories, (2) instructions that operate on the "stack" memory only, and (3) transfer instructions. Note that there are *no* registers such as an AC (accumulator) or GPRs (General Purpose Registers) as on the IBM 7094 or 360.

   We will first discuss the ADD instruction. Assume the "stack" memory has the contents specified in Figure (a) below:

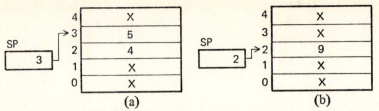

(a)   (b)

The ADD instruction will change the "stack" memory to the contents of Figure (b). Memory locations marked X are not affected by the instruction and may be ignored. Note that the following two actions occurred: (1) the contents of the locations specified by C(SP) and C(SP-1) are added and the result stored in the location specified by C(SP-1) and (2) SP is decreased by 1.

a. Draw a machine organization diagram for this computer (see Fig. 2.1).
b. Draw a micro-flowchart for the ADD instruction. It should be similar in complexity to the preceding flowchart in Figure 2.2, but the actual registers etc., will not necessarily be the same. You should *clearly* specify your notation. Assume the instruction is already in the decoding register. (Hopefully, you noticed that the ADD instruction does *not* have an operand, only an op-code. Assume that the ADD instruction requires only one byte of op-code.)
c. The LOAD instruction operates as described below. Assume that the regular memory has its contents illustrated in Figure (c) and the "stack" memory is still as in Figure (b). The instruction LOAD 100 would result in Figure (d).

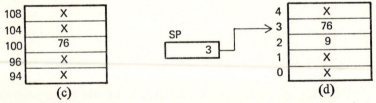

(c)   (d)

Note that the instruction loads into the location specified by C(SP+1) and then increases C(SP) by 1. Assume that the LOAD instruction is four bytes long, i.e.

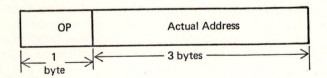

Draw a micro-flowchart for the LOAD instruction.

13. The following 360 assembly language program computes the function:

$$A = 2 * B + 2 * C - 1$$

1)	COMPUTE	START	
2)		USING	*,15
3)		L	1,B
4)		SLA	1,1
5)		L	2,C
6)		SLA	2,1
7)		AR	1,2
8)		S	1, =F'1'
9)		ST	1,A
10)		BR	14
11)	A	DC	F'0'
12)	B	DC	F'5'
13)	C	DC	F'7'
14)		END	

a. Verify that the preceding program works correctly by simulating the instructions one by one and filling in the table below. Indicate the contents of each register and memory location *after* each instruction is executed.

Instruction	Register 1	Contents of register 2	Location A
3			
4			
5			
6			
7			
8			
9			

b. The above program is reasonably efficient; it only requires 44 bytes and cleverly avoids the use of the slow multiply instruction and the literal 2. It is known that by rewriting statements 3 through 9 only, it is possible to reduce the entire program to only 12 statements that require 32 bytes. This new program must compute the same function though not necessarily in the same way.

Fill in the blank spaces in the following program to represent a new program that is more efficient than the preceding one. It need not be optimal nor use all the statements 3 through 9.

1)	COMPUTE	START	
2)		USING	*,15
3)			
4)			
5)			

```
6)
7)
8)
9)
10)              BR        14
11)    A         DC        F'0'
12)    B         DC        F'5'
13)    C         DC        F'7'
                 END
```

14. Obtain the manufacturer's manual for any digital computer and answer the five basic questions of section 2.1.1.

15. †Write a subroutine in 360 assembly language that does the following.

   a. When control is passed to your program, registers 2 and 3 will contain 8 EBCDIC characters (four eight-bit characters in each register).
   b. The subroutine should *count* the number of EBCDIC commas and return the count in register 1.

Example:	Register 2	Register 3
INPUT:	A , B C	D E , F (EBCDIC)
	Register 1	
OUTPUT:	00000002	(HEXADECIMAL)

A reasonable solution to this problem will probably require from 8-20 assembler cards.

There will be a grader[5] to evaluate your program. The format for each program is:

```
      GRADER                           STUDENT
Loads registers 2,3     STUDENT  START 0
L     15, =V(STUDENT)            ENTRY STUDENTN
BALR 14,15                       USING  *,15
Checks for right answer            .
                                   .                      Body of program
                                   .
                                 BR      14             DC and DS
                                   .                    pseudo-ops
                                                        (if any)
                                 LTORG
                        STUDENTN EQU     *
                                 END
```

---

[5]The problem can be done without a grader. The student will have to supply data and a main program. A grading program calls student programs and keeps a record of the results. We specify the grader only as an aid to the instructor or student who wishes to use such a scheme.

The student's program *must not change* the contents of registers 14 or 15.

16. †All data forms are read by the assembler into the machine in character format (EBCDIC), so the assembler or compiler must provide routines for converting the data into the internal representation specified by the programmer.

Your assignment is to write a 360 assembly language subroutine that simulates the data processing performed by an assembler in handling a 'DC' pseudo-op for C, X, P, and F formats. You will be given an EBCDIC character string of specified byte-length in storage and asked to convert it to a specified internal data format.

a. *Communication with the Grading[5] Program* When your program is entered, the general registers will contain the following information.

Register 0:
 The contents of register zero indicate the type of conversion to be performed, as follows:

0	Character
1	Hexadecimal
2	Packed decimal
3	Fullword binary

Register 1:
 The contents of register one indicate the length and location of the data to be converted. Bits 0-7 contain the byte count of the data (including any optional sign as described below) and bits 8-31 contain the absolute address of the data:

```
      ┌──────────┬──────────────────────────────┐
      │          │                              │
      │  Count   │           Address            │
      │          │                              │
      └──────────┴──────────────────────────────┘
      0         7 8                             31
```

Registers 2-12:
 The contents of registers 2-12 are not significant, but must be saved and restored by your program.

Register 13:
 Register 13 contains the address of an 18 fullword area where you may save general registers.

Register 14:
 Register 14 contains the address of the return point in the grading program. You should branch to this address when you have completed processing.

Register 15:
 Register 15 contains the address of the entry point to your program.

When your program returns to the grading program, the contents of registers 2-12 should be the same as when you were called, and register 1 should contain the *address* of a fullword area in your program with the following structure:

Count	Address
0 7	8 31

The "count" will be the length in bytes of the converted data, and the "address" will be the absolute address of an area within your program containing the converted data.

The following restrictions will be placed on the input and output data:

Character data will have a maximum byte count of 40.

Data to be converted to hexadecimal will have a maximum byte count of 40, yielding a maximum answer count of 20, and the byte count will be even. (Thus, you will not have to pad with zeros.)

Data to be converted to packed decimal will have, at most, 16 significant decimal digits not including an optional prefixed plus or minus sign. When you return your answer, it should be as short as possible, that is, with leading zeros removed. You must return the answer with the EBCDIC preferred sign codes C and D.

Data to be converted to fullword binary will also have an optional prefixed plus or minus sign, and a maximum significant digit count of 16. Your answer should be aligned to a fullword boundary.

You must not modify the input strings in any way.

b. *Examples* If you were given the string '110', with a count of 3, your answer would be:

Conversion	Internal code (hexadecimal)	Final count
C	F1F1F0	3
X	0110	2
P	110C	2
F	0000006E	4

Note the zero padding and justification in the X, P, F conversions.

17. †Write a 360 assembly language subroutine that will perform addition and subtraction of mixed base numbers. For example:

					Register	Contents (hex)			
	1 days	22 hours	3 min		R1	+	01	16	03
−(		22 hours	20 min	)	R2	−	00	16	14
	0 days	23 hours	43 min		R3	+	00	17	2B

Registers 1 and 2 contain the operands; register 0 will contain your answer. For each register the first byte is the sign, the second is the number of days, third number of hours, fourth number of minutes.

The student program must have the same form as problem 16.

3

assemblers

An assembler is a program that accepts as input an assembly language program and produces its machine language equivalent along with information for the loader (Fig. 3.1). In this chapter we will discuss the design of an assembler.

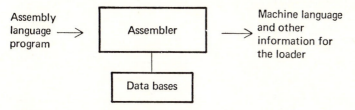

FIGURE 3.1 Function of an assembler

We focus on procedures for producing the machine language. However, the reader must keep in mind that (in all but the most primitive of loading schemes) the assembler must also produce other information for the loader to use. For example, externally defined symbols must be noted and passed on to the loader; the assembler does not know the address (value) of these symbols and it is up to the loader to find the programs containing them, load them into core, and place the values of these symbols in the calling program. Loading is discussed in Chapter 5.

In this chapter we are primarily concerned with the production of machine language. The illustrative examples use a 360-type assembler and mnemonic machine language. In our design of an assembler, and later in our design of a macro processor, many possible algorithms could have been used. We have chosen a way which we feel demonstrates the basic tasks of such programs.

Throughout this book, we will be referring to "decks" and "programs." At one time a "deck" always meant a deck of cards. Today, with the widespread use of other forms of secondary storage and of typewriter terminals, many programs never actually take the form of card decks. A "card" is a convenient unit of information; other devices offer similar divisions into units, or *records*, often of variable lengths. These different forms of storage are essentially interchangeable; a "statement" may be a card or other record, and a "card" may be a record on tape or drum. The term "deck," as used in this book and throughout the computer industry, has become a commonplace for every form of program used as input or output to a computer.

3.1 GENERAL DESIGN PROCEDURE

Before discussing the detailed design of an assembler, let us examine the general problem of designing software. Listed below are six steps that should be followed by the designer:

1. Specify the problem
2. Specify data structures
3. Define format of data structures
4. Specify algorithm
5. Look for modularity (i.e., capability of one program to be subdivided into independent programming units)
6. Repeat 1 through 5 on modules

In this book we have followed this procedure in the design of the assembler, loader, and compiler.

3.2 DESIGN OF ASSEMBLER

3.2.1 Statement of Problem

Let us pretend that we are the assembler trying to translate the program in the left column of Figure 3.2. We read the START instruction and note that it is a pseudo-op instruction (to the assembler) giving JOHN as the name of this program; the assembler must pass the name on to the loader. The next instruction is the USING pseudo-op. This tells the assembler (us) that register 15 is the base register and at execution time will contain the address of the first instruction of the program.

Source program		First pass		Second pass	
		Relative address	Mnemonic instruction	Relative address	Mnemonic instruction
JOHN START	0				
USING	*,15				
L	1,FIVE	0	L 1,–(0,15)	0	L 1,16(0,15)
A	1,FOUR	4	A 1,–(0,15)	4	A 1,12(0,15)
ST	1,TEMP	8	ST 1,–(0,15)	8	ST 1,20(0,15)
FOUR DC	F'4'	12	4	12	4
FIVE DC	F'5'	16	5	16	5
TEMP DS	1F	20	–	20	–
END					

FIGURE 3.2 Intermediate steps in assembling a program

There is no BALR instruction. This program was presumably called by another program that left the address of the first instruction in register 15 (see standard subroutine linkage conventions in Appendix B). Next comes a Load instruction: L 1, FIVE. We can look up the bit configuration for the mnemonic in a table and put the bit configuration for the L in the appropriate place in the machine language instruction. Now we need the address of FIVE. At this point, however, we do not know where FIVE is, so we cannot supply its address. Because no index register is being used, we put in 0 for the index register. We know that register 15 is being used as the base register, but we cannot calculate the offset. The base register 15 is pointing to the beginning of this program, and the offset is going to be the difference between the location FIVE and the location of the beginning of the program, which is not known at this time. We maintain a *location counter* indicating the relative address of the instruction being processed; this counter is incremented by 4 (length of a Load instruction).

The next instruction is an Add instruction. We look up the op-code, but we do not know the offset for FOUR. The same thing happens with the Store instruction. The DC instruction is a pseudo-op directing us to define some data; for FOUR we are to produce a '4'. We know that this word will be stored at relative location 12, because the location counter now has the value 12, having been incremented by the length of each preceding instruction. The first instruction, four bytes long, is at relative address 0. The next two instructions are also four bytes long. We say that the symbol "FOUR" has the value 12. The next instruction has as a label FIVE and an associated location counter value of 16. The label on TEMP has an associated value of 20. We have thus produced the code in the center column of Figure 3.2.

As the assembler, we can now go back through the program and fill in the offsets as is done in the third column of Figure 3.2.

Because symbols can appear before they are defined, it is convenient to make two passes over the input (as this example shows). The first pass has only to define the symbols; the second pass can then generate the instructions and addresses. (There are one-pass assemblers and multiple-pass assemblers. Their design and implications are discussed in this chapter). Specifically, an assembler must do the following:

1. Generate instructions:
   a. Evaluate the mnemonic in the operation field to produce its machine code.
   b. Evaluate the subfields — find the value of each symbol, process literals, and assign addresses.
2. Process pseudo ops

We can group these tasks into two *passes* or sequential scans over the input; associated with each task are one or more assembler modules.

Pass 1: Purpose — define symbols and literals
   1. Determine length of machine instructions (MOTGET1)
   2. Keep track of Location Counter (LC)
   3. Remember values of symbols until pass 2 (STSTO)
   4. Process some pseudo ops, e.g., EQU, DS (POTGET1)
   5. Remember literals (LITSTO)

Pass 2: Purpose — generate object program
   1. Look up value of symbols (STGET)
   2. Generate instructions (MOTGET2)
   3. Generate data (for DS, DC, and literals)
   4. Process pseudo ops (POTGET2)

Figures 3.3 and 3.4 outline the steps involved in pass 1 and pass 2. The specifics of the data bases and a more detailed algorithm are developed in the following sections.

3.2.2   Data Structure

The second step in our design procedure is to establish the data bases that we have to work with.

Pass 1 data bases:
   1. Input source program.
   2. A Location Counter (LC), used to keep track of each instruction's location.
   3. A table, the Machine-Operation Table (MOT), that indicates the symbolic

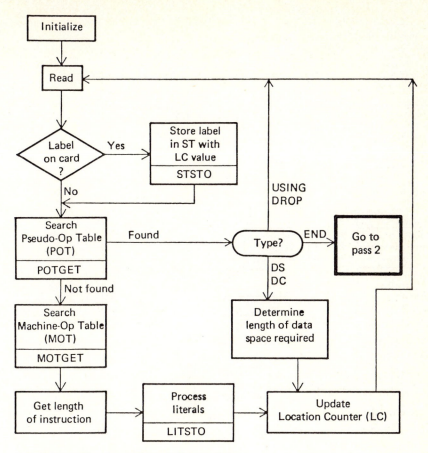

FIGURE 3.3 Pass 1 overview: define symbols

mnemonic for each instruction and its length (two, four, or six bytes).
4. A table, the Pseudo-Operation Table (POT), that indicates the symbolic
   mnemonic and action to be taken for each pseudo-op in pass 1.
5. A table, the Symbol Table (ST), that is used to store each label and its
   corresponding value.
6. A table, the Literal Table (LT), that is used to store each literal encountered
   and its corresponding assigned location.
7. A copy of the input to be used later by pass 2. This may be stored in a
   secondary storage device, such as magnetic tape, disk, or drum, or the
   original source deck may be read by the assembler a second time for pass 2.

Pass 2 data bases:
1. Copy of source program input to pass 1.
2. Location Counter (LC).

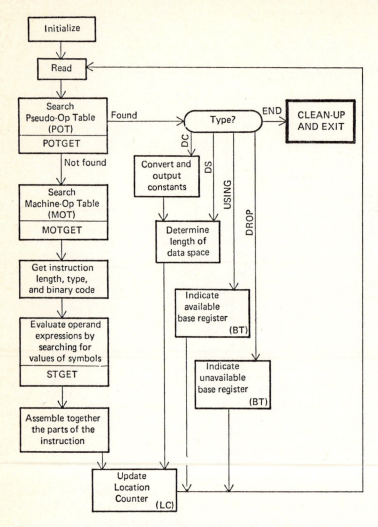

FIGURE 3.4   Pass 2 overview: evaluate fields and generate code

3. A table, the Machine Operation Table (MOT), that indicates for each instruction: (a) symbolic mnemonic; (b) length; (c) binary machine opcode, and (d) format (e.g., RS, RX, SI).

4. A table, the Pseudo-Operation Table (POT), that indicates for each pseudo-op the symbolic mnemonic and the action to be taken in pass 2.

5. The Symbol Table (ST), prepared by pass 1, containing each label and its corresponding value.

6. A table, the Base Table (BT), that indicates which registers are currently

specified as base registers by USING pseudo-ops and what are the specified contents of these registers.

7. A work-space, INST, that is used to hold each instruction as its various parts (e.g., binary op-code, register fields, length fields, displacement fields) are being assembled together.

8. A workspace, PRINT LINE, used to produce a printed listing.

9. A workspace, PUNCH CARD, used prior to actual outputting for converting the assembled instructions into the format needed by the loader.

10. An output deck of assembled instructions in the format needed by the loader.

Figure 3.5 illustrates the interrelation of some of the data bases and the two passes of the assembler.

3.2.3 Format of Data Bases

The third step in our design procedure is to specify the format and content of each of the data bases — a task that must be undertaken even before describing the specific algorithm underlying the assembler design. In actuality, the algorithm, data base, and formats are all interlocked. Their specification is in practical designs, circular, in that the designer has in mind some features of the format and algorithm he plans to use and continues to iterate their design until all cases work.

Pass 2 requires a Machine-Operation Table (MOT) containing name, length, binary code, and format; pass 1 requires only name and length. We could use two separate tables with different formats and contents or use the same table for both passes; the same is true of the Pseudo-Operation Table (POT). By generalizing the table formats, we could combine the MOT and POT into one table. For this particular design, we will use a single MOT but two separate POTs.

Once we decide what information belongs in each data base, it is necessary to specify the format of each entry. For example, in what format are symbols stored (e.g., left justified, padded with blanks, coded in EBCDIC or ASCII) and what are the coding conventions? The Extended Binary Coded Decimal Interchange Code (EBCDIC) is the standard IBM 360 coding scheme for representing characters as eight-bit bytes. The character "A," for instance, is represented in EBCDIC as 1100 0001 binary (C1 in hexadecimal).

The Machine-Op Table (MOT) and Pseudo-Op Tables (POTs) are examples of *fixed tables*. The contents of these tables are not filled in or altered during the assembly process. Figure 3.6 depicts a possible content and format of the machine-op table. The op code is the key and its value is the binary op-code equivalent, which is stored for use in generating machine code. The instruction

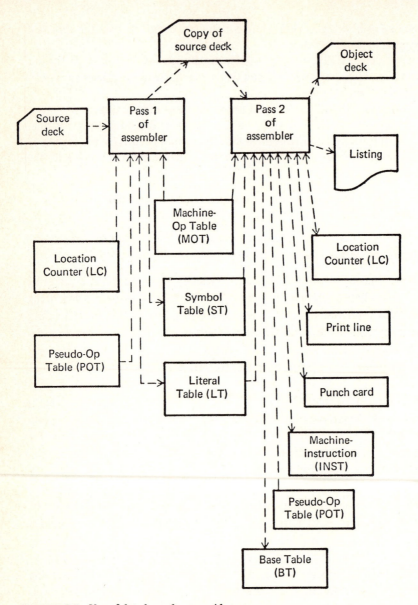

FIGURE 3.5 Use of data bases by assembler passes

length is stored for use in updating the location counter; the instruction format for use in forming the machine language equivalent.

Figure 3.7 depicts a possible pseudo-op table. Each pseudo-op is listed with an associated pointer to the assembler routine for processing the pseudo-op.

<— ——————————————————— 6-bytes per entry ——————————————————— —>

Mnemonic op-code (4-bytes) (characters)	Binary op-code (1-byte) (hexadecimal)	Instruction length (2-bits) (binary)	Instruction format (3-bits) (binary)	Not used in this design (3-bits)
"Abbb"	5A	10	001	
"AHbb"	4A	10	001	
"ALbb"	5E	10	001	
"ALRb"	1E	01	000	
"ARbb"	1A	01	000	
. . .	. . .	. . .	. . .	
"MVCb"	D2	11	100	
. . .	. . .	. . .	. . .	

$b\sim$ represents the character "blank"

Codes:

Instruction length

01 = 1 half-words = 2 bytes
10 = 2 half-words = 4 bytes
11 = 3 half-words = 6 bytes

Instruction format

000 = RR
001 = RX
010 = RS
011 = SI
100 = SS

FIGURE 3.6 Machine-Op Table (MOT) for pass 1 and pass 2

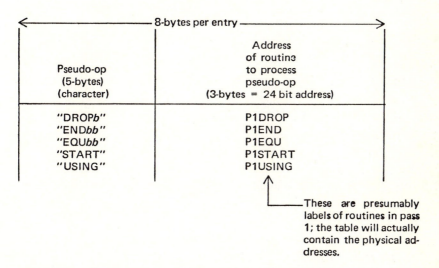

<— ————————————— 8-bytes per entry ————————————— —>

Pseudo-op (5-bytes) (character)	Address of routine to process pseudo-op (3-bytes = 24 bit address)
"DROPb"	P1DROP
"ENDbb"	P1END
"EQUbb"	P1EQU
"START"	P1START
"USING"	P1USING

These are presumably labels of routines in pass 1; the table will actually contain the physical addresses.

FIGURE 3.7 Pseudo-Op Table (POT) for pass 1 (similar table for pass 2)

The Symbol Table and Literal Table (Fig. 3.8) include for each entry not only the name and assembly-time value fields but also a length field and a relative-location indicator. The length field indicates the length (in bytes) of the instruction or datum to which the symbol is attached. For example, consider

```
COMMA      DC      C','
F          DS      F
AD         A       1,F
WORD       DC      3F'6'
```

The symbol COMMA has length 1; F has length 4; AD has length 4 (an add instruction is four bytes long); and WORD has length 4 (the multiplier, 3, is not considered in determining length). The symbol * (current value of location counter) always has a length of 1. If a symbol is equivalent (via EQU) to another, its length is made the same as that of the other. The length field is used by the assembler to calculate length codes used with certain SS-type instructions.

←	14-bytes per entry		→
Symbol (8-bytes) (characters)	Value (4-bytes) (hexadecimal)	Length (1-byte) (hexadecimal)	Relocation (1-byte) (character)
"JOHN*bbbb*"	0000	01	"R"
"FOUR*bbbb*"	000C	04	"R"
"FIVE*bbbb*"	0010	04	"R"
"TEMP*bbbb*"	0014	04	"R"

FIGURE 3.8   Symbol Table (ST) for pass 1 and pass 2

The relative-location indicator tells the assembler whether the value of the symbol is absolute (does not change if the program is moved in core), or relative to the base of the program. The assembler can use a simple heuristic to decide into which class a symbol falls. If the symbol is defined by equivalence with a constant (e.g., 6) or an absolute symbol, then the symbol is absolute. Otherwise, it is a relative symbol. The relative-location field in the symbol table will have an "R" in it if the symbol is relative, or an "A" if the symbol is absolute. In the actual assembler a substantially more complex algorithm is generally used.

Figure 3.9 depicts a possible base table that is used by the assembler to generate the proper base register reference in machine instructions and to compute the correct offsets. Basically, the assembler must generate an address (offset, a base register number, an index register number) for most symbolic references. The symbol table contains the address of the symbol relative to the beginning of the program. When generating an address, the assembler may use the base register table to choose a base register that will contain a value closest to the symbolic reference. The address is then formulated. Base register number = the base register containing a value closest to the symbolic reference. Offset = (value of symbol in symbol table) - (contents of base register).

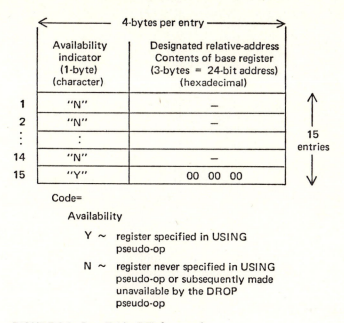

Code=

Availability

Y ~ register specified in USING
pseudo-op

N ~ register never specified in USING
pseudo-op or subsequently made
unavailable by the DROP
pseudo-op

FIGURE 3.9 Base Table (BT) for pass 2

The following assembly program is used to illustrate the use of the *variable tables* (symbol table, literal table, and base table) and to demonstrate the motivation for the algorithms presented in the next section. We are only concerned with the problem of assembling this program; its specific function is irrelevant.

Sample Assembly Source Program

Statement no.

1	PRGAM2	START	0
2		USING	*,15
3		LA	15, SETUP
4		SR	TOTAL, TOTAL
5	AC	EQU	2
6	INDEX	EQU	3
7	TOTAL	EQU	4
8	DATABASE	EQU	13

Sample Assembly Source Program (continued)

Statement no.			
9	SETUP	EQU	*
10		USING	SETUP, 15
11		L	DATABASE, = A(DATA1)
12		USING	DATAAREA, DATABASE
13		SR	INDEX, INDEX
14	LOOP	L	AC, DATA1 (INDEX)
15		AR	TOTAL, AC
16		A	AC, = F'5'
17		ST	AC, SAVE (INDEX)
18		A	INDEX, = F'4'
19		C	INDEX, = F'8000'
20		BNE	LOOP
21		LR	1, TOTAL
22		BR	14
23		LTORG	
24	SAVE	DS	2000F
25	DATAAREA	EQU	*
26	DATA1	DC	F'25, 26, 97, 101 . . . .'
			[2000 numbers]
27		END	

In keeping with the purpose of pass 1 of an assembler (define symbols and literals), we can create the symbol and literal tables shown below.

Variable Tables

Symbol Table

Symbol	Value	Length	Relocation
PRGAM2	0	1	R
AC	2	1	A
INDEX	3	1	A
TOTAL	4	1	A
DATABASE	13	1	A
SETUP	6	1	R
LOOP	12	4	R
SAVE	64	4	R
DATAAREA	8064	1	R
DATA1	8064	4	R

Literal Table

A(DATA1)	48	4	R
F'5'	52	4	R
F'4'	56	4	R
F'8000'	60	4	R

As in the flowchart of Figure 3.3, we scan the program above keeping a location counter. For each symbol in the label field we make an entry in the symbol table. For the symbol PRGAM2 its value is its relative location. By IBM convention its length is 1.

We update the location counter, noting that the LA instruction is four bytes long and the SR is two. Continuing, we find that the next five symbols are defined by the pseudo-op EQU. These symbols are entered into the symbol table and the associated values given in the argument fields of the EQU statements are entered. The location counter is further updated noting that the L instruction is four bytes and the SR is two. (None of the pseudo-ops encountered affect the location counter since they do not result in any object code.) Thus the location counter has a value 12 when LOOP is encountered. Therefore, LOOP is entered into the symbol table with a value 12. It is a relocatable variable and so noted. Its length is 4 since it denotes a location that will contain a four-byte instruction. All other symbols are entered in like manner.

In the same pass all literals are recognized and entered into a literal table. The first literal is in statement 11 and its value is the address of the location that will contain the literal. Since this is the first literal, it will have the first address of the literal area. The LTORG pseudo-op (statement 23) forces the literal table to be placed there, where the location counter is updated to the next double word boundary which equals 48. Thus the value of '=A(DATA1)' is its address, 48. Similarly, the value of the literal F'5' is the next location in the literal table, 52 and so on.

Base table (showing only base registers in use)

1) After statement 2:

base	contents
15	0

2) After statement 10:

base	contents
15	6

3) After statement 12:

base	contents
13	8064
15	6

The literal table and the symbol table being completed, we may initiate pass 2 (Fig. 3.4), whose purpose is to evaluate arguments and generate code. To generate proper address in an instruction, we need to know the base register. To compute the offset, we need to know the content of the base register. The assembler of course does not know the execution time value of the base register, but it does know the value relative to the start of the program. Therefore, the assembler enters as "contents" its relative value. This value is used to compute the offset. Processing the USING pseudo-ops produces the base table shown above.

For each instruction in pass 2, we create the equivalent machine language instruction as shown below. For example, for statement 3 we:

1. Look up value of SETUP in symbol table (which is 6)
2. Look up value of op code in machine op table (binary op code for LA)
3. Formulate address
   a. Determine base register — pick one that has content closest to value of SETUP (register 15)
   b. Offset = value of symbol — content of base register = 6-0 = 6
   c. Formulate address: *offset (index register, base register)* = 6(0,15)
4. Average output code in appropriate formula

Similarly, we generate instructions for the remaining code as shown below.

Generated "machine" code

Corresponding statement no.	Location	Instruction/datum	
3	0	LA	15,6 (0,15)
4	4	SR	4,4
11	6	L	13,42 (0,15)
13	10	SR	3,3
14	12	L	2,0 (3,13)
15	16	AR	4,2
16	18	A	2,46 (0,15)
17	22	ST	2,58 (3,15)
18	26	A	3,50 (0,15)
19	30	C	3,54 (0,15)
20	34	BC	7,6 (0,15)
21	38	LR	1,4
22	40	BCR	15,14
23	48	8064	
	52	X'00000005'	
	56	X'00000004'	
	60	8000	

Generated "machine" code (continued)

Corresponding statement no.	Location	Instruction/datum
24	64	.
	.	.
	.	.
25	8064	X'00000019'
		.
		.
		.

3.2.4 Algorithm

The flowcharts in Figures 3.10 and 3.11 describe in some detail an algorithm for an assembler for an IBM 360 computer. These diagrams represent a simplification of the operations performed in a complex assembler but they illustrate most of the logical processes involved.

PASS 1: DEFINE SYMBOLS

The purpose of the first pass is to assign a location to each instruction and data-defining pseudo-instruction, and thus to define values for symbols appearing in the label fields of the source program. Initially, the Location Counter (LC) is set to the first location in the program (relative address 0). Then a source statement is read. The operation-code field is examined to determine if it is a pseudo-op; if it is not, the table of machine op-codes (MOT) is searched to find a match for the source statement's op-code field. The matched MOT entry specifies the length (2,4 or 6 bytes) of the instruction. The operand field is scanned for the presence of a literal. If a new literal is found, it is entered into the Literal Table (LT) for later processing. The label field of the source statement is then examined for the presence of a symbol. If there is a label, the symbol is saved in the Symbol Table (ST) along with the current value of the location counter. Finally, the current value of the location counter is incremented by the length of the instruction and a copy of the source card is saved for use by pass 2. The above sequence is then repeated for the next instruction.

The loop described is physically a small portion of pass 1 even though it is the most important function. The largest sections of pass 1 and pass 2 are devoted to the special processing needed for the various pseudo-operations. For simplicity, only a few major pseudo-ops are explicitly indicated in the flowchart (Fig. 3.10); the others are processed in a straightforward manner.

We now consider what must be done to process a pseudo-op. The simplest pro-

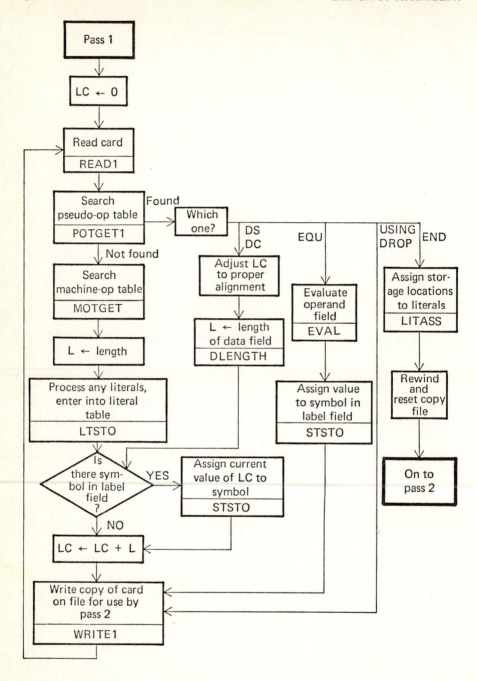

FIGURE 3.10   Detailed pass 1 flowchart

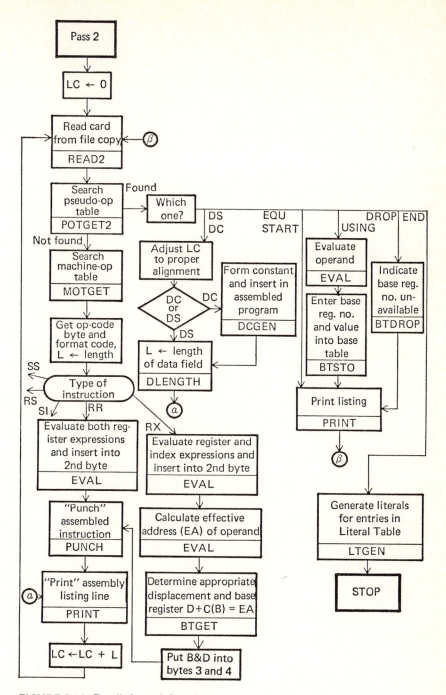

FIGURE 3.11 Detailed pass 2 flowchart

cedure occurs for USING and DROP. Pass 1 is only concerned with pseudo-ops that define symbols (labels) or affect the location counter; USING and DROP do neither. The assembler need only save the USING and DROP cards for pass 2.

In the case of the EQU pseudo-op during pass 1, we are concerned only with defining the symbol in the label field. This requires evaluating the expression in the operand field. (The symbols in the operand field of an EQU statement must have been defined previously.)

The DS and DC pseudo-ops can affect both the location counter and the definition of symbols in pass 1. The operand field must be examined to determine the number of bytes of storage required. Due to requirements for certain alignment conditions (e.g., fullwords must start on a byte whose address is a multiple of four), it may be necessary to adjust the location counter before defining the symbol.

When the END pseudo-op is encountered, pass 1 is terminated. Before transferring control to pass 2, there are various "housekeeping" operations that must be performed. These include assigning locations to literals that have been collected during pass 1, a procedure that is very similar to that for the DC pseudo-op. Finally, conditions are reinitialized for processing by pass 2.

PASS 2: GENERATE CODE

After all the symbols have been defined by pass 1, it is possible to finish the assembly by processing each card and determining values for its operation code and its operand field. In addition, pass 2 must structure the generated code into the appropriate format for later processing by the loader, and print an assembly listing containing the original source and the hexadecimal equivalent of the bytes generated. The Location Counter is initialized as in pass 1, and the processing continues as follows.

A card is read from the source file left by pass 1. As in pass 1, the operation code field is examined to determine if it is a pseudo-op; if it is not, the table of machine op-codes (MOT) is searched to find a match for the card's op-code field. The matching MOT entry specifies the length, binary op-code, and the format-type of the instruction. The operand fields of the different instruction format types require somewhat different processing.

For the RR-format instructions, each of the two register specification fields is evaluated. This evaluation may be very simple, as in:

        AR   2,3

or more complex, as in:

        MR   EVEN , EVEN + 1

The two fields are inserted into their respective four-bit fields in the second byte of the RR-instruction.

For RX-format instructions, the register and index fields are evaluated and processed in the same way as the register specifications for RR-format instructions. The storage address operand is evaluated to generate an Effective Address (EA). Then the base register table (BT) must be examined to find a suitable base register (B) such that $D = EA - c(B) < 4096$. The corresponding displacement can then be determined. The 4-bit base register specification and 12-bit displacement fields are then assembled into the third and fourth bytes of the instruction. Only the RR and RX instruction types are explicitly shown in the flowchart (Fig. 3.11). The other instruction formats are handled similarly.

After the instruction has been assembled, it is put into the necessary format for later processing by the loader. Typically, several instructions are placed on a single card (see Chapter 5 for a more detailed discussion). A listing line containing a copy of the source card, its assigned storage location, and its hexadecimal representation is then printed. Finally, the location counter is incremented and processing is continued with the next card.

As in pass 1, each of the pseudo-ops calls for special processing. The EQU pseudo-op requires very little processing in pass 2, because symbol definition was completed in pass 1. It is necessary only to print the EQU card as part of the printed listing.

The USING and DROP pseudo-ops, which were largely ignored in pass 1, require additional processing in pass 2. The operand fields of the pseudo-ops are evaluated; then the corresponding Base Table entry is either marked as available, if USING, or unavailable, if DROP. The base table is used extensively in pass 2 to compute the base and displacement fields for machine instructions with storage operands.

The DS and DC pseudo-ops are processed essentially as in pass 1. In pass 2, however, actual code must be generated for the DC pseudo-op. Depending upon the data types specified, this involves various conversions (e.g., floating point character to binary representation) and symbol evaluations (e.g., address constants).

The END pseudo-op indicates the end of the source program and terminates the assembly. Various "housekeeping" tasks must now be performed. For example, code must be generated for any literals remaining in the Literal Table (LT).

3.2.5 Look for Modularity

We now review our design, looking for functions that can be isolated. Typically, such functions fall into two categories: (1) multi-use and (2) unique.

In the flowcharts for pass 1 (Fig. 3.10) and pass 2 (Fig. 3.11), we examine each step as a candidate for logical separation. Likely choices are identified in the flowcharts by the shape

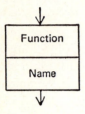

where "name" is the name assigned to the function (e.g., MOTGET, EVAL, PRINT).

Listed below are some of the functions that may be isolated in the two passes.

PASS 1:

1. READ1	— — —	Read the next assembly source card.
2. POTGET1	— — —	*Search* the pass 1 Pseudo-Op Table (POT) for a match with the operation field of the current source card.
3. MOTGET1	— — —	*Search* the Machine-Op Table (MOT) for a match with the operation of the current source card.
4. STSTO	— — —	*Store* a label and its associated value into the Symbol Table (ST). If the symbol is already in the table, return error indication (multiply-defined symbol).
5. LTSTO	— — —	*Store* a literal into the Literal Table (LT); do not store the same literal twice.
6. WRITE1	— — —	Write a copy of the assembly source card on a storage device for use by pass 2.
7. DLENGTH	— — —	*Scan* operand field of DS or DC pseudo-op to determine the amount of storage required.
8. EVAL	— — —	*Evaluate* an arithmetic expression consisting of constants and symbols (e.g. 6, ALPHA, BETA + 4 * GAMMA).
9. STGET	— — —	*Search* the Symbol Table (ST) for the entry corresponding to a specific symbol (used by STSTO, and EVAL).
10. LITASS	— — —	Assign storage locations to each literal in the literal table (may use DLENGTH).

PASS 2:

1.	READ2	———	Read the next assembly source card from the file copy.
2.	POTGET2	———	Similar to POTGET1 (search POT).
3.	MOTGET2	———	Same as in pass 1 (search MOT).
4.	EVAL	———	Same as in pass 1 (evaluate expressions).
5.	PUNCH	———	Convert generated instruction to card format; punch card when it is filled with data.
6.	PRINT	———	Convert relative location and generated code to character format; print the line along with copy of the source card.
7.	DCGEN	———	Process the fields of the DC pseudo-op to generate object code (uses EVAL and PUNCH).
8.	DLENGTH	———	Same as in pass 1.
9.	BTSTO	———	Insert data into appropriate entry of Base Table (BT).
10.	BTDROP	———	Insert "unavailable" indicator into appropriate entry of BT.
11.	BTGET	———	Convert effective address into base and displacement by searching Base Table (BT) for available base registers.
12.	LTGEN	———	Generate code for literals (uses DCGEN).

Each of these functions should independently go through the entire design process (problem statement, data bases, algorithm, modularity, etc.). These functions can be implemented as separate external subroutines, as internal subroutines, or as sections of the pass 1 and pass 2 programs. In any case, the ability to treat functions separately makes it much easier to design the structure of the assembler and each of its parts. Thus, rather than viewing the assembler as a single program (of from 1,000 to 10,000 source statements typically), we view it as a coordinated collection of routines each of relatively minor size and complexity.

We will not attempt to examine all of these functional routines in detail since they are quite straightforward. There are two particular observations of interest: (1) several of the routines involve the scanning or evaluation of fields (e.g., DLENGTH, EVAL, DCGEN); (2) several other routines involve the processing of tables by storing or searching (e.g., POTGET1, POTGET2, MOTGET1, MOTGET2, LTSTO, STSTO, STGET). The section of this book dealing with the implementation of compilers (Chapter 8) will discuss techniques for parsing fields and evaluating arithmetic expressions, many of which are also applicable to the functional modules of the assembler.

Table processing, as discussed in regard to assembler implementation, is found in almost every type of system program, including compilers, loaders, file systems and operating systems, as well as in many application programs. The general topic of processing data structures and data organizations plays a crucial role in systems programming. Since storing and searching for entries in tables often represent the largest expenditures of time in an assembler, the next section examines some techniques for organizing these tasks.

3.3 TABLE PROCESSING: SEARCHING AND SORTING

THE PROBLEM

It is often necessary to maintain large tables of information in such a way that items may be moved in and out quickly and easily. Let us consider the restricted case of a table whose entries are made on the basis of a keyword, such as the *symbol table* maintained by an assembly program.

The assembler symbol table is composed of multiple-word entries in a fixed format. In the table is the symbol name, its value, and various attributes, such as relocatability. The symbol name is the *key*, the string distinguishing each entry from the others that is matched during a search. Each symbol has a corresponding location, its *value*. (Analogously, in a telephone directory a subscriber's name is the key and his telephone number is the value.) There are two important things to notice about the assembler symbol table:

1. The symbols are placed in the table in the order in which they are gathered, so the table is unlikely to be ordered.
2. The symbols and their associated data are placed in consecutive locations in the table. They are all packed starting at one end of the table.

These two statements are true of most tables constructed one entry at a time without an encoding of addresses.

SEARCHING A TABLE

The problem of *searching* is as follows: given a keyword, find an entry in the table that matches, and return its value. The special problems — more than one entry with the same keyword, and no entry found — require individual treatment depending on the function of the table. In the case of an assembler's symbol table, these special cases correspond to multiply defined symbols and undefined symbols.

3.3.1 Linear Search

For a table in which the items have not been ordered (by sorting or otherwise), one way to look for a given keyword is to compare exhaustively every entry in the table with the given keyword. This is known as a *linear search* and is demonstrated in Figure 3.12.

```
           LA      4, SYMTBL          Start of table
LOOP       CLC     0(8,4), SYMBOL     Compare symbols
           BE      SYMFOUND           Equal
           A       4,=F'14'           Move to next symbol
           C       4,LAST             Are we at end of table
           BNE     LOOP               Loop back if not
NOTFOUND           (Symbol not found)
             .
             .
             .
SYMFOUND           (Symbol found)
             .
             .
             .
SYMBOL     DS      CL14               Symbol to be searched for, character
                                         string of length 14
SYMTBL     DS      100CL14            Symbol table space (14 bytes per entry)
LAST       DC      A(———)             Address of current end of symbol table
```

FIGURE 3.12 Sample linear search program

Here the symbols and values are stored in adjacent locations in an array named SYMTBL and defined by a DS. The word LAST contains the location of the current "end of table."

The loop described will compare the keyword (in the location SYMBOL) with each successive item in the table. When a match is found, exit is made via SYMFOUND; if no match is found by the end of the table, execution will go to location NOTFOUND.

On the average we would search half the table, using a linear search, before finding an entry. Therefore, the average length of time to find an entry is

$$T(avg) = [\text{overhead associated with entry probe}] \times \frac{N}{2}$$

Such a *linear search* procedure is fine for short tables and has the great virtue of simplicity, but for long tables it can be very slow. It is comparable to looking up a word in a dictionary whose contents are not ordered. It would provide little comfort to know that on the average you only have to search *half* of the dictionary.

3.3.2 Binary Search

When consulting a dictionary, we don't search every page for the definition of a word. We make a vague estimate of the location of our word in the dictionary (i.e., page number) and we open to that page. If the word is not on it, we go either to the right or left a number of pages and check again. We know which way to go because we are aware of an important property possessed by the dictionary, namely, it is ordered (B follows A, and S comes way after G). Such ordering of letters is called a *lexicographical* order.

A more systematic way of searching an *ordered* table is: Start at the middle of the table and compare the keyword with the middle entry. The keyword may be equal to, greater than, or smaller than the item checked. The next action taken for each of these outcomes is as follows:

1. If equal, the symbol is found.
2. If greater, use the top half of the given table as a new table to search.
3. If smaller, use the bottom half of the table.

This method, effectively divides the table in half on every probe, systematically bracketing the item searched for. The search is terminated with a 'not found' condition when the length of the last subtable searched is down to 1 and the item has not been found.

As an example of this type of search, consider a table of 15 items (Fig. 3.13). Suppose for example that we are searching for item IF (for convenience the values are not shown). We first compare IF with the middle item LO and find that IF must be in the top half of the table; a second comparison with the middle item in this half of the table, FU, shows IF to be in the second quarter; a third comparison with IW shows IF to be in the third eighth of the table (i.e., between items 4 and 6); and a final comparison is made with the item in position 5. A comparison failure on the fourth probe would have revealed that the item did not exist in the table.

This bracketing method of searching a table should be clear in principle although its implementation may be a little more complicated. It is known as a *binary search* or a *logarithmic search*, and it should be clear that since the effective table is halved on each probe, a maximum of about $\log_2(N)$ probes is required to search it.

Comparing the times of the linear search with those of the binary search, where A and B are overhead times associated with each table probe, we obtain

$$T\ (lin)\ =\ A*N$$
$$T\ (bin)\ =\ B*\log_2(N);$$

Since the binary search is more complicated, we can expect the constant B to

Number	Symbol	Probe 1	Probe 2	Probe 3	Probe 4
1	AL				
2	EX				
3	FN				
4	FU		IF $>$ FU		
5	IF				IF $=$ IF
6	IW			IF $<$ IW	
7	LE				
8	LO	IF $<$ LO			
9	NC				
10	OP				
11	OR				
12	RD				
13	RN				
14	TE				
15	TI				

FIGURE 3.13 Illustration of binary search

be considerably larger than A. Thus, a plot of T versus N for the two searching methods might look like Figure 3.14.

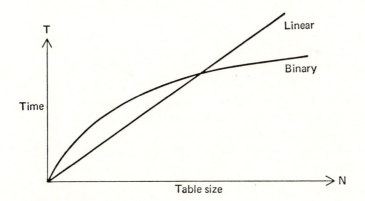

FIGURE 3.14 Search time versus N

Thus for small N we should use linear search while for large N we should use a binary search. The crossover point is generally around 50 - 100 items for machines like the 360. For other computers the number might vary from 10 to 1,000 depending on the available hardware.

Figure 3.15 depicts a sample binary search program. Since the binary process continually divides by 2, for efficiency and simplicity we assume table size is a power of 2 (e.g., 2,4,8,16, . . . etc.). This condition is easily attained by merely adding sufficient "dummy" entries to the end of the table (e.g., entries for the symbol ZZZZ ZZZZ).

```
              L         5,SIZE             Set table size (2^N*14 bytes)
              SRL       5,1                Divide by 2 by shifting
              LR        6,5                Copy into register 6
LOOP          SRL       6,1                Divide table size in half again
              LA        4,SYMTBL(5)        Set address of table entry
              CLC       0(8,4),SYMBOL      Compare with symbol
              BE        FOUND              Symbols match, entry found
              BH        TOOHIGH            SYMTBL entry > SYMBOL
TOOLOW        AR        5,6                Move higher in table
              B         TESTEND
TOOHIGH       SR        5,6                Move lower in table
TESTEND       LTR       6,6                Test if remaining size is 0
              BNZ       LOOP               No, look at next entry
NOTFOUND      (Symbol not found)
                 ⋮
FOUND         (Symbol found)
                 •
```

FIGURE 3.15   Sample binary search program

3.3.3   Sorting

It seems clear that for some purposes a binary search is more efficient than a linear one; but such a search requires an ordered table, which may not be easily obtainable. The Machine-Op Table (MOT) and Pseudo-Op Table (POT) of the assembler are fixed tables that can be manually organized so as to be ordered. Normally, however, a table is not generated in an ordered fashion; indeed, the symbol table created by an assembler is usually far from ordered, the symbols being stored in the exact order in which they appear in label fields.

3.3.3.1   INTERCHANGE SORT

We now address the problem of how to sort a table. There are a number of ways of doing this, some simple and some complicated. Figure 3.16 is a section of coding that performs an *interchange sort* (also known as a *bubble sort*, a *sinking sort* or a *sifting sort*). This simple sort takes adjacent pairs of items in the table and puts them in order (interchanges them) as required. Such a sorting algorithm is not very efficient, but it is simple. Let us take an example to see how it works. Consider the table of 12 numbers shown in Figure 3.17; each column represents one pass over the numbers interchanging any two adjacent numbers that are out of order. This particular table is completely sorted in only seven passes over the data. In the worst case, N-1 (here, 11) passes would be necessary. The interchange sort is thus able to exploit whatever natural order there may be in the table. Moreover, on each pass through the data at least one item is added to the bottom of the list in perfect order (in this case the 31 first, then 27, then 26, etc.). Hence, the sort could be made more efficient by (1) shortening the portion of the sorted list on each pass; and (2) checking for early completion. Such an optimized sort should require roughly N*(N-1)/2 comparisons and thus should take a time roughly proportional to N^2.

```
           L        5,LAST
           LA       4,SYMTBL
LOOP       CLC      0(8,4),14(4)        Compare adjacent symbols — 8 bytes
           BNH      OK                  Correct order
           MVC      TEMP(14),0(4)       Switch entries
           MVC      0(14,4),14(4)       . . .
           MVC      14(14,4),TEMP       . . .
OK         A        4,=F'14'            Move to next entry
           C        4,LAST              Is it last entry
           BNE      LOOP                No
                 .
                 .
                 .
SYMTBL     DS       0F                  Symbol table
           DS       100CL14             14 bytes per entry
TEMP       DS       CL14                Temporary entry
LAST       DC       A(————)             Location of next free entry in table
```

FIGURE 3.16   Interchange sort example in 360 assembly code

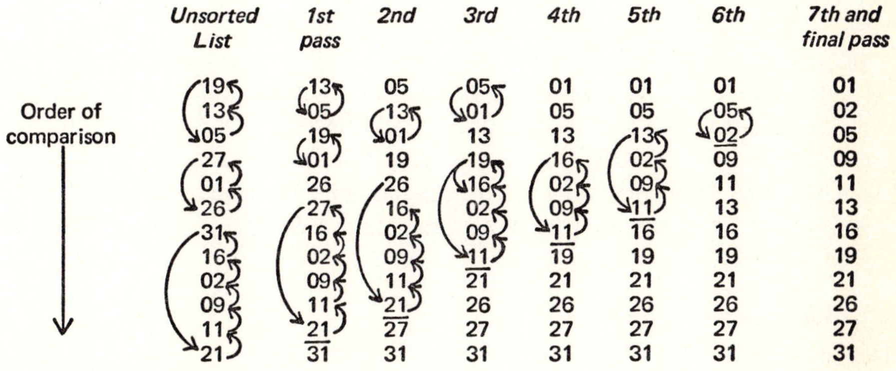

FIGURE 3.17   Illustration of interchange sort

We would like an even better sorting method which requires less time. Sorting methods fall into one of three basic types: (1) *distributive* sorts which sort by examining entries one digit at a time; (2) *comparative* sorts which sort by comparing keywords two at a time; and (3) *address calculation* sorts that transform a key into an address close to where the symbol is expected to end up.

3.3.3.2 SHELL SORT

A fast comparative sort algorithm is due to D.L. Shell (see bibliography, Chapter 10) and is referred to as a *Shell sort*. It approaches optimal performance for a comparative type of sort. The Shell sort is similar to the interchange sort in that it moves data items by exchanges. However, it begins by comparing items a distance "d" apart. This means that items that are way out of place will be moved more rapidly than a simple interchange sort. In each pass the value of d is decreased usually;

$$d_{i+1} = \frac{d_i+1}{2}$$

In every pass, each item is compared with the one located d positions further in the vector of items. If the higher item has a lower value, an exchange is made. The sort continues by comparing the next item in the vector with an item d locations away (if one exists). If an exchange is again indicated, it is made and the comparison is tried again with the next entry. This proceeds until no lower items remain. This process is called bubbling; if you think of low valued items floating to the top, the behavior in the subprocess is like that of a bubble in a water tank. After bubbling can no longer occur with a fixed value of d, the process begins again with a new d.

It is difficult to predict the time requirements of the Shell sort since it is hard to show the effect of one pass on another. It should be obvious that if the above method of calculating d is used, the number of passes will be approximately $\log_2(d)$ since bubbling when d=1 will complete the sort. Empirical studies have shown that the Shell sort takes approximately $B*N*(\log_2 N)^2$ units of time for an N element vector. The constant of proportionality B is fairly small, so for small N the Shell sort will out-perform the radix exchange sort described in section 3.3.3.4 (N up to 1,000). An example of a Shell sort is given in Figure 3.18.

3.3.3.3 BUCKET SORT

One simple distributive sort is called the *radix sort* or *bucket sort*. The sort involves examining the *least* significant digit of the keyword first, and the item is then assigned to a bucket uniquely dependent on the value of the digit. After all items have been distributed, the "buckets" items are merged in order and then the process is repeated until no more digits are left. A number system of base P requires P buckets.

	Pass 1 (d₁ = 6)	Pass 2 (d₂ = 3)	Pass 3 (d₃ = 2)	Pass 4 (d₄ = 1)
19	19	*09	*02	*01
13	13	*01	01	*02
05	*02	02	*09	*05
27	*09	*19	*05	*09
01	01	**11	11	11
26	*21	*05	**13	13
31	31	*27	**16	16
16	16	**13	*19	19
02	*05	*21	***21	21
09	*27	*31	*26	26
11	11	*16	*27	27
21	*26	26	*31	31

* = Exchange

** = Dual exchange

*** = Triple exchange

FIGURE 3.18 Example of a Shell sort

Consider for example the radix sorting of the numbers as shown in Figure 3.19. You should be able to figure out rather quickly how this sort works. In fact, this is precisely the method used on a card sorting machine. However, there are serious disadvantages to using it internally on a digital computer (or on tape sorts for that matter): (1) it takes two separate processes, a separation and a merge; and (2) it requires a lot of extra storage for the buckets. However, this

Original table	First distribution	Merge	Second distribution	Final merge
19		01		01
13	0)	31	0) 01,02,05,09	02
05	1) 01,31,11,21	11	1) 11,13,16,19	05
27	2) 02	21	2) 21,26,27	09
01	3) 13	02	3) 31	11
26	4)	13	4)	13
31	5) 05	05	5)	16
16	6) 26,16	26	6)	19
02	7) 27	16	7)	21
09	8)	27	8)	26
11	9) 19,09	19	9)	27
21		09		31

Separate, based on last digit

Separate, based on first digit

FIGURE 3.19 Demonstration of radix sorting

last disadvantage can be overcome by chaining records within a logical "bucket" rather than pre-allocating maximum size buckets.

3.3.3.4   RADIX EXCHANGE SORT

A considerably better distributive sort is the *radix exchange* sort which is applicable when the keys are expressed (or are expressable) in binary. Sorting is accomplished by considering groups with the same (M) first bits and ordering that group with respect to the (M+1)st bit. The ordering of a group on a given bit is accomplished by scanning down from the top of the group for a one bit and up from the bottom for a zero bit; these two are exchanged and the sort continues. This algorithm requires the program to keep up with a large number of groups and, coded in a bad form, could require an additional table N long. However, with optimal coding it is possible to keep track of the groups by simply monitoring the top of the table and a list of break points, one for each bit of the key-word. (Thus with 32 bit words a table of only 33 entries is required.) An example of the radix exchange sort is shown in Figure 3.20. It is a rather complicated example and somewhat difficult to understand — qualities characteristic of most distributive sorts.

If the sort algorithm is programmed to quit sorting when a group contains only one item, then the time required for the radix exchange sort is proportional to $N*log(N)$ as compared to $N*log_p(K)$ for the bucket sort (here K is the maximum key size and p is the radix). Note that the radix exchange sort does not require extra table space for "buckets."

3.3.3.5   ADDRESS CALCULATION SORT

The last example is of the *address calculation sort*. This can be one of the fastest types of sorts if enough storage space is available. The sorting is done by transforming the key into an address in the table that "represents" the key. For example, if the key were four characters long, one method of calculating the appropriate table address would be to divide the key by the table length in items, multiply by the length of an item and add the address of the table. If the table length is a power of 2, then the division reduces to a shift. This sort would take only N* (time to calculate address) if it were known that no two keys would be assigned the same address. However, in general, this is not the case and several keys will be reduced to the same address.

Therefore, before putting an item at the calculated address it is necessary to first check whether that location is already occupied. If so, the item is compared with the one that is already there, and a linear search in the correct direction is performed to find the correct place for the new item. If we are lucky, there will be an empty space in which to put the items in order. Otherwise, it will be necessary to move some previous entries to make room. It is the search and

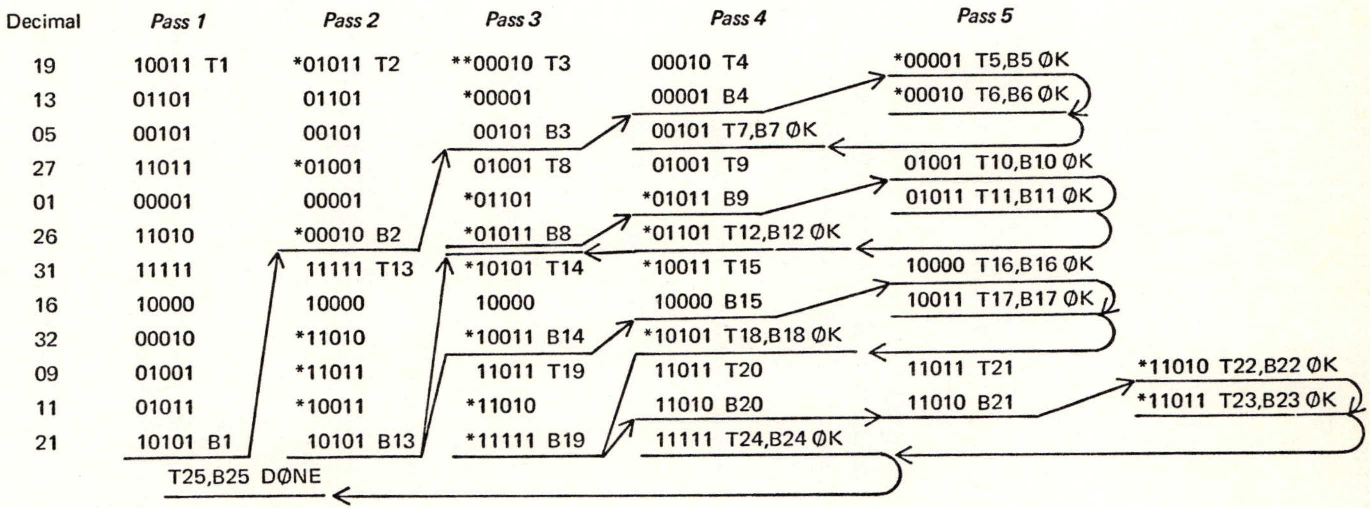

Decimal	Pass 1	Pass 2	Pass 3	Pass 4	Pass 5
19	10011 T1	*01011 T2	**00010 T3	00010 T4	*00001 T5,B5 ØK
13	01101	01101	*00001	00001 B4	*00010 T6,B6 ØK
05	00101	00101	00101 B3	00101 T7,B7 ØK	
27	11011	*01001	01001 T8	01001 T9	01001 T10,B10 ØK
01	00001	00001	*01101	*01011 B9	01011 T11,B11 ØK
26	11010	*00010 B2	*01011 B8	*01101 T12,B12 ØK	
31	11111	11111 T13	*10101 T14	*10011 T15	10000 T16,B16 ØK
16	10000	10000	10000	10000 B15	10011 T17,B17 ØK
32	00010	*11010	*10011 B14	*10101 T18,B18 ØK	
09	01001	*11011	11011 T19	11011 T20	11011 T21
11	01011	*10011	*11010	11010 B20	11010 B21
21	10101 B1	10101 B13	*11111 B19	11111 T24,B24 ØK	

*11010 T22,B22 ØK
*11011 T23,B23 ØK

T25,B25 DØNE

Pass 4 / Pass 5 headings

* indicates where exchanges were made

FIGURE 3.20 Example of radix exchange sort

89

moves that increase the time required for this type of sort.

The time required for the sort can be decreased by making the table bigger than the number of values it will be required to hold. This will provide more open spaces in the table and create less likelihood of address conflicts, long searches or long moves. With a table about 2.2 times the size of the data to sort, this approach (allowing for a final pass to compact the table) uses time proportional to N, making it the fastest type of sort.

An example of an address calculation sort is given in Figure 3.21. The table is of size 12; since it is known that the maximum key is less than 36, the address transformation is to divide the key by 3 and take the integer part (e.g., $19/3 = 6 + 1/3$ so use 6). A "*" indicates a conflict between keys, and an arrow indicates when a move is necessary and in which direction. The associated addresses calculated are given in the second row.

3.3.3.6 COMPARISON OF SORTS

We have discussed five different kinds of sorts: interchange, radix, radix-exchange, Shell, and address calculation. The characteristics for each of these sorts are presented below:

Type	Average time (approx)	Extra storage (wasted space)
Interchange	$A*N^2$	None
Shell	$B*N*(\log_2(N))^2$	None
Radix	$C*N*\log_p(K)$	$N*p$
Radix exchange	$D*N*\log_2(N)$	$k+1$
Address calculation	$E*N$	$2.2*N$ (approximate)

where N is the table size, K is the maximum key size (32 generally, on the 360), and p is the radix of the radix sort. A, B, C, D, and E are the constants of proportionality.

Comparative sorts can take a time from roughly proportional to N^2 down to roughly proportional to $N*\log(N)$. They are insensitive to the distribution of magnitudes; they take good advantage of any natural order in the data; and they generally require no extra storage.

Distributive sorts usually require a time roughly proportional to $N*\log_p(K)$ (where p is the radix of the number system employed and K is the maximum size of the key) because there are N numbers with digits to check and there are $\log_p(K)$ digits per number. However, the distributive sorts are sensitive to the distribution of magnitudes of the entries; they can make scant use of any natural order in the data; and they quite often require considerable additional storage.

Address calculation sorts usually operate quite fast on the first elements entered in the table since address conflicts are unlikely. However, as the table

Data number =	1	2	3	4	5	6	7	8	9	10	11	12
Data =	19	13	05	27	01	26	31	16	02	09	11	21
Calculated address =	6	4	1	9	0	8	10	5	0	3	3	7
Table =												
0		——	——	——	——	01	01	01	01	*01	01	01	01
1		——	——	05	05	05	05	05	05	02	02	02	02
2		——	——	——	——	——	——	——	——	↓05	*05	05	05
3		——	——	——	——	——	——	——	——	——	09	*09	09
4		——	13	13	13	13	13	13	13	13	13	11	11
5		——	——	——	——	——	——	——	16	16	16	16	13
6		19	19	19	19	19	19	19	19	19	19	16	16
7		——	——	——	——	——	——	——	——	——	——	↓19	*19
8		——	——	——	——	——	26	26	26	26	26	26	21
9		——	——	——	27	27	27	27	27	27	27	27	26
10		——	——	——	——	——	——	31	31	31	31	31	27
11		——	——	——	——	——	——	——	——	——	——	——	↓31

FIGURE 3.21 Example of address calculation sort

fills up, the time to add a new entry increases exponentially.

In summary, the *interchange sort* is by far the simplest and should on that account be used whenever speed is not crucial. The *radix* sort is efficient in time but requires an inordinate amount of space so that it is seldom used on a computer; for card sorting, where space is no problem, this is a good sort. The *radix-exchange* sort is very fast and requires very little extra storage (roughly 32 words on the 360), but it is difficult to program and debug. The *address calculation* sort requires the most space to be efficient, but if such space is available, it is faster than any other method.

3.3.4 Hash or Random Entry Searching

Binary search algorithms, while fast, can only operate on tables that are *ordered* and *packed*, i.e., tables that have adjacent items ordered by keywords. Such search procedures may therefore have to be used in conjunction with a sort algorithm which both orders and packs the data.

Actually, it is unnecessary for the table to be ordered and packed to achieve good speed in searching. As we shall presently see, it is possible to do considerably better with an unpacked, unordered table, provided it is sparse, i.e., the number of storage spaces allocated to it exceeds the number of items to be stored.

We have already observed that the address calculation sort gives good results with a sparse table. However, having to put elements in order slows down the process. A considerable improvement can be achieved by inserting elements in a random (or pseudo-random) way. The random entry-number K is generated from the key by methods similar to those used in address calculation. If the Kth position is void, then the new element is put there; if not, then some other cell must be found for the insertion.

The first problem is the generation of a random number from the key. Of course, we don't really want a random number in the sense that a given keyword may yield one position today and another tomorrow. What we want is a procedure that will generate pseudo-random, consistent table positions for keywords. One fairly good prospect for four character EBCDIC keywords is to simply divide the keyword by the table length N and use the remainder. This scheme works well as long as N and the key size (32 bits in our case) have no common factors. For a given group of M keywords, the remainders should be fairly evenly distributed over $0\cdots(N-1)$. Another method is to treat the keyword as a binary fraction and multiply it by another binary fraction:

```
L       1,SYMBOL
M       0,RHO
```

The result is a 64-bit product in registers 0 and 1. If RHO is chosen carefully, the low order 31 bits will be evenly distributed between 0 to 1, and a second multiplication by N will generate a number uniformly distributed over $0\cdots(N-1)$. This is known as the *power residue* method. It has the advantage that the 31-bit first result can be used to generate *another* uniformly distributed number (by multiplying again by RHO) in the event that the first probe of the table is unsuccessful.

The second problem is the procedure to be followed when the first trial entry results in a filled position. There are a number of methods of resolving this problem, three of which will be covered here. These are:

1. *Random entry with replacement* A sequence of random numbers is generated from the keyword (such as by the power residue method). From each of these a number between 1 and N is formed and the table is probed at that position. Probings are terminated when a void space is found. Notice that the random numbers generated are independent and it is perfectly possible (but not likely) to probe the same position twice.

2. *Random entry without replacement* This is the same as above except that any attempt to probe the same position twice is bypassed. This method holds advantage over the above only when *probes* are expensive, e.g., for files on tape or drum.

3. *Open addressing* If the first probe gives a position K and that position is filled, then the next location K+1 is probed, and so on until a free position is found. If the search runs off the bottom of the table, then it is renewed at the top (i.e., the table is considered to be cyclic).

Of these three perhaps the open addressing scheme is the simplest. An example here should serve to illustrate this method.

Consider a table of 17 positions (N=17) in which the following twelve numbers are to be stored: 19, 13, 05, 27, 01, 26, 31, 16, 02, 09, 11, 21. These items are to be entered in the table at a position defined by the remainder after division by 17; if that position is filled, then the next position is examined, etc. Figure 3.22 shows the progress of entry for the 12 items; notice the resolution of conflicts on items 02, 09, and 11. The column 'Probes to find' gives the number of probes necessary to find the corresponding items in the table; thus it takes 3 probes to find items 09, and 1 to find item 26. The column 'Probes to find not' gives the number of probes necessary to determine that an item is not in the table; thus the search for the number 54 would give an initial position of 3 and it would take 4 probes to find that the item is not present. The item is known not to be present when a void position is encountered (position 6 in this case). Notice here that the following figures hold·

Length of table	N	$= 17$
Items stored	M	$= 12$
Density	ρ	$= 12/17 = 0.705$
Probes to store	T_s	$= 16$
Average probes to find	T_p	$= 16/12 = 1.33$
Average probes to find not	T_n	$= 54/16 = 3.37$

The comparative times for a packed table, using radix exchange sort and binary search, are as follows:

Probes to store and sort	T_s	$= M + M*\log_2(M) = 55$
Average probe to find	T_p	$= \log_2(M) = 3.58$
Average probe to find not	T_n	$= \log_2(M) = 3.58$

Thus, it would appear that the open addressing scheme holds considerable advantage in speed, but it pays for this by having a table nearly 50 percent longer than necessary. Furthermore, the table cannot be compressed after its initial assignment nor can the assigned area be easily shared among several tables. One final very serious disadvantage is that it is very difficult to *delete* any item from the table — one cannot simply zero out that location because this might break the addressing chain.

It is interesting to consider the expected probe time, etc., for the random entry

Position	Item	Probes to find	Probes to find not
0			1
1	01	1	6
2	19, 02*	1	5
3	02	2	4
4	21	1	3
5	05	1	2
6			1
7			1
8			1
9	26, 09*	1	7
10	27, 09*	1	6
11	09, 11*	3	5
12	11	2	4
13	13	1	3
14	31	1	2
15			1
16	16	1	1
		$\overline{16}$	$\overline{54}$

FIGURE 3.22 Example of open addressing

methods. The simpler method to evaluate is *random entry with replacement.*
Consider a table of N positions with K-1 elements already inserted. We define
density $\rho = (K-1)/N$.

$$\text{Probes to store } K^{th}: \quad L_K = \frac{1}{1-\rho}$$

$$\text{Probes to search:} \quad T_P = \frac{1}{\rho} \log_e \frac{1}{1-\rho}$$

These figures are very interesting and illustrate well the tradeoff between search
time and table density.

For open addressing the figures are considerably different. As the table becomes denser, the probability of long strings becomes greater so that more
probes are required. In fact, it can be shown that the number of probes to find
is roughly

$$T_P(\rho) = 1 + \frac{\rho}{2} \cdot \frac{1}{1-\rho}$$

and that the time to determine that an item is not in the table is roughly

$$T_N(\rho) = \frac{1}{1-\rho}$$

For a density of p = 12/17 this yields:

$$T_P = 1 + \frac{6}{5} = 2.2$$

$$T_N = \frac{17}{5} = 3.4$$

which compare well with the example shown (see Chapter 10 references for more detailed figures).

GENERATION OF PSEUDO-RANDOM NUMBERS

Many algorithms exist for the generation of pseudo-random numbers, one of the most commonly used being the power residue method. The reader is referred to Hamming's book, Chapter 32, section 5, or Knuth (see bibliography, Chapter 10).

3.4 SUMMARY

A design of a two-pass assembler was presented. Pass 1 defined symbols, and pass 2 generated the object deck. It was emphasized that, in producing the design of an assembler or of any software, six basic steps are followed.

1. Specify the problem.
2. Specify data structures.
3. Define format of data structures.
4. Specify algorithm.
5. Look for modularity.
6. Repeat 1 through 5 on modules.

It was noted that a particularly important component of an assembler is the processing of various data bases (e.g., symbol table, machine-op table). Techniques for organizing, searching, and sorting tables were presented.

3.5 EPILOG

You may have heard the expression "programming is an art, not a science." Of course, there are various programming styles, just as each person has a unique writing or speaking style. But the basic design process, as exemplified by the assembler design, can be and usually is quite straightforward.

It is rather ironic then that many observers interpret the software designer's scientifically motivated actions as evidence of some mysterious "black art." For example, we have devoted a significant portion of this chapter to the presentation of searching and sorting techniques, which are only a portion of the assembler's functions, while ignoring the details of formatting the listing lines and many other assembler modules. This may appear to be an arbitrary decision. In fact, this attention to searching and sorting techniques derives from an awareness of critical performance areas or potential *bottlenecks*. All of the identified assembler functional modules are of comparable programming complexity; whereas the listing format module is used once for every source card, the symbol table search module, for example, contains a loop that may be executed *hundreds* or *thousands* of times for every source card. Since the software designer only has a finite amount of time, it is essential to accentuate those particular modules that yield the highest performance results.

A simple example should illustrate this point. Consider an assembler running on a medium-speed computer, such as an IBM System/360 Model 40, which has a typical instruction time of 12 microseconds (i.e., it averages 83,000 instructions per second). Assume that we wish to assemble a fairly large assembly source program of 5,000 cards, which contains about 2,000 symbols. On an average, each source card has at least one symbolic reference in the operand field. Let us compute the amount of time spent in searching the symbol table.

If a linear search is used and programmed as in Figure 3.12, there will be five instructions executed for each loop of the search. Thus each iteration will take about 5x12=60 microseconds. The number of iterations for each search will be approximately half the symbol table size, 1,000=(1/2) of 2,000. Finally, there will be approximately one search for each of the 5,000 source cards. Thus we can estimate the total time spent searching as:

$$
\begin{aligned}
\text{Total search time} &= \text{number of searches} \\
&\quad \text{x number of iterations per search} \\
&\quad \text{x time per iteration} \\
&= (5\text{x}10^3) \text{ x } (10^3) \text{ x } (60\text{x}10^{-6}) \\
&= 300 \text{ seconds} \\
&= 5 \text{ minutes}
\end{aligned}
$$

On the other hand, if a binary search is used, the average number of iterations per search becomes only $\log_2(2000) -1 \approx 10$, and the time per iteration is about 100 microseconds if programmed as in Figure 3.15.

$$
\begin{aligned}
\text{Total search time} &= (5\text{x}10^3) \text{ x } (10) \text{ x } (100\text{x}10^{-6}) \\
&= 5000 \text{ x } 10^{-3} \\
&= 5 \text{ seconds}
\end{aligned}
$$

Thus, the binary search would reduce the assembly time about 4 minutes 55 seconds (alternately, the linear search technique consumes 6,000 percent more time). Furthermore, since the assembler may be used tens or hundreds of times each day, the time saved may be of major significance to the productivity of the computer system.

This has been a very brief example of bottleneck analysis, but it does point out the importance of searching and sorting techniques. It has been empirically recognized that about 80 percent of the execution time for most programs is spent in less than 20 percent of the modules; thus bottleneck analysis emerges as one of the most important techniques of the software designer.

QUESTIONS[1]

1. What feature of assembly language required us to build a two-pass assembler?

2. What additional features would a three-pass assembler afford the user?

3. Note the number corresponding to the pass or passes (i.e., pass 1, or pass 2) in which the assembly program presented in the book performs the following functions.

Function	Pass	
a. Keeps a base register table	1	2
b. Updates the location counter	1	2
c. Stores symbol definitions	1	2
d. Processes START pseudo-op	1	2
e. Writes collation tape	1	2
f. Punches binary cards	1	2
g. Processes END pseudo-op	1	2
h. Processes L op-code	1	2
i. Processes DS pseudo-op	1	2
j. Processes DC pseudo-op	1	2
k. Searches for symbol which has been defined by EQU and which is in address field of instruction	1	2

4. The Tepid Terminal System (TTS) has just contracted with you to propose a design for a one-pass assembler to be part of their terminal service. It will be implemented on an IBM 360. You are to provide specifications for the assembler. Indicate below whether the feature can be unconditionally implemented, cannot be implemented, or list restrictions under which the feature could be implemented.

    a. USING, DROP
    b. START
    c. EQU
    d. DC, DS
    e. Normal symbolic operation codes
    f. EXTRN
    g. Labels on instructions
    h. The instruction "B LABEL" where LABEL is defined later in the program

5. *a. Can you write an assembler language program without using USING instructions? How? What are the limitations?

    b. Of what use is:

        DS   0D

---

6.   We desire to add the LTORG pseudo-op in the assembler presented in this
      chapter. A LTORG in a program causes all literals used as operands since
      the last LTORG (or since the START if no previous LTORG has occurred)
      to be stored beginning on the next doubleword boundary after the cur-
      rent location. What changes will this require in pass 1 and pass 2? Why
      couldn't the processing of LTORG be completely done in one pass?

7.   a. Why must symbols appearing in the length and repetition factors of the
         DC pseudo-op be self-defining or previously defined symbols?
      b. Why must the operand field of the EQU pseudo-op be evaluated in
         pass 1?
      c. Constants defined in the operand field of a DC pseudo-op are not
         formed and inserted into the program until pass 2. Why couldn't this be
         done in pass 1?

8.   The IBM 360 assembly language "extended mnemonics" allow the user to
      write abbreviations for particular cases of the BC (Branch on Condition)
      instruction. For example,

      BZ   x ≡ BC 8,x
      BM   x ≡ BC 4,x

      where BZ stands for Branch on Zero and BM stands for Branch on Minus.

      a. Discuss briefly a method by which extended mnemonics might be
         added to the assembler discussed in this chapter. Do not add an extra
         pass.
      b. Would the changes effect only pass 1, only pass 2, or both? Why?

9.   For the following programs
      1) Show the symbol table at the end of pass 1.
      2) Show the literal table at the end of pass 1.
      3) Show the changes in the base register table during pass 2.
      4) Show the generated "machine" code from pass 2.

      a.

```
SIMPLE      START
            BALR      15,0
            USING     *,15
LOOP        L         R1,TWO
            A         R1,TWO
            ST        R1,FOUR
            CLI       FOUR+3,4
            BNE       LOOP
            BR        14
R1          EQU       1
TWO         DC        F'2'
FOUR        DS        F
            END
```

*b.

```
SAE         START     484
ARCHON      EQU       1
DEPUTY      EQU       2
TREAS       EQU       3
            BALR      2,0
            USING     *+ARCHON-DEPUTY-TREAS,TREAS
            LM        1,6,POINT
            USING     BETA,ARCHON,DEPUTY
            EXTRN     BACK
            ENTRY     BEACON
BEACON      CR        DEPUTY,ARCHON
            BNH       POINT+SAE-BEACON
            LA        7,=A(BACK)
            CLI       HOLE,X'90'
            BR        6
            DC        H'64',X'40',B'1000000',C' '
            DROP      DEPUTY
            DC        15X'0',6F' '80'
BETA        MVC       POINT+20(4),=H'43'
            MVC       POINT+16,=H'43'
STOMP       EQU       5
            DROP      ARCHON
            L         9,=A(BEACON)
            NR        9,TREAS
            ST        9,=F'482'
            B         POINT+24
            LTORG
HOLE        DS        0D
POINT       DC        CL4'WIN'
            DC        (STOMP)A(BETA),V(FOOTBL)
            CLC       POINT-4,=F'482'
            LA        1,1
            CVB       2,10(DEPUTY*TREAS)
            STC       3,POINT(TREAS*TREAS)
            BR        14
            END
```

10. In this problem, we will explore a feature of the 360 assembly language that we wish to implement in the assembler presented in this chapter.

Suppose that we have a table of information in storage which has a number of entries of the same format. We would address an entry in the table by pointing some base register at it and using displacements from that register to address the various fields of that entry. This has the disadvantage that the programmer has to remember the displacements. What we would like is a way to refer to the fields symbolically, and have the assembler calculate a base and displacement in a similar way to any other symbol encountered.

We use the pseudo-op DSECT to define the displacements. It establishes a *new* location counter, initially sets it at zero, and causes the assembler to assign relative addresses to the symbols following the DSECT, based on the *new* location counter, just as it assigned relative addresses to the symbols preceding the DSECT based on the old location counter. For the purpose of this problem, all DSECTS will be at the end of a program, and another DSECT or END instruction will terminate the use of the most recently established location counter.

We use the pseudo-op USING to indicate the base register to be used in generating instructions referencing symbols defined within a DSECT. The address part of the USING is the label on the DSECT instruction, and the base register is specified in the usual way.

Let us look at an example:

Location counter	Generated code			
0		SUB	START	0
0			USING	SUB,15
0			USING	TABLE,3
0	LH 4, 10(0,15)		LH	4,FIFTY
4	LH 5, 4(0,3)		LH	5,B
8	BCR 15,14		BCR	15,14
10	H'50'	FIFTY	DC	H'50'
0		TABLE	DSECT	
0		A	DS	F
4		B	DS	H
6		C	DS	H
			END	

Notice that the statements following a DSECT update the new location counter and define symbols but they do *not* reserve any storage. Also note that FIFTY was replaced by 10(0,15), while B was replaced by 4(0,3)

We need to modify the assembler in three areas to handle the DSECT concept.

1) Recognizing and processing the DSECT instruction.
   Recognizing and processing labels which are defined within the scope of a DSECT
2) Processing USING instructions which reference DSECTS
3) Generating base-displacement replacements for symbols used as operands of instructions

For each of these areas, answer *(explain in full)* the following questions:

a. Which pass of the assembler will be affected? Why?
b. What additional or modified logic will be required?
c. What modifications to existing data bases will be required? Why?

11. An old computer firm has gone out of business and left you their sole product. The computer has no core memory. It has a drum. It has two

working registers — an AC and MQ (there are no index registers). The AC register is used for addition and subtraction, and the AC/MQ pair for multiplication and division. The machine operates on 26-bit words; there is one instruction format.

Op	Track	Location	Track	Loca-tion

0   5 6   10 11   15 16   20 21   25

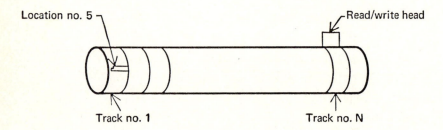

Location no. 5 ⌐   ⌐Read/write head

Track no. 1   Track no. N

The machine interprets bits 0-6 as the op code, bits 7-16 as the location of the operand, and bits 17-25 as the location of the next instruction.

An example of an assembly language program for this computer is:

```
          LOAD    A,LOC1      Load accumulator with A
LOC1      ADD     C,LOC3      Add C to accumulator
A         DC      F'5'
LOC3      STO     D,LOC10     Store accumulator in D
C         DC      F'4'
LOC10     STOP
D         DS      F
          END
```

The first subfield of the variable field is the operand address and the second subfield is the address of the next instruction. The drum is always running. To minimize the execution time, you have found that instructions should be placed four locations apart, on a track. This allows enough time for completion of an instruction before the "read" head of the drum is directly over the next instruction.

Discuss briefly each of the following points, indicating what modifications, if any, would be necessary to the assembler we studied in this chapter.

a. Format of location counter.

b. Updating and maintenance of the location counter.

c. Assume we want to optimize execution time. How would you handle space allocation for each of the following. Which of these place restrictions on the assembler and which on the programmer?

    1) Instructions
    2) DC and DS pseudo-ops
    3) Literals

d. How would the location counter be maintained for such optimization?

e. What modifications are needed to pass 1 or pass 2 of the assembler discussed in the chapter?

f. Do we need a two-pass assembler? Why?

12.   a. Define the following terms in one or two sentences.

    1) Searching
    2) Sorting
    3) Hashing

    b. What is the difference between searching and sorting?

13.   Show the results of each pass for the following lists using:

1) Interchange sort
2) Shell sort
3) Radix sort

a.	b.
81	424
52	887
57	807
22	709
95	882
04	616
83	573
96	413
42	679
32	180
48	975
78	264
82	
65	
16	
66	
14	
77	
87	
67	

14.   The list below is in alphabetical order. Assume that a binary search technique is used to find a name on the list. Indicate the number of probes (steps) required to find each entry. For example, to find DONOVAN

would require three probes (8 = GOODMAN, 4 = BRUNK, 6 = DONO-VAN.)

Number of probes requested

1) ASHTON
2) BERMAN
3) BERNSTEIN
4) BRUNK
5) DAVIS
6) DONOVAN   3
7) FREYBERG
8) GOODMAN
9) KOHN
10) MADNICK
11) MICHELS
12) NANGLE
13) STEEL
14) TURNER
15) ZILLES

15. Show the results of each pass of a radix exchange sort performed upon the following lists, similar to Figure 3.19.

a. 00100
   10001
   01011
   00001
   00010
   00101
   00000
   01001
   10101
   10010
   01111
   11011

b. 100011
   011000
   000111
   010100
   010110
   100010
   111100
   000100
   100001
   101100
   110111
   110011
   110000
   010000
   000110
   111001

16.   The table below lists several methods of sorting and various attributes
       which may or may not apply to the various sorts. To make sure everything
       is clear, the interchange sort referred to is the model which stops when
       nothing was done on its last pass. For each attribute place a mark (✓) in
       each column where the corresponding sorting technique has that attri-
       bute.

Sorts / Attributes	Shell	Radix	Interchange	Radix exchange
Examines all bits (or characters) in key of an item in each probe				
Requires large amounts of extra storage				
Requires only one pass if table is already sorted on entry to sort				
Is a distributive sort				
Requires items to be sorted to be in binary form				

17.   In an assembler it is often convenient to enable pass 1 to access symbols
       from the symbol table before the pass is completed. For example, in the
       following pseudo-op

           A   EQU   B

       it is necessary to obtain the value of B to get a value for A. In view of this
       requirement, suggest the best method of data storage and retrieval for the
       symbol table. Explain your answer.

18.   As head programmer for a small computer company, you have been as-
       signed the task of writing an assembler for the company's latest machine.
       During assembly the symbol table can become arbitrarily long, and you are
       worried about how to build the table and access entries from it.

       You have only enough core to hold 100 symbols, but there is secondary
       storage available that allows storage of symbols in blocks of 100.

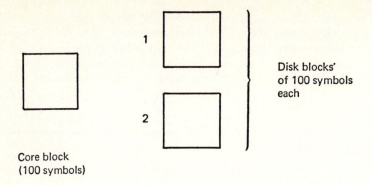

Other considerations:

1) 100 msec (10^{-1} sec) are required to either read or write a disk block.
2) The average instruction time is 10 μsec (10^{-5} sec).

    a. Assuming that the number of entries in the symbol table is < 100, which sorting technique, distributive or comparative, would you use if you were to order it? If the number of entries is > 1000? Why?

    b. For each of the four situations listed across the top of the table below, check both a maintenance and an access technique that you think would require the least overhead to build and obtain entries from the symbol table. There is not necessarily a single correct answer in each case; give two sentences for each situation explaining the criteria you used for your choice.

    (Hint: note that considerable time is spent in switching between blocks of a table larger than 100 entries.)

19.   Below is a flowchart for a hash-coding algorithm to sort the list of names — each to take two fullwords (eight bytes) in a 360-type machine.

    DONOVAN*b*
    MULHERN*b*
    FREYBERG
    MITCH*bbb*
    HARRIS*bb*
    MARY*bbbb*
    MADNICK*b*
    NANGLE*bb*

		Case 1	Case 2	Case 3	Case 4
		Table size <100	Table size <100	Table size >1000	Table size >1000
		Table is accessed infrequently	Table is accessed frequently	Table is accessed infrequently	Table is accessed frequently
Table access techniques	Linear search				
	Binary search				
	Hash search				
	Hash with binary bucket search				
Table maintenance techniques	Sequential entry				
	Sequential entry and then do an interchange sort				
	Sequential entry and then do a radix sort				
	Sequential entry with final Shell sort				
	Hash entry				
	Hash entry, and if multiple entries per bucket then sort bucket				

a. List the contents of locations 22000 through 22160 after sorting.
b. The problem of two or more names being assigned the same location is handled in blocks 1 and 2 by checking the next location. Give other ways of handling the problem, and discuss their advantages and disadvantages.

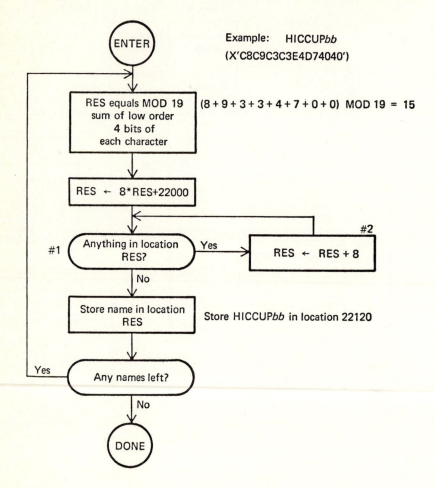

Example: HICCUP*bb*
(X'C8C9C3C3E4D74040')

RES equals MOD 19 sum of low order 4 bits of each character
$(8 + 9 + 3 + 3 + 4 + 7 + 0 + 0)$ MOD 19 = 15

RES ← 8*RES+22000

#1 Anything in location RES?   Yes   →   RES ← RES + 8   #2

No

Store name in location RES
Store HICCUP*bb* in location 22120

Yes   Any names left?

No

DONE

20.   a. Sort this list of names into lexicographical order by using a Shell sort on the last name only. Thus if there are two or more occurrences of one last name, they should be treated as being identical regardless of the first names.

One example of a properly ordered table:

1	DONOVAN	JOHN
2	FAY	REGAN
3	FAY	ELIZABETH
.		
.		
.		
N	QUIMBY	DAVE

←TABLE (3,2) = ELIZABETH

LIST TO BE SORTED:

FREYBERG, DUTCH	DONOVAN, MARILYN
ZILLES, STEVEN	MADNICK, STUART
KOHN, NORMAN	NANGLE, ELLEN
SINNOTT, MARY	GOODMAN, LEONARD
BRUNK, GLEN	DODSON, ORVILLE
DONOVAN, MAUREEN	ASHTON, BENJAMIN
DONOVAN, JAMES	JOHNSON, JERRY
DONOVAN, CAROLYN	HAMMER, MICHAEL
DONOVAN, REBECCA	JACK, MARTIN
DONOVAN, JOHN	BERMAN, HARRIS
	RAMCHANDANI, CHANDER

The following flowchart searches a table for an entry. Use the sorted list of part a for parts b and c.

b. What does the algorithm return for N=22, FIRST=MAUREEN, and LAST=DONOVAN?
c. What searching method(s) does the algorithm use? Explain some attributes of this method or methods (TIME, STORAGE REQUIRE-MENTS, etc.).
d. What is good about this search algorithm?
e. What is wrong with this search algorithm?

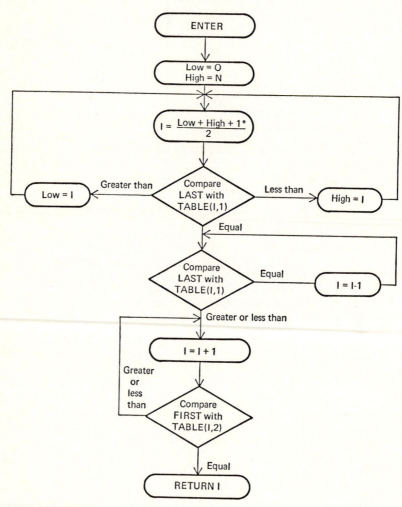

* Truncated to integer if necessary.

4

macro language
and the macro processor

The assembly language programmer often finds it necessary to repeat some blocks of code many times in the course of a program. The block may consist of code to save or exchange sets of registers, for example, or code to set up linkages or perform a series of arithmetic operations. In this situation the programmer will find a macro instruction facility useful. *Macro instructions* (often called *macros*) are single-line abbreviations for groups of instructions. In employing a macro, the programmer essentially defines a single "instruction" to represent a block of code. For every occurrence of this one-line macro instruction in his program, the macro processing assembler will substitute the entire block.

By defining the appropriate macro instructions, an assembly language programmer can tailor his own higher level facility in a convenient manner, at no cost in control over the structure of his program. He can achieve the conciseness and ease in coding of high level languages without losing the basic advantage of assembly language programming. Integral macro operations simplify debugging and program modification and they facilitate standardization. Many computer manufacturers use macro instructions to automate the writing of "tailored" operating systems in a process called *systems generation.*

Macro instructions are usually considered an extension of the basic assembler language, and the macro processor is viewed as an extension of the basic assembler algorithm. As a form of programming language, however, macro instruction languages differ significantly from assembly languages and compiled algebraic languages. Important analogs are to be found in some high level languages and text editing systems.

In this section we will discuss an assembler macro facility. We will treat the use of macro instructions in programming and the implementation of macros within an assembler. Certain features that are characteristic of most macro processors will be introduced and developed.

4.1 MACRO INSTRUCTIONS

In its simplest form, a macro is an abbreviation for a sequence of operations. Consider the following program:

Example 1:

```
             :
             :
   A         1, DATA     Add contents of DATA to register 1
   A         2, DATA     Add contents of DATA to register 2
   A         3, DATA     Add contents of DATA to register 3

             :
             :

   A         1, DATA     Add contents of DATA to register 1
   A         2, DATA     Add contents of DATA to register 2
   A         3, DATA     Add contents of DATA to register 3

             :
             :

DATA  DC     F'5'

             :
             :
```

In the above program the sequence

```
   A         1, DATA
   A         2, DATA
   A         3, DATA
```

occurs twice. A macro facility permits us to attach a name to this sequence and to use this name in its place. We can invent a macro language that allows us to specify the above as a macro definition and allows us to refer to the definition later. We have chosen to use a 360-type macro language.

A macro processor effectively constitutes a separate language processor with its own language.

We attach a name to a sequence by means of a macro instruction definition, which is formed in the following manner:

```
Start of definition  ───────────────────────────────────►  MACRO

Macro name  ─────────────────────────────────────────────►  [      ]

Sequence to be abbreviated                               {  ────────
                                                            ────────
                                                            ────────
End of definition  ──────────────────────────────────────►  MEND
```

The MACRO pseudo-op is the first line of the definition and identifies the following line as the *macro instruction name.* Following the name line is the sequence of instructions being abbreviated—the instructions comprising the 'macro' instruction. The definition is terminated by a line with the MEND ('macro end') pseudo-op.

Once the macro has been defined, the use of the macro name as an operation mnemonic in an assembly program is equivalent to the use of the corresponding instruction sequence. Our example might be rewritten as follows, assigning the name 'INCR' to the repeated sequence.

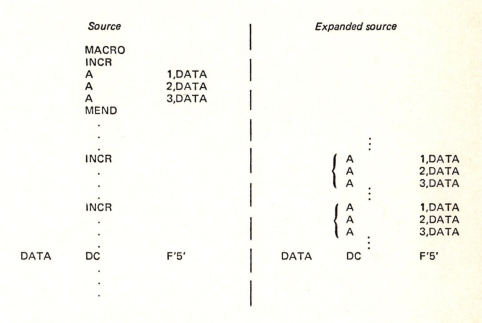

In this case the macro processor replaces each macro call with the lines

```
A            1, DATA
A            2, DATA
A            3, DATA
```

This process of replacement is called *expanding* the macro. Notice that the macro definition itself does not appear in the expanded source code. The definition is saved by the macro processor. The occurrence in the source program of the macro name, as an operation mnemonic to be expanded, is called a *macro call.*

4.2 FEATURES OF A MACRO FACILITY

4.2.1 Macro Instruction Arguments

The macro facility presented thus far is capable of inserting blocks of instructions in place of macro calls. All of the calls to any given macro will be replaced by identical blocks. This macro facility lacks flexibility: there is no way for a specific macro call to modify the coding that replaces it. An important extension of this facility consists of providing for arguments, or parameters, in macro calls. Corresponding *macro dummy arguments* will appear in macro definitions. Consider the following program.

Example 2:

```
                      .
                      .
                      .
          A           1, DATA 1
          A           2, DATA 1
          A           3, DATA 1
                      .
                      .
                      .
          A           1, DATA 2
          A           2, DATA 2
          A           3, DATA 2
                      .
                      .
                      .
  DATA 1  DC          F'5'
  DATA 2  DC          F'10'
```

In this case the instruction sequences are very similar but not identical. The first sequence performs an operation using DATA1 as operand; the second, using DATA2. They can be considered to perform the same operation with a variable parameter, or argument. Such a parameter is called a *macro instruction argument,* or "dummy argument;" it is specified on the macro name line and distinguished (as a macro language symbol rather than an assembly language symbol) by the ampersand (&), which is always its first character. The preceding program could be written as:

	Source			Expanded source	
MACRO		Macro INCR has			
		one argument			
INCR	&ARG				
A	1,&ARG				
A	2,&ARG				
A	3,&ARG				
MEND					
.					
.				:	
.					
INCR	DATA1	Use DATA1 as		A	1,DATA1
		operand		A	2,DATA1
.				A	3,DATA1
.					
.				:	
INCR	DATA2	Use DATA2 as		A	1,DATA2
		operand		A	2,DATA2
.				A	3,DATA2
.					
.					
DATA1 DC	F'5'			DATA1 DC	F'5'
DATA2 DC	F'10'			DATA2 DC	F'10'
.					
.					
.					

It is possible to supply more than one argument in a macro call. Each argument must correspond to a definition ("dummy") argument on the macro name line of the macro definition. When a macro call is processed, the arguments supplied are substituted for the respective dummy arguments in the macro definition.

Consider the following program:

Example 3:

```
                :

LOOP1   A        1, DATA1
        A        2, DATA2
        A        3, DATA3

                :

LOOP2   A        1, DATA3
        A        2, DATA2
        A        3, DATA1

                :

DATA1   DC       F'5'
DATA2   DC       F'10'
DATA3   DC       F'15'
```

In this case the operands in the common sequence are different, as are the labels on the first cards of the sequences. This program could be written as:

	SOURCE			EXPANDED SOURCE	
	⋮				
	MACRO				
&LAB	INCR	&ARG1,&ARG2,&ARG3			
&LAB	A	1,&ARG1			
	A	2,&ARG2			
	A	3,&ARG3			
	MEND				
	⋮			⋮	
LOOP1	INCR	DATA1,DATA2,DATA3	LOOP1	A	1,DATA1
				A	2,DATA2
				A	3,DATA3
	⋮			⋮	
LOOP2	INCR	DATA3,DATA2,DATA1	LOOP2	A	1,DATA3
				A	2,DATA2
				A	3,DATA1
	⋮			⋮	
DATA1	DC	F'5'	DATA1	DC	F'5'
DATA2	DC	F'10'	DATA2	DC	F'10'
DATA3	DC	F'15'	DATA3	DC	F'15'
	⋮				

Here we have specified four arguments, including a *label argument*. Label arguments are treated just like those written as "operands" of a macro instruction; the argument appearing in the label field on the macro name line and in calls to the macro differs from other arguments only in its location. Arguments used as labels within the macro need not appear in the label field of a call, and arguments appearing in the label field of a call may be used as operands within the macro instruction code. Label arguments are convenient but nonessential features that enhance the similarity between macro instructions and ordinary assembly language instructions. Following is another encoding of example 3.

	Source				Expanded source	
	MACRO					
	INCR	&ARG1,&ARG2,&ARG3,&LAB				
&LAB	A	1,&ARG1				
	A	2,&ARG2				
	A	3,&ARG3				
	MEND					

```
                  Source                    |         Expanded source

        MACRO
        INCR    &ARG1,&ARG2,&ARG3,&LAB      |
&LAB    A       1,&ARG1                     |
        A       2,&ARG2                     |
        A       3,&ARG3                     |
        MEND                                |
          .                                 |              .
          .                                 |              .
        INCR    DATA1,DATA2,DATA3,LOOP1     |    LOOP1   A       1,DATA1
          .                                 |            A       2,DATA2
          .                                 |            A       3,DATA3
        INCR    DATA3,DATA2,DATA1,LOOP2     |    LOOP2   A       1,DATA3
          .                                 |            A       2,DATA2
          .                                 |            A       3,DATA1
          .                                 |              .
                                            |              .
```

There are generally two ways of specifying arguments to a macro call. The first, *positional argument,* is demonstrated in the preceding examples. Arguments are matched with dummy arguments according to the order in which they appear. Thus, in a macro call 'INCR A,B,C' A, B, and C replace the first, second, and third dummy arguments. A more general argument facility, *keyword arguments*, allows reference to dummy arguments by name as well as by position. Referring to the dummy arguments appearing in the definition of INCR, we might write

'INCR &ARG1=A,&ARG3=C,&ARG2=B' or 'INCR &ARG1=A,&ARG2=&ARG3=C'.

This can be useful when a macro has arguments—labels, for example—that are not always needed. Any arguments not supplied are presumed blank by the macro processor.

4.2.2 Conditional Macro Expansion

Two important macro processor pseudo-ops, AIF and AGO, permit conditional reordering of the sequence of macro expansion. This allows conditional selection of the machine instructions that appear in expansions of a macro call.

Consider the following program:

Example 4:

```
                    ⋮
LOOP1   A           1, DATA1
        A           2, DATA2
        A           3, DATA3

                    ⋮

LOOP2   A           1, DATA3
        A           2, DATA2

                    ⋮

LOOP3   A           1, DATA1

                    ⋮

DATA1   DC          F'5'
DATA2   DC          F'10'
DATA3   DC          F'15'

                    ⋮
```

In this example, the operands, labels, and the number of instructions generated change in each sequence. This program could be written as follows:

```
                .
                .
                MACRO
&ARG0           VARY        &COUNT,&ARG1,&ARG2,&ARG3
&ARG0           A           1,&ARG1
                AIF         (&COUNT EQ 1).FINI              Test if & COUNT = 1
                A           2,&ARG2
                AIF         (&COUNT EQ 2).FINI              Test if & COUNT = 2
                A           3,&ARG3
.FINI           MEND                                  ┌ ─ ─ ─ ─ ─ ─ ─ ─ ─ ─ ─
                .                                     │       Expanded source
                .                                     │
                .                                     │            ⋮
LOOP1           VARY        3,DATA1,DATA2,DATA3        │ { LOOP1   A    1,DATA1
                .                                     │           A    2,DATA2
                .                                     │           A    3,DATA3
                                                      │            ⋮
LOOP2           VARY        2,DATA3,DATA2             │ { LOOP2   A    1,DATA3
                .                                     │           A    2,DATA2
                                                      │            ⋮
LOOP3           VARY        1,DATA1                    │ { LOOP3   A    1,DATA1
                .                                     │            ⋮
                .                                     │
DATA1           DC          F'5'
DATA2           DC          F'10'
DATA3           DC          F'15'
                .
```

Labels starting with a period (.), such as .FINI, are *macro labels* and do not appear in the output of the macro processor. The statement AIF (&COUNT EQ 1)FINI directs the macro processor to skip to the statement labelled .FINI if the parameter corresponding to &COUNT is a 1; otherwise, the macro processor is to continue with the statement following the AIF pseudo-op.

AIF is a *conditional branch* pseudo-op; it performs an arithmetic test and branches only if the tested condition is true. The AGO is an *unconditional branch* pseudo-op or 'go to' statement. It specifies a label appearing on some other statement in the macro instruction definition; the macro processor continues sequential processing of instructions with the indicated statement. These statements are directives to the macro processor and do not appear in macro expansions. Just as conditional and unconditional branch instructions in a machine language program direct the order of program flow, AIF and AGO control the sequence in which the macro processor expands the statements in macro instructions. This makes it possible to tailor specific occurrences of instructions sequences to their various contexts. If machine language branches and tests are used, they will waste execution time; also, the tests and unused instructions will waste memory space. Branches and tests in the macro instruction language permit the use of highly general macros that assemble selectively, and by testing the parameters to each call, omit code not needed. This facility for selective assembly of highly general macros is one of the systems programmer's most powerful programming tools.

4.2.3 Macro Calls Within Macros

Since macro calls are "abbreviations" of instruction sequences, it seems reasonable that such "abbreviations" should be available within other macro definitions. For example,

Example 5:

```
MACRO
ADD1        &ARG
L           1, &ARG
A           1, =F'1'
ST          1, &ARG
MEND
MACRO
ADDS        &ARG1, &ARG2, &ARG3
ADD1        &ARG1
ADD1        &ARG2
ADD1        &ARG3
MEND
```

Within the definition of the macro 'ADDS' are three separate calls to a previously defined macro 'ADD1'. The use of the macro 'ADD1' has shortened the length of the definition of 'ADDS' and thus has made it more easily understood. Such use of macros results in macro expansions on multiple 'levels'. Thus:

Source	Expanded source (Level 1)	Expanded source (Level 2)
· · ·		
MACRO		
ADD1 &ARG		
L 1,&ARG		
A 1,=F'1'		
ST 1,&ARG		
MEND		
MACRO		
ADDS &ARG1,&ARG2, &ARG3		
ADD1 &ARG1		
ADD1 &ARG2		
ADD1 &ARG3	Expansion of ADDS	Expansion of ADD1
MEND	· · ·	· · ·
· ·		
	ADD1 DATA1	L 1,DATA1 / A 1,=F'1' / ST 1,DATA1
ADDS DATA1,DATA2, DATA3	ADD1 DATA2	L 1,DATA2 / A 1,=F'1' / ST 1,DATA2
	ADD1 DATA3	L 1,DATA3 / A 1,=F'1' / ST 1,DATA3
· ·		· ·
DATA1 DC F'5'		DATA1 DC F'5'
DATA2 DC F'10'		DATA2 DC F'10'
DATA3 DC F'15'		DATA3 DC F'15'
· ·		· ·

Macro calls within macros can involve several levels. For example, the macro ADDS might be called within the definition of another macro. In fact, conditional macro facilities (such as AIF and AGO) make it possible for a macro to call itself. So long as this does not cause an infinite loop—so long as at some point the macro, having been called for the nth time, decides not to call itself again—it makes perfectly good sense. The problems inherent to macro calls within macros will be discussed in the section on *recursion*; the preceding example is treated further in Figure 4.5.

4.2.4 Macro Instructions Defining Macros

We have viewed macros as generalized abbreviations for instruction sequences, noting that it seems reasonable to permit any valid statements in the abbreviated sequence, including macro definitions. In this manner a single macro instruction might be used to simplify the process of defining a group of similar macros.

It is important to realize that the inner macro definition is not defined (i.e., callable) until after the outer macro has been called. This is because of the method by which definitions are implemented. For example, a user might wish to define a group of macros for subroutine calls with some standardized calling sequence. The following example defines a macro instruction DEFINE, which when called with a subroutine name defines a macro with the same name as the subroutine. The individual macros generated bear the names (given through the argument &SUB) of their associated subroutines.

```
                                    MACRO
                                    DEFINE  &SUB            Macro name:  DEFINE
                                    MACRO
                                    &SUB    &Y              Dummy macro name
Definition    Definition           CNOP    0,4             Align boundary
of macro      of macro             BAL     1,*+8           Set register 1 to parameter list pointer
DEFINE        &SUB                 DC      A(&Y)           Parameter list pointer
                                    L       15,=V(&SUB)     Address of subroutine
                                    BALR    14,15           Transfer control to subroutine
                                    MEND
                                    MEND
```

The user might then call this macro with the statement

```
        DEFINE          COS
```

defining a new macro named COS: the statement expands into a new macro definition. The user might subsequently call the COS macro as follows:

```
        COS             AR
```

and the macro processor will generate the calling sequence:

```
BAL          1, *+8
DC           A(AR)              address of AR
L            15,=V(COS)         V denotes address of external symbol
BALR         14,15
```

Macro definitions within macros are sometimes called "macro definitions within macro definitions." (See Section 4.3.2 for further treatment of this example.)

4.3 IMPLEMENTATION

Thus far we have described a macro instruction scheme for extending the basic assembly language. In the remainder of this chapter we will outline a method for implementing such a scheme.

STATEMENT OF PROBLEM

There are four basic tasks that any macro instruction processor must perform.

1. Recognize macro definitions A macro instruction processor must recognize macro definitions identified by the MACRO and MEND pseudo-ops. This task can be complicated when macro definitions appear within macros. When MACROs and MENDs are *nested*, as in the example of the previous section, the macro processor must recognize the nesting and correctly match the last or outer MEND with the first MACRO. All of the intervening text, including nested MACROs and MENDs, defines a single macro instruction.

2. Save the definitions The processor must store the macro instruction definitions, which it will need for expanding macro calls.

3. Recognize calls The processor must recognize macro calls that appear as operation mnemonics. This suggests that macro names be handled as a type of op-code.

4. Expand calls and substitute arguments The processor must substitute for dummy or macro definition arguments the corresponding arguments from a macro call; the resulting symbolic (in this case, assembly language) text is then substituted for the macro call. This text, of course, may contain additional macro definitions or calls.

In summary: the macro processor must recognize and process macro definitions and macro calls.

With regard to arguments, the designer of the macro processor must make several decisions. He must determine where dummy arguments may appear in a macro definition – for example, whether they may appear as op-codes. He must also define the syntax of permissible arguments. Although we do not treat these matters in detail, we present some typical (and reasonable) answers. Dummy arguments may appear *anywhere* in a macro definition — for example, they may appear as op-codes. We want to be able to concatenate macro arguments with fixed strings. For example, we might want to write A&A, which we take to mean A concatenated with the argument replacing &A. This is easy to arrange. It is harder to have arguments inside a string. For this we permit the argument to be enclosed in single quotes. Thus, we take A&AB to mean A concatenated with the argument replacing AB, and A'&A'B to mean the concatenation of A, the argument replacing &A, and *B*. Any string enclosed in parentheses (e.g., (.A&B)) may be used as an argument.

In order for AIF and AGO to work, some arithmetic expressions will have to be evaluated. A symbol defining capability, similar to the EQU facility by which variables may be assigned and reassigned values, is often useful.

4.3.1 Implementation of a Restricted Facility: A Two-Pass Algorithm

We begin by making some simplifying assumptions. We will assume that our macro processor is functionally independent of the assembler and that the output text from the macro processor will be fed into the assembler. Initially we will not permit macro calls or definitions within macro definitions. Because these features introduce complications, we postpone discussion of them until after we have presented the basic macro processor algorithm.

A macro processor, like an assembler, scans and processes lines of a text. In assembly language, lines are interrelated by addressing: a line can refer to another by its address or name, which must be available ("known") to the assembler. Moreover, the address assigned to each line depends upon preceding lines, upon their addresses, and possibly upon their contents as well. If we consider macro definitions to constitute integral entities, we may say that the lines of our macro language are not so closely interrelated. Macro definitions refer to nothing outside themselves, and macro calls refer only to macro definitions. (Remember our restrictions. Remember also that a macro call substitutes *text*, not values, for parameters. Suppose, for example, that a macro call INCR Y is preceded by a statement defining Y—e.g., Y EQU 10. The macro processor substitutes 'Y', not '10' for the macro definition argument—indeed, it never processes the EQU statement at all, except as a complete line of text.)

Our macro processor algorithm will make two systematic scans, or passes, over the input text, searching first for macro definitions and then for macro calls. Just as our assembler cannot process a reference to a symbol before its definition, so the macro processor cannot expand a macro call before having found and saved the corresponding macro definition. Thus we need the two passes over the input text, one to handle definitions and one to handle calls. The first pass, examining every operation code, will save all macro definitions in a Macro Definition Table (MDT) and save a copy of the input text, minus macro definitions, on secondary storage (e.g., magnetic tape) for use in the second pass. The first pass will also prepare a Macro Name Table (MNT) along with the MDT. The second pass will then examine every operation mnemonic and replace each macro name with the appropriate text from the macro definitions. (A separate MNT is not essential, but it facilitates searching for macro names.)

SPECIFICATION OF DATA BASES
The following data bases are used by the two passes of the macro processor.

Pass 1 data bases:
1. The input macro source deck
2. The output macro source deck copy for use by pass 2
3. The Macro Definition Table (MDT), used to store the body of the macro definitions
4. The Macro Name Table (MNT), used to store the names of defined macros
5. The Macro Definition Table Counter (MDTC), used to indicate the next available entry in the MDT
6. The Macro Name Table Counter (MNTC), used to indicate the next available entry in the MNT
7. The Argument List Array (ALA), used to substitute index markers for dummy arguments before storing a macro definition

Pass 2 data bases:
1. The copy of the input macro source deck
2. The output expanded source deck to be used as input to the assembler
3. The Macro Definition Table (MDT), created by pass 1
4. The Macro Name Table (MNT), created by pass 1
5. The Macro Definition Table Pointer (MDTP), used to indicate the next line of text to be used during macro expansion
6. The Argument List Array (ALA), used to substitute macro call arguments for the index markers in the stored macro definition

SPECIFICATION OF DATA BASE FORMAT
The only data bases with nontrivial format are the Macro Definition Table (MDT), the Macro Name Table (MNT), and the Argument List Array (ALA). The others we will not present in detail.

ARGUMENT LIST ARRAY: The Argument List Array (ALA) is used during both pass 1 and pass 2 but for somewhat reverse functions. During pass 1, in order to simplify later argument replacement during macro expansion, dummy arguments in the macro definition are replaced with positional indicators when the definition is stored. The ith dummy argument on the macro name card is represented in the body of the macro by the index marker symbol # where #i is a symbol reserved for the use of the macro processor (i.e., not available to the programmers). These symbols are used in conjunction with the argument list prepared before expansion of a macro call. The symbolic dummy arguments are retained on the macro name card to enable the macro processor to handle argument replacement by name rather than by position.

As an example, consider the macro INCR used in Example 3. The stored macro definition would be:

```
Macro Definition Table MDT

            .
            .
            .

&LAB    INCR        &ARG1,&ARG2,&ARG3
#0      A           1, #1
        A           2, #2
        A           3, #3
        MEND
            .
            .
            .
```

During pass 2 it is necessary to substitute macro call arguments for the index markers stored in the macro definition. Thus upon encountering the call

```
LOOP    INCR        DATA1,DATA2,DATA3
```

the macro call expander would prepare an argument list array:

```
            Argument List Array

                    8 bytes per entry

    Index               Argument
    0                   "LOOP1bbb"
    1                   "DATA1bbb"
    2                   "DATA2bbb"
    3                   "DATA3bbb"
```

(b denotes the blank character)

The list would be used only while expanding this particular call. Suppose that a succeeding call were:

```
INCR        &ARG1=DATA3,&ARG2=DATA2,&ARG3=DATA1
```

The macro processor would find that '&ARG1', '&ARG2', and '&ARG3' occupy argument positions 1, 2, and 3 on the macro name card. The resulting argument list array would be:

Argument List Array	
Index	Argument
0	"bbbbbbbb" (all blank)
1	"DATA3bbb"
2	"DATA2bbb"
3	"DATA1bbb"

MACRO DEFINITION TABLE: The Macro Definition Table (MDT) is a table of text lines; if input is from 80-column cards, the MDT can be a table with 80-byte strings as entries. Every line of each macro definition, except the MACRO line, is stored in the MDT. (The MACRO line is useless during macro expansion.) The MEND is kept to indicate the end of the definition; and the macro name line is retained to facilitate keyword argument replacement. Thus, for example, the INCR macro discussed might be stored as follows:

Macro Definition Table			
	80 bytes per entry		
Index	Card		
⋮	⋮		
15	&LAB	INCR	&ARG1,&ARG2,&ARG3
16	#0	A	1,#1
17		A	2,#2
18		A	3,#3
19		MEND	
⋮	⋮		

MACRO NAME TABLE: The Macro Name Table (MNT) serves a function very similar to that of the assembler's Machine-Op Table (MOT) and Pseudo-Op Table (POT). Each MNT entry consists of a character string (the macro name) and a pointer (index) to the entry in the MDT that corresponds to the beginning of the macro definition. The MNT entry for the INCR macro discussed might be:

	8 bytes	4 bytes
Index	Name	MDT index
⋮	⋮	⋮
3	"INCRbbbb"	15
⋮	⋮	⋮

ALGORITHM

Figures 4.1 and 4.2 are flowcharts of the macro definition and expansion algorithms. Each of the algorithms makes a line-by-line scan over its input. The 'READ' boxes refer to the fetching of successive input lines from secondary storage into a workspace.

PASS 1–MACRO DEFINITION: The algorithm for pass 1 (Fig. 4.1) tests each input line. If it is a MACRO pseudo-op, the entire macro definition that follows is saved in the next available locations in the Macro Definition Table (MDT). The first line of the definition is the macro name line. The name is entered into the Macro Name Table (MNT), along with a pointer to the first location of the MDT entry of the definition. When the END pseudo-op is encountered, all of the macro definitions have been processed so control transfers to pass 2 in order to process macro calls.

PASS 2–MACRO CALLS AND EXPANSION: The algorithm for pass 2 (Fig. 4.2) tests the operation mnemonic of each input line to see if it is a name in the MNT. When a call is found, the call processor sets a pointer, the Macro Definition Table Pointer (MDTP), to the corresponding macro definition stored in the MDT. The initial value of the MDTP is obtained from the "MDT index" field of the MNT entry. The macro expander prepares the Argument List Array (ALA) consisting of a table of dummy argument indices and corresponding arguments to the call. This list is simply a succession of symbols ordered to match the dummy arguments on the name card (the first is the label argument, which is considered to have an index of zero). Arguments not represented in a call are considered blank, and superfluous arguments are ignored. In the case of argument reference by position, this scheme is completely straightforward. For references by name, the macro processor locates the dummy argument on the macro name line (which is available at the beginning of the definition in the MDT) in order to determine the proper index.

Reading proceeds from the MDT; as each successive line is read, the values from the argument list are substituted for dummy argument indices in the macro definition. Reading of the MEND line in the MDT terminates expansion of the macro, and scanning continues from the input file. When the END pseudo-op is encountered, the expanded source deck is transferred to the assembler for further processing.

4.3.2 A Single-Pass Algorithm

Suppose we wanted to provide for macro definitions within macros. The basic problem here is that the inner macro is defined only after the outer one has been called; in order to provide for any use of the inner macro, we would have to re-

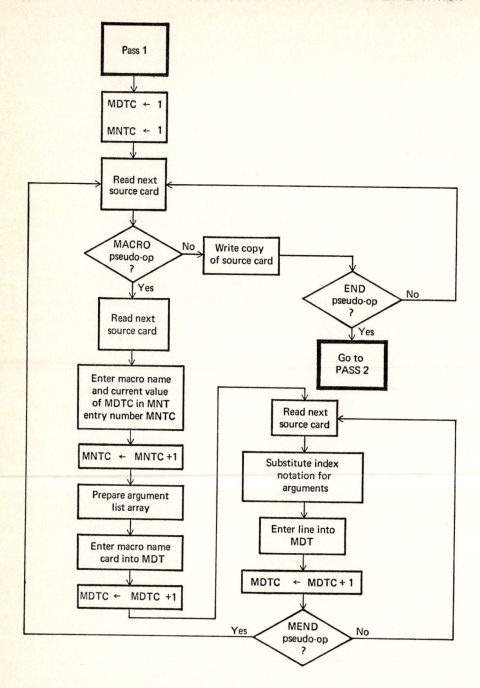

FIGURE 4.1 Pass 1–processing macro definitions

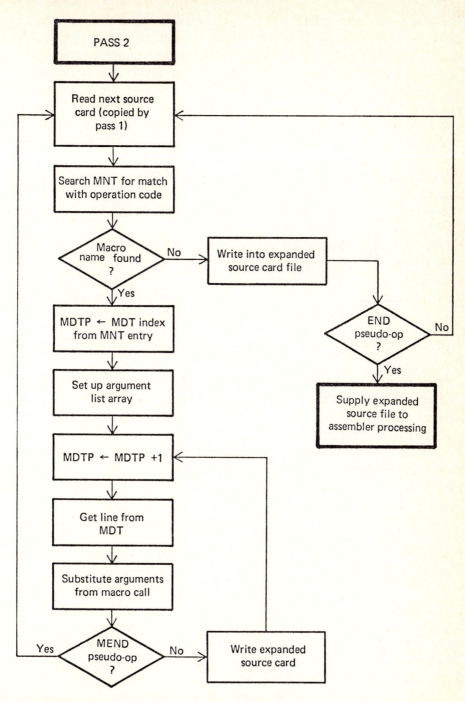

FIGURE 4.2 Pass 2—processing macro calls and expansion

peat both the macro-definition and the macro-call passes. However, there is a simpler solution that has the added advantage of reducing all macro processing to a single pass. Consider again the analogy that we drew to an assembler. Macro definitions must be processed before calls because macros must be defined to the processor before it can expand calls to them. However, if we stipulate the restriction that every macro be defined before it is called, we remove the essential obstacle to a single-pass process. (Notice that the same would be true for assemblers and symbols, except that a similar requirement for symbols would prove unduly restrictive to the program flow.) In the case of macro languages, it is perfectly reasonable to require that all macro definitions precede their calls. This imposes no significant restriction on macro use. It does not even prevent a macro from calling itself, for the call is expanded not during the definition of the macro but during a later call.

The flowcharts in Figures 4.3 and 4.4 combine the algorithms of Figures 4.1 and 4.2 into a single pass and permit macro definitions within macros (but not calls within macros). You should notice considerable similarity between these new flowcharts and those illustrating the earlier two-pass macro processor design. There are two additional variables introduced in the one-pass design: a Macro Definition Input (MDI) indicator and a Macro Definition Level Counter (MDLC). The MDI and MDLC are switches (counters) used to keep track of macro calls and macro definitions.

The MDI indicator has the value "ON" during expansion of a macro call and the value "OFF" at all other times. The actual expansion of macro calls is performed in the READ box, which is detailed in the second flowchart (Fig. 4.4). READ tests the switch MDI. If it is "ON", lines are read from the Macro Definition Table (MDT). The reading of a MEND line indicates the end of a macro and terminates expansion of a call; MDI is reset to "OFF" and the next line is obtained from the regular input stream. Note that lines returned by READ may include macro definitions; expanded macro code comes out of READ looking just like any other code and may therefore include macro definitions.

The Macro Definition Level Counter is incremented by 1 when a MACRO pseudo-op is encountered and decremented by 1 when a MEND pseudo-op occurs.

The MDLC is used to insure that the entire macro definition, including MACROs and MENDs, gets stored in the MDT. This is analogous to treating statements with nested parentheses—e.g., "(2*(A+B)+C)". If a program is to read the entire expression, it must not stop at the first right parenthesis, but rather it must keep a count of left and right parentheses and recognize that the second parenthesis is the true end of the expression. The MDLC acts as a counter for the difference between the numbers of MACROs and MENDs encountered; it

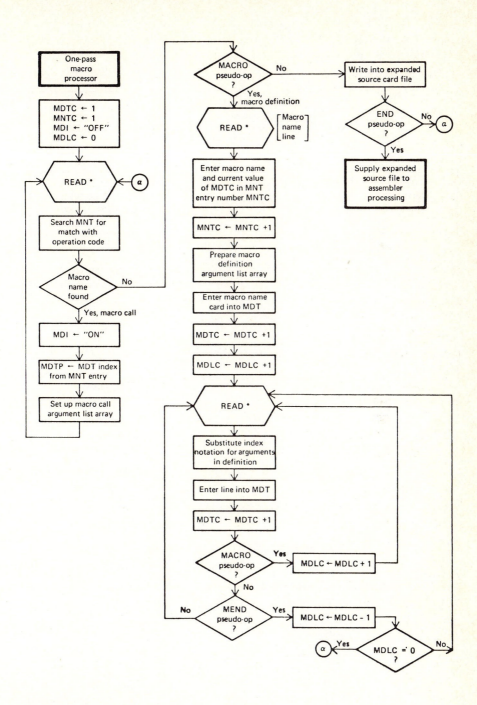

FIGURE 4.3 Simple one-pass macro processor

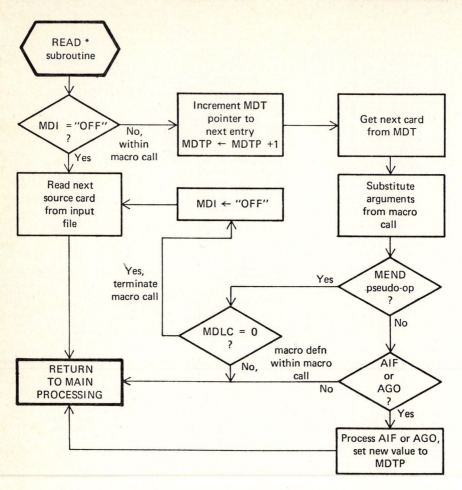

FIGURE 4.4 Detail of READ function used for macro expansion

tells how many more MACROs than MENDs have been read.

Notice that since it is possible to be performing the "macro definition pass" simultaneously with the "macro expansion pass," as is the case when expanding a macro definition with an inner macro definition, there must be two separate Argument List Arrays. One ALA is used for macro definitions. The other is employed for macro call expansion.

Consider now example 6 from section 4.2.4. After definition of the macro DEFINE:

MDT:	*Index*			
	1	DEFINE	&SUB
	2	MACRO	
	3	#1	&Y
	4	CNOP	0,4
	5	BAL	1,*+8
	6	DC	A(&Y)
	7	L	15,=V(#1)
	8	BALR	14,15
	9	MEND	
	10	MEND	

			MDT	
MNT:	*Index*	*Name*	*Index*
	1	DEFINE	1

after processing of statement DEFINE COS:

MDT:

			Lines 1-10 same as above
	.	.	
	.	.	
	.	.	
	11	COS	&Y
	12	CNOP	0,4
	13	BAL	1,*+8
	14	DC	A(#1)
	15	L	15,=V(COS)
	16	BALR	14,15
	17	MEND	

			MDT	
MNT:	*Index*	*Name*	*Index*
	1	DEFINE	1
	2	COS	11

So far no output has been generated by the macro: output lines will be created upon expansion of the statement COS AR. The reader should "simulate" the actions of the macro processor by following through the flowchart for the preceding example.

4.3.3 Implementation of Macro Calls Within Macros

The basic problem in implementing macro calls within macros is that of *recur-*

sion. If a macro call is encountered during the expansion of a macro, the macro processor will have to expand the included macro call and then finish expanding the enclosing macro. The second call might be expanded by a second macro processor, which would look up the macro definition in the MDT and return the expanded code to the first macro processor. Having many macro processors is neither efficient nor general; however, if a single macro processor is to handle such nested macro calls, it must in some way save its status when it encounters nested calls.

Example 5 illustrates this problem. It defines two macros, ADDS and ADD1. The macro definitions in the MDT are shown in Figure 4.5.

Macro Definition Table MDT

Index	Contents	
1	ADD1	&ARG
2	L	1, #1
3	A	1,=F'1'
4	ST	1, #1
5	MEND	
6	ADDS	&ARG1,&ARG2,&ARG3
7	ADD1	#1
8	ADD1	#2
9	ADD1	#3
10	MEND	

FIGURE 4.5   MDT after macro definition of example 5

Consider the action of the macro processor of Figure 4.3 and 4.4 when it encounters the macro call

        ADDS   DATA1, DATA2, DATA3

Our algorithm will prepare a macro call argument list array and set a pointer, MDTP, to line 6 of the MDT; switch MDI is set to "ON". The READ function increments MDTP, gets its next line from the MDT (line 7) and substitutes the argument, yielding the line

        ADD1   DATA1

Now our algorithm is in trouble: it has encountered another macro call. ADD1 is a macro name, so the processor will prepare a new argument list array, set MDTP to line 1 of the MDT, and set MDI to "ON", its current value. The ADD1 macro will expand correctly; at the end MDTP will point to MDT line 5. MDI will be reset to "OFF", and reading will proceed from the input stream.

This of course is wrong: there are unexpanded lines left in the ADDS macro. Three errors have occurred. The switch MDI has been turned off, causing the processor to read from the input stream instead of from the MDT; the value of MDTP before it was reset to process the ADD1 macro has been lost; and the argument list for the call to ADDS has been lost.

To handle macro calls within macros, the macro processor must be able to work recursively—that is, to process one macro before it is finished with another, then to continue with the previous, or 'outer,' one. Recursive procedures usually operate by means of a *stack*, a storage scheme that allocates a separate storage area for the variables associated with each call to the procedure. Because a separate storage space or 'stack frame' is associated with each recursive call, the status of unfinished computations is preserved. Conceptually, a stack is an unbounded array that is treated in a last-in, first-out manner: the last element stored is the first one removed. A Stack Pointer (SP) indicates the position or *frame* at the 'top' of the stack. *(Pointer* is a term that refers to a data item which is an address or index. Intuitively, a pointer points to information stored in core.)

In our example the pointer MDTP and the argument list ALA associated with each call belong in the stack. The switch MDI must also be saved. The Stack Pointer (SP), which indicates the beginning of the current stack frame, can serve in place of MDI; in each succeeding frame, however, we must save the previous value of SP to prevent it from being lost. (Compare this with our use of the Macro Definition Level Counter (MDLC). 'Recursive' handling of macro definitions was easy because the inner definitions do not have any associated data—see the exercises at the end of this chapter). Ignoring the actual method of data representation, we consider the stack to be an array of pointers and character strings; S(SP) refers to the beginning of the current (top) stack frame, the position indexed by SP.

The organization of each stack frame is depicted in Figure 4.6. S(SP) contains the *previous* value of SP; for the first frame, where SP=1,S(SP)=-1. The condition SP=-1, like MDI=0 in the nonrecursive algorithm, tells the macro processor that it is not within a macro call expansion. S(SP+1) contains the current value of MDTP, the MDT pointer; S(SP+2) . . . S(SP+N+1) contain the N (0th through (N-1)th) character strings of the current argument list.

Figures 4.7 and 4.8 depict the macro processor algorithm that handles macro calls within macro definitions as well as macro definitions within macro definitions. Simple "housekeeping" steps, such as incrementing the Macro Name Table Counter (MNTC) and the Macro Definition Table Counter (MDTC) after inserting a new entry, have been omitted to simplify the flowcharts. The reader

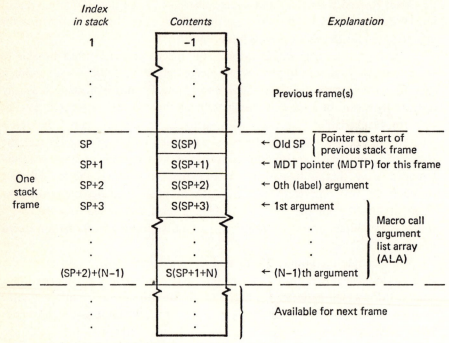

FIGURE 4.6 Stack organization

should confirm the fact that the algorithm described in these new flowcharts is indeed very similar to the previous algorithm (Figs. 4.3 and 4.4). Notice that the number of entries in a stack frame depends upon the number of elements in the argument list (i.e., the number of dummy arguments in the macro definition).

It is desirable for the reader to hand-simulate the operation of the macro processor by using the algorithm to expand a macro source program. Figure 4.9 illustrates the state of the stack and expanded source at various key points in the processing of Example 5. The corresponding Macro Definition Table (MDT) for this example was presented in Figure 4.5. It is strongly recommended that the reader go through all the steps of the macro expansion and compare results with Figures 4.9a and 4.9b.

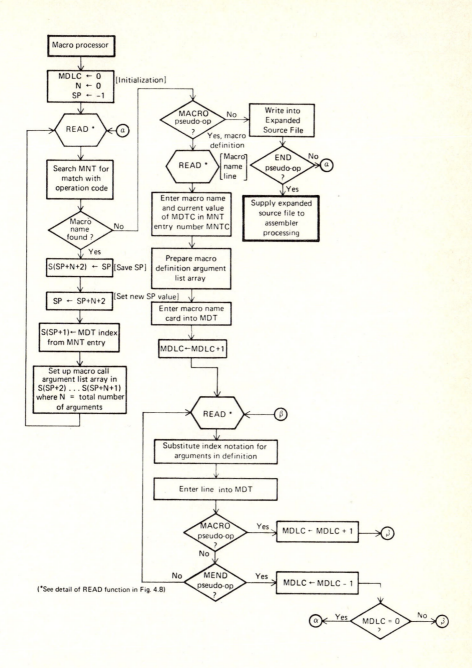

FIGURE 4.7 One-pass macro processor capable of handling macro calls within macro definitions

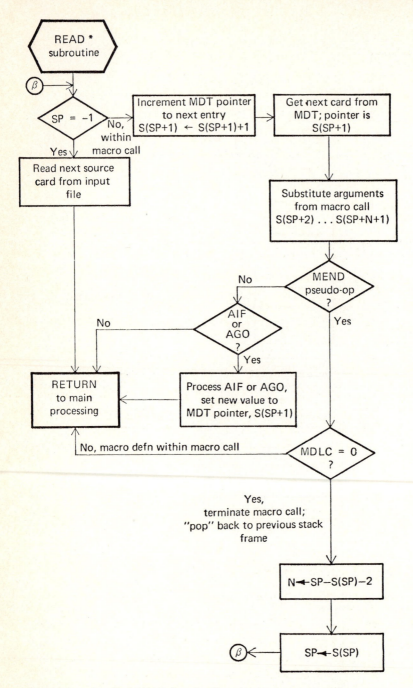

FIGURE 4.8 Detail of READ function for recursive macro expansion

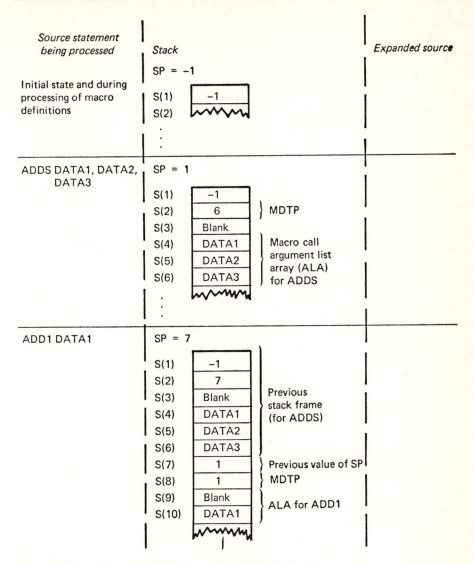

FIGURE 4.9 (a) Chronology of processing example 5 (part 1)

4.3.4 Implementation Within an Assembler

The macro processor can be added as a pre-processor to an assembler, making a complete pass over the input text before pass 1 of the assembler. The macro processor can also be implemented within pass 1 of the assembler.

The implementation of the macro processor within pass 1 eliminates the overhead of intermediate files, and we can improve this integration of macro pro-

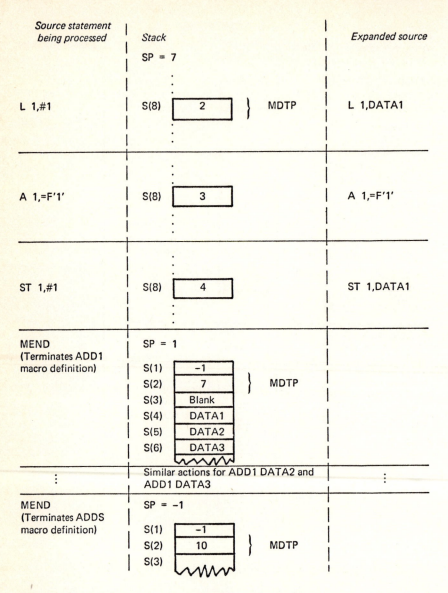

FIGURE 4.9 (b) Chronology of processing example 5 (part 2)

cessor and assembler by combining similar functions. For example, the Macro
Name Table (MNT) can be combined with the assembler's op-code table (MOT
or POT); a flag in each entry indicates whether or not it is a macro name.
MACRO pseudo-ops to the macro processor can be detected by the assembler's

regular pseudo-op handler. The input READ function, which expands macro calls and receives the original source input, will be the same as that of Figure 4.8. Figure 4.10 is a flowchart of this algorithm; compare it with the flowcharts of Chapter 3.

The major advantages of incorporating the macro processor into pass 1 are:

1. Many functions do not have to be implemented twice (e.g., read a card, test for statement type).

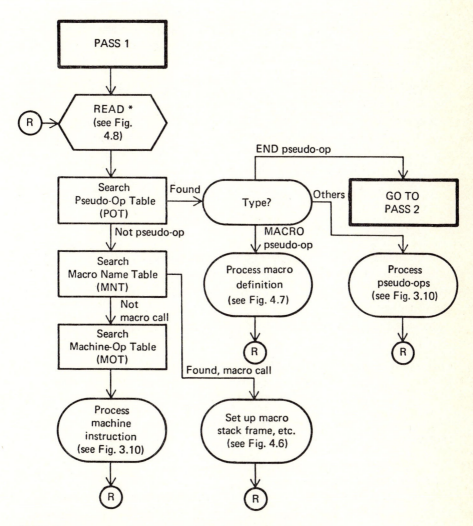

FIGURE 4.10 A macro processor combined with assembler pass 1

2. There is less overhead during processing: functions are combined and it is not necessary to create intermediate files as output from the macro processor and input to the assembler.
3. More flexibility is available to the programmer in that he may use all the features of the assembler (e.g., EQU statements) in conjunction with macros.

The major disadvantages are:

1. The combined pass 1 of the assembler and the macro processor may be too large a program to fit into core of some machines.
2. The complexity of such a program may be overwhelming. Typically, two separate programming groups implement pass 1 of the assembler and the macro processor. The combination of the two functions may be too much for one group or person to coordinate.

Separate from the considerations of implementing the macro facility in the assembler is the consideration of an additional pass. Many macro processors have a "prepass" the function of which is to note certain characteristics of the source program, such as data types. With such a macro processor the programmer may use conditional macro pseudo-ops, which expand a macro conditionally on certain characteristics of the program.

4.4 SUMMARY

Macro languages and their associated processors represent a distinct form of programming languages. When used in conjunction with an assembler, the macro processor provides the programmer with many useful tools and essentially allows him to define his own personal "high level" language.

There are four basic tasks that any macro processor must perform:

1. Recognize macro definitions
2. Save the macro definitions
3. Recognize macro calls
4. Expand macro calls and substitute arguments

A macro processor for assembly language can be implemented in various ways. This chapter presented three variations:

1. Independent two-pass processor
2. Independent one-pass processor
3. Processor incorporated into pass 1 of a standard two-pass assembler

QUESTIONS[1]

1. Describe the input and output of the macro processor. How dependent is it upon the assembler source code format?

2. For the following programs show:

    1) The expanded assembly language programming (i.e., no macros)
    2) The MDT table after macro processing
    3) The MNT table after processing

    The SETA and LCLA pseudo-op used in part b is as defined in problem 9.

    a.

    ```
                    MACRO
                    XYZ         &A
                    ST          1,&A
                    MEND
                    MACRO
                    MIT         &Z
                    MACRO
                    &Z          &W
                    AR          4,&W
                    XYZ         ALL
                    MEND
                    ST          &Z,ALL
                    MEND
    PROG            START
                    USING       *,15
                    MIT         HELLO
                    ST          2,3
                    HELLO       YALE
    YALE            EQU         5
    ALL             DC          F'3'
                    END
    ```

    b. Computes exponentiation, e.g., 5^3

    ```
                    MACRO
                    EXPO        &EXP
                    LCLA        &N
    &N              SETA        &EXP
                    AIF         (&N EQ 1) .STOP
                    MR          0,2
    &N              SETA        &N-1
                    EXPO        &N
    .STOP           ANOP
                    MEND
    ```

---

[1]An * denotes that the question may require the use of IBM 360 manuals.

```
EXPON    START    0
         USING    *,15
         L        2,BASE
         L        1,BASE
         SR       0,0
         EXPO     3
         ST       1,ANS
         BR       14
ANS      DS       F
BASE     DC       F'5'
         END
```

3. The macro assembler presented in this chapter used its data bases in two different ways. It made references to the data (without making any modifications) and it created or adjusted the data (that is, it modified the data). In the matrix below, various data bases used in the assembler are listed in the vertical column. Across the top of the matrix are listed the various forms of data usage. Assume the macro processor has been combined with pass 1 of the assembler as in section 4.3.4.

	Must be built or modified in pass 1	Referenced but not modified in pass 1	Built during pass 1; saved for pass 2	Not modified during pass 2	Built or modified during pass 2	References occur in pass 2
Symbol table						
Literal table						
Base register table						
Collate tape						
Machine Op Table (MOT) includes MNT						
Pseudo-op table						
Input deck						
Macro Definition Table (MDT)						
Location counter						
Macro stack						

4. In a sense, macro expansion is very similar to subroutine calls during program execution. Explain the similarities and differences between them. What is the analog of the stack frame during subroutine calls?

5. a. If the assembler is processing a macro call and this macro contains a macro definition, would a new stack frame be set up? If so, what information would be stored?

    b. Do any other data bases get changed in the handling of this nested definition? If so, which ones and how are they changed?

    c. After processing the MEND card associated with the nested definition, can a macro call to this MACRO appear in the outer macro?

    d. Could it appear anywhere in the outer macro? Could it appear anywhere in the program?

    e. If we did not allow macro definitions within macro definitions, would we be able to remove the macro stack from the assembler? If so, why? If not, why not?

    f. Which macro features required us to have a stack and the need for recursion?

6. If labels are allowed in the macro definition, what modification must be made to the macro processor implementation given in this chapter?

7.   a. In order to be able to process macros in a single pass, we had to restrict the macro language. Describe the restriction and the limitations that it imposes on program organization.

    b. Can a one-pass macro processor successfully handle a macro call with conditional macro pseudo-ops?

    Consider the following case:

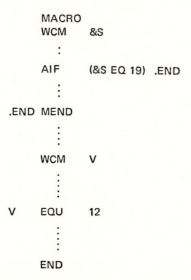

```
        MACRO
        WCM     &S
          :
        AIF     (&S EQ 19)  .END
          :
.END MEND
          :
        WCM     V
          :
          :
V       EQU     12
          :
          :
        END
```

    c. If a one-pass processor cannot, what modifications would be necessary to enable it to handle this type of situation?

8.   a. We wish to implement an assembler using only a macro processor (i.e., the macro processor is to accept assembly language and output hexadecimal machine code). Consider a macro processor with *only* two pseudo-operations (SET,BYTE) and the two macro pseudo-ops MACRO and MEND.

The two pseudo-operations are:

(1)α SET β   The symbol α in the label field is assigned the value of the expression β in the operand field. A symbol's value may be reset by another SET. Symbol LC is used as the assembler's Location Counter.

(2)BYTE expression (radix, size), [expression (radix, size)] ...   The BYTE pseudo-op will generate one 8-bit machine byte at the location corresponding to the current value of the Location Counter (@LC). The bytes are made up of subfields appearing from left to right in the operand field. The *radix* specifies whether the expression is in hex (16) or decimal (10); the *size* specifies the number of bits (out of 8) for that subfield. Example: Define AR-like instruction (add register to register); assume numeric op-code of hexadecimal '1A.'

```
            MACRO
&VAR1       AR          &VAR2, &VAR3
&VAR1       SET         LC
            BYTE        1A (16,8)
LC          SET         LC+1
            BYTE        &VAR2 (10,4), &VAR3 (10,4)
LC          SET         LC+1
            MEND
```

After 'AR' has been defined as a MACRO, this "assembler" can process AR instructions (i.e., accept an AR instruction and produce the equivalent hexadecimal machine instruction). Define SR (subtract register).

b. Define the IBM 360 instructions A, L (add, load — see Chapter 2).

9.   It is often useful when constructing macros to save strings of characters for later use. In order to provide such a facility within the framework of an assembler like that discussed in this chapter we wish to add the following:

1) In addition to introducing dummy or "variable" symbols (those beginning with the character "&") in the prototype statement, it shall be possible to create variable symbols with two other statements: a GLOBAL statement and a LOCAL statement. The syntax of these statements is:

```
GBLA        &symbol
      or
LCLA        &symbol
```

where "&symbol" is a variable symbol called a "set symbol."

The GBLA (*GloBaL A*rithmetic) declares that the symbol has a value which is "global" in the sense that all macros which use the same name will reference the same value. It is much like declaring a label to be an EXTRN in a running program although this "set symbol" only has a value during the macro processing phases of the assembler.

The LCLA (*LoCaL A*rithmetic) declares that the symbol has a value which is initialized to 0 each time the macro containing it is invoked, and that different macros containing "set symbols" of the same name will be referencing unique values.

An arithmetic symbol is stored and processed as a 32-bit fullword binary integer.

2) In order that we may assign values to "set symbols" we will create a statement of the form:

&set-symbol SETA arithmetic-expression

which will assign the value of the expression to the "set symbol."

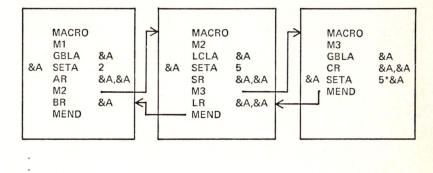

```
           .
           .
           .
     25        M1
     26+       AR      2,2
     27+       SR      5,5
     28+       CR      2,2
     29+       LR      5,5
     30+       BR      10
```

(+denotes a generated statement   not in source code)

Make certain that you understand how the LCLA, GBLA and SETA pseudo-ops work in the above call of M1 before you answer the following questions.

For questions a, b, c, and d below you may assume that the macro processor was implemented in pass 1 of the assembler with a stack similar to that discussed in section 4.3.3.

a. 1) Which passes of the assembler must be modified for each pseudo-op?
   2) Which phases of the macro facility (definition or expansion) must be modified for each pseudo-op?

    b. 1) Could *local* (LCLA) symbols be *efficiently* implemented by merely appending entries to the stack frame, much as macro parameters are handled? If not, how could they be handled? Explain both how your scheme would work and why you would choose it over the other one.

       2) Answer the questions in b. 1) for global (GBLA) symbols.

    c. Describe your method for processing the SETA instruction. Consider specifically both local and global symbols and how to update the correct variable.

    d. 1) Describe how you would process an LCLA statement.

       2) Do the same for the GBLA statement.

10. *Modify the macro processor designs given in this chapter (i.e., one-pass implementation, two-pass implementation, and assembler implementation) so that they can process AIF and AGO statements.

5

loaders

The purpose of this chapter is to discuss various loader schemes and to present the design of a direct-linking loader.

As illustrated in the previous chapter, the user's *source program* decks are usually converted to *object program* decks (machine language) by assemblers and compilers. The *loader* is a program which accepts the object program decks, prepares these programs for execution by the computer, and initiates the execution (see Fig. 5.1).

In particular, the loader must perform four functions:

1. Allocate space in memory for the programs *(allocation)*
2. Resolve symbolic references between object decks *(linking)*
3. Adjust all address dependent locations, such as address constants, to correspond to the allocated space *(relocation)*
4. Physically place the machine instructions and data into memory *(loading)*

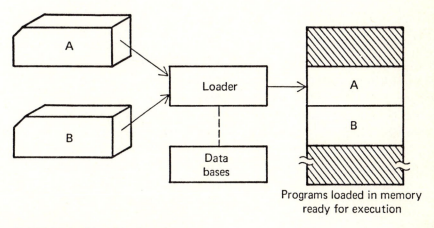

Programs loaded in memory
ready for execution

FIGURE 5.1 General loading scheme

Most of the examples used in this section are based upon the IBM System/370 assembler and loader. Several of the alternative loader schemes discussed are based upon computers with a fixed-word, direct-address instruction format, such as the IBM 7094, IBM 1130, UNIVAC 1108 and GE 635.

For simplicity of presentation, we assume card deck inputs — these of course may actually be card images on tape or any secondary storage.

5.1 LOADER SCHEMES

In this section we discuss various schemes for accomplishing the four functions of a loader. It is desirable to introduce the term *segment*, which is a unit of information that is treated as an entity, be it a program or data. Usually a segment corresponds to a single source or object deck. It is possible to produce multiple program or data segments in a single source deck by means of the assembly CSECT (Control Section) pseudo-op, the FORTRAN COMMON statement, or the PL/I EXTERNAL STATIC data attribute.

5.1.1 "Compile-and-Go" Loaders

One method of performing the loader functions is to have the assembler run in one part of memory and place the assembled machine instructions and data, as they are assembled, directly into their assigned memory locations (Fig. 5.2). When the assembly is completed, the assembler causes a transfer to the starting instruction of the program. This is a simple solution, involving no extra procedures. It is used by the WATFOR FORTRAN compiler and several other language processors.

Such a loading scheme is commonly called "compile-and-go" or "assemble-and-go." It is relatively easy to implement. The assembler simply places the code into core, and the "loader" consists of one instruction that transfers to the starting instruction of the newly assembled program.

However, there are several apparent disadvantages. First, a portion of memory is wasted because the core occupied by the assembler is unavailable to the object program. Second, it is necessary to retranslate (assemble) the user's program deck every time it is run. Third, it is very difficult to handle multiple segments, especially if the source programs are in different languages (e.g., one subroutine in assembly language and another subroutine in FORTRAN or PL/I). This last disadvantage makes it very difficult to produce orderly modular programs as discussed in the design of assemblers.

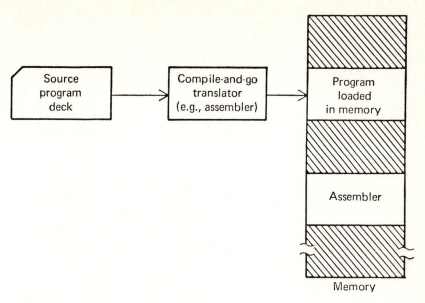

FIGURE 5.2 "Compile-and-go" loader scheme

5.1.2 General Loader Scheme

Outputting the instructions and data as they are assembled circumvents the problem of wasting core for the assembler. Such an output could be saved and loaded whenever the code was to be executed. The assembled programs could be loaded into the same area in core that the assembler occupied (since the translation will have been completed). This output form, which may be on cards containing a coded form of the instructions, is called an *object deck*.

The use of an object deck as intermediate data to avoid one disadvantage of the preceding "compile-and-go" scheme requires the addition of a new program to the system, a loader (Fig. 5.3). The *loader* accepts the assembled machine instructions, data, and other information present in the object format, and places machine instructions and data in core in an executable computer form. The loader is assumed to be smaller than the assembler, so that more memory is available to the user. A further advantage is that reassembly is no longer necessary to run the program at a later date.

Finally, if all the source program translators (assemblers and compilers) produce compatible object program deck formats and use compatible linkage conventions, it is possible to write subroutines in several different languages since the object decks to be processed by the loader will all be in the same "language" (machine language).

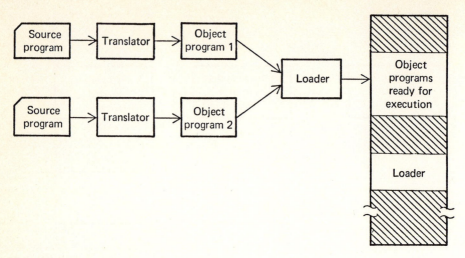

FIGURE 5.3 General loader scheme

5.1.3 Absolute Loaders

The simplest type of loader scheme, which fits the general model of Figure 5.3, is called an absolute loader. In this scheme the assembler outputs the machine language translation of the source program in almost the same form as in the "assemble-and-go" scheme, except that the data is punched on cards (object deck) instead of being placed directly in memory. The loader in turn simply accepts the machine language text and places it into core at the location prescribed by the assembler. This scheme makes more core available to the user since the assembler is not in memory at load time.

Absolute loaders are simple to implement but they do have several disadvantages. First, the programmer must specify to the assembler the address in core where the program is to be loaded. Furthermore, if there are multiple subroutines, the programmer must remember the address of each and use that absolute address explicitly in his other subroutines to perform subroutine linkage.

Figure 5.4 illustrates the operation of an absolute assembler and an absolute loader. The programmer must be careful not to assign two subroutines to the same or overlapping locations.

The MAIN program is assigned to locations 100-247 and the SQRT subroutine is assigned locations 400-477. If changes were made to MAIN that increased its length to more than 300 bytes, the end of MAIN (at 100 + 300 = 400) would overlap the start of SQRT (at 400). It would then be necessary to assign SQRT

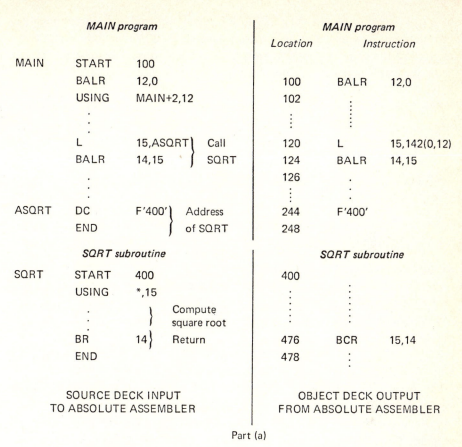

	MAIN program				MAIN program	
					Location	Instruction
MAIN	START	100				
	BALR	12,0			100	BALR 12,0
	USING	MAIN+2,12			102	
		.				.
		.				
	L	15,ASQRT	} Call		120	L 15,142(0,12)
	BALR	14,15	} SQRT		124	BALR 14,15
		.			126	.
		.				
ASQRT	DC	F'400'	} Address		244	F'400'
	END		} of SQRT		248	

	SQRT subroutine				SQRT subroutine	
SQRT	START	400			400	
	USING	*,15				
		.	} Compute			
		.	square root			
	BR	14	} Return		476	BCR 15,14
	END				478	

SOURCE DECK INPUT   OBJECT DECK OUTPUT
TO ABSOLUTE ASSEMBLER   FROM ABSOLUTE ASSEMBLER

Part (a)

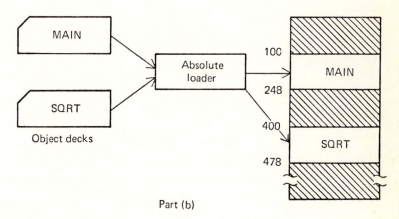

Part (b)

FIGURE 5.4 Absolute loader example

to a new location by changing its START pseudo-op card and reassembling it. Furthermore, it would also be necessary to modify all other subroutines that referred to the address of SQRT. In situations where dozens of subroutines are being used, this manual "shuffling" can get very complex, tedious, and wasteful of core.

The four loader functions are accomplished as follows in an absolute loading scheme:

1. Allocation — by programmer
2. Linking — by programmer
3. Relocation — by assembler
4. Loading — by loader

5.1.4 Subroutine Linkages

In this section we briefly discuss, from a programmer's point of view, the special mechanism for calling another subroutine in an assembly language program.

The problem of subroutine linkage is this: a main program A wishes to transfer to subprogram B. The programmer, in program A, could write a transfer instruction (e.g., BAL 14,B) to subprogram B. However, the assembler does not know the value of this symbol reference and will declare it as an error (undefined symbol) unless a special mechanism has been provided.

This mechanism is typically implemented with a relocating or a direct-linking loader. The assembler pseudo-op EXTRN followed by a list of symbols indicates that these symbols are defined in other programs but referenced in the present program. Correspondingly, if a symbol is defined in one program and referenced in others, we insert it into a symbol list following the pseudo-op ENTRY. In turn, the assembler will inform the loader that these symbols may be referenced by other programs. For example, the following sequence of instructions may be a simple calling sequence to another program:

```
MAIN        START
            EXTRN       SUBROUT
            ———
            ———
            L           15,=A(SUBROUT))
                                        }  CALL SUBROUT
            BALR        14,15          )
             .
             .
             .
            END
```

The above sequence of instructions first declares SUBROUT as an external variable, that is, a variable referenced but not defined in this program. The load instruction loads the address of that variable into register 15. The BALR instruction branches to the contents of register 15, which is the address of SUBROUT, and leaves the value of the next instruction in register 14. In most assemblies we may simply use a CALL SUBROUT macro, which is translated by the assembler into a calling sequence as shown above.

Now we may see the reason for programming conventions, since it is necessary for both the caller and called subprograms to cooperate. On a 360 we observe the convention that register 15 is used as a linkage and base register. Note that the caller in the above program has loaded register 15 with the beginning address of the subroutine being called. Thus the called subroutine does not have to load a base register. Register 14 contains the return address of the caller. The programmer must not use register 14 within a subprogram unless he saves its contents and restores them before he returns. A typical sequence for subroutines is:

```
SUBROUT        START
               USING        *,15
                 :
               BR           14
               END
```

No BALR instruction is necessary at the beginning since register 15 was already loaded with the address of the start of this program. The BR 14 instruction is an unconditional branch to the address contained in register 14, which is the return address of the calling program. In Appendix B we present in more detail the methods that are typically used on a 360 and discuss further the calling sequences. The following discussion introduces the basic mechanism used.

ASSEMBLER LINKAGE PSEUDO-OPS

Subroutine and Entry Naming (START and ENTRY Pseudo-ops)

```
A              START         defines subroutine A.
               ENTRY         B1,B2,B3, . . . defines locations B1, . . .,
                                          Bn as additional subroutine
                                          entry points
B1             -----
B2             -----
```

The uses of multiple entry points are:

1. Common coding.
   Example: SIN and COS involve basically the same computations and could employ different entry points of the same routine.

2. Collecting together related routines for convenience.
3. Better or convenient access to common data base.

SUBROUTINE REFERENCE (EXTRN PSEUDO-OP)

Assembler symbols are either internal or external. External means that their value is not known to the assembler but will be provided by the loader — the action of the loader will be discussed in the following section.

    EXTRN E1,E2,etc.

defines E1, E2, etc. as external symbols to be used in address constants.

    Example: CALL BETA becomes:
                               EXTRN   BETA
                               ⋮
                               L   15,ABETA
                               BALP   14,15
                               ⋮
                    ABETA DC   A(BETA)

5.1.5 Relocating Loaders

To avoid possible reassembling of all subroutines when a single subroutine is changed, and to perform the tasks of allocation and linking for the programmer, the general class of *relocating loaders* was introduced. An example of a relocating loader scheme is that of the Binary Symbolic Subroutine (BSS) loader such as was used in the IBM 7094, IBM 1130, GE 635, and UNIVAC 1108. The BSS loader allows many procedure segments, yet only one data segment (common segment). The assembler assembles each procedure segment independently and passes on to the loader the text and information as to relocation and interseg-ment references.

The output of a relocating assembler using a BSS scheme is the object program and information about all other programs it references. In addition, there is information (relocation information) as to locations in this program that need to be changed if it is to be loaded in an arbitrary place in core, i.e.. the locations which are dependent on the core allocation.

For each source program the assembler outputs a text (machine translation of the program) prefixed by a *transfer vector* that consists of addresses containing names of the subroutines referenced by the source program. For example, if a Square Root Routine (SQRT) was referenced and was the first subroutine called, the first location in the transfer vector would contain the symbolic name SQRT.

The statement calling SQRT would be translated into a transfer instruction indicating a branch to the location of the transfer vector associated with SQRT.

The assembler would also provide the loader with additional information, such as the length of the entire program and the length of the transfer vector portion. After loading the text and the transfer vector into core, the loader would load each subroutine identified in the transfer vector. It would then place a transfer instruction to the corresponding subroutine in each entry in the transfer vector. Thus, the execution of the **call** SQRT statement would result in a branch to the first location in the transfer vector, which would contain a transfer instruction to the location of SQRT.

The BSS loader scheme is often used on computers with a fixed-length direct-address instruction format. For example, *if* the format of the 360 RX instruction were:

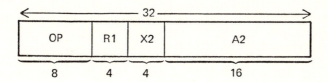

where A2 was the 16-bit absolute address of the operand, this would be a *direct address* instruction format. Such a format works if there are less than $2^{16} =$ 65,536 bytes of storage, as was the case with most of the early computers and is still true for many of the current "minicomputers" and "midicomputers."

Since it is necessary to relocate the address portion of every instruction, computers with a direct-address instruction format have a much more severe relocation problem than the 360. In the absence of 360-type base registers, this problem is often solved by the use of *"relocation bits."* The assembler associates a bit with each instruction or address field. If this bit equals one, then the corresponding address field must be relocated; otherwise the field is not relocated. These relocation indicators, surprisingly enough, are known as relocation bits and are included in the object deck.

Figure 5.5 illustrates a simple assembly language program written for a hypothetical "direct-address" 360 that uses a BSS loader. The function of the program is not important; it supposedly calls the SQRT subroutine to get the square root of 9. If the result is not 3, it transfers to a subroutine called ERR. Since this is a direct-address computer, there is no base register field in the object code and no need for a USING pseudo-op in the source program. The EXTRN pseudo-op identifies the symbols SQRT and ERR as the names of other subroutines; since the locations of these symbols are not defined in this subroutine, they are called *external symbols.* For each external symbol the assembler generates a four-

byte fullword at the beginning of the program, containing the EBCDIC characters for the symbol (for simplicity, we are assuming that symbols are not more
than four characters long). These extra words are called transfer vectors. Every
reference to an external symbol is assigned the address of the corresponding
transfer vector word. In addition, for every halfword (two bytes) in the program, the assembler produces a separate relocation bit. For example, the assembled instruction ST 14,36 is assigned relocation bits 01 since the first
halfword contains the op-code, register field, and index field which should not
be relocated but the second halfword contains the relative address 36, which
must be relocated.

	Source program				Program length = 48 bytes		
					Transfer vector = 8 bytes		
				Rel.			
MAIN	START			addr.	Relocation	Object code	
	EXTRN	SQRT		0	00	'SQRT'	
	EXTRN	ERR		4	00	'ERR*b*'	
	ST	14,SAVE	Save return address	8	01	ST	14,36
	L	1,=F'9'	Load test value	12	01	L	1,40
	BAL	14,SQRT	Call SQRT	16	01	BAL	14,0
	C	1,=F'3'	Compare answer	20	01	C	1,44
	BNE	ERR	Transfer to ERR	24	01	BC	7,4
	L	14,SAVE	Get return address	28	01	L	14,36
	BR	14	Return to caller	32	0	BCR	15,14
				34	0	(Skipped for alignment)	
SAVE	DS	F	Temp. loc.	36	00	(Temp location)	
	END			40	00	9	
				44	00	3	

FIGURE 5.5 Assembly of program for "direct-address" 360

Figure 5.6 illustrates the contents of memory after the programs have been
loaded by the BSS loader. Based upon the relocation bits, the loader has
relocated the address fields to correspond to the allocated address of MAIN
which is 400. Using the program length information, the loader placed the subroutines SQRT and ERR at the next available locations which were 448 and
526, respectively. Finally, the transfer vector words were changed to contain

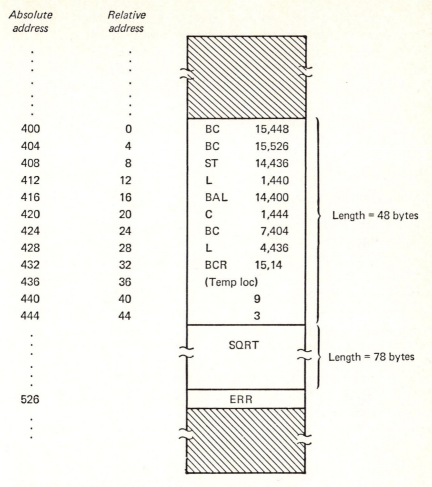

FIGURE 5.6 BSS loading of programs for "direct access" 360

branch instructions to the corresponding subroutines. Thus, the four functions of the loader (allocation, linking, relocation, and loading) were all performed automatically by the BSS loader.

It should be noted that the relocation bits are used to solve the problem of relocation; the transfer vector is used to solve the problem of linking; and the program length information is used to solve the problem of allocation.

There are several disadvantages to the BSS loader scheme. First, the transfer vector linkage is only useful for transfers, and is not well-suited for loading or storing external data (data located in another procedure segment). Second, the transfer vector increases the size of the object program in memory. Finally, the BSS loader, as described, processes procedure segments but does not facilitate access to data segments that can be shared. This last shortcoming is overcome in many BSS loaders by allowing one common data segment, often called *COMMON*. This facility is usually implemented by extending the relocation bits scheme to use two bits per halfword address field: if the bits are 01, the halfword is relocated relative to the procedure segment, and if they are 10, it is relocated relative to the address of the single common data segment. If the bits are 00 or 11, the halfword is not relocated.

5.1.6 Direct-Linking Loaders

A direct-linking loader is a general relocatable loader, and is perhaps the most popular loading scheme presently used. Throughout our discussion of compilers in later sections, we will assume that the system employs such a loader.

The direct-linking loader has the advantage of allowing the programmer multiple procedure segments and multiple data segments and of giving him complete freedom in referencing data or instructions contained in other segments. This provides flexible intersegment referencing and accessing ability, while at the same time allowing independent translations of programs.

A design of a direct-linking loader will be given later in this chapter. In this section we present a general format for the assembler output with such a loading scheme, patterned after those used in the IBM 370. While the formats themselves are somewhat arbitrary, the information that the assembler must give to the loader is not. The assembler (translator) must give the loader the following information with each procedure or data segment:

1. The length of segment
2. A list of all the symbols in the segment that may be referenced by other segments and their relative location within the segment
3. A list of all symbols not defined in the segment but referenced in the segment
4. Information as to where address constants are located in the segment and a description of how to revise their values
5. The machine code translation of the source program and the relative addresses assigned

A simple example using a direct-linking loading scheme is presented in Figure 5.7. A source program (left-hand column) is translated by an assembler to produce the object code depicted in the right column. Mnemonic machine codes have again been used in the translation shown.

	Program				Translation	
Card no.				Rel. loc.		
1.	JOHN	START				
2.		ENTRY	RESULT			
3.		EXTRN	SUM			
4.		BALR	12,0	0	BALR	12,0
5.		USING	*,12			
6.		ST	14,SAVE	2	ST	14,54(0,12)
7.		L	1,POINTER	6	L	1,46(0,12)
8.		L	15,ASUM	10	L	15,58(0,12)
9.		BALR	14,15	14	BALR	14,15
10		ST	1,RESULT	16	ST	1,50(0,12)
11.		L	14,SAVE	20	L	14,54(0,12)
12.		BR	14	24	BCR	15,14
				26	——	
13.	TABLE	DC	F'1,7,9,10,3'	28	1	
				32	7	
				36	9	
				40	10	
				44	3	
14.	POINTER	DC	A(TABLE)	48	28	
15.	RESULT	DS	F	52	——	
16.	SAVE	DS	F	56	——	
17.	ASUM	DC	A(SUM)	60	?	
18.		END		64		

FIGURE 5.7 Assembly source program and its translation

Card number 14 of Figure 5.7 contains a Define Constant (DC) pseudo-operation which instructs the assembler to create a constant with the value of the address of TABLE, and causes this constant to be placed in the location labelled POINTER. At this point the assembler does not know the final absolute address of TABLE since it has no idea where the program is going to be loaded. It knows, however, that the address is the 28th byte from the beginning of this program. The assembler will put a 28 in POINTER and inform the loader that the content of location POINTER is incorrect if this program is loaded anywhere except absolute location 0. For instance, if this program were loaded in location 2000, the loader would have to change the contents of POINTER to be a 2028.

Card number 17 of Figure 5.7 is another DC pseudo-op, which instructs the assembler to create a constant with the value of the address of the subroutine SUM and cause this constant to be placed in the location labelled ASUM. Since the assembler has no idea where the procedure SUM will be loaded, it cannot generate this constant. Thus, the assembler must provide information to the loader that will cause it to put the final absolute address of SUM at the designated location (ASUM) when the programs are loaded.

We have named the program JOHN. Hence, JOHN is a symbol that may be referenced externally or "called" by other programs. We also have stated that the symbol RESULT may be referenced by other programs. These facts must be passed on to the loader.

The design of the direct-linking loading scheme we present is similar to the standard IBM 370 scheme. The assembler produces four types of cards in the object deck: ESD, TXT, RLD, and END. External Symbol Dictionary (ESD) cards contain information about all symbols that are defined in this program but that may be referenced elsewhere, and all symbols referenced in this program but defined elsewhere. The text (TXT) cards contain the actual object code translated version of the source program. The Relocation and Linkage Directory (RLD) cards contain information about those locations in the program whose contents depend on the address at which the program is placed. For such locations the assembler must supply information enabling the loader to correct their contents. The END card indicates the end of the object deck and specifies the starting address for execution if the assembled routine is the "main" program. Figure 5.8 depicts the information that would appear for the preceding program on the ESD, TXT, RLD, and END cards.

The reference numbers in Figure 5.8 do not actually appear on the cards. They are for the benefit of the reader, and each denotes the card number of the original program that resulted in the object deck card; e.g., the first RLD card resulted from card number 14 in the original program.

As shown in Figure 5.8, three ESD cards are needed for the program JOHN. The first card contains the name of the program JOHN, which may be referenced externally. The "type" mnemonic we have used is SD, which means the symbol is a Segment Definition. The relative address of JOHN is 0, and the length is of the program that JOHN denotes, 64. On the next ESD card appears the symbol RESULT, which is a Local Definition (LD); its relative address is 52. The final ESD card specifies that the symbol SUM is an External Reference (ER). We will see in a later section how the ER symbols are actually used in conjunction with the RLD cards.

The TXT cards contain the actual assembled program. The format and use of these cards are similar to those for the absolute loader.

The RLD cards contain the following information:

1. The location of each constant that needs to be changed due to relocation
2. By what it has to be changed
3. The operation to be performed

The first RLD card of our example contains a 48, denoting the relative loca-

ESD cards

Reference no.	Symbol	Type	Relative location	Length
1	JOHN	SD	0	64
2	RESULT	LD	52	— —
3	SUM	ER	— —	— —

TXT cards

Reference no.	Relative location	Object code	
4	0	BALR	12,0
6	2	ST	14,54(0,12)
7	6	L	1,46(0,12)
8	10	L	15,58(0,12)
9	14	BALR	14,15
10	16	ST	1,50(0,12)
11	20	L	14,54(0,12)
12	24	BCR	15,14
13	28	1	
13	32	7	
13	36	9	
13	40	10	
13	44	3	
14	48	28	
17	60	0	

RLD cards

Reference no.	Symbol	Flag	Length	Relative location
14	JOHN	+	4	48
17	SUM	+	4	60

Object deck

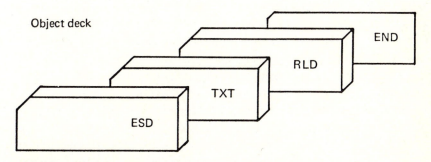

FIGURE 5.8   Example object deck for a direct-linking loader

tion of a constant that must be changed; a plus sign denoting that something must be added to the constant; and the symbol field indicating that the value of external symbol JOHN must be added to relative location 48. The relative value of JOHN is 0. When the program is loaded, the loader will determine its absolute value.

The second RLD card of our example contains a 60, denoting the relative location of a constant that must be changed. The symbol field indicates that the value of the external symbol SUM must be added to relative location 60. Although the assembler does not know the absolute address of SUM, the loader will later be able to fill in the correct value.

The process of adjusting the address constant of an internal symbol, such as TABLE, is normally called relocation; while the process of supplying the contents of an address constant for an external symbol, such as SUM, is normally referred to as linking. Significantly, the RLD card mechanism is used for both cases, which explains why they are called relocation *and* linkage directory cards. The reader may wish to compare this technique with the mechanisms used in the BSS relocating loader described earlier in this chapter.

5.1.7 Other Loader Schemes — Binders, Linking Loaders, Overlays, Dynamic Binders

There are numerous variations to the previously presented loader schemes.

One disadvantage of the direct-linking loader, as presented, is that it is necessary to allocate, relocate, link, and load all of the subroutines each time in order to execute a program. Since there may be tens and often hundreds of subroutines involved, especially when we include utility routines such as SQRT, etc., this loading process can be extremely time-consuming. Furthermore, even though the loader program may be smaller than the assembler, it does absorb a considerable amount of space. These problems can be solved by dividing the loading process into two separate programs: a binder and a module loader.

A *binder* is a program that performs the same functions as the direct-linking loader in "binding" subroutines together, but rather than placing the relocated and linked text directly into memory, it outputs the text as a file or card deck. This output file is in a format ready to be loaded and is typically called a *load module*. The *module loader* merely has to physically load the module into core. The binder essentially performs the functions of allocation, relocation, and linking; the module loader merely performs the function of loading.

There are two major classes of binders. The simplest type produces a load module that looks very much like a single absolute loader deck. This means that the specific core allocation of the program is performed at the time that the subroutines are bound together. Since this kind of module looks like an actual "snapshot" or "image" of a section of core, it is called a *core image module* and the corresponding binder is called a *core image builder*. A more sophisticated binder, called a *linkage editor*, can keep track of the relocation information so that the resulting load module, as an ensemble, can be further relocated and thereby loaded anywhere in core. In this case the module loader must perform additional allocation and relocation as well as loading, but it does not have to worry about the complex problems of linking.

In both cases, a program that is to be used repeatedly need only be bound once and then can be loaded whenever required. The core image builder binder is relatively simple and fast. The linkage editor binder is somewhat more complex but allows a more flexible allocation and loading scheme.

DYNAMIC LOADING

In each of the previous loader schemes we have assumed that all of the subroutines needed are loaded into core at the same time. If the total amount of core required by all these subroutines exceeds the amount available, as is common with large programs or small computers, there is trouble! There are several hardware techniques, such as paging and segmentation, that attempt to solve this problem; these are discussed in Chapter 9. In this section we will present conventional dynamic loading schemes based upon the use of a binder prior to loading.

Usually the subroutines of a program are needed at different times: for example, pass 1 and pass 2 of an assembler are mutually exclusive. By explicitly recognizing which subroutines call other subroutines it is possible to produce an *overlay structure* that identifies mutually exclusive subroutines. Figure 5.9a illustrates a program consisting of five subprograms (A,B,C,D and E) that require 100K bytes of core. The arrows indicate that subprogram A only calls B, D and E; subprogram B only calls C and E; subprogram D only calls E; and subprograms C and E do not call any other routines. Figure 5.9b highlights the interdependencies between the procedures. Note that procedures B and D are never in use at the same time; neither are C and E. If we load only those procedures that are actually to be used at any particular time, the amount of core needed is equal to the longest path of the overlay structure. This happens to be 70K for the example in Figure 5.9b — procedures A, B, and C. Figure 5.9c illustrates a storage assignment for each procedure consistent with the overlay structure.

In order for the overlay structure to work it is necessary for the module loader to load the various procedures as they are needed. We will not go into their specific details, but there are many binders capable of processing and allocating an overlay structure. The portion of the loader that actually intercepts the "calls" and loads the necessary procedure is called the *overlay supervisor* or

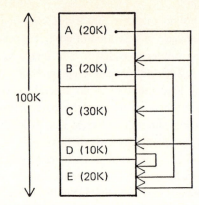

(a) Subroutine calls between the procedures

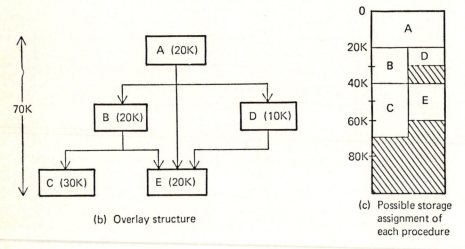

(b) Overlay structure

(c) Possible storage assignment of each procedure

FIGURE 5.9 Other loading schemes

simply the *flipper*. This overall scheme is called *dynamic loading* or *load-on-call* (LOCAL).

DYNAMIC LINKING

A major disadvantage of all of the previous loading schemes is that if a subroutine is referenced but never executed (e.g., if the programmer had placed a call statement in his program but this statement was never executed because of a condition that branched around it), the loader would still incur the overhead of linking the subroutine.

Furthermore, all of these schemes require the programmer to explicitly name all procedures that might be called. It is not possible to write programs as follows:

$$\vdots$$

```
READ       SUBNAME, ARGUMENT
ANSWER  =  SUBNAME(ARGUMENT)
PRINT      ANSWER
```

$$\vdots$$

where the name of the subroutine (e.g., SQRT, SINE, etc.) is an input parameter, SUBNAME, just like the other data.

A very general type of loading scheme that we will discuss in Chapter 9 is called dynamic linking. This is a mechanism by which loading and linking of external references are postponed until execution time. That is, the assembler produces text, binding, and relocation information from a source language deck. The loader loads only the main program. If the main program should execute a transfer instruction to an external address, or should reference an external variable (that is, a variable that has not been defined in this procedure segment), the loader is called. Only then is the segment containing the external reference loaded.

An advantage here is that no overhead is incurred unless the procedure to be called or referenced is actually used. A further advantage is that the system can be dynamically reconfigured. The major drawback to using this type of loading scheme is the considerable overhead and complexity incurred, due to the fact that we have postponed most of the binding process until execution time.

5.2 DESIGN OF AN ABSOLUTE LOADER

We introduce the general topic of loader design by presenting a design of an absolute loader.

With an absolute loading scheme the programmer and the assembler perform the tasks of allocation, relocation, and linking. Therefore, it is only necessary for the loader to read cards of the object deck and move the text on the cards into the absolute locations specified by the assembler.

There are two types of information that the object deck must communicate from the assembler to the loader. First, it must convey the machine instructions that the assembler has created along with the assigned core locations. Second, it must convey the entry point of the program, which is where the loader is to transfer control when all instructions are loaded. Assuming that this information is transmitted on cards, a possible format is shown in Figure 5.10.

Note that in the card format shown the instructions are stored on the card as one core byte per column. For each of the 256 possible contents of an eight-bit byte there is a corresponding punched card code (e.g., hexadecimal 00 is a column punched with five holes, 12-0-1-8-9, whereas a hexadecimal F1 is a column with a single punch in row 1). Thus, when a card is read, it is stored in core as 80 contiguous bytes.

Text cards (for instructions and data)

Card column	Contents
1	Card type = 0 (for text card identifier)
2	Count of number of bytes (1 byte per column) of information on card
3-5	Address at which data on card is to be put
6-7	Empty (could be used for validity checking)
8-72	Instructions and data to be loaded
73-80	Card sequence number

Transfer cards (to hold entry point to program)

Card column	Contents
1	Card type = 1 (transfer card identifier)
2	Count = 0
3-5	Address of entry point
6-72	Empty
73-80	Card sequence number

FIGURE 5.10 Card formats for an absolute loader

The algorithm for an absolute loader is quite simple. The object deck for this loader consists of a series of text cards terminated by a transfer card. Therefore, the loader should read one card at a time, moving the text to the location specified on the card, until the transfer card is reached. At this point the assembled instructions are in core, and it is only necessary to transfer to the entry point specified on the transfer card. A flowchart for this process is illustrated in Figure 5.11.

5.3 DESIGN OF A DIRECT-LINKING LOADER

In this section a design of an IBM 360-type direct-linking loader is presented. Certain obscure features (primarily related to the IBM PL/I implementation and overlay structures) have been omitted, and where alternative formats are possible, only the simplest is given.

The design steps followed will parallel those taken in the design of an assembler (Chapter 3). Note that because the direct-linking loader needs to know

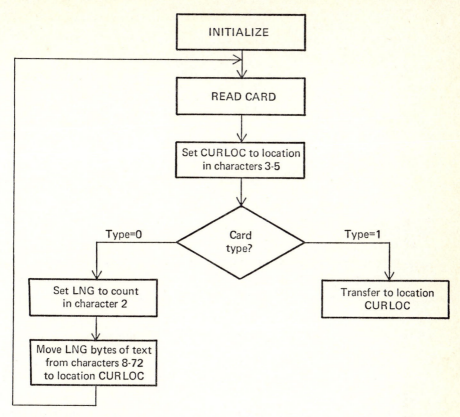

FIGURE 5.11 Absolute loader

the absolute (load time) values of some external symbols before it can perform the modifications on address constants, it requires two passes.

5.3.1 Specification of Problem

The organization of the IBM 360 facilitates the tasks to be performed by its relocating loader. On the IBM 7094, a direct access machine, it was necessary to relocate the address portion on almost all instructions. In the 360, instruction relocation is accomplished by the use of the base register, which is set by neither the assembler nor the loader. Therefore, the 360 relocating loader can treat instructions *exactly* like nonrelocatable data (full word constants, characters, etc.). However, address constants must still be relocated.

For example, the following instructions:

```
TEST       START
           USING        *,15
           L            1,DATA
             ⋮

DATA       DC           F'5'
           END
```

might be assembled as:

Rel. loc.	Instruction/data
0	L 1,96(0,15).
⋮	⋮
96	5

Regardless of where the program is loaded, the L instruction will be unchanged as long as DATA remains 96 bytes from the beginning of the program. The contents of the base register (15) obviously will be different, depending upon the program's load location.

On the other hand, consider modifying the above example:

```
             ⋮
DATA       DC           F'5'
DATALOC    DC           A(DATA)
           END
```

DATALOC must contain the absolute address of DATA. The assembler knows only that DATA is 96 bytes from the beginning of the program, so the loader must add to this the load address of the program in finding the actual absolute address to be contained in DATALOC.

Let us clarify the scope of the address constant problem. An address constant may be (1) absolute; (2) simple relocatable; or (3) complex relocatable.

For example, the address constant A(LOC1-LOC2) will be:

1. *Absolute* if LOC1 and LOC2 are two relocatable symbols defined internal to program — the assembler can calculate the actual value, their difference.
2. *Simple relocatable* if LOC1 is a relocatable symbol within this procedure and LOC2 is an absolute number (e.g., LOC2 EQU 5). The assembler can calculate the difference between relative location of LOC1 and value of LOC2, but the loader must perform relocation by adding the program load address.
3. *Complex relocatable* if LOC1 and LOC2 are entries to some other program. The assembler can do nothing, and the value must be calculated by the loader.

The 360 direct-linking loader processes programs generated by the assembler, FORTRAN compiler, or PL/I compiler. Recall that neither the original source program nor the assembler symbol table is available to the loader. Therefore, the object deck must contain all information needed for relocation and linking.

There are four sections to the object deck (and four corresponding card formats):

1. External Symbol Dictionary cards (ESD)
2. Instructions and data cards, called "text" of program (TXT)
3. Relocation and Linkage Directory cards (RLD)
4. End card (END)

The ESD cards contain the information necessary to build the external symbol dictionary or symbol table. External symbols are symbols that can be referred beyond the subroutine level. The normal labels in the source program are used only by the assembler, and information about them is not included in the object deck.

EXAMPLE

Assume program B has a table called NAMES; it can be accessed by program A as follows.

```
A               START
                EXTRN       NAMES
                :
                L           1,ADDRNAME get address of NAME table
                :
ADDRNAME        DC          A(NAMES)
                END
                ───────────────────
B               START
                ENTRY       NAMES
                :
NAMES           DC          ─────
                END
```

There are three types of external symbols, as illustrated in the above:

1. *Segment Definition* (SD) — name on START or CSECT card.
2. *Local Definition* (LD) — specified on ENTRY card. There must be a label in same program with same name.
3. *External Reference* (ER) — specified on EXTRN card. There must be a

corresponding ENTRY, START, or CSECT card in another program with same name.

Each SD and ER symbol is assigned a unique number (e.g., 1,2,3, . . .) by the assembler. This number is called the symbol's *identifier*, or *ID*, and is used in conjunction with the RLD cards.

The TXT cards contain blocks of data and the relative address at which the data is to be placed. Once the loader has decided where to load the program, it merely adds the *Program Load Address* (PLA) to the relative address and moves the data into the resulting location. The data on the TXT card may be instructions, nonrelocated data, or initial values of address constants.

EXAMPLE

Relative address		Instruction	
A		START	
		EXTRN	NAMES
		USING	*,15
		:	
40		L	1,ALPHA
44		BCR	15,14
46		————————————	(Skipped by assembler)
48	ALPHA	DC	F'5'
52	ALLOC	DC	A(ALPHA)
56	ADDRNAME	DC	A(NAMES)
		:	

The TXT card produced is:

Relative address = 40
Data portion = *58 10 F0 30 07FE XX XX 00 00 00 05 00 00 00 30 00 00 00 00*
Length of data portion = 20 bytes

The RLD cards contain the following information.

1. The location and length of each address constant that needs to be changed for relocation or linking
2. The external symbol by which the address constant should be modified (added or subtracted)
3. The operation to be performed (add or subtract)

Rather than using the actual external symbol's name on the RLD card, as implied in section 5.1.6 and Figure 5.8, the external symbol's identifier, or ID, is used. There are various reasons for this, the major one probably being that the ID is only a single byte long, compared to the eight bytes occupied by the symbol name, so that a considerable amount of space is saved on the RLD cards. Unfortunately, this space-saving technique causes increased loader complexity as will be shown later.

The preceding program segment used as an example for TXT cards would result in the following RLD cards

ID	Flag	Length	Rel. loc.
01	+	4	52
02	+	4	56

if we assume that A's assigned ID is 01 and NAMES' assigned ID is 02. This RLD information tells the loader to add the absolute load address of A to the contents of relative location 52 and then add the absolute load address of NAMES to the contents of relative location 56.

The END card specifies the end of the object deck. If the assembler END card has a symbol in the operand field, it specifies a start of execution point for the entire program (all subroutines). This address is recorded on the END card.

There is a final card required to specify the end of a collection of object decks. The 360 loaders usually use either a loader terminate (LDT) or End of File (EOF) card.

```
                          ┌ ESD
                          │ TXT
        Subroutine A      ┤ RLD
                          └ END

                          ┌ ESD
                          │ TXT
        Subroutine B      ┤ RLD
                          └ END

                          ┌ ESD
                          │ TXT
        Subroutine C      ┤ RLD
                          └ END

                            EOF or LDT
```

The simple programs PG1 and PG2 in Figure 5.12 illustrate a wide range of relocation and linking situations. Figures 5.13 and 5.14 display the ESD, TXT, and RLD cards produced by the assembler for PG1 and PG2, respectively. Finally, Figure 5.15 depicts the contents of main storage after the programs have been allocated space, relocated, linked, and loaded. The reader should examine these figures carefully and validate the correctness and reasons for each value.

A few specific points in these examples should be noted. Both PG1 and PG2 contain an address constant of the form A(PG1ENT2-PG1ENT1-3). It should be

Source card reference	Relative address		Sample program (source deck)		
1	0	PG1	START		
2			ENTRY	PG1ENT1,PG1ENT2	
3			EXTRN	PG2ENT1,PG2	Procedure PG1
4	20	PG1ENT1	≡		
5	30	PG1ENT2	≡		
6	40		DC	A(PG1ENT1)	
7	44		DC	A(PG1ENT2+15)	
8	48		DC	A(PG1ENT2-PG1ENT1-3)	
9	52		DC	A(PG2)	(a)
10	56		DC	A(PG2ENT1+PG2-PG1ENT1+4)	
11			END		
12	0	PG2	START		
13			ENTRY	PG2ENT1	Procedure PG2
14			EXTRN	PG1ENT1,PG1ENT2	
15	16	PG2ENT1	≡		
16	24		DC	A(PG1ENT1)	
17	28		DC	A(PG1ENT2+15)	
18	32		DC	A(PG1ENT2-PG1ENT1-3)	(b)
19			END		

FIGURE 5.12   Sample procedures PG1 and PG2

reassuring to note in Figure 5.15 that both instances of this address constant (location 152, 200) have the same value − 7. Since both PG1ENT2 and PG1ENT1 are symbols internal to PG1, the assembler, processing PG1, can compute the entire expression and determine the value of 7. We see in Figure 5.13 that the TXT card for location 48-51 contains the 7 and there are no associated RLD cards for this address constant. On the other hand, these symbols are external to PG2; thus, the assembler, while processing PG2, has no means of evaluating the address constant. This is illustrated in Figure 5.14. The TXT card for relative locations 32-35 contains a -3, the only part of the address constant that can be calculated by the assembler. The last two RLD cards tell the loader to add the value of ID 03, which is PG1ENT2, to locations 32-35 and then subtract the value of ID 02, which is PG1ENT1. When processed by the loader, this address constant in PG2 will indeed have the same value as the one in PG1.

Since the direct-linking loader may encounter external references in an object deck which cannot be evaluated until a later object deck is processed, this type of loader requires two passes. Their functions are very similar to those of the two passes of an assembler. The major function of pass 1 of a direct-linking loader is to allocate and assign each program a location in core and create a

ESD cards					
Source card reference	Name	Type	ID	Relative address	Length
1	PG1	SD	01	0	60
2	PG1ENT1	LD	––	20	––
2	PG1ENT2	LD	––	30	––
3	PG2	ER	02	––	––
3	PG2ENT1	ER	03	––	––

TXT cards			
(only the interesting ones, i.e. those involving address constants)			
Source card reference	Relative address	Contents	Comments
6	40-43	20	
7	44-47	45	= 30 + 15
8	48-51	7	= 30-20-3
9	52-55	0	unknown to PG1
10	56-59	-16	= -20 + 4

RLD cards				
Source card reference	ESD ID	Length (bytes)	Flag + or –	Relative address
6	01	4	+	40
7	01	4	+	44
9	02	4	+	52
10	03	4	+	56
10	02	4	+	56
10	01	4	–	56

FIGURE 5.13 Object deck program PG1

symbol table filling in the values of the external symbols. The major function of pass 2 is to load the actual program text and perform the relocation modification of any address constants needing to be altered.

The first pass allocates and assigns storage locations to all segments and stores the values of all external symbols in a symbol table. These external symbols appear as local definitions on the ESD cards of another assembled program. For every external reference symbol there must be a corresponding internal symbol in some other program. The loader inserts the absolute address of all of these external symbols in the symbol table. In the second pass, the loader places the text into the assigned locations and performs the relocation task, modifying relocatable constants. Figure 5.16 depicts the interplay between the passes of a loader in a direct-linking loading scheme.

ESD cards					
Source card reference	Name	Type	ID	ADDR	Length
12	PG2	SD	01	0	36
13	PG2ENT1	LD	––	16	––
14	PG1ENT1	ER	02	––	––
14	PG1ENT2	ER	03	––	––

TXT cards (only the interesting ones)		
Source card reference	Relative address	Contents
16	24-27	0
17	28-31	15
18	32-25	-3

RLD cards				
Source card reference	ESD ID	Length flag (bytes)	Flag + or –	Relative address
16	02	4	+	24
17	03	4	+	28
18	03	4	+	32
18	02	4	–	32

FIGURE 5.14 Object deck program PG2

5.3.2 Specification of Data Structures

The next step in our design procedure is to identify the data bases required by each pass of the loader.

Pass 1 data bases:

1. Input object decks.
2. A parameter, the Initial Program Load Address (IPLA) supplied by the programmer or the operating system, that specifies the address to load the first segment.
3. A Program Load Address (PLA) counter, used to keep track of each segment's assigned location.
4. A table, the Global External Symbol Table (GEST), that is used to store each external symbol and its corresponding assigned core address.
5. A copy of the input to be used later by pass 2. This may be stored on an auxiliary storage device, such as magnetic tape, disk, or drum, or the original object decks may be reread by the loader a second time for pass 2.
6. A printed listing, the *load map*, that specifies each external symbol and its assigned value.

Assume:

PG1 loaded at location 104
PG2 loaded at location 168

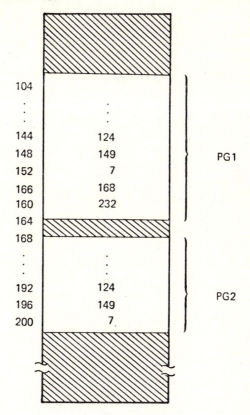

FIGURE 5.15   Main storage after loading programs PG1 and PG2

Pass 2 data bases:

1. Copy of object programs inputted to pass 1
2. The Initial Program Load Address parameter (IPLA)
3. The Program Load Address counter (PLA)
4. The Global External Symbol Table (GEST), prepared by pass 1, containing each external symbol and its corresponding absolute address value
5. An array, the Local External Symbol Array (LESA), which is used to establish a correspondence between the ESD ID numbers, used on ESD and RLD cards, and the corresponding external symbol's absolute address value

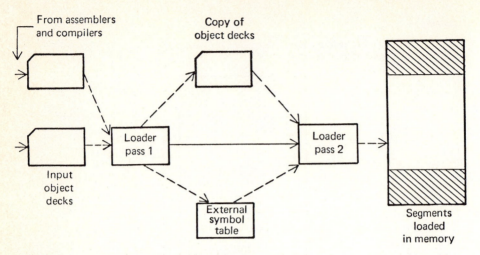

FIGURE 5.16 Two pass direct-linking loader scheme

5.3.3 Format of Data Bases

The third step in our design procedure is to specify the format and content of
each of the data bases. The major data bases are depicted in Figure 5.17.

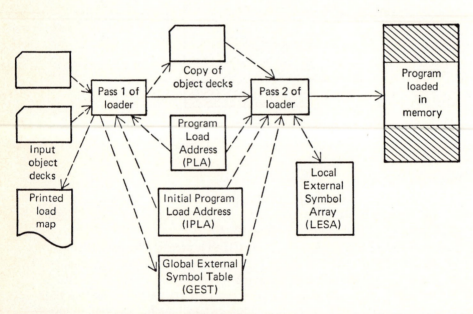

FIGURE 5.17 Use of data bases by loader passes

OBJECT DECK

The object deck has been discussed several times; Figures 5.18, 5.19, 5.20 and 5.21, depict in detail the actual card deck format that is used by various IBM 370 or 360 direct-linking loaders. The specific card format is not crucial, but these figures present a good example of the various techniques used to encode information.

GLOBAL EXTERNAL SYMBOL TABLE

The Global External Symbol Table (GEST) is used to store the external symbols defined by means of a Segment Definition (SD) or Local Definition (LD) entry on an External Symbol Dictionary (ESD) card. When these symbols are encountered during pass 1, they are assigned an absolute core address; this address is stored, along with the symbol, in the GEST as illustrated in Figure 5.22.

The reader may wish to review the discussion on symbol tables and searching/sorting techniques presented in Chapter 3 in conjunction with the design of an

Columns	Contents
1	Hexadecimal byte X'02' (card punch 12-2-9)
2-4	Characters ESD
5-14	Blank
15-16	ESD identifier (ID) for program name (SD) or external symbol (ER) (IDs unique within program) or blank for entry (LD), see box below
17-24	Name, padded with blanks
25	ESD type code (TYPE)
26-28	Relative address or blank (ADDR), see box below
29	Blank
30-32	Length of program otherwise blank (LENGTH)
33-72	Blank
73-80	Card sequence number

TYPE	Hexadecimal code
SD	01
LD	02
ER	03

ESD forms and conventions

	Type	ID	ADDR	Length
Program name (segment definition)	SD	01	Zero	Length of program
Entry (local definition)	LD	--	Relative address	--
External reference	ER	Unique number	--	--

(The unique ID numbers are usually assigned sequentially.)

FIGURE 5.18 ESD card format

Columns	Contents
1	Hexadecimal byte X'02'
2-4	Characters TXT
5	Blank
6-8	Relative address of first data byte (ADDR)
9-10	Blank
11-12	Byte Count (BC) = number of bytes of information in cc. 17-72
13-16	Blank
17-72	From 1 to 56 data bytes (instructions and "data" look the same)
73-80	Card sequence number

FIGURE 5.19   TXT card format

Columns	Contents
1	Hexadecimal byte X'02'
2-4	Characters RLD
5-18	Blank
19-20	ID corresponding to a number assigned to SD or ER on ESD card
21	Flag byte (see box below)
22-24	Relative address of first byte of address constant (ADDR)
25-72	Blank
73-80	Card sequence number

Flag byte conventions	
bits	
0-3	Not used
4-5	Length (in bytes) of address constant
	00 = one byte
	01 = two bytes
	10 = three bytes
	11 = four bytes
6	0 means add ESD address to address constant
	1 means subtract ESD address from address constant

FIGURE 5.20   RLD card·format

Columns	Contents
1	Hexadecimal byte X'02'
2-4	Characters END
5	Blank
6-8	Start of execution entry (ADDR), if other than beginning of program (specified on assembly END card)
9-72	Blank
73-80	Card sequence number

FIGURE 5.21   END card format

$\xleftarrow{\hspace{3cm}}$ 12 bytes per entry $\xrightarrow{\hspace{3cm}}$

External symbol (8-bytes) (characters)	Assigned core address (4-bytes) (decimal)
"PG1bbbbb"	104
"PG1ENT1b"	124
"PG1ENT2b"	134
"PG2bbbbb"	168
"PG2ENT1b"	184

Notation: This sample GEST content is based upon the example in Figures 5.12 and 5.15.

FIGURE 5.22   Global External Symbol Table (GEST) format

assembler. The GEST has the same general use and characteristics as the assembler's Symbol Table.

LOCAL EXTERNAL SYMBOL ARRAY

As mentioned earlier, the external symbol to be used for relocation or linking is identified on the RLD cards by means of an ID number rather than the symbol's name. The ID number must match an SD or ER entry on the ESD cards. This technique both saves space on the RLD cards and speeds processing by eliminating many searches of the Global External Symbol Table.

It is necessary to establish a correspondence between an ID number on an RLD card and the absolute core address value. The ESD cards contain the ID numbers and the symbols they correspond to, while the information relating these symbols to absolute core address values may be found in the GEST. In pass 2 of the loader the GEST and ESD information for each individual object deck is merged to produce the local external symbol array that directly relates ID number and value. In principle it is necessary to create a separate LESA for each segment, but since the LESAs are only produced one at a time, the same array can be reused for each segment. Figure 5.23 depicts the format of the Local External Symbol Array (LESA). Note that unlike the case with the GEST, it is not necessary to *search* the LESA; given an ID number, the corresponding value is written as LESA(ID) and can be immediately obtained.

5.3.4 Algorithm

The following two flowcharts (Figs. 5.24 and 5.25) describe an algorithm for a direct-linking loader for an IBM System/360-type computer While they illustrate

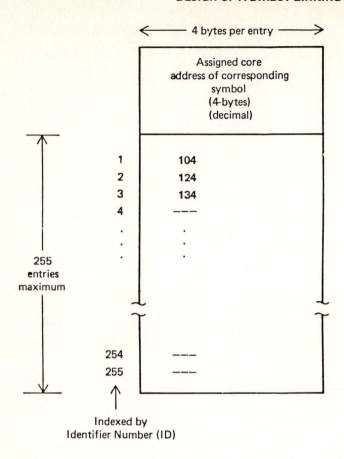

FIGURE 5.23   Local External Symbol Array (LESA) format

most of the logical processes involved, these flowcharts are still a simplification of the operations performed in a complex loader. In particular, many "special" features, such as COMMON segments, library processing, dynamic loading and dynamic linking, are not explicitly included (many of them are discussed in the problems section and in later chapters).

Pass 1 – allocate segments and define symbols   The purpose of the first pass is to assign a location to each segment, and thus to define the values of all external symbols. Since we wish to minimize the amount of core storage required for the total program, we will assign each segment the next available location after the

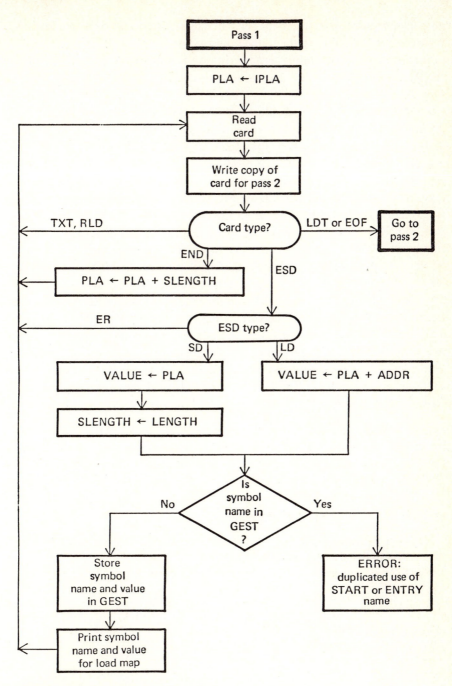

FIGURE 5.24 Detailed pass 1 flowchart

preceding segment. It is necessary for the loader to know where it can load the first segment. This address, the Initial Program Load Address (IPLA), is normally determined by the operating system. In some systems the programmer may specify the IPLA; in either case we will assume that the IPLA is a parameter supplied to the loader.

Initially, the Program Load Address (PLA) is set to the Initial Program Load Address (IPLA). An object card is then read and a copy written for use by pass 2. The card can be one of five types, ESD, TXT, RLD, END, or LDT/EOF. If it is a TXT or RLD card, there is no processing required during pass 1 so the next card is read. An ESD card is processed in different ways depending upon the type of external symbol, SD, LD or ER. If a segment definition ESD card is read, the length field, LENGTH, from the card is temporarily saved in the variable, SLENGTH. The value, VALUE, to be assigned to this symbol is set to the current value of the PLA. The symbol and its assigned value are then stored in the GEST; if the symbol already existed in the GEST, there must have been a previous SD or LD ESD with the same name – this is an error. The symbol and its value are printed as part of the load map. A similar process is used for LD symbols; the value to be assigned is set to the current PLA plus the relative address, ADDR, indicated on the ESD card. The ER symbols do not require any processing during pass 1. When an END card is encountered, the program load address is incremented by the length of the segment and saved in SLENGTH, becoming the PLA for the next segment. When the LDT or EOF card is finally read, pass 1 is completed and control transfers to pass 2.

Pass 2 – load text and relocate/link address constants After all the segments have been assigned locations and the external symbols have been defined by pass 1, it is possible to complete the loading by loading the text and adjusting (relocation or linking) address constants. At the end of pass 2, the loader will transfer control to the loaded program. The following simple rule is often used to determine where to commence execution:

1. If an address is specified on the END card, that address is used as the execution start address.
2. Otherwise, execution will commence at the beginning of the first segment.

At the beginning of pass 2 the program load address is initialized as in pass 1, and the execution start address (EXADDR) is set to IPLA. The cards are read one by one from the object deck file left by pass 1. Each of the five types of cards is processed differently, as follows:

ESD CARD
Each of the ESD card types is processed differently.

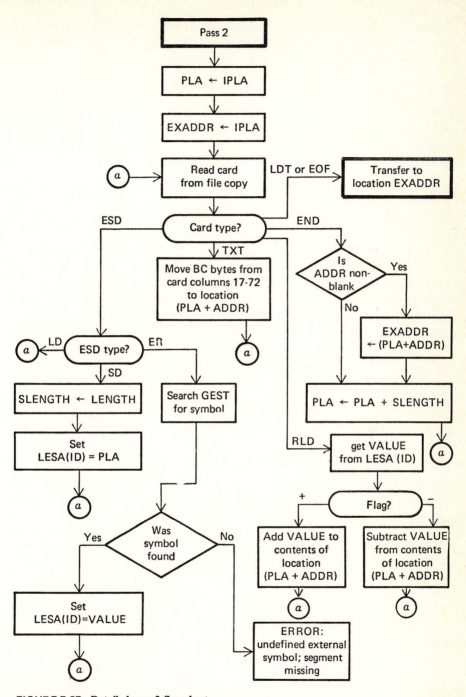

FIGURE 5.25   Detailed pass 2 flowchart

SD-type ESD   The LENGTH of the segment is temporarily saved in the variable SLENGTH. The appropriate entry in the local external symbol array, LESA(ID), is set to the current value of the Program Load Address.

LD-type ESD   The LD-type ESD does not require any processing during pass 2.

ER-type ESD   The Global External Symbol Table (GEST) is searched for a match with the ER symbol. If it is not found, the corresponding segment or entry must be missing — this is an error. If the symbol is found in the GEST, its value is extracted and the corresponding Local External Symbol Array entry, LESA(ID), is set equal to it.

TXT CARD

When a TXT card is read, the text is copied from the card to the appropriate relocated core location (PLA + ADDR).

RLD CARD

The value to be used for relocation and linking is extracted from the local external symbol array as specified by the ID field, i.e., LESA(ID). Depending upon the flag setting (plus or minus) the value is either added to or subtracted from the address constant. The actual relocated address of the address constant is computed as the sum of the PLA and the ADDR field specified on the RLD card.

END CARD

If an execution start address is specified on the END card, it is saved in the variable EXADDR after being relocated by the PLA. The Program Load Address is incremented by the length of the segment and saved in SLENGTH, becoming the PLA for the next segment.

LDT/EOF CARD

The loader transfers control to the loaded program at the address specified by current contents of the execution address variable (EXADDR).

5.4 SUMMARY

The four basic functions of a loader are allocation, linking, relocation, and loading. The various types of loaders (e.g., "compile-and-go," absolute, relocating, direct-linking, dynamic loading, and dynamic linking) differ primarily in the manner in which the four basic functions are accomplished.

A typical direct-linking loader requires two passes. The first pass allocates space for the segments and defines the values of the external symbols. The second pass actually loads the text and uses the global external symbol table, produced by pass 1, to relocate and link the address constants.

Although their purposes are quite different, the design of the direct-linking loader has many similarities to the design of an assembler. In particular, the use of a symbol table is important in both cases.

QUESTIONS

1. Give an example of each of the following types of address constants.

   a. Simple relocatable
   b. Absolute
   c. Complex relocatable

2.

```
PROG        START       0
            ENTRY       PLACE
            EXTRN       SIN
ONE         EQU         1

              ⋮

LOOP        - - -
PLACE       - - -

              .

KOHN        - - -

              ⋮

            END
```

Using the above program as a reference, identify each of the address constants below as absolute, simple relocatable, or complex relocatable. Also, explain how the value of each address constant would be calculated. You need not show the object deck cards.

   a. A(SIN)
   b. A(KOHN - LOOP + ONE)
   c. A(PLACE)
   d. A(SIN - LOOP)

3.   a. For the types of loading schemes discussed in this chapter, binding takes place at various points during the life of a process. Define the term "bind," and give an example.
     b. At what point in time do each of the following loading schemes perform binding?

        1) BSS loader
        2) Direct linking loader
        3) Absolute loader
        4) Dynamic binder
        5) Dynamic linking loader
        6) Overlay
        7) Linkage editor

    c. 1) List two advantages of binding at load time over binding at assembly time.

       2) List two disadvantages.

    d. 1) List two advantages of binding at execution time over binding at load time.

       2) List two disadvantages.

4. Describe the function of each of the RLD, ESD, TXT, and END cards.

5. What is the order of the RLD, ESD, TXT, and END cards in an object deck and why are they in this order?

6. What is the purpose of the ID number on the ESD cards? Why is it not needed for locally defined symbols?

7. Consider deleting the address constant facility from the IBM 360 assembler language.

    a. What parts of the object deck could be simplified or excluded?

    b. In what ways could the loader be simplified?

8. Consider the following three simple programs:

```
PGA        START
           ENTRY      PGA1
           EXTRN      PGB, PGC, PGC2
           DC         A(PGA), A(PGB + 4)
PGA1       DC         A(PGA1 - PGA), A(PGC2 - PGC)
           END

PGB        START
           ENTRY      PGB1
           EXTRN      PGA, PGC1
PGB1       DC         A(PGC1 - 4), A(PGB1)
PGB2       DC         A(PGB + 4), A(PGB1 - PGB)
PGB3       DC         A(PGC1 + PGB - PGA - 16)
           END

PGC        START
           ENTRY      PGC1, PGC2
           DC         A(PGC2 - PGC)
PGC1       DC         A(PGC1 - 4), A(* + 4)
PGC2       DC         A(PGC + PGC2 - PGC1)
           END
```

    a. Assume that these three programs are to be loaded starting at location 400 (decimal) in the order PGA, PGB, then PGC. Fill out the Global External Symbol Table (GEST) for each symbol. (Hint: Remember that each program must start on a double-word boundary.)

Symbol	Absolute Address
PGA	400
PGA1	
PGB	
PGB1	
PGC	
PGC1	
PGC2	

b. Why are the symbols PGB2 and PGB3 excluded from the GEST? (Give one or two brief sentences.)

c. Illustrate the contents of memory after the three programs have been loaded and linked.

Location	Contents
400	
404	
408	
412	
416	
420	
424	
428	
432	
436	
440	
444	
448	
452	
456	
460	

9.   In this section, we discussed a two-pass direct-linking loader.

a. What is the function of pass 1?

b. What is the function of pass 2?

c. Suppose you were restricted to a one-pass loader. What facilities would you be able to give to the user?

Examples:

1) Simple address relocation?
2) External symbol?
3) Etc.

Justify your answers and describe the restrictions that are applicable.

d. Define possible output cards from the assembler for a one-pass loader and what the information would be on these cards (e.g., cards corresponding to ESD, RLD, TXT, END).

e. Give a flowchart for your loader.

10. a. Given the object deck below, produce as much as possible of the symbolic code from which the object was assembled.

ESD

SYMBOL	TYPE	ID	REL-LOC	LENGTH
PGM	SD	01	0	92
ENT1	LD	–	20	- -
ENT2	LD	--	40	- -
SQRT	ER	02	- -	- -
TAN	ER	03	- -	- -
COS	ER	04	- -	- -

TXT

REL-LOC	VALUE
80	-40
84	0
88	20

RLD

REL-LOC	+/-	ID
80	+	02
80	+	03
80	-	01
84	+	04
88	+	01
88	-	02

b. Is this solution unique? Why?

11. To make it possible to produce code for absolute loading, a new pseudo-op has been added to the assembler. This pseudo-op has the operation code ABS and one operand which specifies where the start of the program is to be loaded. The function of the pseudo-op is to tell the assembler to produce code for input to an absolute loader.

    a. Where must the ABS card occur within the input deck? That is, what things can occur before the ABS card and what things must follow the ABS card. Why?

    b. In what pass (or passes) of the assembler would the ABS pseudo-op be processed? Why?

    c. What data bases would be affected by assembly in ABS (absolute) mode? Describe the changes (assume the assembler correctly generates code for the DLL), being fairly specific, and give reasons for the changes.

    d. Would it still be necessary to use the relocatable-absolute flag in the symbol table? If so, why? If not, why not?

12. Describe the overall design for a simple relocating loader that will load a single segment with no external references. Since the machine is very small, there is no room for frills, so your design should include only information which is necessary. To maintain compatibility, we suggest that you begin your design using the absolute loader card specifications given in Figure 5.10.

    a. Either modify the absolute loader cards or design new cards which contain the additional information (if any) which you will need. Be careful not to include unnecessary information. Do not worry about designing different card formats. The assembler can be redesigned to produce whatever kind of card you design.

    b. Indicate how you expect the cards to be organized in a typical object deck. For example, which cards must occur first, what cards come next, etc.

13. For efficiency reasons, it is often useful to combine several segments into a single segment for use at a later time or to save loading time. In part a. of this problem, you are to prepare the object decks for segments SOLN and GRADER from the source programs for these segments. The object deck for the segment STUDENT has been prepared below as an example for you to follow.

    a. Schematically, the first part of the problem consists of the following:

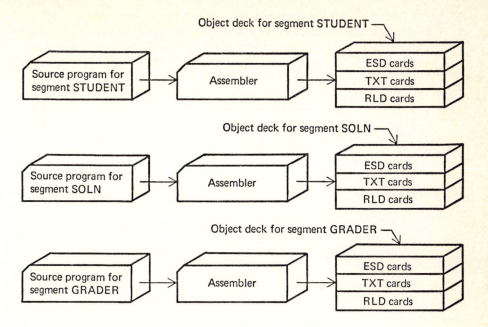

EXAMPLE

1) Source program for segment STUDENT

```
STUDENT     START       0
            ENTRY       A
            EXTRN       SOLN,DELTA
            BALR        15,0
            USING       STUDENT +2,15
            SR          4,4
            L           4,TWO
            L           5,TWO
            ST          5,SAVE
            BR          14
            DC          5F'01'
            DC          A(A+10)
SAVE        DC          12C'0'
A           DC          A(DELTA)
TWO         DC          F'2'
            DC          A(STUDENT-SOLN)
            END
```

EXAMPLE

2) Object deck for segment STUDENT

	Symbol	Type	ID	Relative address	Length
	STUDENT	SD	01	0	68
ESD	A	LD	- -	56	- -
	SOLN	ER	02	- -	- -
	DELTA	ER	03	- -	- -

	Opcode	Relative address	Address constants	Actual value of addr. Constants
	BALR	0	- -	- -
	SR	2	- -	- -
	L	4	- -	- -
	L	8	- -	- -
TXT	ST	12	- -	- -
	BR	16	- -	- -
	DC	20	- -	- -
	DC	40	A(A+10)	66
	DC	44	- -	- -
	DC	56	A(DELTA)	0
	DC	60	- -	- -
	DC	64	A(STUDENT-SOLN)	0

	ID	FLAG(length)	FLAG (+ -)	Relative address
RLD	01	4	+	40
	03	4	+	56
	02	4	-	64
	01	4	+	64

Prepare the object deck for segments SOLN and GRADER from the following source program for segment SOLN and GRADER shown in the example.

Source program for segment SOLN			Source program for segment GRADER		
SOLN	START	0	GRADER	START	0
	EXTRN	A,C2		ENTRY	C2
	BALR	15,0		BALR	15,0
	USING	*,15		USING	*,15
	SR	4,4		SR	4,4
	SLL	1,2		L	6,C3
	L	0,ANS(1)		ST	1,C3+4
	BR	14		LA	1,C3
	DC	A(A+10)		L	2,JOHNSN
CODE	DC	2C'JJ'	JOHNSN	BR	14
	DC	A(C2)	C2	DC	A(GRADER)
	DC	12C'2'	C3	DC	8F'3'
ANS	DC	5H'0'		END	
	END				

b. In part b of this problem, you are to combine the object decks for segments STUDENT, SOLN, and GRADER into a composite segment and answer several questions about the composite segment. To be able to use the DLL described in the notes, it is necessary for the composite segment to be in the same format as the original segments. Thus the composite segment will be of the form shown below:

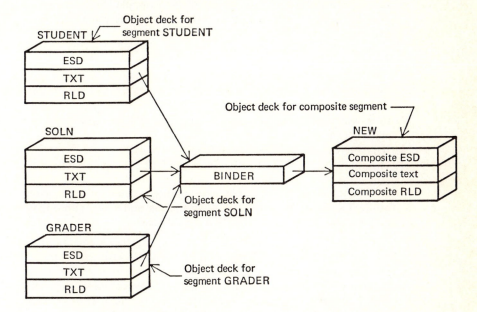

The composite ESD has one entry for each unique name occurring in the combined segments and an additional entry for the new segment name, in this case "NEW."

The composite text is the text for the combined segments in the order they were presented to the BINDER (i.e., STUDENT, SOLN, GRADER). Segments must begin on a doubleword boundary.

The composite RLD is the merging of all the RLD cards which now refer to the composite ESD and composite text.

QUESTIONS

1) In combining the segments, it will be necessary to merge the three separate parts of each segment. When forming the composite text, will it be necessary to modify the text cards in any way? If so, how? If not, why not?

2) Since the ESD section may have only a single SD card (to be named "NEW"), what can be done to represent the SDs for the separate segments? Note that segment STUDENT refers to the symbol SOLN so that they cannot be ignored.

3) What fields of the RLD cards will have to be modified when the composite RLD is built? How will these fields be modified?

4) In the example shown, which RLD cards of the composite segment still refer to symbols which are external and what symbols would they reference?

5) Draw the composite segment in the same form as the object deck for the segment STUDENT, presented in the example. Note: You *may* omit all rows of the composite text that do not refer to address constants.

6) Show in the composite segment the actual value that the address constants in the TXT cards would contain. For example, in segment STUDENT, the value of the constant DC A(DELTA) would be $\emptyset$ since there is no relative offset from the symbol and the symbol DELTA is external to STUDENT.

7) How many passes would the program to build the composite segment require? Give reasons for your answer.

8) What are the required data bases for the BINDER?

9) How does the BINDER differ from the DLL? A few sentences are sufficient.

10) Is it possible to eliminate common address references in the composite TXT, e.g., DC A(A+10)? Give reasons, and where appropriate give methods for your answer. Is it a good idea?

14. It is often useful, in saving loading time, to bind together segments which reference one another. In debugging, it is equally useful for saving re-assembly time to be able to unbind or delink these segments again in order to remove a bug-ridden culprit. However, these combined segments cannot be unbound. The reason is that information which existed in the original segments, such as old SD cards and ERs which become resolved, was not needed by the direct-linking loader to load the combined segment, and so was thrown away (refer to question 5.13).

The ABC manufacturing company has come up with the design criteria and format changes they feel would be easiest to make on the binder in your homework problem so that it could successfully delink any segment. However, several critical design problems still remain. Your job is to help resolve these problems by deciding just what extra information needs to be kept and on which cards.

a. Note that in making the old SDs into new LDs, the segment length was dropped.

1) If this field were to be kept, would it be useful in delinking?

a) The ESD cards? How?
b) The TXT cards? How?
c) The RLD cards? How?

2) If this field were still dropped, could the original length for each segment still be calculated from the available information remaining on all the ESDs? Why?

3) In view of the above answers, is the segment length field necessary to have for delinking?

b Note that in resolving any old ERs with their old LD, all the ERs are thrown away and the LD is placed into the ESD. To unbind, however, the LD must be rematched with its original segment and all the ERs must again be created and rematched with theirs. For LDs that were old LDs, this suggests the need to create two new data fields: one of fixed length called FROM containing the ID of the segment from which it came, and one of varying length called IN, each entry of which is the ID of a segment in which it occurred as an ER.

1) Consider these two fields for LDs that were old SDs. Does the FROM field need to be filled in? Does the IN field? Why?

2) Consider ERs and answer the questions in 1).

c. Without adding new data to the completed LD cards, what criteria could the binder use to distinguish those that were old SDs from those that were only old LDs. Base your answer solely on differentiating the content of each of the LD card fields.

15. We wish to consider a system that uses a separate program binder and simple loader.

a. What functions could you remove from the DLL and have performed in the binder instead? Be specific; the idea is to make the loader as simple as possible.

b. What functions must still be performed in the simplified loader?

c. How many passes will be needed in your simplified loader? Why?

d. Considering all of the loaders which were discussed, how would you characterize the new loader you have designed?

6

programming languages

Chapters 6, 7, and 8 are concerned with high level programming languages. The purpose of Chapter 6 is threefold:

1. To present important features of high level languages
2. To briefly discuss the use of these features for systems programming
3. To introduce PL/I, the example source language for our compiler design

We have chosen PL/I as our source language because most languages are subsets of it, and moreover because it is a real language, not a synthetic one created for teaching purposes. PL/I[1] possesses advanced features such as data structures, string manipulations, pointers, storage classes, and conditions, all of which are important to systems programmers and may become commonplace in languages of the future. Further, the features we discuss here are the ones that present difficult problems to the compiler designer.

This chapter was written mainly for the reader who is already familiar with some of the earlier high level languages, such as FORTRAN, ALGOL, and CO-BOL. We present the extensions to these that have been developed in modern languages like PL/I and ALGOL 68. It is recommended that the reader study these extensions in more detail in the various reference manuals and books.

In Chapter 7 we give formal descriptions of high level languages and some of the theoretical work that is being done in this area. The design of compilers for high level languages is discussed in Chapter 8.

---

[1] In view of its relationship to the proposed advanced FORTRAN IV, nicknamed FOR-TRAN VIII (designed for scientific use) and the latest versions of COBOL (designed for commercial use), it was suggested that this new language be called VIII-BOL.

6.1 IMPORTANCE OF HIGH LEVEL LANGUAGES

High level languages are becoming increasingly important in programming. They are being effectively used to perform tasks that hitherto were thought to belong exclusively to the domain of assembly language. As an example, the MULTICS[2] timesharing system at M.I.T. Project MAC and the new Burroughs systems are written primarily in a PL/I-type and ALGOL high level language respectively. We discuss here some of the advantages that have been found in using such languages. Some of the points made are not obvious and they are possibly controversial; the reader may investigate the references in Chapter 10 for further details and explanations.

The advantages inherent to using high level languages are as follows:

1. Fewer people, less management

    Various studies have indicated that a programmer completes roughly the same number of lines of debugged final code per unit time-independent of the language he is using. Since a high level language is often 10 times more expressive than assembly language (i.e., one statement in a high level language would typically require 10 assembly language statements to accomplish the same result), it is possible to operate with a relatively small personnel pool and fewer levels of management. The effectiveness of a small group often results in an even greater increase in efficiency.

2. Shorter transition in learning time

    New staff members are readily assimilated into the project and produce useful work more quickly due to a greatly reduced learning time. The programs and modules are much more brief and lucid to a new reader.

3. Improved debugging capability

    Attention is focused on the bugs in the algorithms and the flaws in the design, rather than on detailed machine language bugs and tricks (i.e., on content rather than form).

4. Superior documentation

    A PL/I program is to a large extent self-documenting. For example, a description of a module may consist of the PL/I data structure and a brief statement of the manipulations of this data. It has been said that most operating systems are just simple programs with complicated data structures.

5. A greater degree of machine independence

    High level languages, such as PL/I, are much less sensitive to the peculiarities of the hardware than is machine language. This makes it possible to use the same program on different machines. Most importantly, it forces the programmer to "design" rather than "bit twiddle."

---

[2]MULTICS = Multiplexed Information and Computing Service

6. Possible improved code efficiency

Code efficiency is perhaps the most controversial issue in the use of high level language. It is true that in the microscopic sense (statement by statement), a good machine language programmer can produce more efficient code than can a compiler. However, in a system that is comprised of millions of words of code, the efficiency issues are not so clear cut. An experienced machine language programmer recoding a PL/I program might gain speed or space efficiency factors of two to three. The important point here is that it is not clear that saving a byte or a word occasionally is a true savings when one considers efficiency in the macroscopic sense. It is easier to view an algorithm macroscopically when it is made more explicit, as occurs if a high level language is used. These points must be considered in light of the fact that machine language programmers in "real life" seldom have the time to optimize their programs to the fullest extent.

7. Getting the system operational

We usually cannot predict the inefficiencies of software. Ultimately, we hand-code those segments where speed and efficiency are found to be critical. In a large system it is quite typical to find that 80 percent of the execution time is spent in less than 20 percent of the code (e.g., error routines, etc., are seldom used). Unfortunately, there is no algorithmic technique available to determine in advance which portions of the code are the most critical. Thus, it is important to get a prototype version completed as early as possible, determine the bottlenecks, and then optimize.

These are the seven areas in which the advantages of using a high level language seem apparent. To fully exploit these areas requires us to accept the following constraints:

1. We must have a high level language that is powerful enough for systems programming.
2. We must have a compiler for the high level language (Chapter 8).
3. We must have a machine and operating system that can support such a high level language (Chapter 9).

6.2 FEATURES OF A HIGH LEVEL LANGUAGE

In this section we discuss important features of high level languages as they appear in PL/I or ALGOL 68. Some are also to be found in such languages as FORTRAN, COBOL, ALGOL, GPL (e.g., COBOL-data structures, ALGOL-block structures and recursion, GPL-pointers), although none of these languages contains all of them. We believe that these features will become standard in future languages, and that the compilers of tomorrow must be flexible enough to handle them. The difficult areas in compiler writing are not associated with parsing arithmetic statements, as has so often been the focus in the literature. Rather, we will see that the compilation of storage allocation, recursion, and the close interface with an operating system may be quite complicated to implement for most machines.

PL/I represents an attempt to effectively merge all of the desirable features of earlier languages. In the following sections we will introduce the features of PL/I that are especially relevant to systems programming, such as:

1. Extensive data types and organization (6.3)
   a. Character strings
   b. Bit strings
   c. Data structures
2. Storage allocation and scope of names (6.4)
   a. Storage classes
   b. Block structure
3. Accessing flexibility (6.5)
   a. Pointers
   b. Label variables and label arrays
4. Functional modularity (6.6)
   a. Procedures (internal and external)
   b. Recursion
5. Asynchronous operation (6.7)
   a. Condition handling
   b. Signals
   c. Multi-tasking
6. Extensibility (6.8)
   a. Compile-time macro
   b. Data structures
   c. Subroutines
7. Miscellaneous (6.9)

6.3 DATA TYPES AND DATA STRUCTURES

In most programming languages there are a limited number of data types that can be explicitly manipulated. In FORTRAN, for example, integers (fixed point numbers) and reals (floating point numbers) are the basic data types; complex numbers and logical variables are available in some implementations. Although it is possible to manipulate character data in FORTRAN, it is very awkward and cumbersome since the data must be treated as either integers or reals. As we have seen in the design of the assembler and loader, character and bit data processing is basic to most systems programming operations. Furthermore, the data bases used are much more complex than simple arrays. In particular, each entry consists of several fields of possibly different data types. The bit string, character string, and data structure facilities of PL/I greatly assist many systems programming endeavors.

Figure 6.1 depicts a PL/I program segment. The data structure declaration defines a symbol table consisting of 100 entries in the same format as the assembler's symbol table described in Figure 3.8 of Chapter 3. The brief section of actual PL/I code in Figure 6.1 illustrates a linear search through the table, looking for the entry whose symbol matches the contents of the variable FIND_SYMBOL[3]. We will discuss this example again in later sections.

```
DECLARE     FIND_SYMBOL    CHARACTER(8);
DECLARE     1 SYMBOL_TABLE(100),
               2 SYMBOL CHARACTER(8),
               2 VALUE FIXED BINARY,
               2 LENGTH BIT(8),
               2 RELOCATION CHARACTER(1);

            ⋮

            /* search for symbol */
            DO I = 1 TO 100;
            IF SYMBOL_TABLE(I).SYMBOL = FIND_SYMBOL
               THEN GO TO FOUND;
            END;

            ⋮

            /* symbol found */
FOUND.

            ⋮
```

FIGURE 6.1   PL/I program segment illustrating data types and data segments

6.3.1   Character String

PL/I has three basic character string operations:

---

[3]Note: FIND_SYMBOL denotes a single variable. The underscore _ is frequently used to give more mnemonic names to variables as in SYMBOL_TABLE. Further note that PL/I is free format in that columns are not important, statements end in semicolons and comments are enclosed in the symbols /* comment */.

1. Length operator, which accepts a string as an argument and produces the length of the string denoted by that argument
2. Concatenation operator, which when used between two strings produces a third which is equal to the first string adjacent to the second string
3. Substring operator, which is used to insert or extract strings

The following examples demonstrate the use of these features:

```
1.    DECLARE   S      CHARACTER(9);
2.    DECLARE   T      CHARACTER(6) VARYING;
3.                     T  =  'ABCDE';
4.                     S  =  T ∥ 'IS A STRING';
5.                     T  =  SUBSTR(S,6,2);
6.                     SUBSTR(S,1,3) = 'DEF';
7.                     X  =  LENGTH(T);
```

Statements 1 and 2 declare the variable S to denote a character string of fixed length, always 9 characters, and T to be a character string whose length may vary from 0 to 6. The next statement assigns a value to T. The next sets variable S equal to the string T concatenated with 'IS A STRING'. The result is truncated to the leftmost 9 characters, i.e., 'ABCDEIS A'. The next statement is an assignment statement that sets T equal to a substring of S, starting with the sixth character of length 2, i.e., the string 'IS'. Statement 6 shows the first three characters of S being replaced with the string DEF so that S now has the value 'DEFDEIS A'. Statement 7 assigns the length of string T, which is 2, to the variable X.

It should be observed that declaring T as a varying length string (VARYING) may be inefficient because of the difficulty the compiler has in storage allocation and manipulation. This is the kind of problem with which the compiler designer is often confronted.

6.3.2 Bit String—Boolean

In addition to the three basic string operations mentioned in section 6.3.1., the three following operations are possible in a bit string.

1. The logical AND operation between bit strings
2. The logical OR operation between bit strings
3. The logical NOT operation, which is a unary operator resulting in the bit-by-bit reversal of 0s and 1s

The AND and OR operations are defined in Figure 6.2.

```
DECLARE      B        BIT(1);
DECLARE      L        BIT(1);
DECLARE      R        BIT(1);

             ⋮

             R = ¬B;        /* R = NOT OF B */
             R = ¬L;        /* R = NOT OF L */
             R = B&L;       /* R = B AND L */
             R = B|L;       /* R = B OR L */
```

table of boolean operations

B	L	NOT B	NOT L	B AND L	B OR L
0	0	1	1	0	0
0	1	1	0	0	1
1	0	0	1	0	1
1	1	0	0	1	1

FIGURE 6.2 Example of bit string operations

6.3.3 Data Structures

A data structure is a method of declaring relationships among variables and is found in programming languages such as PL/I and COBOL. For example, Figure 6.1 illustrates the declaration of a symbol table, called SYMBOL_ TABLE. Each entry in the symbol table is defined to consist of four fields labelled SYMBOL, VALUE, LENGTH, and RELOCATION respectively. These fields may represent different data types. For instance, SYMBOL is a character string whereas VALUE is an integer. The particular declaration in Figure 6.1 produces an array of data structures (a table) consisting of 100 entries. Such a table can be manipulated in its entirety; a single entire entry can be manipulated; or a single field of an entry can be accessed. For example, SYMBOL_TABLE refers to the entire table whereas SYMBOL_TABLE(10) refers to the tenth entry in the table. Conventional manipulations are usually performed upon single fields, such as SYMBOL_TABLE(10).VALUE which refers to the VALUE field of the tenth entry in the table.

At this time it is worth noting that PL/I has many pleasing "human factors," such as allowing long and descriptive names like SYMBOL_TABLE rather than forcing the programmer to invent awkward abbreviations, like SYMTBL, as he must when using most other programming languages.

6.4 STORAGE ALLOCATION AND SCOPE OF NAMES

In most programming projects it is important to minimize the program size and data space required. There are two ways of achieving substantial reductions in data space:

1. Reserve data space only when it is needed. For example, in the design of the assembler there were some data bases used only during pass 1 and others only during pass 2.
2. Reserve only as much data space as is needed. In many circumstances, the size of arrays and tables are not known in advance (i.e., size depends upon input data) and it is advantageous to delay reserving space for them, if the compiler permits it.

The storage classes and block structure facilities of PL/I provide mechanisms for achieving these controls.

6.4.1 Storage Classes

PL/I offers the programmer three classes of storage: (1) static, (2) automatic, and (3) controlled.

Static storage is permanent and is assigned at compile time. Static is the only storage available in many programming languages, such as FORTRAN.

Automatic storage is allocated only when the procedure or block referencing it is being executed. For example, if there is a procedure SUBR with an automatic variable A, on the first call SUBR will be assigned a location for A. When the procedure is exited, A's space will be released for possible use by other procedures. It is possible that a different location will be assigned to A for each call to SUBR. A is automatic storage and is assigned automatically at execution time.

Controlled storage allows the programmer to explicitly control space allocation at execution time. He may allocate a block of storage when he needs it and then may de-allocate or free that block of storage during execution. We will give an example of this in our discussion on pointers.

6.4.2 Block Structure

When a declaration of a variable is made in a program, there is a certain well-defined region of the program to which this declaration is applicable. The block structure facility, in programming languages such as PL/I and ALGOL, controls the scope of declaration of variables. Figure 6.3 illustrates the use of these features. (The reference numbers are not part of the program. They are only used to refer to specific lines in the explanation.)

```
Reference
numbers
   1        BEGIN;      /* outer block 1*/
   2            DECLARE  (S,X,N) FIXED BINARY;
                  ⋮
   3            BEGIN;   /* inner block 2*/
   4                DECLARE   A(N), X FLOAT;
   5                X=S;
   6            END;      /* end block 2*/
                  ⋮
   7        END;          /* end block 1*/
```

FIGURE 6.3 Example of block structure

In the outer block of the PL/I program in Figure 6.3, the variables S, X and N are defined as integers (fixed-point binary numbers); by default all variables in PL/I are assumed to be automatic unless explicitly declared otherwise. This program has an inner block that extends from reference numbers 3 to 6. In the inner block the array A and variable X are declared to be real floating-point numbers; since these variables are automatic storage, they are only allocated space when the inner block is entered. This example illustrates several points:

1. This program has two different variables named X but only one is in use at any time, as defined by the block structure.
2. The array A is declared to be N locations long where N is an integer that was already defined in the outer block.
3. The statement X=S sets the variable X, defined in statement 4, equal to the current value of the variable S, defined in statement 2. Since these variables are of different data types, PL/I will automatically convert the value of S to a floating-point representation.

6.5 ACCESSING FLEXIBILITY

Flexibility in both data accessing and transfers is essential to effective systems programming. Data accessing flexibility refers to the ability to manipulate self-defining data structures and complex data organizations, such as list structures. Transfer flexibility pertains to the facility to alter or set the transfer destination based upon input data and previous processing. The pointer data type, in conjunction with based storage, provides significant data access flexibility. Program access flexibility is furnished by the facilities of label variables and label arrays.

6.5.1 Pointers

Pointers may be thought of as qualifiers to a variable. In the case of based storage, for example, a programmer may allocate a block of storage, which he names A, and at a later time allocate another block of storage, which he also calls A. Since the blocks have the same name, a further qualifier is needed in order to distinguish between them. When he allocates the first block, the programmer can set a pointer pointing to it, setting another pointer when he allocates the second block. He may then distinguish between the two blocks by simply naming the appropriate pointer. Recall that variables whose allocation is explicitly controlled by the programmer are in "controlled storage."

Figures 6.4 and 6.5 illustrate some of the uses of pointers and controlled storage. The program shown is intended to be similar to the symbol table processing example given in Figure 6.1. In the earlier example we defined a symbol table of 100 entries. In practice we usually do not know in advance the number of symbol entries required; therefore, it is advantageous to allocate the entries one at a time as they are needed. Since they would no longer be part of a contiguous array, it is necessary to keep track of the location of each entry. This can be accomplished by adding a field to each entry, specifying the address of the "next" entry. The NEXT field which is defined to be a pointer in Figure 6.4 fulfills this role. The program segments labelled ENTER and SEARCH illustrate the process of creating a new entry and searching for a specific entry, respectively. Figure 6.5 represents a possible symbol table data base produced by this program. This process of "linking" or "chaining" together parts of a complex data base is often called *list processing*. We will find many more uses of such organization when we discuss the details of compiler implementation.

In Figure 6.4 we have defined a symbol table entry with the data structure SYMBOL_TABLE. The program creates new entries and links the entries together. Another portion of the program finds entries stored in the table. The ALLOCATE statement causes the data structure SYMBOL_TABLE, which is to be a single new entry, to be allocated and its address to be stored in the pointer P. Then, as shown in Figure 6.5, the pointer SYMBOL_TABLE_START specifies the address of the "first" entry, all other entries being "linked" together via the NEXT fields. In fact, the entries are linked together in reverse chronological order—but that is merely a convenient "programming trick." The entity called NULL represents a special value for a pointer, meaning that it does not "point" to anything; this is used to signify the end of the chain.

6.5.2 Label Variables and Label Arrays

Just as pointers allow us to treat the location of data as a variable, label variables

```
DECLARE        FIND_SYMBOL    CHARACTER(8);
DECLARE        1 SYMBOL_TABLE      BASED(P),
                    2  SYMBOL CHARACTER(8),
                    2  VALUE FIXED BINARY,
                    2  LENGTH BIT(8),
                    2  RELOCATION CHARACTER(1),
                    2  NEXT POINTER;
DECLARE        SYMBOL_TABLE_START POINTER;
               SYMBOL_TABLE_START = NULL;

                   ⋮

ENTER:     /*    create new entry in table */
                 ALLOCATE SYMBOL_TABLE SET(P);
           /*    link new entry to beginning of table */
                 P→SYMBOL_TABLE.NEXT = SYMBOL_TABLE_START;
                 SYMBOL_TABLE_START = P;
           /*    fill in new entry */
                 P→SYMBOL_TABLE.SYMBOL = etc.

                   ⋮

           /*    search for symbol */
SEARCH:          P = SYMBOL_TABLE_START;
LOOP:            IF  P = NULL THEN GO TO NOT_FOUND;
                 IF  P→SYMBOL_TABLE.SYMBOL = FIND_SYMBOL
                         THEN GO TO FOUND;
                 P = P→SYMBOL_TABLE.NEXT;
                 GO TO LOOP;

                   ⋮
```

FIGURE 6.4   Example of pointers and controlled storage

allow us to treat the location of instructions in the same way. Figure 6.6 illustrates the use of both label variables and label arrays. The symbols L(1), L(2), . . . , L(5) represent labels on five different statements of the program. Let us assume that each label identifies the code in pass 2 of an assembler to handle the five types of instruction formats. If the integer INST_TYPE specifies the instruction type, the statement GO TO L(INST_TYPE) will cause control to transfer to one of L(1),..., L(5). If INST_TYPE contains a value other than 1 through 5, an error is flagged.

The variable PROCESS is a label variable, which may be set equal to a label or another label variable. Depending upon the instruction type, PROCESS may be set equal to the labels TWO_BYTE, FOUR_BYTE, or SIX_BYTE. When the statement GO TO PROCESS is encountered, control will transfer to the appropriate label. Since it is possible to pass label variables as parameters and transfer from an inner block to an outer block or external procedure, label variables can

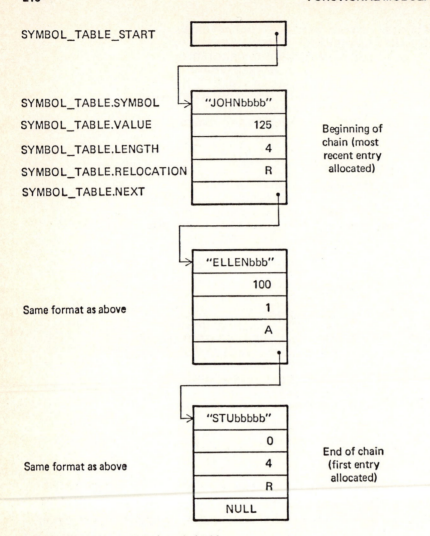

FIGURE 6.5 List structured symbol table

be very difficult to implement in the most general situation. This will be discussed in more detail in later chapters.

6.6 FUNCTIONAL MODULARITY

One of the most important aspects of system design is the ability to design,
implement, and debug separate modules of the system. The mechanisms pro-

```
DECLARE      L(5) LABEL;
DECLARE      PROCESS LABEL;
DECLARE      INST_TYPE FIXED BINARY;

             .
             .
             .

             GO TO L(INST_TYPE);

             .
             .
             .

L(1):        /* RR_TYPE INSTRUCTION */
             PROCESS=TWO_BYTE;

             .
             .
             .

L(2):        /* RS_TYPE INSTRUCTION */
             PROCESS=FOUR_BYTE;

             .
             .
             .

L(3):        /* RX_TYPE INSTRUCTION */
             PROCESS=FOUR_BYTE;

             .
             .
             .

             GO TO PROCESS;
TWO_BYTE:

             .
             .
             .

FOUR_BYTE:

             .
             .
             .
```

FIGURE 6.6   Example of label variables and label array

vided by loaders as discussed in Chapter 5, allow us to bind together separate program modules also called *subroutines* or *procedures*. Although the subroutine feature is quite common, many programming languages, such as basic ALGOL and basic COBOL, do not include it.

6.6.1 Procedures

PL/I allows procedures and functions which may be either internal or external. An internal procedure is included as part of a single program module. An external procedure is a separate program module that is compiled separately and is linked together with the other program modules by means of the loader. Furthermore, PL/I procedures may have multiple entry-points. This feature can be very useful for subroutines that are very similar, such as the SINE and COSINE routines.

6.6.2 Recursion

Recursion, which is facilitated by automatic storage, is an important feature that allows the user to handle a broad range of problems. Many of the routines we must write are recursive, as we will see in the construction of a compiler. We observed previously in the implementation of a macroprocessing facility that recursion was a convenient way to implement macro calls within macro definitions.

Furthermore, many algorithms are much more convenient to describe and program in a recursive manner. For example, the standard mathematical definition of factorial is as follows:

$$n! = \begin{cases} 1 & \text{if } n = 0 \\ n*(n-1)! & \text{if } n \neq 0 \end{cases}$$

A straightforward implementation of this function is shown in Figure 6.7.

```
N_FACTORIAL:  PROCEDURE (N)      RECURSIVE;
         IF  N=0 THEN RETURN(1)
             ELSE  RETURN (N* N_FACTORIAL(N-1));
         END;
```

FIGURE 6.7   Example of recursive procedure

6.7 ASYNCHRONOUS OPERATION

Most programming languages are based upon simple *sequential synchronous operation* (e.g., one instruction at a time, execute statements in sequential order except when a GO TO statement temporarily alters the sequential flow). There are various situations encountered in systems programming that result in nonsequential or nonsynchronous operation, such as:

1. Processing of internal and external interrupts (i.e., interruption of normal program flow due to a program condition—*external interrupt*—such as an I/O completion or error)
2. Simulated interruptions, such as invalid results detected by a procedure that must be signaled to another procedure
3. Multitasking (multiprogramming) operating systems that allow more than one task to be executed at the same time

6.7.1 Conditions

PL/I represents one of the first attempts to implement nonsequential program flow in a high level programming language. *Conditions* are a facility that allows the programmer to process and handle various interrupts and special circumstances. The program in Figure 6.8 illustrates the use of conditions.

```
DEMO:          PROCEDURE;
S1:            ON ENDFILE (INPUT) GO TO END_PROG;

                 ⋮

S2:            ON OVERFLOW BEGIN;
                   PUT EDIT ('OVERFLOW OCCURRED') (A(18) );
                   GO TO END_PROG;
                   END;

                 ⋮

S3:            ON OVERFLOW SYSTEM;

                 ⋮

END_PROG:

                 ⋮

               END DEMO;
```

FIGURE 6.8 Example of conditions

In Figure 6.8 there are three condition-handling statements: S1, S2, and S3. S1 states that when an input operation (e.g., PL/I GET statements) reaches the end of the input data, control will immediately transfer to the statement labelled END_PROG. When the condition handler in S2 is activated, any subsequent hardware overflow interrupt (signifying that a result is computed that is too large for the machine register) will cause control to transfer to the instruction sequence PUT EDIT (corresponds to a WRITE), etc. When the ON OVERFLOW SYSTEM statement is executed, any subsequent overflow interrupt will cause the default action specified in the system, such as termination of the program.

6.7.2 Signals

The conditions and actions, as described in section 6.7.1., remain in effect until redefined by subsequent ON statements, even when subroutines are called. Signals are simulated interrupts caused by the programmer. For example, Figure 6.9 illustrates a possible program flow.

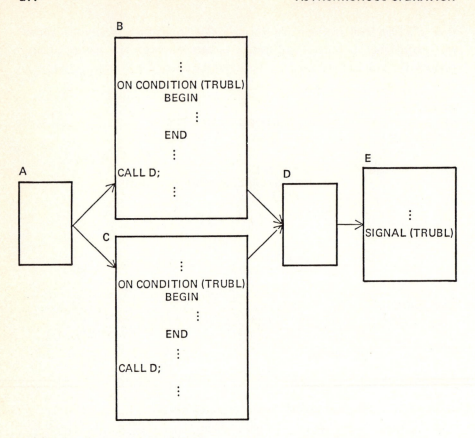

FIGURE 6.9 Example of signal statement

Procedure A may call either procedures B or C which will in turn call procedure D which calls procedure E. Procedure E may detect an error or questionable situation; what does it do? Procedures B and C define a condition called TRUBL; if procedure E needs help it SIGNALS TRUBL. Control will then transfer within procedure B or C, depending upon which procedure's ON statement is in effect. The condition handlers, which are probably different, may decide that the trouble was irrelevant and can cause control to return to procedure E immediately after the SIGNAL statement.

An advantage of using signals here is that if TRUBL is different in B and C, the activation of the signal will cause the appropriate TRUBL to be executed depending on how D was called.

6.7.3 Multitasking

There is a multitasking feature in PL/I, which facilitates programming in a multi-processing environment. The following procedure demonstrates how this feature works:

```
P1:      PROCEDURE;
         ⋮
         CALL P2 EVENT (EP2);

         ⋮
         WAIT (EP2);/*SUSPEND UNTIL EVENT (EP2)*/

         ⋮
         END;
```

In the preceding program the WAIT statement suspends the execution of the procedure P1 until the procedure P2 sends the event EP2. Presumably, P1 is being executed by one CPU, and procedure P2 is being executed by another CPU.

6.8   EXTENSIBILITY AND COMPILE-TIME MACROS

The various mechanisms of PL/I, such as data types, data structures, etc., make it possible to perform a wide range of functions. The compile-time macro feature of PL/I allows the programmer to create more powerful programming constructs from the basic capabilities of the language.

Many languages have facilities that allow a programmer to declare a sequence of statements as a definition and give that definition a name, much in the same way as macros are declared in assembly language. The programmer can have these statements inserted into his program by simply naming the definition. This feature has been helpful to those, for example, who are writing closely related programs, many of which use the same data bases. One programmer may write the data structure with the appropriate declaration statements and then define these as a macro definition. His colleagues, rather than repeating the same declaration statement in every program, may simply write a macro call and allow the compiler to substitute appropriate declaration statements.

In particular, it is possible to essentially add new statement types to PL/I by appropriate use of the macro processor. In this way PL/I may be extended to produce more powerful or specialized languages suitable for specific projects.

6.9 MISCELLANEOUS

As in other modern languages, PL/I has features that are peculiar to a particular application. For instance, the declaration "sterling" was helpful to British brokers until Great Britain switched to the decimal system in 1971. The declarations "floating point" and "complex variables" are helpful to the engineer.

6.10 SUMMARY

The features that have been presented do not include all the capabilities of PL/I, but only those which differentiate it from most common languages. We believe that these features will play an important part in languages of the future and systems programming in particular.

QUESTIONS[4]

1. Explain when variables are allocated and freed for each of the following storage classes.

   a. Static
   b. Controlled
   c. Automatic
   d. Based

2. What are the similarities and differences between controlled and based storage?

3. *What is the difference between a do-group, a begin-block, and a procedure block (if any)? Can they replace each other? Give reasonable examples to support your answers.

4. *How do each of the following affect the scope of a variable? How are they executed? How do they end?

   a. Function procedure
   b. Begin block
   c. Do group
   d. Subroutine (called procedure)

5. What control does the PL/I programmer have over the scope of a variable and why is this control a useful feature of the language?

6. *List three ways in which values may be transmitted to a procedure in PL/I.

7. *The following program is to be hand simulated. Each time a statement is executed, that line number is to be written down. At the same time write down the names and values of any variables changed or created in that statement.

```
Line no.

  1      WHAT_IS:  PROCEDURE OPTIONS (MAIN);
  2          DCL     (X,Y) FIXED BINARY INITIAL (-2),
                     (W,Z) FIXED BINARY INITIAL (0),
                     M       FIXED BINARY CONTROLLED;
  3      I: PROCEDURE (J);
  4          DCL (J,X) FIXED BINARY;
  5          X=Z;
  6          RETURN (Z*X-J);
  7      END I;
  8      L1: ALLOCATE M;
  9          M=X*Y+W-Z;
 10      L2: Z=X+Y
 11          IF Z=0 THEN Z=I(Z);
 12          BEGIN;
```

---

[4]An * denotes that the question may require the use of a PL/I reference manual. A †
denotes that the question is a machine problem.

Line no.

```
13              DCL W INITIAL (2) FIXED BINARY;
14      L3: Z=I(W);
15              IF X=Z THEN GO TO L2;
16              IF X < Z THEN GO TO L1;
17              W=W+1;
18              GO TO L3;
19      L1: END;
20              X=W=M;
21              IF X > 0 THEN GO TO L1;
22              Z,Y,W=X;
23              END WHAT_IS;
```

8. *This exercise is intended to make you read about PL/I beyond what was presented in this chapter. Several new syntactic forms are introduced, and a good understanding of them can be obtained by reading the PL/I reference manual.

```
 1.      BETA : ALPHA : PROC OPTIONS (MAIN) ;
 2.              DECLARE  X FIXED BIN EXTERNAL;
 3.              DCL       Z FLOAT DECIMAL INITIAL (12) ;
 4.              DCL       LABEL_X LABEL ;
 5.              DCL       MESSAGE CHAR (24) VARYING STATIC
                          INITIAL ('NEVER-AGAIN') ;
 6.              X = 5 ;
 7.              ZED = X + Z ;
 8,9.            IF ZED < 4 * Z  THEN  DO ;
10,11.           X = 1 ; LABEL_X = LABEL_1 ;
12.              GO TO LABEL_X ;
13.              END ;
14.              ELSE TRY : BEGIN;
15.              DCL LAMBDA CHAR (0) ;
16.              SUBSTR (MESSAGE, 6, 6) = LAMBDA ;
17.              Z = Z - LENGTH (MESSAGE) ;
18.              UPTO : PROCEDURE ;
19.              DCL Z CHAR (5) INITIAL ('JOHNS') ;
20.              DCL X CHAR (20) VARYING INITIAL (LAMBDA) ;
21.              X = Z ‖ 'TRY-AGAIN' ;
22.              END UPTO ;
23.              NEW = X = Z ;
24.              END TRY ;
25.      LABEL_1 : CALL DELTA ;
26.      GAMMA: PROC ;
27.              DCL X FIXED BINARY EXTERNAL ;
28.              DCL Z FIX BIN (31) CONTROLLED ;
29.              ALLOCATE Z ;
30.              X = 4 ;
31.              Z = X * * 2 ;
32.              X = X + Z ;
33.              FREE Z ;
```

```
34.                END GAMMA ;
35.                UPDATE : AGAIN : PROCEDURE ;
36.                X = X + 4 ;
37.                DELTA : ENTRY ;
38.                Z = X * * 2 ;
39.                Z = Z - 40 ;
40.                END AGAIN ;
41.                CALL UPDATE ;
42.                CALL GAMMA ;
43.                Z = X + SQ (X) ;
44.                SQ : PROC (P) FIX BIN ;
45.                DCL P FIX BIN ;
46.                STR = P + P * 2 ;
47.                RETURN (STR) ;
48.                END ;
49.                END BETA ;
```

Examine the PL/I program above and answer the following question:
Trace the flow of control through the above program and show the value
of the variables X, Z and ZED after each statement. *Note*: The sequence
in which the statements are "executed" does not coincide with the
numbering shown. Read about flow of control through begin blocks,
procedures, etc. Give your answer in the form of a table as shown. We
have filled up the first few entries to show you what we require:

No.	Statement "executed"	Value of variables		
		X	Z	ZED
1	1	Unknown	Unknown	Unknown
2	2	"	"	"
3	3	"	12	"
4	4	"	12	"
5	5	"	12	"
6	6	5	12	"
7	7	5	12	17
	,	,	,	,
	,	,	,	,
	,	,	,	,
	,	,	,	,

The term "executed" is enclosed in quotes because a declare statement is
not really executed. We are using the term in the sense that an interpreter
would handle the above program.

9. †You are to write a PL/I procedure to convert binary integers to roman
   numerals. The roman numerals will be represented by a character string,
   since the attribute ROMAN as an alternative to BINARY and DECIMAL
   does not exist in PL/I. The numerals should be right-justified in the character string, with as many blanks as necessary filling out the string on the

left. Your output should be compact (note that 19 is represented by XIX). The numbers that you will be asked to convert will be positive and less than 4000. The roman numerals that you will need to know are as follows: I~1, V~5, X~10, L~50, C~100, D~500, and M~1000.

Your procedure should be named SPQR. It will be called as follows:

```
ROMAN = SPQR (BINARY)
```

10. †In the course of software implementation, there is a need for a number of "utility routines." In the assembler loader and compiler, frequent reference is made to the symbol and literal tables. In order to build these tables and retrieve information from them, a set of utility routines called SYMSTO and SYMGET may be used. Your job is to code, in PL/I, SYMSTO and SYMGET.

a. The grading program[5] will call SYMSTO to store the value of a new symbol and SYMGET to get the value of an already-stored symbol. One of the arguments to each of your entry points will be an ordered symbol table containing zero or more non-empty entries, all at the top of the table. You may assume the following about the table you are passed:

1) It is a PL/I structure of the form as declared TABLE at the end of this program.

2) An entry in the table is empty if the SYM element of that entry is equal to 'þþþþþþþþ' where þ represents a single blank (i.e., the character string of 8 blanks).

3) The table may contain from zero (empty) to 100 non-empty entries (full) when you are called.

4) All non-empty entries are at the top of the table — one immediately after another — starting at the first entry.

5) The entries are ordered inversely by their spellings (i.e., SYM).

6) No symbol appears twice in the table.

Example: You might be called with the following table:

---

[5]The problem can be done without a grader. The students will have to supply data and a main program. The grading program calls students' programs and keeps a record of the results.

SYM	VALUE	ATTRIBUTES			
		LENGTH	TYPE	REL_ABS	
TERM	44	16	1	0	1st entry
NEXT1	12	4	5	1	2nd entry
FIND2	16	2	4	1	3rd entry
ARG	26	8	2	0	4th entry
bbbbbbbb	0	0	0	0	5th entry - empty
. . .	empty	entries			
bbbbbbbb	0	0	0	0	100th entry - empty

b. SYMSTO

Your SYMSTO entry point will be called by:

N = SYMSTO (SYMBOL,TABLE,VALUE,LENGTH,TYPE,MODE)

(Note that the above statement will occur in the grading program and your program should be written to return the value to be assigned to N.)

SYMSTO must do the following:

1) Return the following fixed binary (31,0) values to the grader:

-1 if SYMBOL already in TABLE.
0 if TABLE is already full.
1 if SYMBOL added successfully.

2) Add an entry in TABLE for SYMBOL if the symbol is not already in TABLE and if TABLE is not already full. The new entry *must* be added as follows: introduce the new entry into the first empty

location following the used portion of the table, and compare it with the entry just above it; if the latter is smaller, interchange the two entries (i.e., the whole structured entry is interchanged). Continue this process until the new entry has reached its correct location, as determined by the six constraints listed earlier.

3) Set the VAL,LENGTH,TYPE and REL_ABS elements of SYMBOL's entry to the VALUE,LENGTH,TYPE and MODE arguments respectively.

c. SYMGET

Your SYMGET entry will be called as:

VALUE = SYMGET (SYMBOL,TABLE,ITEM)

(again, this is how the grading program will use your routine).

SYMGET must do the following:

1) If SYMBOL is found in TABLE, return one of the elements of SYMBOL's entry according to ITEM:

if ITEM is:	SYMGET returns
'VALUE'	the VAL element.
'LENG'	the LENGTH element.
'TYPE'	the TYPE element.
'MODE'	the REL_ABS element.

2) If the symbol is not found in the table, return the value -6251.

3) Note: SYMGET must not modify the table TABLE.

ENTRY POINT AND PARAMETER DECLARATIONS

To correctly establish the entry points and parameters in your procedure, your program should be in the following format:

```
SYMSTO:   PROCEDURE(SYMBOL,TABLE,VALUE,LENGTH,TYPE,MODE)
               FIXED BIN(31);
DECLARE   SYMBOL    CHAR(8),
               (VALUE,LENGTH,TYPE,MODE) FIXED BINARY(31),
               1  TABLE(100),
                   2  SYM CHAR(8),
                   2  VAL FIXED BINARY(31),
                   2  ATTRIBUTES,
                       3  LENGTH FIXED BINARY(31),
                       3  TYPE FIXED BINARY(31),
                       3  REL_ABS FIXED BINARY(31);
          [Declarations for both SYMSTO and SYMGET and body]
                         for SYMSTO
          [SYMSTO body should end with a return statement]
SYMGET:   ENTRY(SYMBOL,TABLE,ITEM) FIXED BINARY(31);
DECLARE   ITEM CHARACTER(4),
               [body for SYMGET]
END SYMSTO
```

11. †In the upcoming discussion of compilers, you will learn that there are six components in a modern compiler. You are to write a PL/I program that is one such component — a lexical processor. This processor will be specialized to handle a simple lexical structure — one containing only operators and identifiers (symbols) and no constants. The purpose of lexical analyzers is to read an input stream of characters and group the characters into the lexical entities (called *tokens*). Thus the following line of 36 characters

FOO: IF ALPHA = BETA THEN GOTO EXIT;

would be formed into the following sequence of 10 tokens:

You are to write a PL/I program with two entry points named NEXTKN and NEWLINE. The entry NEWLINE will be used by the grader to simulate an input card stream. It will call NEWLINE each time it wishes to give your program a new input line. The entry NEXTKN will be used by the grader to transmit the current versions of the two data bases, SYMTAB and OPTAB, and to invoke your analyzer routine. It will make several calls per current line to NEXTKN to obtain the successive tokens, one token for each call.

In particular, NEWLINE will be called via:

CALL NEWLINE(PL/I character string).

When it is called, your program must save this argument in a STATIC (why?) string variable as the new input line to be processed. The lines passed will vary in length but satisfy the pseudo-PL/I expression:

$1 \leq \text{LENGTH(NEW\_LINE)} \leq 80.$

The entry NEXTKN will be called via:

CALL NEXTKN(SYMTAB,OPTAB,UNIFSYM).

When it is called, your program must take the following action:

a. Isolate as a character string the next token from the current input line.
b. Determine whether the token is an operator or a symbol by searching the arguments OPTAB and SYMTAB. By default, if it is in neither table, it is assumed to be a new symbol.
c. If it is a new symbol, store it into SYMTAB at the first entry that is all blanks. If it is in SYMTAB already, note its position. If it is an operator, note its position in OPTAB.

d. Before you return, store two values in argument UNIFSYM passed to you:

1) Set structure element UNIFSYM.TYPE to the single letter:

'O' if the token is an operator
'I' if it is an identifier
'L' if it is a literal

Note that in SYMTAB, an entry can be of two types: 'I' or 'L'. The distinction your program must make here is that a literal is a character string composed only of numeric characters (an integer), whereas an identifier must have at least one non-numeric character in it.

2) Set the structure element UNIFSYM.INDEX to the numeric value of the position of the token in its respective table.

e. Return to the grader by executing: RETURN. Note that this pair of values (TYPE,INDEX) is a uniform symbol representation of the token and uniquely identifies it.

SPECS

The entry NEWLINE has been adequately described above. However, some additional areas of detail are needed about NEXTKN.

1) The tables: The two data bases of concern to NEXTKN are OPTAB and SYMTAB. Both are simple arrays of character strings — the strings being spellings of the operators and keywords, identifiers and literals. The PL/I declarations of these tables are:

```
DECLARE      SYMTAB(*)      char(20),
             OPTAB(*)       char(8)
```

These two arrays will vary in dimension, as indicated by the '*' in the declaration, but will satisfy the pseudo-PL/I expression:

$1 \leq DIM(EITHER\_TAB,1) \leq 16;$

2) Isolating the token: When called, NEXTKN will start scanning the current input line from the first non-blank character beyond the last recognized token. To isolate the current token, it should scan until the end of the token is found. These rules define the end of a token:

a) A blank character terminates a token.

b) The end of a line terminates a token. Remember lines vary in size up to 80 characters.

c) The following set of 14 break characters terminates a token and the characters themselves are separate tokens: $\{ : , ; , + , - , \leftarrow , \rightarrow , > , |$ (vertical slash), || (two slashes), **, (,), ,(comma), $< \}$

3) Returned values: NEXTKN classifies the token as one of three types and sets the passed structure element UNIFSYM.TYPE to the corresponding CHAR(1) letter described above. The structure element

UNIFSYM.INDEX is then set to the "position" value of the token. "Position" will be a FIXED BIN(31) value between 1 and 16 and is the index (subscript) of the token in its particular table. Remember that a newly found symbol will also have to be stored in SYMTAB.

EXAMPLE

The grader will first transmit an input line to your analyzer via:

CALL NEWLINE(' IHTFP :TUITION = 2500 ‖ 'IS TOO DARN MUCH';');

This line contains eight tokens. Let us assume the following tables:

SYMTAB(7)		OPTAB(9)	
1	TUITION	1	:
2	2150	2	←
3	USAGNP	3	DO
4	NOV4	4	=
5	' '	5	‖
6	' '	6	END
7	' '	7	'
		8	BEGIN
		9	;

The next eight calls to NEXTKN will return these values:

CALL #	(TYPE,INDEX)	
1	('I',5)	IHTFP was stored
2	('O',1)	
3	('I',1)	
4	('O',4)	
5	('L',6)	2500 was stored
6	('O',5)	
7	('I',7)	'IS TOO DARN MUCH' was stored
8	('O',9)	

LINKAGE TO THE GRADER[5]

To correctly establish entry points and parameters, your program should have the following format[6]:

---

[6]Note that the declarations under both NEXTKN and NEWLINE apply throughout the entire procedure. The entry NEWLINE is simply a means for allowing external execution of your program to start at this point rather than at the beginning entry NEXTKN. Writing particular declarations under their related entry simply makes the program more logically organized and thus adds to its readability and comprehension.

```
col 2
↓
NEXTKN:PROC(SYMTAB,OPTAB,UNIFSYM);
          DCL SYMTAB(*)   CHAR(20),
              OPTAB(*)     CHAR(8),
              1 UNIFSYM,
              2 TYPE CHAR(1),
              2 INDEX FIXED BIN(31);
```

          [declarations and code for NEXTKN]

```
col 2
↓
NEWLINE:ENTRY(NEW_LINE);
          DCL NEW_LINE CHAR(80) VAR;
```

          [declarations and code for NEWLINE]

```
END NEXTKN;
```

12. †a. Define a subset of IBM 360 assembly language.
    b. Write an assembler for it in PL/I.

13. †a. Specify a macro language.
    b. Write a macro processor for it in PL/I.

7

formal systems and programming languages: an introduction

The objectives of this chapter are to:

1. Provide an informal introduction to formal systems and grammars
2. Demonstrate the relevance of theoretical to practical work in the area of programming languages
3. Present formal systems and terminology that are commonly used in the literature
4. Present theoretical tools relevant to compiling techniques
5. Describe two methods for programming language specification: Backus-Naur Form and canonic systems
6. Present an example of research being conducted in this area and pose some theoretical questions that are being asked about programming languages and formal systems

This chapter presents a brief view of a complicated and varied subject; more complete treatments will be found in the references (Chapter 10).

Except for the description of Backus-Naur Form in section 7.5, and problem 1, this chapter may be omitted from presentations of systems programming with a purely practical orientation.

7.1 USES OF FORMAL SYSTEMS IN PROGRAMMING LANGUAGES

A formal system is an uninterpreted calculus or logistic system. It consists of an alphabet, a set of words called axioms, and a finite set of relations called rules of inference. Examples of formal systems are: set theory, boolean algebra, propositional and predicate calculus, Post systems, Euclid's plane geometry, Backus Normal Form, and Peano arithmetic. A formal system is uninterpreted in the sense that no meaning is formally attached to the symbols of the system; there is for each of the above-mentioned systems a standard informal interpretation of the symbols, but other interpretations are generally valid so far as the systems themselves are concerned.

We generally construct formal systems in order to have formalized models of informal, intuitive notions. A formal model can be studied mathematically; and if the model is appropriate, the results may tell us much about the notions that it portrays.

Formal systems are becoming important in the design, implementation, and study of programming languages. Specifically, various sorts of formal systems are used for syntax specification, syntax-directed compilation, compiler verification, complexity studies, and analysis of the structure of languages.

7.1.1 Language Specification

Formal systems are used to define the form (the *syntax*) of a programming language. Such definition is important both to the user and to the implementer of the language. The user needs (for reference) a clear description of the language. The implementer is faced with the problems of transferability and maintenance. If the same language is to be implemented (transferred) on different machines, the legal strings of the language must be well-defined so that the user-level appearance is, so far as is practicable, invariant. Further, the implementer must be concerned with maintenance. Both the user and the maintainer of a compiler need an exact specification of the acceptable strings of the corresponding language.

7.1.2 Syntax-Directed Compilers

A syntax-directed compiler uses a data base containing the syntactical rules of a source language to *parse* (recognize - find the sequence of rules that generate the string) the source-language input. Formal systems are used as the data base. Because of the increase in the number of programming languages and machines, researchers have been looking into automatic generation of compilers. Their approach has been to have formal definitions of both the input or source language L_{source} and the output language L_{object}. The output of the compiler generator would be a translator $T: L_{source} \rightarrow L_{object}$.

A problem similar to that of automatic compiler-writing is the problem of generating test programs to validate a language processor. If the source language is formally defined, the generative techniques described in the next section provide a method for automatically producing such test programs. This can be useful in testing software since a computer can be more pedantic than a human tester.

7.1.3   Complexity Structure Studies

Formal systems are used to study the complexity of programming languages and of their compilers. Compiler writers and language designers want to know which features of language inordinately increase the complexity of a compiler's recognition phase. A compiler writer also wants a basis for evaluating the performance of a compiler. He would like to know the theoretically optimum level of performance (in terms of number of steps) that he could expect for the process of translation. After implementing a version of the compiler, he could compare its performance to the theoretical limit; if it was within some tolerance, he could forego further effort. But if the performance was two orders of magnitude worse than the theoretical bound, improvement would clearly be in order.

Analogies will be found in the work surrounding Shannon's information theory. Shannon determined a measure for information and applied it to the coding of information. The resulting theory gave bounds on efficiency in information coding and transmission. Bell Telephone Laboratories researchers devising coding techniques for transmission of information could compare the performance of their schemes with Shannon's bound, using it as a yardstick. Shannon's theory does not determine coding schemes. It merely provides a measure of how efficient they can be. Similarly, in complexity studies, the compiler writer would not be told what method to use, but merely whether a better method might exist.

7.1.4   Structure Analysis

Formal systems are used in attempts to prove the equivalence and the validity of programs. The work in proving the equivalence of programs is motivated by the prospect of global optimization. If there were an algorithm which recognized the equivalence of two different programs, the faster program could be used in place of the slower-running one.

A formal theory also provides a framework for analyzing and comparing various languages. It helps answer questions such as:

1. What are the basic language features?
2. What constructs can exist in the language? How can the features be combined to build new constructs?
3. What categories of problems can be programmed in the language?
4. What is the cost or difficulty of writing a program?

These key questions may be approached through formalization. The answers are also of interest in the field of machine design; the ideal computer should efficiently perform the operations corresponding to the basic features of a language.

7.2 FORMAL SPECIFICATION

7.2.1 Approaching a Formalism

Before going deeper into formalism it is useful to analyze some of the problems in formally defining a language and to look into the intuitive basis for the definitions. A language may be thought of as a set of sentences or formulae — strings of symbols — with well-defined structures and, usually, meaning. The rules specifying valid constructions of a language are its *syntax*: the syntax of a language describes its form. For example, when we say that x+2 is an expression, but x2+ is not, we are referring to the syntax of algebra. The assignment of a meaning, or *interpretation*, to symbols and formulae is the *semantics* of a language. When we say, for example, that the value of x+2 is the sum of the values of x and 2 — or that 2·x = x+x is true — we are referring to the usual semantics of algebra.

If all languages consisted of a finite number of legal sentences or formulae, syntactic definition would not pose a problem; it would suffice merely to list all legal sentences — a string of symbols would be a sentence only if it appeared in the list. The problem of definition exists because almost all languages of any utility contain an unlimited (or very large) number of valid sentences. It is not possible to store a list of all valid strings for infinite languages. But it is not necessary to store the list of sentences if any member of the list can be generated whenever it is needed, even though to generate all sentences may be endless. If an algorithm exists that will successively produce legal strings, an arbitrary string is in the language if it ever occurs in the list that is generated: if it is a legal string, it will be generated after some finite (but possibly long) time. Such a listing algorithm is called a *generative specification* of the language.

If the algorithm generates sentences in such an order that each new sentence is at least as long (has at least as many symbols) as the previous sentence, it is clearly possible to determine whether or not a given string is in the language. Whenever the algorithm begins to generate sentences longer than the string being tested, that string cannot be in the language unless it has already been generated. This type of algorithm enables us to decide after a finite number of steps whether or not a string is a legal sentence. If such a decision can be made in finite time for every string, the language is called *decidable*.

An alternative type of algorithm could be used to specify languages. In this second approach the string to be tested is fed as data into the algorithm. The algorithm then analyzes the input, performs whatever computation is necessary, and produces an answer indicating "yes, the string is legal," or "no, it is not legal." This is called an *analytic* specification. A language with an analytic specification is decidable if the analyzer always stops after finitely many steps for every input string. Unfortunately, formal analytic specifications are often very difficult to derive; this chapter will deal primarily with generative specifications.

English is not suitable for defining languages formally because it is too vague and leads to ambiguous definitions. It is necessary to develop a formalism in which language definitions can be stated. This defining language is the *syntactic meta-language*. When we employ a language to talk about some language (itself or another) we shall call the latter the *object language* and the former the *meta-language*. A formal system is a meta-language. Symbols of the object language are called *terminal symbols*. Symbols of a meta-language that denote strings in the object language are called *nonterminals*. To formally define the meta-language would require a meta-meta-language; therefore, we hope that the meta-language is intuitively clear.

The first step of the definition process is to establish the *universe of discourse*. That is, it is necessary to specify the objects being discussed. The most elementary object is a symbol. Symbols are concatenated to form strings, which may or may not belong to the language.

Definition 1:   An *alphabet* T is a finite set of symbols ("terminal symbols"). A formula (also called a string or a sentence) is a concatenation of symbols.

It is useful to have a notation for the class of all possible finite strings on an alphabet T. This is designated by T*. For any set U, U* represents the set of all possible finite concatenations of elements of the set U. Small Greek letters are used to denote strings. We commonly write λ to represent the "null" or "empty" string (i.e. the string which contains no elements).

Generally, a language does not include all possible strings on its alphabet. Only certain strings are valid formulae in the language. Thus:

Definition 2:   A *language*, L, is a subset of the set of finite concatenations of symbols in an alphabet T. We write this L ⊂ T*.

7.2.2 Development of Formal Specification

Let us turn for an example to English syntax. English is not just a collection of groups of words — there is an underlying structure connecting the words. Given the sentence

"The student studies hard."

one can construct the sentence structure shown in Figure 7.1. In particular, one can separate the Noun Phrase (NP) from the Verb Phrase (VP) and then complete the analysis by subdividing these phrases into individual words. Since all sentences have some structure, it should be possible to generate this structure in small steps and thus build up to complex sentences. We can represent structure graphically with a syntax tree; branches from each node on the tree indicate its logical subdivisions.

For example, we might begin with the classification "sentence" and replace it by the pair NP and VP to construct one possible form that a sentence might have. It is notationally convenient to write this as

sentence → NP VP

It is clear from the context that NP represents the linguistic class "noun phrase." In Figure 7.1 we must distinguish between the string "NP", which may be replaced by the string "article", and the string "The", which cannot be replaced. We distinguish the names of classes from words in the language by placing the meta-brackets "⟨"and"⟩" around symbols used to represent linguistic classes. The first structure rule then becomes:

(1) ⟨sentence⟩ → ⟨NP⟩ ⟨VP⟩
(2) ⟨NP⟩ → ⟨article⟩ ⟨noun⟩

Similarly, a verb-phrase consists of a verb possibly modified by an adverb.

(3) ⟨VP⟩ → ⟨verb⟩
(4) ⟨VP⟩ → ⟨verb⟩ ⟨adverb⟩

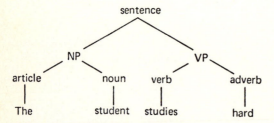

FIGURE 7.1 Syntax tree for "the student studies hard"

The way these structure transformations or rewriting rules are written allows a ⟨VP⟩ to have optionally one adverb while an ⟨NP⟩ must have exactly one adjective.

The last step is to list possible terminal-symbol replacements for the class representatives, ⟨article⟩, ⟨adverb⟩, ⟨noun⟩, and ⟨verb⟩:

(5) ⟨article⟩ → The
(6) ⟨noun⟩ → student
(7) ⟨verb⟩ → studies
(8) ⟨adverb⟩ → hard
(9) ⟨adverb⟩ → slowly

Using these rewriting rules, it is possible to build a sentence by replacing the linguistic class symbols with the structures that they represent. Figure 7.2 gives a derivation of "The student studies hard." By changing the last step and using

⟨adverb⟩ → slowly

it is possible to generate instead "The student studies slowly." The structure rewriting rules or *transformations* determine the form of the language generated. In our example, the language is a very small subset of English.

Such a system of rewriting rules constitutes an algorithm for generating sentences. By changing the symbols from words to phonemes and allowing for more complex structure transformations, one can describe much of English syntax in a similar manner. This scheme can handle most programming-language features as well. However, features that require more specification power will lead us to seek other, more discriminating methods of language specification.

7.3 FORMAL GRAMMARS

The above example indicated a way to formalize the process of generating the

Step	Structure	Rule applied
a)	⟨sentence⟩	
b)	⟨NP⟩ ⟨VP⟩	(1)
c)	⟨article⟩ ⟨noun⟩ ⟨VP⟩	(2)
d)	⟨article⟩ ⟨noun⟩ ⟨verb⟩ ⟨adverb⟩	(4)
e)	The ⟨noun⟩ ⟨verb⟩ ⟨adverb⟩	(5)
f)	The student ⟨verb⟩ ⟨adverb⟩	(6)
g)	The student studies ⟨adverb⟩	(7)
h)	The student studies hard	(8)

FIGURE 7.2 Steps in a derivation

strings of a language: before considering a formal definition, it is useful to analyze the structure of a sentence. We used two classes of symbols: one, enclosed in brackets, to represent linguistic classes (grammatical units used as intermediate steps in the formal generation process); and another, composed of Roman letters, from which the generated sentence was eventually formed. Because the symbols of one set are in the sentence when generation terminates, while those of the other appear only in intermediate steps, they are referred to as *terminal* and *nonterminal* symbols, respectively. One nonterminal symbol, the *starting symbol* (in our example, ⟨sentence⟩) is distinguished as the symbol with which the generation process begins.

Definition 3: The *terminal symbols* are the symbols of the alphabet T. The *nonterminal symbols* are a set N of symbols not in T that represent intermediate states in the generation process. The *starting symbol* is a distinguished nonterminal symbol from which all strings of the language are derived.

The generation process itself consisted of applying, at each step, any one of the set of rewriting rules or productions. This process transforms the string into a new string; the process stops when there is no production that can be applied or when the string consists solely of terminal symbols.

Definition 4: A *production*[1] is a string transformation rule having a left-hand side that is a pattern to match a substring (possibly all) of the string to be transformed, and a right-hand side that indicates a replacement for the matched portion of the string.

It is important to realize that any substring of the current string may be replaced by an applicable production and that only that part of the string matched by the left-hand side of the production is affected. Productions can totally replace substrings, or they may merely rearrange the symbols of the matched substring.

Definition 5: A formal grammar G is a 4-tuple G = (N,T,Σ,P) where
   (1) N is the set of nonterminal symbols
   (2) T is the set of terminal symbols
   (3) Σ is the starting symbol; Σ ∈ N

---

[1]The term production is due to the mathematician Emil Post who first used similar rules to define languages. The formal grammars presented here are essentially the same as Post's canonical systems with some restrictions on the use of symbols in productions.

(4) P is the set of productions $\alpha \to \beta$ where $\alpha, \beta \, \epsilon \, (N \cup T)^*$, $\alpha \neq \lambda$ (i.e., α is not null)

(5) $N \cap T$ is empty

Requirement (5) assures that it is always possible to distinguish nonterminals from terminals.

7.3.1 Examples of Formal Grammars

To clarify the notion of formal grammar we consider two examples. The non-terminals will be capital Roman letters (A,B,C) and Σ; the terminal symbols will be small Roman letters (a,b,c).

Example 1: $N = \{A,B,\Sigma\}$ $T = \{a,b\}$

$$P = \{ \begin{array}{ll} \Sigma \to AB & (1) \\ A \to aA & (2) \\ A \to a & (3) \\ B \to Bb & (4) \\ B \to b\} & (5) \end{array}$$

Notice that in production (2) the nonterminal A occurs on both sides of the rule; (2) indicates that the class of strings corresponding to A is closed under prefixing with "a". Since the only other production indicating the structure of class A is production 3, it is easy to see that A is closed under concatenation and consists of the class of finite strings of "a"s: a,aa,aaa,aaaa, . . . Likewise, the class B consists of finite strings of "b"s: b,bb,bbb,bbbb, . . . The language produced by the grammar consists of all strings formed from a string of "a"s followed by a string of "b"s.

Example 2: $N = \{A,\Sigma\}$ $T = \{a,b\}$

$$P = \{ \begin{array}{l} \Sigma \to A \\ A \to aAb \\ A \to ab\} \end{array}$$

Since the terminal alphabets are the same in examples 1 and 2, both languages are subsets of the set of strings containing "a"s and "b"s. There is a difference, however. In the language of example 1 an arbitrary number of "a"s may precede an equally arbitrary number of "b"s. But in example 2 every time an "a" is generated, a "b" is also generated. Therefore, the legal sentences of example 2 consist of a string of "a"s followed by an equal number of "b"s.

7.3.2 The Derivation of Sentences

So far we have indicated that formal grammars provide a generative specification of a language, but we have not formally defined the process of generating a string.

Definition 6:   A string γ is *immediately derived* from a string
μ (write $\mu \Rightarrow \gamma$) in a grammar G if and only if
$\mu = \sigma\, \alpha\, \tau, \quad \gamma = \sigma\, \beta\, \tau, \quad$ and
$\alpha \to \beta \in P$ of G
where σ and τ represent arbitrary (possibly empty) strings.

Referring to example 1 above, suppose that μ = aABb and γ = aaBb. aABb $\Rightarrow$ aaBb is then an immediate derivation with σ = a, α = A, τ = Bb, β = a, and the production A $\to$ a. We now define proof in a grammar.

Definition 7:   A string γ is *derived* from a string μ (write $\mu \Rightarrow^* \gamma$) in a grammar G if and only if there is a sequence of strings $\omega_0, \omega_1, \ldots, \omega_{n-1}, \omega_n$, for $n \geqslant 0$, such that
$\mu = \omega_0,$
$\gamma = \omega_n$
and for every $0 \leqslant i < n \qquad \omega_i \Rightarrow \omega_{i+1}$
(i.e. $\mu = \omega_0 \Rightarrow \omega_1 \Rightarrow \ldots \Rightarrow \omega_{n-1} \Rightarrow \omega_n = \gamma$)
with $\omega_i \in (N \cup T)^* \text{-}\lambda$ for every i.
The list $\{\omega_i\}$ is a *proof* of γ in G.

This is a formal statement that each new string in the derivation process must come from some previously derived string by application of a production of G. The last condition rules out deriving a string from the *empty string* λ (i.e., a string without symbols). A typical derivation in the grammar of example 1 is $\Sigma \Rightarrow AB \Rightarrow aAB \Rightarrow aABb \Rightarrow aaBb \Rightarrow aabb$ hence $\Sigma \Rightarrow^*$ aabb (also aAB $\Rightarrow^*$ aaBb, etc).

7.3.3 Sentential Forms and Sentences

The above definitions specify formally the generation process. It is now necessary to designate which of the set of possible derivations terminate on strings of the language.

Definition 8:   A *sentential form* is any string which can be derived from the starting symbol Σ.

Examples of sentential forms in the grammar of example 1 are aAB and aabb. The sentential or sentence-like forms include formulae which have nonterminal symbols in the final string.

Definition 9: A *sentence* is a sentential form containing only terminal symbols.

Therefore, aabb is a sentence, but aAB is not.

Definition 10:   A language L defined by a grammar G (write L(G)) is the set of sentences that can be derived from Σ in G:
$$L(G) = \left\{ \omega \ \epsilon \ T^* \ | \ \Sigma \ \Rightarrow^* \ \omega \right\}.$$
L is called *ambiguous* if it contains a formula for which there is more than one distinct proof in which the left-most nonterminal is replaced at each step.

7.4   HIERARCHY OF LANGUAGES

The definition of production allows for a wide variety of string transformations. Certain restrictions on the form of productions give grammars producing subclasses of the class of formal languages — e.g., linear grammars, producing regular languages. Noam Chomsky has constructed a system of four language types that classify some languages according to such restrictions.

The most general type of grammar imposes no restrictions on the productions. In particular, productions that eliminate ("erase") symbols are permitted. This allows the intermediate strings to expand and contract. An example of an erasing production is aAB → aB, in which A is erased from the context aAB. A grammar (as we have defined it) without restrictions is called a type 0 grammar.

The simplest restriction which produces a strictly smaller class of languages is to require the right-hand side of every production to have at least as many symbols as the left-hand side. A grammar with this restriction is called a type 1 or noncontracting context-sensitive grammar because $\alpha \Rightarrow \beta$ is possible only if length $(\beta) \geqslant (\alpha)$. Examples of productions in a type 1 grammar are

bB → Bb   (interchange symbols)
$\sigma\alpha\tau \rightarrow \sigma\beta\tau$ (where length $(\beta) \geqslant$ Length (α)

Definition 11:   The *length* of a string is the number of symbols in the string. If α consists of a single symbol, length $(\alpha) = 1$; length $(\lambda) = 0$ (the null string). For strings α,β, length $(\alpha\beta) =$ length $(\alpha) +$ length (β).

In both type 0 and type 1 grammars α can be any string. "Context-sensitive" refers to the fact that some productions may recognize context — e.g., in the case of $\sigma\alpha\tau \rightarrow \sigma\beta\tau$, the transformation $\alpha \rightarrow \beta$ occurs only in the context $\sigma\alpha\tau$. An example of a type 1 grammar is:

Example 3: $N = \{A,B,\Sigma\}$ $T = \{a,b,c\}$
$$P = \{\Sigma \rightarrow Abc$$
$$Ab \rightarrow aAbB$$
$$Bb \rightarrow bB$$
$$Bc \rightarrow bcc$$
$$A \rightarrow a\}$$

This grammar generates strings of the form $a^n b^n c^n$ for $n \geqslant 1$.

If the left-hand side of the production is restricted to a single nonterminal symbol, its application cannot be dependent on the context in which the symbol occurs. Grammars with this restriction (and nonblank right-hand strings) are called *type 2, context-free* or *simple phrase-structure* grammars. The latter name comes from an analogy to the method that we used to generate the sentence "The student studies hard." Our grammar satisfied the single-symbol restriction, and every nonterminal symbol expanded into a word or phrase — for example, ⟨sentence⟩ became the concatenation of a Noun Phrase ⟨NP⟩ and a Verb Phrase ⟨VP⟩. Two more context-free grammars appeared in examples 1 and 2 above. A subclass of context-free languages called *bounded-context languages* has become important in practical compiling.

A third type of restriction on productions restricts the number of terminals and nonterminals that each step can create. When, at most, one nonterminal symbol is used in both the right- and left-hand sides of a production, the production is said to be *linear*. If the nonterminal occurs to the right of all other symbols on the right-hand side of a production, the production is called a *right-linear production*. Similarly, if the nonterminal occurs to the left of all other symbols the production is called a *left-linear production*. A grammar is called right- (left-) linear if each of its productions is right- (left-) linear; a language is called *regular* if it can be generated by a right- or left-linear grammar.

Each of the above restrictions includes those above it. These types form a hierarchy that is summarized in Figure 7.3. We remark without proof that no type 3 grammar can generate the language defined in example 2, so type 3 is a strict subset of type 2. Similarly, no type 2 grammar can generate the language of example 3, so type 2 is a strict subset of type 1. Finally, type 1 is a strict subset of type 0. We classify languages according to the type of grammar that can generate them: a type i language is a language that can be generated by a grammar of type i (but not by one of type i+1, for i=0,1, or 2).

Languages can also be defined in terms of the machines (e.g., translators, interpreters) that accept them. To each of these general language types there is a corresponding type of abstract machine: for example, regular languages are languages that can be recognized by finite-state machines; while type 0 languages are all languages that can be recognized by a class of machines called Turing machines. The table in Figure 7.3 indicates the type of abstract machine corresponding to each class of formal grammar.

Type	Type of language and recognizing automation	Production form and restrictions
0	Contracting context-sensitive (Post systems): Turing machines	$\alpha \to \beta$ $\alpha,\beta \in (N \cup T)^*;$ $\alpha \neq \lambda$
1	Noncontracting context-sensitive: non-deterministic linear-bounded automata	$\sigma\,\alpha\,\tau \to \sigma\,\beta\,\tau$ $\sigma,\tau \in (N \cup T)^*; \alpha,\beta \in (N \cup T)^* - \lambda$ and length $(\alpha) \leqslant$ length (β)
2	Context-free: non-deterministic push-down storage automata	$A \to \beta$ $\beta \in (N \cup T)^* - \lambda; A\epsilon N$
3	Regular or finite-state: finite-state automata	Right-linear Left-linear $A \to aB$ $A \to Ba$ $A \to a$ $A \to a$ $a \epsilon T; A,B \epsilon N$

Notation: By convention X* consists of all finite strings of symbols from the set X including the empty string λ.

FIGURE 7.3 Basic formal grammars

7.5 BACKUS-NAUR FORM — BACKUS NORMAL FORM — BNF

BNF is a notation for writing grammars that is commonly used to specify the syntax of programming languages. In BNF nonterminals are written as names enclosed in corner-brackets '⟨ ⟩'. The sign → is written ::= (read "is replaced by"). Alternative ways of rewriting a given nonterminal are separated by a vertical bar, |, (read "or"). Using BNF notation, example 1 of the last section would be written

⟨Σ⟩::= ⟨A⟩ ⟨B⟩   — read "the sign Σ is replaced by A followed by B"
⟨A⟩::= a ⟨A⟩ | a   — read "A is replaced by 'a' followed by A or by 'a'"
⟨B⟩::= ⟨B⟩ b | b

As an example of BNF, we specify in Figure 7.4 a FORTRAN-like language consisting only of GO TO statements. The GO TO statements have statement labels and reference labels of arbitrary length. It would of course be desirable to have all the reference labels appear among the list of statement labels. We will see that we cannot impose this restriction on a language using Backus Normal Form.

```
       ⟨letter⟩ ::= A | B | C | . . . | Z   — (reader reads "letter is replaced by A or B. . .)
   ⟨identifier⟩ ::= ⟨letter⟩ | ⟨letter⟩ ⟨identifier⟩
    ⟨go to stm⟩ ::= GO TO ⟨identifier⟩;
      ⟨program⟩ ::= ⟨identifier⟩ ⟨go to stm⟩ | ⟨identifier⟩ ⟨go to stm⟩ ⟨program⟩
```

FIGURE 7.4   A BNF specification of a subset of FORTRAN-like language

An example of a program in this language would be:

```
  AB      GO TO      XY;
  XY      GO TO      WXYZA;
WXYZA     GO TO      AB;
```

According to the specification it is possible to generate a program such as "A GO TO B; C GO TO D;" where no statements are labelled B or D. We would like to exclude such programs. However, there is no way to do this formally in a BNF specification. The set ⟨program⟩ is much larger than the set that we wish to call valid programs. BNF notation is equivalent to context-free (or phrase-structure) grammar, so class symbols expand without reference to surrounding context. We would like to distinguish a subset of programs in which every reference label occurs as a statement label. To express such a relationship or function, we need a more powerful formal system, one with the capability of cross-reference between elements of the sentence structure that it generates. Cross-reference is a context-sensitive feature.

7.6 CANONIC SYSTEMS

We present canonic systems as another more powerful method for defining languages. The author feels that canonic systems provide a useful vehicle for a theoretical approach to language. They also exemplify some of the theoretical work currently being done, and the same basic questions that we pose about them may be directed at any formal language specification.

A *canonic system* is a type of formal system that operates on several sets of strings over a finite alphabet. Canonic systems (equivalent to Smullyan's *ele-*

mentary formal systems) are a variant of Post's canonical systems. In canonic systems the general framework of productions, or string-transformation rules, is replaced by a system of axioms (*canons*) and by the logical rules of substitution for variables and detachment (modus ponens). A canonic system defines a set of interrelated predicates, each of which is a set of strings.

Canonic systems have been used to specify the syntax and the translation of programming languages (More[3]; Donovan and Ledgard, 1967). They have served as a data base for a generalized translator for computer languages (Alsop, 1967; Altman[4]); later theorems as to their mathematical power and their formal properties have been proven (Doyle[4], Mandl[4]); and they have been used to study the complexity of translators and languages (Haggerty, 1969). The ultimate goal of this research has been to say something about programming languages. The author hopes to use this system to prove things about programming languages and their translators.

Consider the inadequacies of the Backus-Naur Form (BNF) specification of the syntax of programming languages. In BNF it is impossible to describe many of the constraints that exist in programming languages, such as the restriction that a "legal program" is not acceptable to a translator, even though correct in form, unless all of the reference labels in the program correspond to statement labels. These features are sometimes referred to as "context-sensitive features." Some people feel that they really refer to the meaning of a language and that they are semantic and not syntactic. However, these features *must* be specified in specifying the translation of a language. The distinction between syntax and semantics is not always clear. For example, the statement

```
20 GO TO 20
```

may be syntactically a legal statement, but is it semantically correct? (One might argue that this statement is useful for determining how long a computer will run before making an error.)

The translation of a programming language is specified by a canonic system that generates a set of ordered pairs of the form

⟨*statement in source language, its translation in the target language*⟩

Such a set of rules would specify the translation of a computer language. If the target language is understood, such a specification could be said to define the semantics of the language.

Like BNF, canonic systems *generate* the strings of a language. The *recognition* process is a different problem: An algorithm that uses a canonic system specification of a programming language to recognize and produce the transla-

---

[3]More, Yale classnotes, 1963.
[4]Unpublished M.S. Theses, M.I.T., 1970.

tion of strings has been developed and implemented.

The issue of whether or not canonic systems specifying the context-sensitive code parts of a programming language specify the syntax or the semantics of a language is academic; the real goal is to use a specification of a language to say something about the language and its translation. If we are to define the translation of a language, we must specify *all* the legal strings that get translated in that language. We need a system powerful enough to exclude illegal strings, whether on the basis of syntax or of semantics; hence, the motivation for a more powerful system than BNF. Yet, in their most general form, canonic systems are so powerful that they introduce many undecidability problems. A requirement exists, therefore, to determine more precisely the power of canonic systems and to restrict their power to the point at which they are adequate to handle the features we wish to define, but not powerful enough to introduce problems we cannot cope with in our models.

We will first introduce canonic systems informally. A canonic system consists of a number of *canons*, logical rules which state that certain *premises* imply certain *conclusions*. A *predicate* is a name given to a well-defined set of strings over the alphabet of the object language. For a programming language these sets are defined in such a way as to aid the user of the canonic system.

The assertion sign $\vdash$ is used to separate the premises from the conclusions. The general form of a canon is

$$a;b; \ldots ;c \vdash z$$

and is read "from the premises a;b; . . . ; c can be asserted z." For example, we might define a set *number:*

$$\vdash 1 \; digit$$
$$\vdash 2 \; digit$$
$$\vdash 3 \; digit$$
$$x \; digit \vdash x \; number$$
$$x \; digit; \; y \; number \vdash yx \; number[5]$$

This system defines *number* as the set of strings over the symbols 1, 2, and 3. Any terminals may be substituted for the variables x and y, but no conclusion can be drawn unless the resulting premises are true — that is, unless the resulting premise statements have been previously reached as conclusions. The first three canons, which have no premises, are "axioms": their conclusions are immediate.

---

[5] When writing a canon the underline may be used in place of italics, e.g.
x digit; y number $\vdash$ yx number

PREDICATE, VARIABLE, TERM, REMARK, CANON

In the above example, *digit* and *number* are predicates of degree 1 that name certain sets of strings. A predicate of degree 2 names a set of ordered pairs of strings. A *term* is a string of concatenated variables and terminal symbols; a *remark* is a term followed by a predicate symbol. If $R_1, \ldots, R_{n-1} \vdash R_n$ is a canon, $R_1, \ldots, R_{n-1}$ are premises and R_n is the conclusion. Each of the R_i is a remark.

The following notation will be used:

1. Lower case letters will be used as variables.
2. Italicized strings of letters will be used as predicate symbols.
3. The notation $\langle x_1 < x_2 < \ldots x_n \rangle$ will be used to denote n-tuples. Terms of degree 1 will be denoted by their single component without the brackets.
4. A series of canons with identical premises $R_1, \ldots, R_n$ and different conclusions $\alpha_1 P, \ldots, \alpha_m P$ will be abbreviated (see Fig. 7.5 for example)

$$R_1; \ldots; R_n \vdash \alpha_{1+} \ \alpha_{2+} \ \alpha_{3+} \ \ldots \ \alpha_n P$$

FORMAL DEFINITION

Definition 12: A canonic system is a sextuple
$$\mathscr{C} = (\,C\,,V\,,M\,,P\,,S\,,D\,)$$
where

C   is a finite set of *canons*

V   is an alphabet of terminal symbols used to form the strings generated (i.e., provable) by $\mathscr{C}$

M   is a finite set of *variable symbols* (variables)

P   is a finite set of *predicate symbols* (predicates) used to name sets of n-tuples. The number of components in the n-tuples denoted by a predicate is the *degree* of the predicate

S   is a finite set of punctuation signs used in writing canons

D   ($\subseteq$ P) is a set of *sentence predicates*, the union of which will be defined to be the *language specified by the canonic system*

The usual punctuation signs are $\vdash, \langle, \rangle, <$, and ;.

SUBSTITUTION AND DETACHMENT

An *instance* of a canon is the result of substituting strings from V* for the variables that appear in the canon. Substitution must be uniform: occurrences of a single variable must all be replaced by the same string. The rule of inference (called *modus ponens*, or *detachment*) states that if $R_1; \ldots; R_{n-1} \vdash R_n$ is an instance of a canon, the remark R_n can be derived (in the canonic system) only if the premises $R_1; \ldots; R_{n-1}$ are all in the system. (Note that in the case of an "axiom" there are no premises). R_n is then immediately derived from $R_1, \ldots, R_{n-1}$. A *proof* or derivation of a remark R in a canonic system $\mathscr{C}$ is a finite sequence of remarks $R_1, \ldots, R_n$, R every member of which can be immediately derived from one or more of the preceding remarks. R is in $\mathscr{C}$ (can be derived or proven in $\mathscr{C}$) if and only if there exists a proof for R in $\mathscr{C}$.

7.6.1 Example: Syntax Specification

In this section we present an example of the use of canonic systems to specify the syntax of a programming language. Our example defines the same FORTRAN subset that was used to demonstrate the use of Backus Naur Form. A canonic system specification of this same subset is given in Figure 7.5.

```
1  ⊢ A+B+C . . . +Z letter
2  ℓ letter ⊢ ℓ identifier
3  ℓ letter; y identifier | yℓ identifier
4  y identifier ⊢ GO TO y go to stm
5  i identifier; x go to stm ⊢ ix program
6  i identifier; x go to stm; p program ⊢ ixp program
```

FIGURE 7.5 Canonic system specification of syntax

We can generate programs using this specification. For example, the string

    A GO TO B

may be generated using the fifth canon with the terminal string substituted as below:

    A identifier; GO TO B go to stm ⊢ A GO TO B program

A is in *letter* by the axiom (1) and so by (2) is in *identifier*. Therefore, the first premise of canon 5 is satisfied. The second premise may be satisfied by using canons 4, 2, and 1. Therefore, the following sequence using substitutions and modus ponens repeatedly derives A GO TO B *program*: (see Fig. 7.6).

```
1  A letter              C.1, MP
2  A identifier           1,C.2, MP
3  B letter
4  B identifier
5  GO TO B gotostm        4,C.4, MP
6  A GO TO B program      5,2,C.5, MP
```
(k, Cn, MP ~ Mp = Modus Ponens; Cn = canon in fig. 7.5; k = line in this fig.)

FIGURE 7.6 Derivation of a string in a canonic system

We now construct a canonic system that specifies the same language but with the restriction that all reference labels appear among the statement labels. Thus the program below

```
A  GO TO  B
C  GO TO  D
```

will not be a legal program because the reference labels B and D are not among the statement labels A and C. To effect this restriction, we will eventually generate a set of ordered triples: a program, a list of reference labels in the program, and a list of statement labels in the program. Out of this set we want only the programs containing reference labels bearing the relationship *in* to the list of statement labels. To accomplish this, we rewrite the canonic system of Figure 7.5, as follows:

7 ⊢ A+B+C . . .+Z *letter*
8 ℓ *letter* ⊢ ℓ *identifier*
9 ℓ *letter;* y *identifier* ⊢ yℓ *identifier*
10 y *identifier* ⊢ ⟨GO TO y<y⟩ *go to stm with ref label*

Canons 7-9 are similar to those used previously. However, 10 differs in that it defines a set of ordered pairs. Each member of this set consists of a pair of strings, GO TO y and y. That is, each element consists of a GO TO statement with a reference label, and the reference label. When generating the code for legal GO TO statements, we also must keep track of the reference labels.

11 s *identifier;* ⟨x<r⟩ *go to stm with ref label* ⊢ ⟨s x<s,<r,⟩ *prog with stm labels and ref labels*

The above canon defines a set of ordered triplets. The first element of one of the members of this set is a string consisting of an identifier followed by a GO TO statement; the second element is the statement label; the third element is the reference label.

An instance of the canon scheme number 11 is

A *identifier;* ⟨GO TO MZ<MZ⟩ *go to stm with ref label* ⊢
⟨A GO TO MZ<A,<MZ,⟩ *prog with stm labels and ref lables*

12 i *identifier;* ⟨x<ℓ⟩ *go to stm with ref label;*
⟨p<s<r⟩ *prog with stm labels and ref labels*
⊢ ⟨i x p<si,<rℓ,⟩ *prog with stm labels and ref labels*

Canon 12 above generates the set of ordered triplets of which the first element is a program consisting of GO TO statements; the second element is a list of statement labels; and the third element is a list of reference labels (elements of the lists are separated by commas).

13 $\langle p_<s_<r \rangle$ *program with stm labels and ref labels;* $\langle r_<s \rangle$ *in* ⊢ p *program*

The above canon states that given an ordered triplet of which the first element is a program, the next element is a list of statement labels, and the third is a list of reference labels; given also that the list of reference labels bears the relationship *in* to the list of statement labels, then the program is a legal program. We now define the relationship *in* as a set of ordered pairs of which the first element is a list and the second element is a list of labels containing those of the first list.

Canons 14-16 define *list*:

14   ⊢ λ *list*
15   i *identifier* ⊢ i, *list*
16   x *list;* y *list* ⊢ xy *list*

Canons 17 and 18 define the predicate *in*:

17   x *list;* y *list;* z *list* ⊢ $\langle y_<xyz \rangle$ *in*
18   $\langle a_<\ell \rangle$ *in;* $\langle b_<\ell \rangle$ *in* ⊢ $\langle ab_<\ell \rangle$ *in*

Canons 7-18 together define the set of legal programs.

7.6.2 Specification of Translation

Canonic systems may be used to specify the translation of a language. A translation is a function and may be defined by a set of ordered pairs, of which the first element is a legal program and the second element is its translation into the target language. For example, a specification of the translation of PL/I into 360 assembly language ultimately specifies the set of ordered pairs:

$\langle$legal PL/I program $_<$ 360 assembly-language program$\rangle$

Figure 7.7 is a canonic system specifying the translation of the GO TO subset of FORTRAN into the assembly language of the IBM 360 (BAL). For simplicity of this specification, we have not included the restriction that reference labels be in the list of statement labels, nor, as would be the case in real BAL, have we limited the length of identifiers.

$\vdash$ A$_+$B$_+$C$_+$ . . . Z *letter*
ℓ *letter* $\vdash$ ℓ *identifier*
ℓ *letter*; y *identifier* $\vdash$ yℓ *identifier*
y *identifier* $\vdash$ ⟨GO TO y$_<$B y⟩ *go to stm with translation*
i *identifier*; ⟨x$_<$y⟩ *go to stm with translation* $\vdash$ ⟨ix$_<$iy⟩ *translation*
i *identifier*; ⟨x$_<$y⟩ *go to stm with translation*; ⟨p$_<$t⟩ *translation* $\vdash$ ⟨ixp$_<$iyt⟩ *translation*

FIGURE 7.7 A canonic system specification of the translation of a subset of FORTRAN to BAL

7.6.3 Recognition and Translation Algorithm

Canonic systems specify a language by a set of rules that may generate legal strings. An interesting problem arises: can a canonic system be used as a basis for recognizing strings from the defined set? In addition, if the members of the defined set are ordered pairs, triplets, etc., can the algorithm be used to produce the missing terms corresponding to a given term? One straightforward recognition algorithm would be simply to generate all possible strings until a match is found. This section discusses a more efficient algorithm, which is capable of recognizing strings produced by a Backus-Naur Form system. It was developed by Alsop as an extension of an algorithm presented by Cheatham and Sattley.

The algorithm, which has been implemented on a timesharing system at M.I.T., allows a user to type in a canonic system specification of a language and its translation and to type in strings of the language. The program will proceed to recognize the strings and produce the corresponding translation. The algorithm is presented in this chapter in order to illustrate techniques used in syntax directed compilers and recursion.

The program has two phases. A preliminary phase checks the syntax of the canonic system used. The principal phase scans the input string, determines whether it satisfies the canonic-system definition, and generates any associated translations. The algorithm is principally *top-down*; it attempts first to match the input string against the sentence predicate of the canonic system (e.g., *program*), and it arrives only through recursion at a lower-level predicate (e.g., *integer* or *digit*).

The following is a simplified statement of the algorithm for canonic systems involving only predicates of degree 1. The simplified algorithm (Fig. 7.8) will later be expanded to include more general cases.

Imagine an arbitrary character string with an imaginary pointer to the left of the first character, and a canonic system defining a set of strings. We wish to determine whether the character string is a member of the set.

Step 1. The program considers in sequence those canons directly defining the string in question, and performs the following steps (2 through 6) for each such canon.

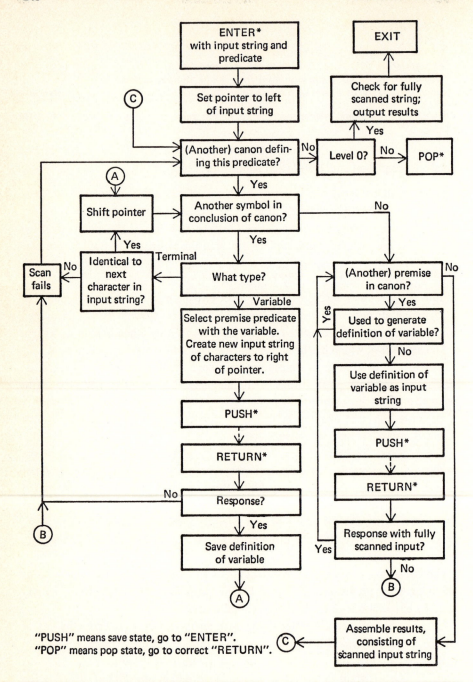

FIGURE 7.8 Flowchart of simplified algorithm

Step 2. The conclusion of the canon is matched, item by item, against the input string. If the item in the conclusion is a terminal character, step 3 is performed; if a variable, step 4 is performed. If the end of the canon is reached, the algorithm proceeds to step 5.

Step 3. The item in the conclusion is a terminal character. It is compared with the character in the input string to the right of the pointer. If they are identical, the program returns to step 2 to consider the next item in the conclusion, with the pointer shifted one position to the right. If not, the scan fails and the program returns to step 1 to consider any remaining canons that might produce the string.

Step 4. The item in the conclusion is a variable, and the program must determine by recursion the definition of the variable in terms of the input string. In other words, it must determine the number of characters from the input string, commencing with the character to the right of the pointer, which should be allotted to the definition of this variable. To accomplish this, the program assembles a new input string, which is a copy of all input characters to the right of the pointer, and picks a predicate among the premises of the canon that contains the variable. After saving its present state in a stack ("pushing"), the program returns to step 1 to determine the definition of the variable by examining the canons defining the premise predicate chosen. If there is no response upon return, the scan fails and the program returns to step 1 to consider alternative definitions of the string. If there is a response, the program compares it with the original input string to determine the definition of the variable and moves the pointer to its new position following the definition. The algorithm returns to step 2.

Step 5. The scan of the conclusion is complete, and the definition (in terms of the input characters) of the variables appearing in the conclusion has been recorded. The algorithm now inspects the premises. Those premises used in step 4 to determine the definitions of the variables in the conclusion may already be asserted, since they were used to generate the definitions. However, a variable may appear twice in the premises, and we must insure that the string which forms the definition of the variable is a member of both sets. The algorithm forms an input string from the definition of the variable and operates recursively to determine if the other premise containing the variable is also true; i.e., if the string which is the definition of the variable is also a member of the second set named as a premise predicate. Upon return, if there is no response, the algorithm returns to step 1 to pursue alternatives as before. If there is a response, the program insures that the string has been fully scanned. If there are still more unchecked premises, it treats them in the same manner. After all such premises have been successfully verified, the simplified algorithm proceeds to the last step.

Step 6. The results of the scan at this level, which constitute the response for the next higher level of calling are assembled. There are no results if the scan failed. Otherwise, they consist of the input string with the mental pointer resting at the spot where the scan of the conclusion was completed. The algorithm now returns to step 1 if there are more canons directly defining the set of which the input string is possibly a member. Since each canon could conceivably add to the results, the program must actually be equipped to handle multiple results and hence multiple responses at the next higher level, and check out each possibility. The example which follows will serve to clarify the problem. If there are no further canons, the program proceeds to step 7.

Step 7. The program "pops" its state — that is, it returns to pick up where it left off at the next higher level. If the highest level has been reached, then the results are examined for a completely scanned input string. If such a condition is found, the input string is a member of the originally defined set. If not, there exists a syntax error in the string. It is not clear that the set of all syntactically incorrect strings will be detected by the algorithm; this recognition problem is unsolvable in general.

A simple example will serve to illustrate the process and the problems involved in multiple answers. Consider the following canonic system:

1 ⊢ 1 *digit*
2 ⊢ 2 *digit*
3 ⊢ 3 *digit*
4 d *digit* ⊢ d *integer*
5 d *digit*; i *integer* ⊢ di *integer*

We wish to determine by use of the algorithm whether the string 31 is in *integer*. The process is described in the shorthand fashion below (Fig. 7.9). For simplicity and efficiency in the algorithm, canons are not allowed to be right-recursive (e.g., the canon

i *integer*; d *digit* ⊢ id *integer*

is not allowed)

Figure 7.10 outlines an extension of the algorithm that handles predicates of degree greater than 1, for which one or more of the terms are not known and are desired as translated output.

Step	Recursion level	Input string	Canon considered	Result(s)	Next action
1	0	↓ 31	4	—	Push for *digit*
2	1	↓ 31	1	Fails	Next canon
3	1	↓ 31	2	Fails	Next canon
4	1	↓ 31	3	3↓1 *digit*	Pop
5	0	3↓ 1	4	3↓1 *integer*	Next canon
6	0	↓31	5	—	Push for *digit*
7	1	↓31	1	Fails	Next canon
8	1	↓31	2	Fails	Next canon
9	1	↓31	3	3↓ 1 *digit*	Pop
10	0	3↓1	5	—	Push for *integer*
11	1	↓1	4	—	Push for *digit*
12	2	↓1	1	↓1 *digit*	Next canon
13	2	↓1	2	Fails	Next canon
14	2	↓1	3	Fails	Pop
15	1	1↓	4	1↓ *integer*	Next canon
16	1	↓1	5	—	Push for *digit*
17	2	↓1	1	1↓ *digit*	Next canon
18	2	↓1	2	Fails	Next canon
19	2	↓1	3	Fails	Pop
20	1	1↓	5	—	Push for *integer*
21	2		4	—	Push for *digit*
22	3	↓	1	Fails	Next canon
23	3	↓	2	Fails	Next canon
24	3	↓	3	Fails	Pop
25	2	↓	4	Fails	Next canon
26	2	↓	5	—	Push for *digit*
27	3	↓	1	Fails	Next canon
28	3	↓	2	Fails	Next canon
29	3	↓	3	Fails	Pop
30	2		5	Fails	Pop
31	1		5	1↓ *integer*	Pop
32	0		5	31 ↓ *integer*	
				3↓1 *integer*	Done

FIGURE 7.9 Steps in the recognition of a string

7.7 CANONIC SYSTEMS AND FORMAL SYSTEMS

Robert Mandl has proven a general theorem relating canonic systems to various types of formal grammars.

THEOREM: For every type of grammar there exists a class of canonic systems with the property that for every grammar of the type under consideration there exists a canonic system that generates the same

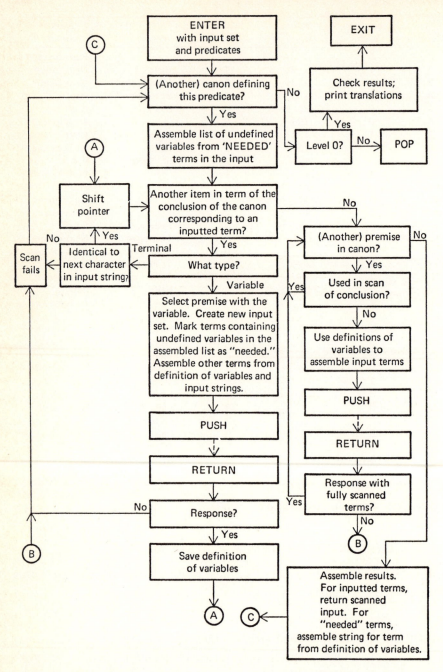

FIGURE 7.10 Flowchart of general algorithm to recognize and generate missing terms

language and that belongs to a corresponding class. Further, that class of canonic systems can be constructed.

We give one example of an equivalence proof: the equivalence of a class of canonic systems to linear grammars. First we establish a correspondence of elements of a canonic system (C, V, M, P, S, D) to elements of a grammar (N, T, P, Σ). Then we show that both systems generate the same strings.

We also choose D = $\{\Sigma\}$, and call Σ the *sentence symbol* (*sentence predicate*).

Definition 13:   A canonic system is a right-linear single-premise canonic system (RLCS) if each canon is of the form $\vdash$ a A or xA $\vdash$ ax B, where xϵM; A, B ϵP; aϵV.

THEOREM: For every regular grammar there is a right-linear single-premise canonic system that generates the same language and, conversely, for every RLCS there is a regular grammar generating the same language. (A similar result holds for LLCS, the left-linear counterpart.) In other words, the class of RLCS is equivalent in generative power to the class of regular grammars.

Proof: 1) Let G = (N_G, T_G, P_G, Σ), be a regular grammar. Construct the following RLCS: $\mathscr{C}$ = (C, V, M, P, S, Σ), where

$V = T_G$
$M = \{x\}$
$P = \{A \mid A \epsilon N_G\}$
$S = \{; , \vdash\}$
$C = \begin{cases} \vdash aA \text{ for every production A} \rightarrow \text{a in } P_G \\ xB \vdash axA \text{ for every production A} \rightarrow \text{aB in } P_G \end{cases}$

To prove that the grammar and the canonic system generate the same set, we show by construction how a derivation in either of these two formal systems can be simulated step-by-step by a derivation in the other system. The proof will be by induction on the number of steps used in the derivation.

BASIS OF INDUCTION A one-step derivation in $\mathscr{C}$ must be of the form $\vdash$ a A, and when a A is assertable in a derivation in $\mathscr{C}$; A $\rightarrow$ a is then applicable in a derivation in G.

A one-step derivation in G must be of the form A $\rightarrow$ a (this is a derivation "from A"). When this production is applicable, $\vdash$ a A is assertable and is the corresponding one-step derivation in $\mathscr{C}$.

INDUCTION STEP   We assume for derivations of up to k-1 steps that the simulation is possible, in both directions. By hypothesis a k-1 step canonic-system derivation of $\omega\, B$ corresponds to a proof in G: B $\Rightarrow$* ω; and vice versa. At the kth step of the derivation, if a canon $\vdash a\, A$ (a production A $\rightarrow$ a) is used, we are in a situation similar to that considered above, under "Basis of induction;" if the other type of canon (production) is used, we distinguish between the two directions of simulation:

a) (Derivation in the canonic system simulated by the grammar)   Assume that a canon of the form x $B \vdash ax\, A$ is used in the kth step of a derivation; its applicability implies the existence of a proof in $\mathscr{C}$ of ωB. Since this derivation takes only k-1 steps, by the induction hypothesis we have B $\Rightarrow$* ω in G.

An instance of x $B \vdash ax\, A$ with x = ω completes a proof of a$\omega\, A$ in $\mathscr{C}$. The corresponding rule A $\rightarrow$ a B in G yields A $\Rightarrow$* aω.

Therefore all derivations in $\mathscr{C}$ can be simulated step-by-step by derivations in G, including in particular the Σ-derivations. This proves L($\mathscr{C}$) = L(G).

b) (Derivation in the grammar, simulated by the canonic system)   Consider a k-step derivation A $\Rightarrow$* ω. Suppose that the first production applied is A $\rightarrow$ aB; its applicability implies the existence of a string ω', $\omega' \epsilon T*_G$, such that B $\Rightarrow$* ω' in G is k-1 steps long and ω=aω'. By the induction hypothesis this k-1 step derivation in G can be simulated by a k-1 step derivation in $\mathscr{C}$. The canon corresponding to the rule A $\rightarrow$ aB is

    x $B \vdash$ ax A

Substituting ω' for x yields a k-step proof ... ωA in $\mathscr{C}$. Hence $\Sigma \Rightarrow$* ω in G implies that $\omega \Sigma$ is in $\mathscr{C}$, and L($\mathscr{C}$) = L(G).

Proof: 2) Let $\mathscr{C}$ = (C , V , M , P , S , Σ) be a RLCS. Construct G, G = (N_G , T_G , P_G , Σ)

$$N_G = \{A \mid A \epsilon P\}$$
$$T_G = V$$
$$P_G = \begin{cases} A \rightarrow a, \text{ for every } \vdash a\, A \text{ in C;} \\ A \rightarrow aB, \text{ for every } x\, B \vdash ax\, A \text{ in C} \end{cases}$$

Σ corresponds to Σ

This argument gives L($\mathscr{C}$) = L(G). QED

Notice that these systems are strongly equivalent (derivation-for-derivation equivalent), thus

THEOREM: The class of RLCS and the class of regular grammars are strongly equivalent.

Much of the research into formal systems and grammars concerns their generative power and the structure and complexity of their languages; these qualities are interrelated. We described at the beginning of this chapter some of the motivation behind complexity studies. Underlying all such work is the desire to simplify linguistics into a form that can be productively used and analyzed. Language is too complicated and varied, so we turn to formal systems. But the mere existence of a formalism does not solve our problems.

Many formal systems — for example, canonic systems and type 0 grammars — have inherent undecidability problems: in general, there is no algorithm capable of telling after a finite amount of time whether or not a given string is in the language of a given grammar. (Recall our definition of decidability in section 7.2.) Studies of generative power help us to understand how characteristics of a grammar correspond to structural features of languages and to choose the weakest grammar suitable to a given situation. At the same time, by exploring restrictions we learn about the structure of language.

Figure 7.11 is an inclusion diagram of the relationships between certain classes of grammars. Classes of systems in the diagram include all classes below them (that is, at nodes below them in the tree). The diverging branches represent classes for which inclusion either does not exist or is not presently known.

Complexity is an intuitive notion, and no satisfactory measure for it has yet been proposed. We use the term "complexity" of a formula to mean some measure of the difficulty involved in generating or recognizing it; complexity *measures* will be used to compare formulae or languages. Possible measures are the length of proof; the length of a string; or the "height" (length of longest path of branches) of the tree-diagram of a derivation. In the case of canonic systems, one might count the number of remarks considered in a proof. These measures all deal with aspects of *structure*. Another way of getting at structure is to consider a machine, or automaton corresponding to a formal system: a complexity measure might be given in terms of some characteristic of the machine, for example, the amount of memory it requires, or the number of steps it takes.

Alternately, a measure might treat the meaning or "depth" of formulae — semantic notions. Another sort of measure might involve the difficulty of recognizing a formula, and perhaps of constructing a derivation for it. In this latter case a short or structurally simple formula might have a high measure of complexity if it involved ambiguities or if it were similar, superficially or structurally, to many other formulae.

It is obvious that these proposed measures are not in complete agreement: they lead to very different orderings of the formulae in a language and of different languages. In the case of language-translating systems, we can consider the complexity measures of equivalent formulae in different languages; we might

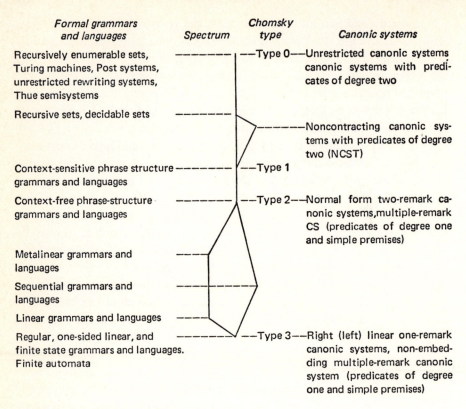

FIGURE 7.11 Corresponding hierarchies

ask, for example, whether a given translation algorithm preserves the ordering of complexities under a given measure.

The structure of a formula or sentence is important because in it lies much of the meaning of the sentence. (See the phrase-structure example in section 7.2.1.) Ambiguity is thus of special interest. (For example, there is a theorem that states that some context-free languages are inherently ambiguous, that is, they have no unambiguous context-free grammars.) When we say that two grammars both generate a given sentence, we may want to know also whether they give the same structure for the sentence. This question relates to complexity because complexity is a structural notion.

7.8 SUMMARY

We have explored the practical use of formal systems in defining, studying, and implementing programming languages and language processors. We defined some terminology of *formal linguistics* (the study of grammars, formal systems, and languages). BNF was presented as a method of defining syntax and translation and of studying programming languages.

As an example of research currently being conducted in this area, canonic systems were defined, some formal properties were investigated, and their power was diagrammed. We showed how canonic systems can be used to define language features that BNF, a context-free grammar, cannot specify. Finally, we discussed the notion of a complexity measure.

QUESTIONS

1. Consider the following BNF specification of simple arithmetic expressions
    such as A + 2 ∗ C:

    (1)   ⟨arith⟩ : := ⟨arith⟩ + ⟨term⟩ I ⟨term⟩
    (2)   ⟨term⟩ : := ⟨factor⟩*⟨term⟩ I ⟨factor⟩
    (3)   ⟨factor⟩ : :=⟨symbol⟩ I ⟨number⟩
    (4)   ⟨number⟩ : := 0 I 1 I 2 I 3
    (5)   ⟨symbol⟩ : := [⟨letter⟩]$_1^8$
    (6)   ⟨letter⟩ : := A I B I C I D

    Note: [⟨letter⟩]$_1^8$ means 1 to 8 letters. It is shorthand for
    ⟨letter⟩ I⟨letter⟩ ⟨letter⟩ I⟨letter⟩ ⟨letter⟩ ⟨letter⟩ I . . .).

Now consider:

THETA + SIGMA + 2 ∗ 4 ∗ ALPHA + MOO

and its "parse tree":

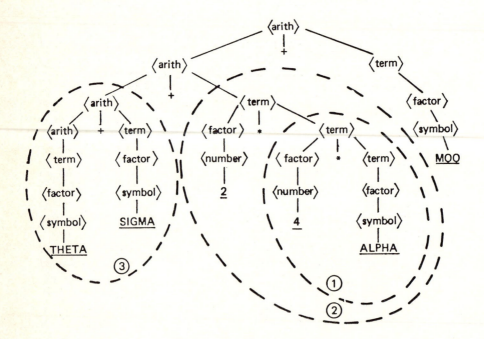

or its "compact parse tree":

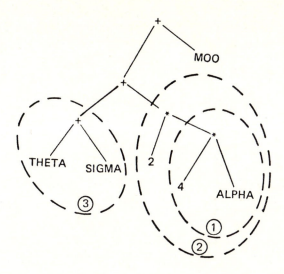

Each dashed circle encloses a sub-tree (headed by one node) of the entire tree. These three sub-trees show examples of left-recursion, right-recursion, and precedence in BNF. Precedence is the implied order of computation of the operators in the sub-trees.

a. Sub-tree ① must be evaluated before the "*" operation of sub-tree ② can be done. Thus in "2 * 4 * ALPHA", the "4 * ALPHA" is computed first and the parse is (2 * (4 * ALPHA)). Thus multiplication proceeds *right to left*. This results from the *right recursion* in rule (2) of the BNF above. There ": := ⟨factor⟩*⟨term⟩" says ⟨term⟩ (which can contain multipliers) is an input on the right side to "*" and must be performed before the "*" can. ⟨factor⟩ on the left can contain no operators. Right recursion yields right to left evaluation of the operator.

b. Sub-tree ③ shows the *left recursion* of "+" which results from rule (1) of the BNF above. Rule (1) says ": :=⟨arith⟩+⟨term⟩ . . ." meaning ⟨arith⟩ (which can contain additions) is input on the left side to "+" and must be performed. Thus addition proceeds left to right. Left recursion yields left to right evaluation of the operator.

c. Sub-tree ② illustrates the precedence (or higher priority) of "*" over "+" since the ②* (sub-tree ①) of sub-tree ② must be evaluated before the "+" from which the tree hangs can be performed. This precedence of "*" over "+" is expressed in rule (1) of the above BNF when ": := ⟨arith⟩ + ⟨term⟩" states ⟨term⟩ which can contain multiplications is input to "+" and must be evaluated before "+". In general, if

⟨foo⟩ is input to operator ∝ and a ⟨foo⟩ can contain operator λ then λ has precedence over ∝.

Finally, recursion and precedence relate. In our example, the right "*" has precedence over (is performed before) the left "*"; the left "+" has precedence over the right "+".

PROBLEM
Concerning the language defined by the following BNF:

   (1)   ⟨sentence⟩ : := ⟨clause⟩ Δ ⟨sentence⟩ I ⟨clause⟩
   (2)   ⟨clause⟩ : := ⟨clause⟩ □ ⟨foo⟩ I ⟨word⟩ $ ⟨cough⟩
   (3)   ⟨foo⟩ : := ⟨word⟩ I ⟨mumble⟩
   (4)   ⟨word⟩ : := ⟨word⟩ $ ⟨char⟩ I ⟨char⟩
   (5)   ⟨mumble⟩ : := ⟨char⟩ Δ ⟨char⟩
   (6)   ⟨cough⟩ : := ⟨cough⟩ Δ ⟨char⟩ I ⟨char⟩ □ ⟨char⟩
   (7)   ⟨char⟩ : := A I B I C I D

  a. Which rules contain recursion? Identify it as left or right and quote the part(s) of the rule that contain the recursion. Please identify the rules by number.
  b. Which rules express a precedence relation between different operators? Quote the part (parts) of the rule and state what relationship(s) they imply.
  c. If you did (b) correctly you found different rules implying opposite relationships between the same two operators. This is not wrong or even ambiguous or inconsistent. Why? (Hint: When does a relationship expressed by a rule apply? Not everywhere!) (See next question.)
  d. Show the "parse tree" of "A $ C □ D Δ D"

2. List four ways in which formal systems are useful in compilers or programming languages.

3. a. Differentiate among:

    1) A grammar
    2) A language
    3) A machine

  b. Which of the above describes the behavior of a BNF specification? Of a canonic system?
  c. What is the relationship between a BNF and a canonic system?

4. What is the difficulty in using a generative grammar (capable of describing language in question) to determine the legality of a particular string?

5. a. Why is BNF unsatisfactory for completely describing some languages?
  b. How do canonic systems overcome this deficiency?

6. The following Backus-Naur form grammar generates "string expressions" which contain string operands and binary operators. The transformations indicated by these operators are:

Operator	Description	Definition
‖	Concatenate - -	ABC ‖ DE ‖ G $\triangleq$ ABCDEG
*	Imbedded in - -	AB * CD $\triangleq$ CDABCD
		X * AB $\triangleq$ ABXAB
-	Less all	ABCDBABC - BC $\triangleq$ ADBA
	occurrences of - -	XX-X $\triangleq$ Λ

The BNF specification is:

```
<string expression>: :=
      <partial string>|<string expression>‖<partial string>
<partial string>: :=
      <partial string>-<nested strings>|<nested string>
<nested string>: :=
      <basic string>|<nested string>*<basic string>
<basic string>: :=Λ|<basic string> <letter>
<letter>: := A | B | . . . | Y | Z
      where Λ represents the null string.
```

a. Generate two examples of legal string expressions (showing the parse tree). Use every rule at least once.
b. List the operators in order of precedence, highest precedence first (see problem 7.1 for definition of precedence).

In an arithmetic expression A+B*C, the rules for parsing this statement must make us pass over the + and examine the *. In other words, the rules must recognize that B is the left operand of * and not the right operand of +. In order to make this decision, in the absence of parentheses, we must look at the operators on both sides of an operand to see which operator it belongs to. It belongs to the operator with the highest precedence, or if both operators have the same precedence, it belongs to the left-most operator of the two. One may depict the relative precedence of operators in a two-dimensional array where the left operator is the one to the left of the operand.

c. Fill in the precedence array indicating the relative precedence of each pair of operators:

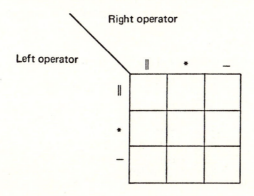

7. In Chapter 8 (Compilers), Figure 8.16, there is a BNF specification of a very small subset of PL/I.

   a. Show the parse tree of:

   COST = RATE*(START-FINISH)+2*RATE*(START-FINISH-100)

   b. Show the parse tree of the program in Figure 8.1.
   c. Is there any precedence expressed between the arithmetic operators (+,-,*,/) of this subset? In what order are arithmetic operations performed in an expression? Is this order ambiguous? Are parenthesized expressions legal?
   d. Extend the BNF to have regular arithmetic precedence.

8. The following is a canonic system description of a language L.

   (1) $\vdash P_+ Q_+ R_+ S_+$ *letter*
   (2)   j *letter* $\vdash$ j *id*
   (3)   i *id* $\vdash$ i *primary*
   (4)   j *letter* ; i *id* $\vdash$ ij *id*
   (5)   q *primary* $\vdash$ q *term*
   (6)   t *term* ; q *primary* $\vdash$ t*q *term*
   (7)   t *term* $\vdash$ t *exp*
   (8)   t *term* ; e *exp* $\vdash$ e+t *exp*
   (9)   e *exp* $\vdash$ (e) *primary*

   a. Are any precedence relations expressed between "+" and "*"? If so, which cannon(s) express them and what are they?
   b. L already has parenthesized expressions (by cannon (9)). Add the exponentiation operator "$" to L. "$" has precedence over "*" and "+". "$" should evaluate right to left. Thus:

           P + Q * R $ S   *means*   P + (Q * (R $S))
   and   P + Q $ R $ S   *means*   P + (Q $ (R $S))

9. Any BNF system may be written as an equivalent canonic system and sometimes a canonic system can be written as an equivalent BNF system. The canonic system of problem 8 can be written in BNF. One technique to write the BNF equivalent is to:

   1) For every canon, write one BNF rule.
   2) Let the canonic system's predicates (the italicized names) be the nonterminals in BNF (the bracketed names).

   EXAMPLES

Canonic system	BNF
$\vdash P_+Q_+R_+S$ *letter*	⟨letter⟩ : := P | Q | R | S
j *letter* $\vdash$ j *id*	⟨id⟩ : := ⟨letter⟩
j *letter* ; i *id* $\vdash$ ij *id*	⟨id⟩ : := ⟨id⟩ ⟨letter⟩

a. Following our example, write the BNF equivalent of the canonic system of problem 8.

b. A canonic system can express a language more complex than BNF (or context free) languages. Such a language cannot have a BNF equivalent. Does the following have a BNF equivalent? If so, write it. If not, indicate which canons and predicates cannot be expressed in BNF.

$$
\begin{aligned}
&(1) \quad \vdash A_{+}B_{+}C_{+}D \text{ } letter \\
&(2) \quad \vdash 0_{+}1_{+}2_{+}3 \text{ } digit \\
&(3) \quad \text{a } letter \vdash \text{a } thing \\
&(4) \quad \text{a } letter \text{ \& b } thing \vdash \text{ab } thing \\
&(5) \quad \vdash \wedge \text{ } list \\
&(6) \quad \text{i } thing \vdash \text{i, } list \\
&(7) \quad a_{+}\text{b } list \vdash \text{ab } list \\
&(8) \quad a_{+}b_{+}\text{c } list \vdash \text{b } in \text{ abc} \\
&(9) \quad \text{a } in \text{ m \& b } in \text{ m} \vdash \text{ab } in \text{ m} \\
&(10) \quad \text{t } thing \vdash \text{GOTO t } goto\text{-}stmt \\
&(11) \quad \text{t } thing \text{ \& s } thing \vdash \text{s=t } assign\text{-}label\text{-}stmt \\
&(12) \quad \text{s } goto\text{-}stmt \vdash \text{s } stmt\text{-}seq \\
&(13) \quad \text{s } assign\text{-}label\text{-}stmt \vdash \text{s } stmt\text{-}seq
\end{aligned}
$$

10. Suggest a possible measure of complexity for a language or a translator specified by a canonic system.

11. Take as a simple measure $m(C,t)$ of a theorem t in a canonic system C as the number of remarks in the shortest proof of t in C. That is, if r_1, $r_2, \ldots$, rk is the shortest proof of t in C then $m(C,t)=k$.

a. If t is a theorem of C, then prove $m(C,t)$ is computable.

b. Take a new measure function $m'(C,n)=\text{maximum} \left\{ m(C,t) \mid t \text{ is provable in C and } |t| = n \right\}$;

under what conditions is m' computable?

c. Prove that all canonic systems can be reduced to a canonic system of only single premise canons.

d. Find a correspondence between this measure function and the number of steps it may take to *recognize* a string t defined by a canonic system C.

12. a. For your measure function of problem 10, prove the theorems of problems 11a and 11b.

b. Find a closed form for upper and lower bounds of your measure function.

8

compilers

This chapter has two purposes:

1. To present a general model of a compiler that may be used as a basis for designing and studying compilers.
2. To create an appreciation of the difficulty and 'cost' of implementing and using particular features of languages.

To accomplish this, we have divided the chapter into three parts.

PART 1   presents a simple example and introduces a general model of a compiler.

PART 2   elaborates upon the model and explains its inner workings in detail.

PART 3   uses the model to demonstrate the implementation of advanced features discussed in Chapter 6 (e.g., data structures, recursion, storage allocation, block structure, conditions, and pointers).

PART 1

8.1   STATEMENT OF PROBLEM

A compiler accepts a program written in a higher level language as input and produces its machine language equivalent as output. Here in Part 1, we examine a simple PL/I program and become familiar with the issues we must face in trying to compile it.

```
WCM: PROCEDURE (RATE,START,FINISH);
      DECLARE (COST,RATE,START,FINISH) FIXED BINARY (31)STATIC;
      COST = RATE * (START-FINISH) + 2 * RATE * (START-FINISH - 100);
      RETURN (COST);
END;
```

FIGURE 8.1 MINI-PL/I program example

What must the compiler do in order to produce the machine language equivalent of WCM?

1. Recognize certain strings as basic elements, e.g., recognize that COST is a variable, WCM is a label, PROCEDURE is a keyword, and "=" is an operator
2. Recognize combinations of elements as syntactic units and interpret their meaning, e.g., ascertain that the first statement is a procedure name with three arguments, that the next statement defines four variables to be fixed binary numbers of 31 bits, that the third statement is an assignment statement that requires seven computations, and that the last statement is a return statement with one argument
3. Allocate storage and assign locations for all variables in this program
4. Generate the appropriate object code

8.1.1 Problem No. 1 − Recognizing Basic Elements

The action of parsing the source program into the proper syntactic classes is known as *lexical analysis*. The program is scanned and separated as shown in Figure 8.2. The operational details for this step involve conceptually simple string processing techniques. The source program is scanned sequentially. The basic elements or tokens are delineated by blanks, operators, and special symbols, and thereby recognized as identifiers, literals, or terminal symbols (operators, keywords).

The basic elements (identifiers and literals) are placed into tables. As other phases recognize the use and meaning of the elements, further information is entered into these tables (e.g., precision, data type, length, and storage class).

Other phases of the compiler use the attributes of each basic element and must therefore have access to this information. Either all the information about each element is passed to other phases, or typically, the source string itself is converted into a string of "uniform symbols." Uniform symbols are of fixed size and consist of the syntactic class and a pointer to the table entry of the associated basic element. Figure 8.3 depicts uniform symbols for users.

Because the uniform symbols are of fixed size, converting to them makes the later phases of the compiler simpler. Also, testing for equality is now just a matter of comparing syntactic classes and pointers rather than comparing long character strings.

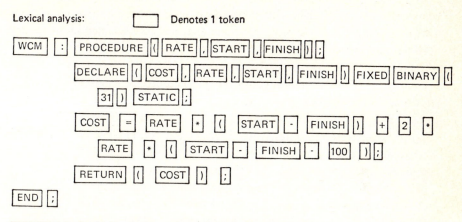

FIGURE 8.2 Lexical analysis — tokens of example program

This lexical process can be done in one continuous pass through the data by creating an intermediate form of the program consisting of a chain or table of tokens. Alternatively, some schemes reduce the size of the token table by only parsing tokens as necessary, and discarding those that are no longer needed. Current compilers use both of these approaches. Either method of lexical analysis will discover and note lexical errors (e.g., invalid characters and improper identifiers). The lexical phase also discards comments since they have no effect on the processing of the program.

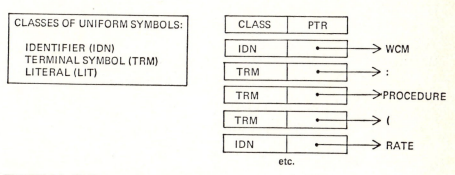

FIGURE 8.3 Uniform symbols of first statement

Notice that the uniform symbol is the same length whether the token is 1 or 31 characters long. Other phases of the compiler deal mainly with the small uniform symbol, but they may access any attribute of the token by following the pointer.

8.1.2 Problem No. 2 — Recognizing Syntactic Units and Interpreting Meaning

Once the program has been broken down into tokens or uniform symbols, the compiler must (1) recognize the phrases (syntactic construction); each phrase is a semantic entity and is a string of tokens that has an associated meaning; and (2) interpret the meaning of the constructions.

The first of these two steps is concerned solely with recognizing and thus separating the basic syntactical constructs in the source program. This process is known as *syntax analysis*. For our example, we arbitrarily take the statements as phrases. The program is scanned and separated as shown in Figure 8.4.

Syntactic analysis also notes syntactic errors and assures some sort of recovery so that the compiler can continue to look for other compilation errors. Some compilers attempt to guess what the programmer did wrong and correct it.

Once the syntax of a statement has been ascertained, the second step is to interpret the meaning (semantics). Associated with each syntactic construction is a defined meaning. This may be in the form of actual code or an intermediate form of the construction.

There are many ways of operationally recognizing the basic constructs (syntactical analysis) and interpreting their meaning. In Part 2, we chose to use very general methods. They use rules *(reductions)* which specify the syntax form of the source language. These reductions define the basic syntax constructions and the appropriate compiler routine *(action* routine) to be executed when a construction is recognized. The action routines interpret the meaning of the constructions and generate either code or an intermediate form of the construction. For example, a reduction might specify: "if an identifier is followed by an "="

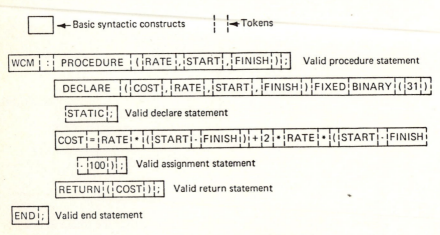

FIGURE 8.4 Syntax analysis — syntactic units of example program

sign, then call the action routine 'ARITHMETIC_STM'."

8.1.3 Intermediate Form

Once the syntactic construction is determined, the compiler can generate object code for each construction. Typically, however, the compiler creates an intermediate form of the source program. The intermediate form affords two advantages: (1) it facilitates optimization of object code; and (2) it allows a logical separation between the *machine-independent* phases (lexical, syntax, interpretation) and the *machine-dependent* phases (code generation and assembly).

Using an intermediate form raises two questions: (1) what form? and (2) what are the rules for converting source code into that form? The form depends on the syntactic construction, e.g., arithmetic, nonarithmetic, or nonexecutable statements.

8.1.3.1 ARITHMETIC STATEMENTS

One intermediate form of an arithmetic statement is a *parse tree*. From the formal methods of the previous chapter, e.g., the general syntax tree of problem 1, Chapter 7, we can obtain the parse tree of Figure 8.5. The rules for converting an arithmetic statement into a parse tree are:

1. Any variable is a terminal node of the tree.
2. For every operator, construct (in the order dictated by the rules of algebra) a binary (two-branched) tree whose left branch is the tree for operand 1 and whose right branch is the tree for operand 2.

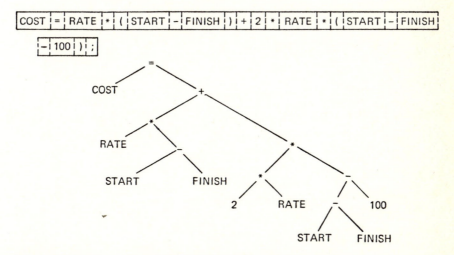

FIGURE 8.5 Tree − intermediate form of example arithmetic statement

The tree for the arithmetic statement of the example program is depicted in Figure 8.5.

Although this picture makes it easy for us to visualize the structure of the statement, it is not a practical method for a compiler.

The compiler may use as an intermediate form a linear representation of the parse tree called a *matrix*. In a matrix, operations of the program are listed sequentially in the order they would be executed. Each matrix entry has one operator and two operands.

The operands are uniform symbols denoting either variables, literals, or other matrix entries Mi (*i* denotes a matrix entry number). The matrix that would be generated for the arithmetic statement is depicted in Figure 8.6. (For ease of reading we use the actual symbols as entries instead of their uniform symbols.)

The tree (Fig. 8.5) and the matrix (Fig. 8.6) are equivalent representations of the assignment statement. The reader can form the tree of such a statement using rules of elementary algebra. The process of constructing a tree or matrix from an arithmetic statement is the subject of many compiler books. We leave it as an exercise for the reader (see question 1 of Chapter 7).

8.1.3.2 NONARITHMETIC STATEMENTS

The problem of creating an accurate intermediate form for nonarithmetic executable statements is similar to that for arithmetic ones. The statements DO, IF, GO TO, etc., can all be replaced by a sequential ordering of individual matrix entries (Fig. 8.7). The operators in the matrix are defined in later phases of the compiler so that proper code can be produced.

```
COST = RATE * ( START - FINISH ) + 2 * RATE * ( START - FINISH
- 100 ) ;
```

Matrix line no.	Operator	Operand 1	Operand 2
1	−	START	FINISH
2	*	RATE	M1
3	*	2	RATE
4	−	START	FINISH
5	−	M4	100
6	*	M3	M5
7	+	M2	M6
8	=	COST	M7

FIGURE 8.6 Matrix for example arithmetic statement

Source		*Matrix*		
		Operator	Operand 1	Operand 2
RETURN (COST);	→	Return	COST	
END;	→	End		

FIGURE 8.7 Example matrix for RETURN and END statement

8.1.3.3 NONEXECUTABLE STATEMENTS

Nonexecutable statements like DECLARE or FORTRAN's DIMENSION give the compiler information that clarifies the referencing or allocation of variables and associated storage. There is no intermediate form for these statements. Instead, the information contained in a nonexecutable statement is entered into tables, to be used by the other parts of the compiler. For instance, for the DECLARE statement in our example the interpretation phase would note the data type, precision, and storage class (FIXED BINARY, 31 bits, STATIC) in the identifier table for each of the variables COST, RATE, START, and FINISH (as in Fig. 8.8).[1]

In a high-powered language like PL/I where some storage allocation and data definition are delayed until execution time, certain tables are used by the object program as well as by the compiler. Therefore, some declarative information is passed on to the object program to be used at execution time.

So far we have discussed lexical analysis, syntactical analysis, and interpretation (semantics). Now we will discuss how the last two general problems associated with the PL/I example may be solved.

8.1.4 Problem No. 3 – Storage Allocation

At some time we must reserve the proper amounts of storage required by our program. In our example the DCL statement gives us the proper information:

```
DECLARE|(|COST|,|RATE|,|START|,|FINISH|)|FIXED|BINARY|(|31|)|
|STATIC|;|
```

The interpretation phase constructs the entries in the table of Figure 8.8.[1]

The storage allocation routine scans the identifier table and assigns a location to each scalar. In the case of fixed binary numbers of 32 bits, it will assign the first to relative location 0, the second to location 4, and so on. The absolute ad-

[1]For the variables RATE, START, FINISH the expression "STATIC" may cause an error warning by a full PL/I compiler. PL/I views them as a special storage class PARAMETER. For further details on how parameters may be implemented in full PL/I, one may wish to refer to Appendix B, section 5, Page 469.

Name	Base	Scale	Precision (bits)	Storage class	Location
COST	BINARY	FIXED	31	STATIC	0
RATE	BINARY	FIXED	31	STATIC	4
START	BINARY	FIXED	31	STATIC	8
FINISH	BINARY	FIXED	31	STATIC	12

FIGURE 8.8 Identifier table

dress is unknown until load time. The storage assignment phase must also assume that 4 words of 31 binary digits and 1 sign bit are allocated at load time. The compiler uses these relative assigned addresses in later phases for proper accessing.

Similarly, storage is assigned for the temporary locations that will contain intermediate results of the matrix (e.g., M1, M2, M3, M4, M5, M6, M7).

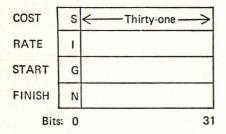

For a language like FORTRAN where all storage is assigned at compilation time, this is a straightforward procedure. We would look at an entry in the table, find its base, scale, and precision, and reserve the proper amount of storage. However, in a language like PL/I only STATIC storage is assigned this way. There are three other types of storage (AUTOMATIC, CONTROLLED, and BASED) that are not.

For variables declared as automatic, controlled, or based, information about each variable is included in the object deck and thus is available at execution time.

Further, the compiler generates for statements such as PROCEDURE, BEGIN, and ALLOCATE the proper object code to reserve the necessary storage for these variables. In a similar way, END, RETURN, and FREE statements must generate object code to free this dynamic storage for other use. This requires that these statements have associated entries in the matrix that will in turn cause the proper code to be generated.

Accessing this type of storage is difficult. Typically, the compiler doesn't even know whether or not it will be allocated, much less the location at which it is to be allocated. References to this type of data may be made relative to registers that can be updated at execution time to point at the dynamically allocated data.

8.1.5 Problem No. 4 — Code Generation

Once the compiler has created the matrix and tables of supporting information, it may generate the object code.

One scheme is to have a table (code production table) defining each type of matrix operation with the associated object code (Fig. 8.9). The code generation phase would scan the matrix and generate, for each entry, the code defined in the table using the operands of the matrix entries to further specialize the code. This process is depicted in Figure 8.10 using the code definitions of Figure 8.9. One way to view this scheme is that we are treating operators in the matrix as macro calls, operands as arguments, and the production table as macro definitions.

When we examine Figure 8.10 carefully, three questions arise.

1. Was it a good idea to generate code directly from the matrix? Lines 1 and 4 of our matrix are identical and thus resulted in redundant code.

2. Have we made the best use of the machine we have at our disposal? Lines 12 (ST 1,M4) and 13 (L 1,M4) of the generated code are wasteful; they do

Standard code definitions for -, *, +, =

-	L	1,&OPERAND1
	S	1,&OPERAND2
	ST	1,M&N
*	L	1,&OPERAND1
	M	0,&OPERAND2
	ST	1,M&N
+	L	1,&OPERAND1
	A	1,&OPERAND2
	ST	1,M&N
=	L	1,&OPERAND2
	ST	1,&OPERAND1

where &OPERAND1 is the first operand of the matrix, &OPERAND2 is the second operand, &N is the line number of the matrix entry being examined

FIGURE 8.9 Code definitions – productions for -, *, +, =

Matrix					*Generated code*	
1	–	START	FINISH		L S ST	1,START 1,FINISH 1,M1
2	*	RATE	M1		L M ST	1,RATE 0,M1 1,M2
3	*	2	RATE		L M ST	1,=F'2' 0,RATE 1,M3
4	–	START	FINISH		L S ST	1,START 1,FINISH 1,M4
5	–	M4	100		L S ST	1,M4 1,=F'100' 1,M5
6	*	M3	M5		L M ST	1,M3 0,M5 1,M6
7	+	M2	M6		L A ST	1,M2 1,M6 1,M7
8	=	COST	M7		L ST	1,M7 1,COST

FIGURE 8.10 Example code generation

not change the results of any computation. Also we have used only 2 out of the 16 registers and only one type instruction (RX) of the five types available on the 360. The RR instructions, which are faster, have not been used.

3. Can we generate machine language directly? The example used assembly language. What would have happened if one of the operands in the matrix was a label on a statement that wasn't generated yet?

The first two of these questions are issues of optimization. The first refers to the optimality of the matrix as an intermediate form (machine-independent) and the second to the optimality of the actual machine code (machine-dependent). A compiler resolves the issues raised in question 1 before those raised in question 2, since if the compiler eliminates the redundant code of question 1 it will not waste time trying to improve the eliminated code in question 2.

8.1.5.1 OPTIMIZATION (MACHINE-INDEPENDENT)

The issue raised by question 1 provides an example of one type of machine-independent optimization problem. Operationally, when a subexpression occurs in the same statement more than once (a common subexpression), we can delete all duplicate matrix entries and modify all references to the deleted entries so that they refer to the remaining copy of that subexpression (Fig. 8.11). The resulting code shown in the middle column of Figure 8.12 is an improvement over that in Figure 8.10.

Matrix with common subexpression / Matrix after elimination of common subexpression

1	–	START	FINISH		1	–	START	FINISH
2	*	RATE	M1		2	*	RATE	M1
3	*	2	RATE		3	*	2	RATE
4	–	START	FINISH		4			
5	–	M4	100		5	–	M1	100
6	*	M3	M5		6	*	M3	M5
7	+	M2	M6		7	*	M2	M6
8	=	COST	M7		8	=	COST	M7

FIGURE 8.11 Elimination of common subexpressions

Other machine-independent optimization steps are:

1. Compile time computation of operations, both of whose operands are constants

2. Movement of computations involving nonvarying operands out of loops

3. Use of the properties of Boolean expressions to minimize their computation

These will be discussed in more detail in Part 2. At this point it is important to realize that *machine-independent* optimization of the matrix is possible and that logically it should occur before we use the matrix as a basis for code generation. Such a process is called the optimization phase and is logically separated from code generation.

8.1.5.2 OPTIMIZATION (MACHINE-DEPENDENT)

The problems raised by question 2 can best be illustrated by comparing two possible versions of the code that can be generated from our optimized matrix example:

	Optimized matrix			First try		Improved code			
1	–	START	FINISH	L S ST	1,START 1,FINISH 1,M1	L S	1,START 1,FINISH	M1 → R1	
2	*	RATE	M1	L M ST	1,RATE 0,M1 1,M2	L MR	3,RATE 2,1	M2 → R3	
3	*	2	RATE	L M ST	1,=F'2' 0,RATE 1,M3	L M	5,=F'2' 4,RATE	M3 → R5	
4									
5	–	M1	100	L S ST	1,M1 1,=F'100' 1,M5	S	1,=F'100'	M5 → R1	
6	*	M3	M5	L M ST	1,M3 0,M5 1,M6	LR MR	7,5 6,1	M6 → R7	
7	+	M2	M6	L A ST	1,M2 1,M6 1,M7	AR	3,7	M7 → R3	
8	=	M7	COST	L ST	1,M7 1,COST	ST	3,COST		
					80 bytes		36 bytes		

FIGURE 8.12 Machine-dependent optimized code

Figure 8.12 depicts the matrix that we previously optimized by eliminating a common subexpression (M4). Next to each matrix entry is the code generated using the operators as defined in Figure 8.9. The third column is even better code in that it uses less storage and is faster due to a more appropriate mix of instructions. How did we get this more efficient version?

1. We made better use of temporary storage by employing as many of the 360's 16 registers as we could and by not storing our intermediate results unless necessary. This reduced the number of loads and stores from 14 to 5.
2. We used shorter and faster 360 instructions whenever possible (MR instead of M).

This example of machine-dependent optimization has reduced both the memory space needed for the program and the execution time of the object program by a factor of 2. Machine-dependent optimization is typically done while generating code. Operationally, we can extend the previous scheme of a code generator to that of a sophisticated macro processor with conditional macro pseudo-ops. In this way we could vary the instructions generated according to the availability and contents of temporary storage. This type of scheme would incorporate machine-dependent optimization into the code generation phase.

8.1.5.3 ASSEMBLY PHASE

In the beginning of this section we stated that the task of a compiler was to produce the *machine language* equivalent of a source program. Yet in our examples of code generation we have been producing assembly language. Literals and symbolic addresses are easier for the reader, but the compiler must create the actual machine language.

The compiler can generate references to actual core locations in place of literals and variables assigned by a storage allocation routine. However, labels cannot be assigned values until the final code has been generated. Therefore, coupled with code generation are:

1. Generating code
2. Defining labels and resolving all references

We separate (1) the code generation phase, and (2) the assembly phase since they are logically distinct and are often implemented as such. Operationally, the assembly phase is similar to pass 2 of the assembler.

8.1.6 General Model of Compiler

In analyzing the compilation of our simple PL/I program we have found seven distinct logical problems as follows and summarized in Figure 8.13.

1. *Lexical analysis* – recognition of basic elements and creation of uniform symbols
2. *Syntax analysis* – recognition of basic syntactic constructs through reductions
3. *Interpretation* – definition of exact meaning, creation of matrix and tables by action routines
4. *Machine independent optimization* – creation of more optimal matrix
5. *Storage assignment* – modification of identifier and literal tables. It makes entries in the matrix that allow code generation to create code that allo-

cates dynamic storage, and that also allow the assembly phase to reserve the proper amounts of STATIC storage.

6. *Code generation* – use of macro processor to produce more optimal assembly code
7. *Assembly and output* – resolving symbolic addresses (labels) and generating machine language

These will be the names of the seven phases in our model compiler. Phases 1 through 4 are machine-independent and language-dependent. Phases 5 through 7 are machine-dependent and language-independent. For reasons of efficiency, in actual implementations these phases may not be separate modules of code.

We might evaluate a compiler not only by the object code produced but also by the amount of core it occupies and the time it takes to execute. Unfortunately, these dimensions of optimality are often inversely proportional to each other. Likewise, the optimality of the code typically is inversely proportional to the complexity, size, and execution time of the compiler itself. These are tradeoffs that we must be aware of throughout this chapter.

We also mentioned or assumed the following data bases which are used by the compiler and which form the lines of communication between the phases:

A. *Source code* – in our example the simple PL/I program in Figure 8.1
B. *Uniform symbol table* – consists of a full or partial list of the tokens as they appear in the program. Created by lexical analysis and used for syntax analysis and interpretation (Fig. 8.3)
C. *Terminal table* – a permanent table which lists all key words and special symbols of the language in symbolic form (pointed to by uniform symbols in Fig. 8.3)
D. *Identifier table* – contains all variables in the program (four in example) and temporary storage and any information needed to reference or allocate storage for them; created by lexical analysis, modified by interpretation and storage allocation, and referenced by code generation and assembly (Fig. 8.8). The table may also contain information of all temporary locations that the compiler creates for use during execution of the source program (e.g., temporary matrix entries).
E. *Literal table* – contains all constants in the program (two in example). Creation and use similar to D above
F. *Reductions* – permanent table of decision rules in the form of patterns for matching with the uniform symbol table to discover syntactic structure
G. *Matrix* – intermediate form of the program which is created by the action routines, optimized, and then used for code generation (Fig. 8.6)
H. *Code productions* – permanent table of definitions. There is one entry defining code for each possible matrix operator (Fig. 8.9).

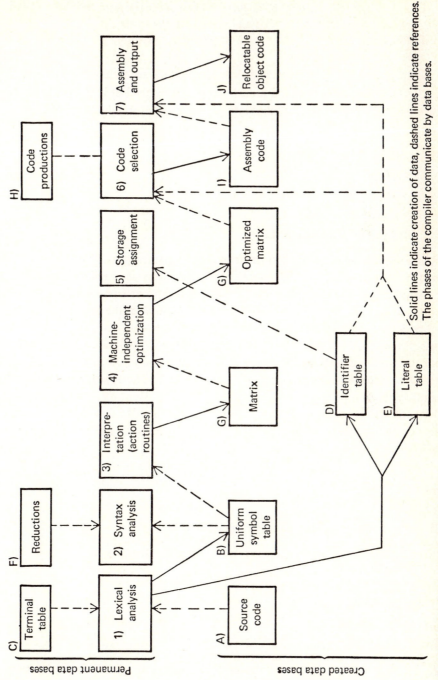

FIGURE 8.13 Structure of a compiler

Solid lines indicate creation of data, dashed lines indicate references. The phases of the compiler communicate by data bases.

C) Terminal table

F) Reductions

H) Code productions

1) Lexical analysis

2) Syntax analysis

3) Interpretation (action routines)

4) Machine-independent optimization

5) Storage assignment

6) Code selection

7) Assembly and output

A) Source code

B) Uniform symbol table

D) Identifier table

E) Literal table

G) Matrix

G) Optimized matrix

I) Assembly code

J) Relocatable object code

Permanent data bases

Created data bases

I. *Assembly code* – assembly language version of the program which is created by the code generation phase and is input to the assembly phase

J. *Relocatable object code* – final output of the assembly phase, ready to be used as input to loader

These phases and data bases and their interactions are summarized in Figure 8.13. This figure represents the model compiler described in Part 2 and used in Part 3 of this chapter. In reading these parts the reader should refer back to the figure for an overview.

PART 2

8.2 PHASES OF THE COMPILER

In this part of the chapter we examine in detail the seven phases of the compiler model. Each phase (Fig. 8.13) is described chronologically, and data bases are introduced into the discussion as the compiler creates or first references them. For reasons of efficiency or because of particular features of the source languages, actual implementations may use more or less elaborate data bases and algorithms than those presented. For example, FORTRAN- or COBOL-like languages may not require the compiler to establish as many attributes in the identifier table as would be needed for languages like PL/I or ALGOL. The algorithms presented similarly may not be the best for a particular situation. However, they do provide the basic guidelines to be followed in compiler design. We feel that the reader may extend the data bases easily to include the exceptions and special cases he will encounter when implementing his own compiler.

8.2.1 Lexical Phase

8.2.1.1 TASKS

The three tasks of the lexical analysis phase are:

1. To parse the source program into the basic elements or tokens of the language
2. To build a literal table and an identifier table
3. To build a uniform symbol table

8.2.1.2 DATA BASES

These tasks involve manipulations of five data bases. Possible forms for these are:

1. Source program – original form of program; appears to the compiler as a string of characters

2. Terminal table – a permanent data base that has an entry for each terminal symbol (e.g., arithmetic operators, keywords, nonalphameric symbols). Each entry consists of the terminal symbol, an indication of its classification (operator, break character), and its precedence (used in later phases). See problem 1 of Chapter 7.

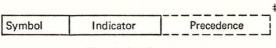

Terminal table entry

3. Literal table – created by lexical analysis to describe all literals used in the source program. There is one entry for each literal, consisting of a value, a number of attributes, an address denoting the location of the literal at execution time (filled in by a later phase), and other information (e.g., in some implementation we may wish to distinguish between literals used by the program and those used by the compiler, such as the literal 31 in the expression BINARY FIXED (31)). The attributes, such as data type or precision, can be deduced from the literal itself and filled in by lexical analysis.

Literal	Base	Scale	Precision	Other information	Address

Literal table entry

4. Identifier table – created by lexical analysis to describe all identifiers used in the source program. There is one entry for each identifier. Lexical analysis creates the entry and places the name of the identifier into that entry. Since in many languages identifiers may be from 1 to 31 symbols long, the lexical phase may enter a pointer in the identifier table for efficiency of storage. The pointer points to the name in a table of names. Later phases will fill in the data attributes and address of each identifier.

Name	Data attributes	Address

Identifier table entry

5. Uniform Symbol table – created by lexical analysis to represent the program

---

‡Solid lines enclose fields filled in either by the phase presently under discussion or phases previously discussed. Dotted lines enclose fields filled in by later phases.

as a string of tokens rather than of individual characters. (Spaces and comments in the source are not represented by uniform symbols and are not used by future phases. There is one uniform symbol for every token in the program.) Each uniform symbol contains the identification of the table of which the token is a member (e.g., a pointer to the table or a code) and its index within that table.

Table	Index

Uniform symbol table entry

8.2.1.3 ALGORITHM

The first task of the lexical analysis algorithm is to parse the input character string into tokens. The second is to make the appropriate entries in the tables. A *token* is a substring of the input string that represents a basic element of the language. It may contain only simple characters and may not include another token. To the rest of the compiler, the token is the smallest unit of currency. Only lexical analysis and the output processor of the assembly phase concern themselves with such elements as characters. Uniform symbols are the terminal symbols for syntax analysis.

There are many ways of implementing this phase. One way is described below. Figure 8.15 depicts the results of the lexical phase for our example PL/I program.

The input string is separated into tokens by break characters. Break characters are denoted by the contents of a special field in the terminal table. Source characters are read in, checked for legality, and tested to see if they are break characters. Consecutive nonbreak characters are accumulated into tokens. Strings between break characters are tokens, as are nonblank break characters. Blanks may serve as break characters but are otherwise ignored.

Lexical analysis recognizes three types of tokens: terminal symbols, possible identifiers, and literals. It checks all tokens by first comparing them with the entries in the terminal table. Once a match is found, the token is classified as a terminal symbol and lexical analysis creates a uniform symbol of type 'TRM', and inserts it in the uniform symbol table. If a token is not a terminal symbol, lexical analysis proceeds to classify it as a possible identifier or literal. Those tokens that satisfy the lexical rules for forming identifiers are classified as "possible identifiers." In PL/I these are strings that begin with an alphabetic character and contain up to 30 more alphameric characters or underscores. If a token does not fit into one of these categories, it is an error and is flagged as such.

After a token is classified as a "possible identifier," the identifier table is examined. If this particular token is not in the table, a new entry is made. Since the only attribute that we know about an identifier is its name, that is all that goes into the table. The remaining information is discovered and inserted by later phases. Regardless of whether or not an entry had to be created, lexical analysis creates a uniform symbol of type 'IDN' and inserts it into the uniform symbol table. The reader should refer to Figure 8.15 for example.

Numbers, quoted character strings, and other self-defining data are classified as "literals." After a token has been classified as such, the literal table is examined. If the literal is not yet there, a new entry is made. In contrast to the case of identifiers, lexical analysis can determine the attributes and the internal representation of a literal by looking at the characters that represent it. Thus each new entry made in the literal table consists of the literal and all its attributes. Regardless of whether or not a new entry is made, a uniform symbol of type 'LIT' is created and put into the uniform symbol table.

The lexical analysis may make one complete pass over the source code and produce the entire uniform symbol table. Another scheme is to have the lexical analyzer called only when the syntax phase needs the next token.

8.2.1.4 EXAMPLE

$$\langle idn \rangle ::= \langle letter \rangle \mid \langle letter \rangle \langle letter\_digit \rangle_1^{30}$$
$$\langle letter\_digit \rangle ::= \langle letter \rangle \mid \langle digit \rangle$$
$$\langle letter \rangle ::= A \mid B \mid \ldots \mid Z$$
$$\langle digit \rangle ::= 0 \mid 1 \mid 2 \mid 3 \mid 4 \mid 5 \mid 6 \mid 7 \mid 8 \mid 9$$
$$\langle lit \rangle ::= \langle digit \rangle_1^{15}$$
$$\langle trm \rangle ::= \langle op \rangle \mid DECLARE \mid END \mid PROCEDURE \mid RETURN \mid (\mid) \mid ; \mid : \mid , \mid$$
$$\qquad\qquad STATIC \mid FIXED \mid BINARY \mid b$$
$$\langle op \rangle ::= + \mid - \mid * \mid \div \mid ** \mid =$$

FIGURE 8.14 BNF representation of lexical rules

Figure 8.14 specifies the form for our example of three classes of symbols (idn, lit, trm), which result in uniform symbols (IDN, LIT, TRM). A uniform symbol is created for each token and an entry is made in the identifier or literal table for each unique identifier or literal (see Figure 8.15 for example).

8.2.2 Syntax Phase

The function of the syntax phase is to recognize the major constructs of the language and to call the appropriate action routines that will generate the intermediate form or matrix for these constructs. In some compilers this phase is

Terminal table

	Symbol	Break	Other
1	:	Yes	
2	;	Yes	
3	(	Yes	
4	)	Yes	
5	,	Yes	
6	b̸	Yes	
7	PROCEDURE	No	
8	DECLARE	No	
9	RETURN	No	
10	END	No	
	+		
	−		
	⋮		
etc.			

Uniform symbol table

Class	Index	Tokens
IDN	1	WCM
TRM	1	:
TRM	7	PROCEDURE
TRM	3	(
IDN	2	RATE
TRM	5	,
IDN	3	START
TRM	5	,
IDN	4	FINISH
TRM	4	)
TRM	2	;
TRM	8	DECLARE
TRM	3	(
IDN	5	COST
TRM	5	,
IDN	2	RATE
⋮		⋮
etc.		

Identifier table

	Name	Attributes
1	WCM	
2	RATE	
3	START	Filled in by later phases
4	FINISH	
5	COST	

Literal Table

Literal	Base	Scale	Precision	Other	Address
31	DECIMAL	FIXED	2		
2	DECIMAL	FIXED	1		
100	DECIMAL	FIXED	3		

FIGURE 8.15 Lexical phase – terminal, identifier, uniform symbol tables for example

implemented by one large program that recognizes each construct. We choose to present a more general implementation. Our syntax phase will be an interpreter for general rules or reductions that define the major constructs of the language and the appropriate action to be taken for each construct.

The reductions are dependent upon the syntax of the source language and thus must be modified should the syntax of the source language change. The format of the reductions is quite arbitrary, but the information contained in them is essential. We will see later that there is a tradeoff between how much is done in the syntactic phase and how much is done by the action routines of the interpretation phase. For reasons of efficiency many compilers do not have interpreters as their syntactic phase. Rather, the phase consists of fixed code. If one wished to make the compiler more efficient, one could "compile" the reductions. We find that writing reductions is a systematic approach to implementing the syntax phase; if the designer wishes, he may then hand-translate reductions into a single program.

8.2.2.1 DATA BASES

Uniform symbol table — created by the lexical analysis phase and containing the source program in the form of uniform symbols. It is used by the syntax and interpretation phases as the source of input to the stack. Each symbol from the UST enters the stack only once.

Table	Index

Uniform symbol table entry

Stack — the stack is the collection of uniform symbols that is currently being worked on by the syntax analysis and interpretation phases. Additions to or deletions from the stack are made by the phases that use it. The stack is organized on a *Last In-First Out* (LIFO) basis. This book always shows the top of the stack toward the bottom of the page, representing the way a stack might be organized in a computer. Actually the term 'Top of Stack' refers to the most recent entry and 'Bottom of Stack' to the oldest entry. The stack may be incorporated into the uniform symbol table or vice versa.

Reductions — the syntax rules of the source language are contained in the reduction table. The syntax analysis phase is an interpreter driven by the reductions. The general form of the rule or reduction is:

label: Old Top of Stack/Action Routines/New Top of Stack/Next Reduction

The following conventions are used:

1. Label — optional
2. Old Top of Stack — to be compared to top of stack
   a. Blank or null — always a match, regardless of what is on the stack
   b. Nonblank — one or more items from the following categories.
      1) ⟨syntactic type⟩ such as identifier or literal — matches any uniform symbol of this type

2) ⟨any⟩ – matches a uniform symbol of any type

3) Symbolic representation of a keyword, such as "PROCEDURE" or "IF" or ":" – matches only the uniform symbol for this keyword

3. Action Routines – to be called if Old Top of Stack matches Top of Stack
   a. Blank or null – no action routines called
   b. Name of action routine(s) – call the routine(s)

4. New Top of Stack – changes to be made to Top of Stack after action routines are executed
   a. Blank or null – no change
   b. " – delete Top of Stack (i.e. pattern that has been matched)[2]
   c. Syntactic type, keyword or stack item (Sm) – delete Old Top of Stack (i.e. pattern that has been matched in 2)[2] and replace witn this item(s)
   d. * – get next uniform symbol from uniform symbol table and put it on top of stack

5. Next Reduction
   a. Blank or null – interpret the next sequential reduction
   b. n – interpret reduction n

Within the reductions we have written both stack fields with the oldest item on the left and the newest on the right. $S_m \ S_{m-1} \ldots S_2 \ S_1$ denotes a field m long, where S_1 refers to the top of the stack, S_2 to the second item on the stack, etc. The S_n notation will be used in the New Top of Stack field to represent the nth item on the stack. We have also placed the symbolic representation of the terminal symbols into the Old Top of Stack field, instead of the uniform symbols that may be the actual stack elements in efficient implementation of reductions.

8.2.2.2 ALGORITHM

The algorithm for the syntax analysis phase is as follows:

1. Reductions are tested consecutively for match between Old Top of Stack field and the actual Top of Stack, until match is found
2. When match is found, the action routines specified in the action field are executed in order from left to right
3. When control returns to the syntax analyzer, it modifies the Top of Stack to agree with the New Top of Stack field
4. Step 1 is then repeated starting with the reduction specified in the next reduction field

8.2.2.3 EXAMPLE

A detailed example of the analysis of our sample program from Part 1 will

---

[2]Note: This does not necessarily mean delete all elements on the stack – rather delete only the elements that were matched in the Old Top of Stack field of the reduction.

follow the description of the interpretation phase. For now we will just explain the workings of the following three reductions.

```
     /  /  *** /
2: ⟨idn⟩:  PROCEDURE  /  bgn_proc  /  S1  ****  /  4
   ⟨any⟩ ⟨any⟩ ⟨any⟩  /  ERROR  /  S2 S1*  /  2
```

These three reductions will be the first three of the set defined for the example in the next section. If the reader pretends he is the syntax phase and interprets these, he will:

1. Start by putting the first three uniform symbols from the UST onto the stack.
2. Test to see if top three elements are ⟨idn⟩: PROCEDURE. If they are, call the begin procedure (bgn_proc) action routine, delete the label and the ":" and get the next four uniform symbols from the UST onto the stack and go to reduction 4. If not, call action routine ERROR, remove the third uniform symbol from the stack, get one more from the UST, and go to reduction 2.

In effect, the reductions state that all programs must start with a '⟨label⟩: PROCEDURE'. After recognizing the PROCEDURE statement, the action routine, bgn_proc, classifies the identifier table entry for ⟨label⟩ as a label. Then the syntax phase deletes the label and the ':', gets four more tokens, and interprets reduction 4, which will start the parsing of the body of the procedure. If the first statement is not a ⟨label⟩: PROCEDURE, an error is noted by calling ERROR, which will print a diagnostic message. Then S3 is deleted, a new token is placed on the stack and reduction 2 is tried again. This checks for ⟨label⟩: PROCEDURE until a match is found or until all the symbols in the UST have been tried.

8.2.3 Interpretation Phase

The interpretation phase is typically a collection of routines that are called when a construct is recognized in the syntactic phase. The purpose of these routines (called action routines) is to create an intermediate form of the source program and add information to the identifier table.

The separation of the syntactic phase from the interpretation phase is a logical division. The former phase recognizes syntactic constructs (phrases that have an associated meaning, e.g., statements or clauses) while the latter interprets the precise meaning into the matrix or identifier table. In actual situations it may not be obvious where the recognizing of a construct ends and the interpretation of its meaning begins. In other words, it may be arbitrary to what size phrase one wishes to assign a meaning. This may be illustrated by the problem of handling arithmetic expressions. An entire arithmetic expression may be considered a syntactic entity, so that its recognition should be a problem for syntax analysis and its parsing a problem for an action routine. However, each subexpression (two operands and an operator) can also be considered a syntactic entity and therefore should be recognized by the syntax analysis phase. For the first case the action routine may construct matrix entries for the entire expression, and for the second case the action routines would only construct one entry for a subexpression. The tradeoff is between how much computation is performed by the syntax phase versus how much by the action routines.

In the example that follows this section, we have separated the functions of the reductions from those of the action routines in different places for the parsing of different statements. In so doing, we hope to illustrate the diversity of approaches to the problem. In general, a compiler writer would try for an efficient division of labor, i.e., one that results in the lowest complexity for the two phases taken as a unit. In general he gives to syntax analysis the task of recognizing constructs and to the interpretation phase the more specific task of the parsing that results directly in matrix entries or modifications to the identifier table.

8.2.3.1 DATA BASES

Uniform symbol table

Stack — contains the tokens currently being parsed by the syntax and interpretation phases.

Identifier table — initialized by lexical analysis to completely describe all identifiers used in the source program. The lexical phase entered the identifier (or pointer to its character string) in the name field. The interpretation phase enters all the attributes. The storage assignment phase will enter the address. This information is used in later phases for assignment of storage and for generating the proper code for accessing storage associated with these entries. Most attributes may be determined during the parsing of the declaration statement.

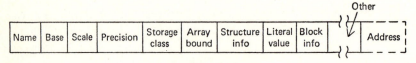

Identifier table entry

Matrix — the primary intermediate form of the program. There are two reasons for having a matrix: (1) it allows the first four phases of the compiler to be machine-independent; (2) it allows machine-independent optimization of the program to occur before the code generation phase. A simple form of a matrix entry consists of a triplet where the first element is a uniform symbol denoting the terminal symbol or operator and the other two elements are uniform symbols denoting the arguments. The code generation phase will be driven by this matrix and will produce the appropriate object code.

There may also be fields reserved for chaining of entries that can be utilized by the optimization phase to add or delete entries.

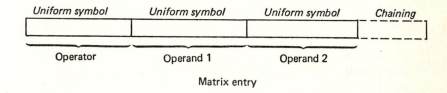

Matrix entry

Although the entries in the matrix are uniform symbols, for clarity in our examples we will show the symbol itself. Some of the matrix operators do not have a direct parallel in either the source language or the machine language. For example, a compound statement such as IF THEN. . .ELSE, may be translated into multiple matrix entries, each of which is translated into several machine instructions.

Matrix operands are uniform symbols of the type IDN, LIT, or TRM, and a fourth form, MTX. A uniform symbol $\boxed{\text{MTX} \mid \text{n}}$ denotes the result of the nth matrix entry and points to the corresponding entry in the temporary storage area of the identifier table line.

Temporary storage table — (may be implemented as part of the identifier table).

The interpretation phase enters into the temporary storage table all information about the associated values of MTX symbols, i.e., the attributes of the temporary computations resulting from matrix lines, such as data type, precision, source statement in which it is used, etc. This information will be used in storage assignment and in generating code for accessing.

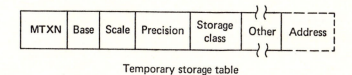

Temporary storage table

8.2.3.2 ALGORITHM

There is no one algorithm for this phase since it is a collection of individual action routines that accomplish specific tasks when invoked by the syntax analysis phase. In particular these routines may:

1. Do any necessary additional parsing — this permits action routines to add symbols to or delete them from the stack as they deem necessary.
2. Create new entries in the matrix or add data attributes to the identifier table. In the former case the routines must be able to determine the proper operator and operands and insert them into the matrix. In the latter case, they must decide exactly what attributes have been declared and put them into the identifier table. In both these cases the complexity of the action routines will depend on how much has been done by the reductions and vice versa.

The following example will illustrate some complex action routines and some simple ones, demonstrating that there is no unique answer as to what should be covered in what phase.

8.2.3.3 EXAMPLE

We will now show an example of the workings of the syntactic analysis and interpretation phases as they compile our sample program from Part 1. In order to make the example more understandable we have created a compiler that will handle only a small subset of PL/I (MINI-PL/I).

Verbally we could define MINI-PL/I as follows.

There are only five types of statements. Their formats are:

(1) label: PROCEDURE (list of arguments);
(2) DECLARE followed by a string AB where
    A) ⟨idn⟩ or (list of ⟨idn⟩s)
    B) FIXED BINARY (precision) STATIC
    where AB's phrases can be further separated by commas and the statement
    is ended by a ;
(3) ⟨idn⟩ = legal arithmetic expression;
(4) RETURN (argument);
(5) END;

Our example is a legal program of MINI-PL/I. Anything not agreeing with the above rules is illegal. Further, a legal MINI-PL/I program must start with statement of the form (1) and end with statement (5) and have only statements (2) through (4) in between.

It is difficult to write a compiler from such a verbal definition because it is imprecise. For example, is a PROCEDURE statement with no arguments legal? We now formally define MINI-PL/I in BNF in Figure 8.16. If you do not under-

stand this definition, reread Section 7.5, and question 1 of Chapter 7. Note
that the BNF definitions utilize three classes that were defined in the lexical
phase. Also note that there is no arithmetic operator precedence in these rules.
That issue is covered in questions 1 and 7 of Chapter 7.

```
⟨procedure⟩ : : = ⟨proc⟩ ⟨body⟩ ⟨end⟩                          Procedure
⟨proc⟩ : : = ⟨idn⟩ : PROCEDURE ( ⟨var⟩ );                      Procedure statement
⟨end⟩ : : = END ;                                              End statement
⟨var⟩ : : = ⟨idn⟩ I ⟨idn⟩ , ⟨var⟩
⟨body⟩ : : = ⟨stmnt⟩ I ⟨stmnt⟩ ⟨body⟩                          Body of a procedure
⟨stmnt⟩ : : = ⟨assign⟩ I ⟨return⟩ I ⟨dcl⟩                      Statements
⟨assign⟩ : : = ⟨idn⟩ = ⟨exp⟩ ;                                 Assignment
⟨exp⟩ : : = ⟨lit⟩ I ⟨idn⟩ I ⟨exp⟩ ⟨op⟩ ⟨exp⟩ I ( ⟨exp⟩ )      statement
⟨return⟩ : : = RETURN ( ⟨idn⟩ ) ;                              Return statement
⟨dcl⟩ : : = DECLARE ⟨dcl element⟩ ;
⟨dcl element⟩ : : = ⟨var list⟩ ⟨attribute list⟩ I ⟨var list⟩
                    ⟨attribute list⟩ , ⟨dcl element⟩
⟨attribute list⟩ : : = FIXED BINARY ( ⟨lit⟩ ) STATIC           Declare statement
⟨var list⟩ : : = ⟨idn⟩ I ( ⟨var⟩ )
Terminal classes: (for syntax phase — these are defined in the lexical phase)
⟨idn⟩
⟨lit⟩          Defined in Figure 8.14
⟨op⟩
```

FIGURE 8.16   BNF definition of MINI-PL/I

Once we have formally defined our source language, we establish the syntax
constructs (phrases) to be recognized. We define an action routine associated
with each phrase and write a set of reductions that will recognize and parse the
syntax constructs and call the appropriate action routine. In practice the task of
defining phrases and action routines and writing the reductions is an interactive
and subjective one. That is, we would first postulate a set of action routines, and
while writing the reductions, change or add action routines. Figure 8.17 lists the
reductions we have chosen for MINI-PL/I. Section 8.2.3.2 explained the first
three of these reductions. (Review that explanation if you do not understand
them.)

Figure 8.18 lists the action routines we have chosen. There is a diversity of
complexity in these action routines. For example, the routine var_name is very
simple. All it does is add one identifier to a list. The action routines base_scale
and precision_class use this list to enter the attributes for each identifier on the
list. Since precision_class is the last routine to insert attributes for a particular

```
1:   //***/
2:   ⟨idn⟩ : PROCEDURE / bgn_proc/ S1 **** / 4           ⎫   INITIALIZE STACK
     ⟨any⟩ ⟨any⟩ ⟨any⟩ / error / S2 S1 * / 2            ⎬     PROCEDURE?
4:   ( ⟨idn⟩ , ⟨any⟩ / arg / S4 S1 ** / 4                ⎫   ARGUMENT LIST
5:   ( ⟨idn⟩ ) ; / arg / " ** / 7                        ⎬
     ⟨any⟩ ⟨any⟩ ⟨any⟩ ⟨any⟩ / error / S2 S1 / 7
7:   DECLARE ⟨any⟩ / / S1 ** / 14                        ⎫
     RETURN ⟨any⟩ / return / S1 *** / 5                  ⎪   DECLARE?
     ⟨idn⟩ = /op_prec/ / 12                              ⎬   RETURN?
     PROCEDURE END; /end_proc/ " *** / 2                 ⎪   ASSIGNMENT?
     ⟨any⟩ ⟨any⟩ / error / S1 * / 7                      ⎭   END?
12:  ⟨idn⟩ = ⟨any⟩ ; / assign / " ** / 7                 ⎫   ASSIGNMENT
     ⟨any⟩ ⟨any⟩ ⟨any⟩ ⟨any⟩ / error / S2 S1 / 7        ⎭
14:  ⟨idn⟩ FIXED BINARY / var_name base_scale / " ***** / 18   ⎫
15:  ( ⟨idn⟩ , /var_name / S3 ** / 15.                   ⎪   DECLARE
     ( ⟨idn⟩ ) / / S2 ** / 14                            ⎬   name base scale
     ⟨any⟩ ⟨any⟩ ⟨any⟩ / error / S2 S1 / 7               ⎭
18:  ( ⟨lit⟩ ) STATIC , / precision_class / " *** / 14   ⎫   DECLARE
     ( ⟨lit⟩ ) STATIC ; / precision_class / " ** / 7     ⎬   precision and class
     ⟨any⟩ ⟨any⟩ ⟨any⟩ ⟨any⟩ ⟨any⟩ / error / S2 S1 / 7   ⎭
```

FIGURE 8.17   Reductions for syntax phase – MINI-PL/I

group of identifiers, it deletes the list after using it.

Action routines:

1 arg – place '.arg ⟨idn⟩' into matrix
2 assign – place '= ⟨idn⟩ ⟨any⟩' into matrix
3 base_scale – place 'base = binary' into proper identifier table entry(ies)
4 bgn_proc – (note identifier is a label in IDN table) place '.procbgn ⟨idn⟩' into matrix
5 end_proc – place '.procend' into matrix
6 error – print out error msg and top of stack
7 op_prec – parse arithmetic expression and generate matrix entries using rules of
            operator precedence, leave ⟨result⟩ on stack
8 precision_class – place proper precision and 'STATIC' into proper idn table entry
            (ies)
9 return – put ' rtn' into matrix
10 var_name – put name on temporary list

FIGURE 8.18   Action routines

The routine op_prec is more sophisticated since it parses an entire arithmetic expression. It uses the rules of operator precedence (explained in Chapter 7, questions 1 and 7) to associate the proper operands with an operator and then to put the operations into the matrix in the sequence they should be executed. It stops parsing when it finds a ";" and leaves both the last matrix line and the ";" on the stack. Var_name and op_prec are extreme examples of the possible division of labor between the interpretation and syntax phases.

We will now follow the reductions as they translate the sample program of Part 1 from the data bases created by the lexical phase into the intermediate form (see Fig. 8.19). The reader is strongly encouraged to work through Fig. 8.19.

For the reader's convenience in Figure 8.19, all uniform symbols in the uniform symbol table, the reductions, the stack, and the matrix are replaced by the symbols they denote. In an actual compiler they would all be in the form of

Table	Index

. Also, for conciseness we have abbreviated PROCEDURE as PROC.

Figure 8.19 enumerates the exact steps that these two phases go through in the compilation of our sample program. Figure 8.20 summarizes the interaction between the first three phases of the compiler as they create the MATRIX, identifier, and literal tables for the last four phases.

8.2.4 Optimization

In Part 1 we differentiated between the two types of optimization performed by a compiler, machine-dependent and machine-independent.

Machine-dependent optimization is so intimately related to the instructions that get generated that it was incorporated into the code generation phase, whereas machine-independent optimization was done in a separate optimization phase. In this section we will discuss the optimization phase and the four commonly used types of machine-independent optimization techniques mentioned in section 8.1.5.1 (Part 1).

In deciding whether or not to incorporate any of these optimization schemes into a compiler, it is necessary to weigh the gains it would bring in increased efficiency for the object program against the increased cost in compilation time and complexity. The outcome of the decision should depend heavily on the circumstances under which the compiler is being produced and on the use to which it will be put.

8.2.4.1 DATA BASES

Matrix — This is the major data base used by the optimization phase. To facilitate the elimination or insertion of entries into the matrix, we add to each entry chaining information, forward and backward pointers. This avoids the necessity of reordering and relocating matrix entries when an entry is added or deleted. The forward pointers allow the code generation phase to go through the matrix in the proper order. The backward pointer allows backward sequencing through

Syntax/interpretation phases:

Reduction # of Fig. 8.17	Match?	Action routine – action	Matrix line #	Matrix	Stack
1	Yes	none			WCM: PROCEDURE
2	Yes	bgn_proc — (note WCM is a label in IDN table) enter procedure name into matrix	M1	.procbgn WCM	PROC (RATE,START
4	Yes	arg — enter first argument into matrix	M2	.arg RATE	PROC (START,FINISH
4	Yes	arg — enter second argument into matrix	M3	.arg START	PROC (FINISH);
4	No				
5	Yes	arg — enter third argument into matrix	M4	.arg FINISH	PROC DECLARE (
7	Yes	none			PROC (COST,
14	No				
15	Yes	var_name — put COST on list of entries to be updated			PROC (RATE,
15	Yes	var_name — put RATE on list of entries to be updated			PROC (START,
15	Yes	var_name — put START on list of entries to be updated			PROC (FINISH)
15	No				

FIGURE 8.19 Steps of syntax and interpretation phase

Syntax/interpretation phases: *(continued)*

Reduction # of Fig. 8.17	Match?	Action routine — action	Matrix line #		Matrix		Stack
16	Yes	none					PROC FINISH FIXED BINARY
14	Yes	var_name — put FINISH on list of entries to be updated					
(14 cont'd)		base_scale — set scale = FIXED and base = BINARY for all entries in IDN_TBL with flags turned on					PROC (31) STATIC ;
18	No						
19	Yes	precision_class = set precision = 31, class = STATIC and turn flag off for all IDN_TBL with flags turned on					PROC COST =
7,8	No	op_prec — parse arithmetic expression (until;) and generate the proper matrix entries, using the rules of operator precedence. This will reference a right and left precedence associated with each operator in the terminal table.					
9	Yes		M5	—	START	FINISH	
			M6	*	RATE	MTX5	
			M7	*	2	RATE	
			M8	—	START	FINISH	
			M9	—	MTX8	100	
			M10	*	MTX7	MTX9	
			M11	+	MTX6	MTX10	PROC COST = MTX11;

Fig. 8.19 (continued)

Syntax/interpretation phases: *(continued)*

Reduction # of Fig. 8.17	Match?	Action routine — action	Matrix line #	Matrix			Stack
12	Yes	assgn — enter = COST expression value into matrix	M12	=	COST	MTX11	PROC RETURN (
7	No						
8	Yes	return — enter .rtn onto matrix	M13	.rtn			PROC (COST);
5	Yes		M14	.arg	COST		PROC END;
7,8,9	No						
10	Yes	end_proc — enter .procend into matrix	M15	.procend			End of uniform symbol table

Fig. 8.19 (continued)

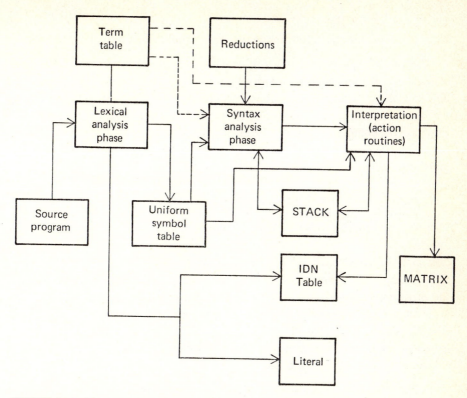

FIGURE 8.20 The interaction of the lexical, syntax, and interpretation phases

the matrix as may be needed by the optimization technique that moves invariant computations outside DO_LOOPS.

A matrix entry now looks like:

Operator	Operand 1	Operand 2	Forward pointer	Backward pointer

where forward pointer is the index of the next matrix entry in the program and backward pointer is the index of the previous one.

Identifier table — accessed to delete un-needed temporary storage and obtain information about identifiers.

Literal table — new literals that may be created by certain types of optimization.

8.2.4.2 ALGORITHM

We discuss possible algorithms for four optimization techniques.

1. Elimination of common subexpressions — In Section 8.1.5.1 we saw how the elimination of duplicate matrix entries can result in a more concise·and efficient object program. The common subexpressions must be identical and must be in the same statement. For example, in the following program we could not eliminate the common matrix entries associated with the second START-FINISH since the value of START is changed in between the evaluation of the two expressions.

```
COST   = RATE * (START - FINISH);
START = START / 2;
COST2 = RATE * (START - FINISH - 100);
```

In some languages such as PL/I where interrupts may change the value of variables at any time, elimination of common subexpressions can be done only if the programmer specifies that none of his own interrupt routines change the value of any variables. For example, in PL/I a programmer may declare ON OVERFLOW (FINISH=0). This could possibly make our two subexpressions unequivalent even if they occurred in the same statement.

The elimination algorithm must:

1. Place the matrix in a form so that common subexpressions can be recognized
2. Recognize two subexpressions as being equivalent
3. Eliminate one of them
4. Alter the rest of the matrix to reflect the elimination of this entry.

Once it has modified entries within a given statement, this algorithm might also want to check to see if its modifications have created any additional common subexpressions.

For example, Figure 8.21 represents the matrix created for several statements of a program. A possible algorithm for the elimination of common subexpressions would:

1. Order the operands of the + and * operators alphabetically — check each entry and change those that are backwards (only M3 and M4 need to be switched)
2. Realize statement boundaries — in this case merely separate them using the = operators
3. Look for common subexpressions — compare M2 with M3, M4, M5. M3 is the only match so delete M3 by changing the pointers of M2 and M4

4. Alter rest of matrix to reflect deleted entry, e.g., change all references of M3 to M2
5. Rescan matrix for possible created common subexpressions – repeat 1 through 5 until no changes occur
6. Eliminate from the temporary storage table any MTX entries that are no longer needed.

Source code

```
B = A
A = C * D * (D * C + B)
```

Matrix before optimization

M1	=	B	A	0	2
M2	*	C	D	1	3
M3	*	D	C	2	4
M4	+	M3	B	3	5
M5	*	M2	M4	4	6
M6	=	A	M5	5	?

Matrix after step 1 and 2

M1	. =	B	A	0	2
M2	*	C	D	1	3
M3	*	C	D	2	4
M4	+	B	M3	3	5
M5	*	M2	M4	4	6
M6	=	A	M5	5	?

} Statement
} Statement

Matrix after step 4

M1	=	B	A	0	2
M2	*	C	D	1	(4)
M3	*	C	D	2	4
M4	+	B	(M2)	(2)	5
M5	*	M2	M4	4	6
M6	=	A	M5	5	?

FIGURE 8.21 Example of elimination of common subexpressions

2. *Compile time compute* – Doing computations involving constants at compile time saves both space and execution time for the object program. This is especially helpful if there is such an arithmetic computation within a loop. For example, if we had the statement

```
A = 2 * 276 / 92 * B
```

the compiler could perform the multiplication and the division so indicated and substitute 6 * B for the original expression. This would enable it to delete two matrix entries, thus reducing the amount of object code that is generated. For example, see Figure 8.22:

Matrix	Before optimization		
M1	*	2	276
M2	/	M1	92
M3	*	M2	B
M4	=	A	M3

Matrix	After optimization		
M1			
M2			
M3	*	6	B
M4	=	A	M3

FIGURE 8.22 Compile-time-compute

A simple algorithm for this optimization technique would first scan the matrix, looking for operators, both of whose operands were literals. Whenever it found such an operation, it would evaluate it, create a new literal, delete the old lines and replace all references to it with the uniform symbol for the new literal, and then continue scanning the matrix for more possible computations.

3. Boolean expression optimization — We may use the properties of Boolean expressions to shorten their computation; e.g., in a statement IF a OR b OR c, THEN . . . . . when a, b, and c are expressions. Rather than generate code that will always test each of the expressions a, b, c, we generate code so that if a is computed as true, then b OR c is not computed, and similarly for b.

4. Move invariant computations outside of loops — If a computation within a loop depends on a variable that does not change within that loop, the computation may be moved outside the loop.

This involves a reordering of a part of the matrix. There are three general problems (a, b, c) that need to be solved in an algorithm of this type.

a. Recognition of invariant computations

For example, in the following program what should we try to move outside a loop?

```
            DO   I = 1 TO 10;
OUTLOOP:  =
            DO   J = 1 TO 10;
      LA:  A = 10;
      LB:  B = Y(I + 2);
      LC:  C = C + 10;
           END;
           END;
```

The statement LA will always produce the same result and thus could be moved outside the loop. In LB the subscript $I + 2$ is also invariant and could be moved outside the inner loop. We might also want to check if the value of Y is changed inside the inner loop. In this case it is not, so this too is an invariant computation which can be moved. LC is a computation that involves C, which is a variable that is changed in the inner loop so it cannot be moved to the outer one. Note that if there are any statements (within the loop) before LA that reference A or B, we could not move their assignment statements out of the inner loop; all we could move would be the computation of the subscript.

b. Discovering where to move the invariant computation

In general we want to move the computation to a position directly preceding the LOOP from which it comes. This requires us to find the starting points of DO_LOOPS by examining the matrix. The interpretation phase would have to place a unique matrix entry at the beginning of every DO_LOOP. It would also have to supply backward pointers in the matrix so that the optimization phase could work its way back to outer loops.

c. Moving the invariant computation

Using the same methods of chaining discussed in the elimination of common subexpressions, we would delete the invariant computation from its original position in the matrix and insert it into the appropriate place.

8.2.5 Storage Assignment

The purpose of this phase is to:

1. Assign storage to all variables referenced in the source program.
2. Assign storage to all temporary locations that are necessary for intermediate results, e.g., the results of matrix lines. These storage references were reserved by the interpretation phase and did not appear in the source code.
3. Assign storage to literals.
4. Ensure that the storage is allocated and appropriate locations are initialized (literals and any variables with the initial attribute).

To do this, it must insert information for the code generation phase into the identifier table, the literal table, and the matrix.

8.2.5.1 DATA BASES

Identifier table — created by lexical analysis and furnished with all attribute entries by interpretation phase. Storage assignment designates locations to all identifiers that denote data. The next two phases use this information to generate accesses to the identifiers.

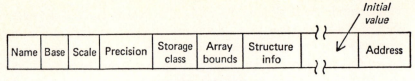

Identifier table entry

Temporary storage table — (part of identifier table) created by the interpretation phase to describe the temporary results of computations in the matrix. This table may be implemented as part of the identifier table since much of the information is of the same format. Further, note that all storage of this type is implemented as automatic, e.g., it is not physically allocated until the procedure is activated. This is satisfactory since no other procedure ever references it, nor is the space needed unless the procedure that contains the storage is activated.

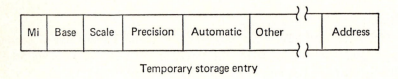

Temporary storage entry

Literal table — The storage assignment phase assigns all literal addresses and places an entry in the matrix to denote that code generation should allocate this storage.

Matrix — storage assignment places entries into the matrix to ensure that code generation creates enough storage for identifiers, temporary storage, and literals. It also ensures that the appropriate ones are initialized.

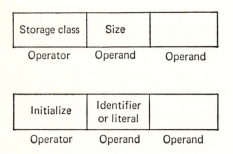

Matrix entries by storage allocation

8.2.5.2 ALGORITHM
Before creating an algorithm for the storage assignment phase, consideration

must be given to the format we wish storage to appear in at execution time to allow efficient accessing. We must ask certain questions about the machine on which the object code is to be run: What registers are available? How is storage accessed? Is indirect addressing permissible? Are index or base registers available? The layout of the user's storage depends on the answers to these questions. (Here we consider .only static storage and leave the more complicated classes, such as automatic, controlled, and based storage until Part 3.)

On a 360-type machine, with base and index registers, it is particularly desirable to lay out the user's storage in continuous blocks, with a register pointing to the beginning of each storage block.

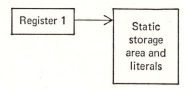

This requires storage assignment to calculate only the offsets for all static storage. The code generation phase will (1) use these offsets to generate the address used in instructions; and (2) generate appropriate code that will load a register with a pointer to the appropriate storage block at execution time and before that storage is accessed.

The storage allocation phase first scans tnrough the identifier table, assigning locations to each entry with a storage class of static. It uses a location counter, initialized at zero, to keep track of how much storage it has assigned. Whenever it finds a static variable in the scan, the storage allocation phase does the following four steps:

1. Updates the location counter with any necessary boundary alignment.
2. Assigns the current value of the location counter to the address field of the variable.
3. Calculates the length of the storage needed by the variable (by examining its attributes).
4. Updates the location counter by adding this length to it.

Once it has assigned relative addresses to all identifiers requiring STATIC storage locations, this phase creates a matrix entry:

STATIC	Size	

This allows code generation to generate the proper amount of storage. For each variable that requires initialization, the storage allocation phase generates a matrix entry:

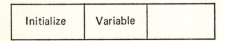

This tells code generation to put into the proper storage location the initial value that the action routines saved in the identifier table.

A similar scan of the identifier table is made for automatic storage and controlled storage. The scan enters relative locations for each entry. An "automatic" entry and a "controlled" entry are also made in the matrix. Code generation uses the relative location entry to generate the address part of instructions. No storage is generated at compile time for automatic or controlled. However, the matrix entry automatic does cause code to be generated that allocates this storage at execution time, i.e., when the generated code is executed, it allocates automatic storage.

The literal table is similarly scanned and locations are assigned to each literal, and a matrix entry | LIT | size | | is made. Code generation generates storage for all literals in the static area and initializes the storage with the values of the literals.

Temporary storage is handled differently since each source statement may reuse the temporary storage (intermediate matrix result area) of the previous source statement. A computation is made of the amount of temporary storage that is required for *each* source statement. The statement requiring the greatest amount of temporary storage determines the amount that will be required for the entire program. A matrix entry is made of the form | AUTOMATIC | size | | This enables the code generation phase to generate code to create the proper amount of storage. Temporary storage is automatic since it is only referenced by the source program and only needed while the source program is active.

EXAMPLE

The identifier and temporary storage table, literal table, and some matrix entries for our example program are depicted in Figure 8.23. Note that all the variables in the identifier table are fixed binary numbers. Thus they are assigned a full word each. The literals are decimal numbers and on the 360 we assign them in packed form, two digits per byte. The matrix entry for the literal storage area explicitly states that this area is three bytes long and implicitly indicates to code generation that it must be initialized with the values in the literal table.

Identifier table

	Name	Base	Scale	Precision	Storage class	Other	Address
1	WCM	proc name					
2	RATE	Binary	Fixed	31	Static		0
3	START	Binary	Fixed	31	Static		4
4	FINISH	Binary	Fixed	31	Static		8
5	COST	Binary	Fixed	31	Static		12
	MTX5	Binary	Fixed	31	Automatic		0
	MTX6	Binary	Fixed	31	Automatic		4
	MTX7	Binary	Fixed	31	Automatic		8
	MTX8	Binary	Fixed	31	Automatic		12
	MTX9	Binary	Fixed	31	Automatic		16
	MTX10	Binary	Fixed	31	Automatic		20
	MTX11	Binary	Fixed	31	Automatic		24

Literal table

Literal	Base	Scale	Precision	Other	Address
31	Decimal	Fixed	2		0
2	Decimal	Fixed	1		1
100	Decimal	Fixed	3		

Matrix

Operator	Operand 1	Operand 2	Chaining
STATIC	16		
AUTOMATIC	28		
LITERALS	3		

FIGURE 8.23 Identifier, literal tables, matrix – after storage assignment

Looking ahead, one can foresee complications emerging in the area of accessing. Later phases have to generate a physical address for each variable referenced. For static storage we at least know the relative location of each variable. But for controlled storage we don't even know at compile time or at load time if this storage will exist, much less know its location.

Note also the problems of handling mixed data types. The literals are decimal numbers; the identifiers are fixed binary. Code generation must examine not only the operators of the matrix but the data types of the operands, and depending on their use, code generation must create appropriate conversion routines.

8.2.6 Code Generation

The purpose of the code generation phase is to produce the appropriate code (assembly or machine language). We have again chosen a general way of depicting this phase, but one which exhibits the issues of code generation and certain machine-dependent optimization techniques. Many modern compilers employ the methodology described here. Referring to Figure 8.13, the code generation phase has the matrix as input. It uses the code productions (macro definitions) which define the operators that may appear in the matrix to produce code. It also references the identifier tables and literal tables in order to generate proper address and code conversions.

It will be recalled that in the example illustrated in Figure 8.12, the code in the center column was generated using the simple definitions of Figure 8.9. More flexible definitions are required that will allow us to generate the more efficient code contained in the last column of Figure 8.12. To accomplish this, we introduce macro pseudo-ops in the definitions.

8.2.6.1 DATA BASES

Matrix — each entry has its operator defined in the code pattern data base. Code generation examines each entry and looks up the code to be generated in the code patterns. In other words, the operator of each entry serves as a macro with the operands as arguments.

Identifier table, literal table — are used to determine the data type and locations of the variables (operands of the matrix) so that proper accessing code with the correct address is generated. Also if there are mixed data type expressions, code generation must generate proper code for conversions.

Code productions (macro definition) — a permanent data base defining all possible matrix operators. Figure 8.9 of Part 1 depicts some simple code productions for the operators -, *, +, =. We will redefine the + operator using an enhanced code production language to allow some machine-dependent optimization. For our code production language we use 360 macro language; in practical implementation the designer may wish to invent his own specialized language.

8.2.6.2 ALGORITHM

We implement the code generation process in a way analogous to that used for the assembler macro processor. The operation field of each matrix line is treated as a "macro-call" and the matrix operands on the line are used as "macro arguments." In Chapter 4 we discussed the issues of a macro processor; here we will focus on methods of defining the operators to allow machine-dependent optimization.

8.2.6.2.1 SIMPLE MACHINE-DEPENDENT OPTIMIZATION Figure 8.24 depicts the matrix for the source statement A=B+C+D. The center column is the code generated using the simple definitions of + and = of Figure 8.9. Let us discuss methods of achieving the better code contained in the third column.

Matrix	"Original code"	"Better code"
+ B C	1) L 1,B	1) L 1,B
	2) A 1,C	2) A 1,C
	3) ST 1,M1	——
+ M1 D	4) L 1,M1	——
	5) A 1,D	3) A 1,D
	6) ST 1,M2	——
= A M2	7) L 1,M2	——
	8) ST 1,A	4) ST 1,A

FIGURE 8.24 Code for statement A = B + C + D

There are two types of optimization involved. *First,* if a value is already contained in a register, there is no need to reload; this allows us to eliminate the L 1,M1, and L 1,M2 references. *Second,* careful consideration of the matrix generation process will show that a matrix temporary, Mi, is used once at most. (This may not be true if matrix optimization occurs, but even that problem can be overcome. We will assume no intermediate matrix optimization.) Therefore, if we are going to immediately use the value of Mi that was left in the register, there is no need to store its value. This allows us to eliminate the ST 1,M1 and ST 1,M2 instructions.

There are three possible ways to perform this code generation optimization: (1) during matrix optimization, (2) during code generation, or (3) during a postpass after assembly code is generated. The matrix, even when optimized, is still intended to be a machine-independent representation of the source program. If we optimize register usage in the matrix, it becomes *machine-dependent*; for example, what does it mean to a machine without "registers" such as the IBM 1620 and 1401? For aesthetic and practical reasons, we wish to keep the matrix machine-independent.

Using a post-generation optimization has many shortcomings. For example, a 1000-line matrix would generate about 4000 assembly cards. Whereas, we might fit the entire matrix in core memory, it would be necessary to write out and then reread the assembly cards to eliminate the unnecessary instructions – a time-consuming process. The best solution is to eliminate unnecessary instructions *before* they are generated (i.e., during the code selection pass).

8.2.6.2.2 SIMPLE MACHINE-DEPENDENT OPTIMIZATION ALGORITHM
Figure 8.25 depicts an algorithm we could use to eliminate unnecessary load (**L**) and store (ST) instructions for the "+" operation.

There are two points that should be noted about the algorithm. First, if an operand, Mi, is (at execution time) already in the register, it is not reloaded. Second, the responsibility for storing the matrix temporary is left to the *next* matrix line code generation since it is the only line that knows whether the previous temporary will be needed immediately.

Rather than write a separate assembler subroutine for the code generation of each operator, a code pattern language is used to represent the appropriate algorithm.

For the "+" operator the code pattern of Figure 8.26 may be employed. Standard 360-like macro language conventions are used in this pattern for simplicity.

It is assumed that the variables &i, &r1, &M, and &lastM were initialized at the beginning of code generation as follows (using 360 macro language notation):

```
          GBLA    &i
          GBLC    &r1, &M, &lastM
&i        SETA    1
&r1       SETC    'null'
&M        SETC    'M1'
&lastM    SETC    'null'
```

The macro NEXTM used in the code pattern for "+" can be defined as follows:

```
          MACRO
          NEXTM
&lastM    SETC    'M&i'      set new value for Mi-1
&i        SETA    &i+1       set new value for i
&M        SETC    'M&i'      set new value for Mi
          MEND
```

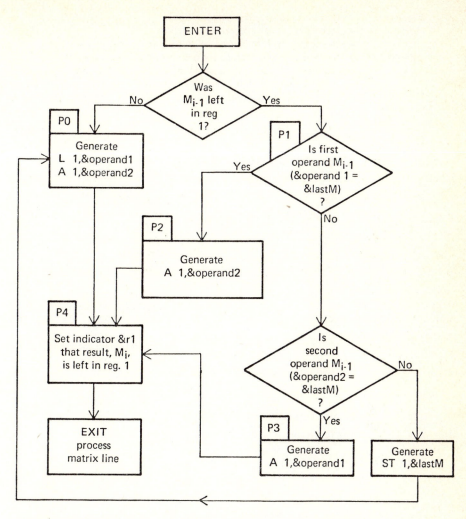

FIGURE 8.25 Code generation language for "+" operator with optimized register usage

The labels P0, P1, etc. used in the code pattern for "+" correspond to the labeled boxes in the flowchart of Figure 8.25. The reader should compare the flowchart with the code pattern definition and note that they perform the same actions. It is strongly recommended that the reader "hand simulate" the action of the code generation phase by processing the matrix presented earlier using the code pattern shown above.

8.2.6.2.3 MULTIPLE REGISTER OPTIMIZATION Conditional code patterns

&operand1   — first operand of current matrix line
&operand2   — second operand of current matrix line
&M   — temporary storage associated with current matrix line (M_i)
&lastM   — temporary storage associated with previous matrix line (M_{i-1})
&r1   — indicator of current contents of register 1 (i.e. the (M_i) which is presently left in register 1, if any).
&i   — current matrix number

		Code pattern for +		Meaning
	AIF	('&lastM' EQ '&r1').P1		If M_{i-1} in R1, go to P1
.P0	L	1,&operand1		Generate instruction
	A	1,&operand2		Generate instruction
	AGO	.P4		Go to EXIT sequence
.P1	AIF	('&operand1' EQ '&lastM').P2		If &operand1 = M_{i-1}, go to P2
	AIF	('&operand2' EQ '&lastM').P3		If &operand2 = M_{i-1}, go to P3
	ST	1,&lastM		Generate instruction
	AGO	.P0		Go to P0 and continue
.P2	A	1,&operand2		Generate instruction
	AGO	.P4		Go to EXIT sequence
.P3	A	1,&operand1		Generate instruction
.P4	ANOP			Start of EXIT sequence
&r1	SETC	'M&i'		Set &r1 to M_i
	NEXTM			Update &i, &M, and &lastM
	MEND			Go on to next matrix entry

FIGURE 8.26 Code pattern for + macro with some optimization

generate much more efficient code than the simple patterns used at the beginning, but they do have shortcomings.

Consider the matrix of Figure 8.27 for

A = B * C + E * F:

Matrix			Code			Better code	
1) *	B	C	1) L	1,B		1) L	1,B
2) *	E	F	2) M	0,C		2) M	0,C
3) +	M1	M2	3) ST	1,M1		3) L	3,E
4) =	A	M3	4) L	1,E		4) M	2,F
			5) M	0,F		5) AR	1,3
			6) A	1,M1		6) ST	1,A
			7) ST	1,A			

FIGURE 8.27 Optimization code for A = B * C + E * F

Assuming code language specifications for "*", similar to "+" of last section, we might expect to generate the "optimized" code shown in the middle column. Although unnecessary loads and stores have been eliminated, the code of the last column is even "better."

Admittedly, the improvement is not as great as the 50 percent we got by eliminating the loads and stores. But we can eliminate one instruction and change an ADD to an ADD Register, which might be as much as 15 percent more effective.

The major difference is that we are using the fact that the 360 has more than one register in which arithmetic may be performed. Some of the 16 registers will have to be set aside for bases and indices, but we could probably arrange for at least 2 or 3 register pairs for arithmetic.

Figure 8.28 depicts an algorithm for the code generation process for the "+" operator. Basic to its operation is the notion of register indicators very similar in function to the assembler's base register table. For each register that is to be used for arithmetic, there is a separate indicator that states (1) that the register presently contains no intermediate results, or (2) that a certain Mi has been left in the register.

The symbols &R1 and &R2 are "register variables" that could take on values from 0 to 15. If the result of matrix line i is to be left in register j, we would have set &rj = "Mi" and &R1 = j. For example, the instruction AR &R1,&R2 would generate AR 3,1 if &R1 has value 3 and &R2 has value 1.

The instruction ST &R1,&r&R1 calls for an instruction to store a register into its corresponding matrix temporarily. For example, if &R1 has value 3 and register 3 contains the intermediate results of matrix line 39, the instruction generated would be:

```
ST   3,&r3   which would be   ST   3,M39
```

This means that a store into Mi may occur hundreds of instructions after the value was actually calculated.

8.2.6.2.4 PRACTICAL CONSIDERATIONS In this section we have discussed some of the problems that must be handled by the code generation phase and, for simplicity, have described the mechanism in the form of a 360 macro processor (as presented in Chapter 4). In many ways code generation may be the most complex phase of a compiler.

One of the most difficult tasks for the compiler writer is to produce efficient code pattern definitions for every possible matrix operator, including non-

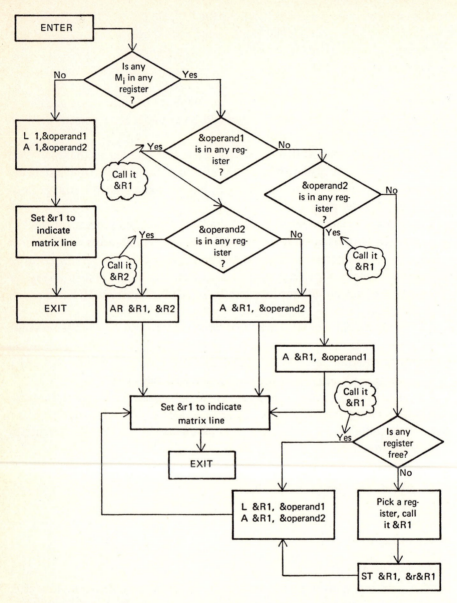

FIGURE 8.28 Code generation process for the "+" operator – improved

numerical operators such as PROC-BGN, RTN and many others. Furthermore, for numerical matrix operators, such as "+ A B", it is necessary to handle data conversion if A and B are not identical data types (e.g. binary and decimal) or not compatible with the "+" operator (e.g. character string or bit string).

These problems can, reassuringly, be handled by sufficiently powerful and flexible conditional code pattern definitions. But, in order to obtain the power and flexibility needed as well as increased speed and efficiency of compilation, a specialized code generation process and code pattern language is often used instead of a general purpose macro processor.

Depending upon the sophistication of the code generation phase, the remaining phases may be greatly simplified. E.g., if code generation produces assembly source code, it is necessary to use a one- or two-pass assembler to produce the necessary machine language object deck. A one-pass assembler would be adequate if the compiler symbol table information is supplied intact; if only DS and DC statements are supplied an entire two-pass assembler would be necessary. For simplicity, several compilers, such as AED/360 and early 7090 FORTRAN, actually produce assembly source code and use the standard system assembler to complete the translation process. Most high-speed high-performance compilers, such as 7090 MAD, attempt to eliminate the assembly phase entirely by producing machine language directly as output from the code generation phase.

8.2.7 Assembly Phase

The task of the assembly phase depends on how much has been done in code generation. If a lot of work has been done in code generation, then the assembly phase (simple) must resolve label references in the object program, format the object deck, and format the appropriate information for the loader (e.g., for direct linking loading schemes prepare TXT, RLD, ESD cards; see Chapter 5).

At the other extreme, if code generation has simply generated symbolic machine instructions and labels, the assembly phase (complicated) must: (1) resolve label references; (2) calculate addresses; (3) generate binary machine instructions; and (4) generate storage, convert literals.

8.2.7.1 DATA BASES

Identifier table — The simple assembly phase uses this data base to enter the value of all labels into the identifier table.

Literal table — The complicated assembly phase would initialize all literal locations, that is, place the literals on the appropriate TXT cards.

Object code — The output of the code generation.

8.2.7.2 ALGORITHM

The simple assembly phase scans the object code, resolving all label references and producing the TXT cards. It then scans the identifier table to create the ESD cards. The RLD cards are created using the object code, the ESD cards, and the identifier table.

A more complicated assembly phase would be an assembler similar to that described in Chapter 3. In actual implementation, certain functions and data bases may be eliminated as they are duplicated in the other phases of the compiler, e.g., the symbol table is similar to the identifier table.

8.2.8 Passes of a Compiler

Instead of viewing the compiler in terms of its seven logical phases, we could have looked at it in terms of the N physical passes that it must make over its data bases.

Figure 8.29 is an overview of a flowchart of a compiler, depicting its passes.

Pass 1 corresponds to the lexical analysis phase. It scans the source program and creates the identifier, literal, and uniform symbol tables.

Pass 2 corresponds to the syntactic and interpretation phases. Pass 2 scans the uniform symbol table, produces the matrix, and places information about identifiers into the identifier table. Passes 1 and 2 could be combined into one by treating lexical analysis as an action routine that would parse the source program and transfer tokens directly to the stack as they were needed.

Passes 3 through N-3 correspond to the optimization phase. Each separate type of optimization may require several passes over the matrix. The optimization techniques implemented for a particular compiler vary and may even be, as in PL/I, controlled by the programmer.

Pass N-2 corresponds to the storage assignment phase. This is a pass over the identifier and literal tables rather than the program itself.

Pass N-1 corresponds to the code generation phase. It scans the matrix and creates the first version of the object deck.

Pass N corresponds to the assembly phase. It resolves symbolic addresses and creates information for the loader. Notice that pass N corresponds roughly to pass 2 of the assembler from Chapter 3. The addition of a macro facility or other advanced features to our compiler may require additional passes.

8.2.9 Preview

In Part 3 we use our model to handle multiple data types, multiple storage classes, and other features. We expand the amount of information in our data bases and increase the complexity of our action routines.

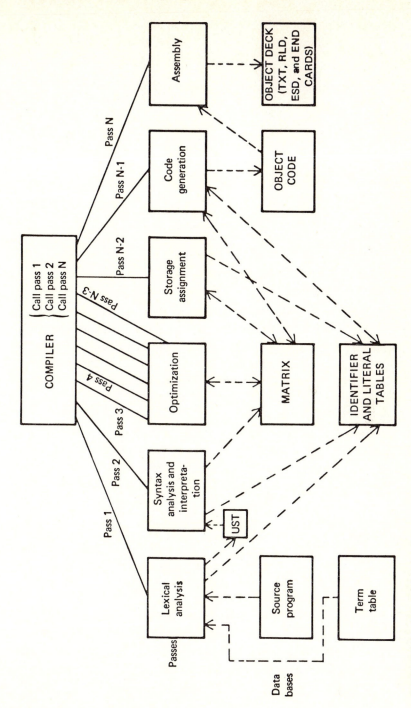

FIGURE 8.29 Passes of a compiler

PART 3

In this part we use our model to implement the more advanced features:

1. Data structures
2. Recursion
3. Storage classes
4. Block structures
5. Conditions
6. Non-local go-to's
7. Pointers

8.3 DATA STRUCTURES

In Figure 8.30 we have declared a structure A to be *static*. This structure has six scalar quantities: C, whose contents have been declared as a fixed binary number; E character string; F bit string; G fixed binary, etc. This structure may be visualized as a tree in which A and B are nodes and C is a scalar. The access to C would consist of its path name, i.e., A.B.C. This structure may also be thought of as an n-tuple consisting of six locations, each containing individual pieces of data denoted by C,E,F,G,J, and K. The entire structure A would denote all the locations. We have declared the structure to be an array of 100 entries, thus there are 100 such trees or n-tuples. A statement that might appear in a program following this declaration structure is A (2).B.D.E = 'NO'. Note that in PL/I the subscript may also be placed at the end of the reference, e.g., A.B.D.E(2).

8.3.1 Statement of Problem

To process a data structure and the statements referencing it, the compiler performs four tasks:

1. Store information contained in the structure declaration into the identifier table. This information will be used by storage assignment to allocate storage and by code generation to create proper accessing and conversion code. The compiler enters the following for all identifiers in the structure (e.g., A,B,C,D,E, ..., K)

Name	Base	Scale	Precision	Storage class	Array bounds	Block info	Structure name? node? scalar?	Connectivity info

	Initial value	Length	Address

entry for all identifiers

Data structure

```
DECLARE      1    A(100)    STATIC,
                    2 B,
                      3 C FIXED BIN,

                      3 D,

                            4 E  CHAR(2),
                            4 F  BIT(4),

                      3 G  FIXED BIN,

                    2 H,

                      3 J  BIT(12),
                      3 K  FIXED BIN;
```

Tree

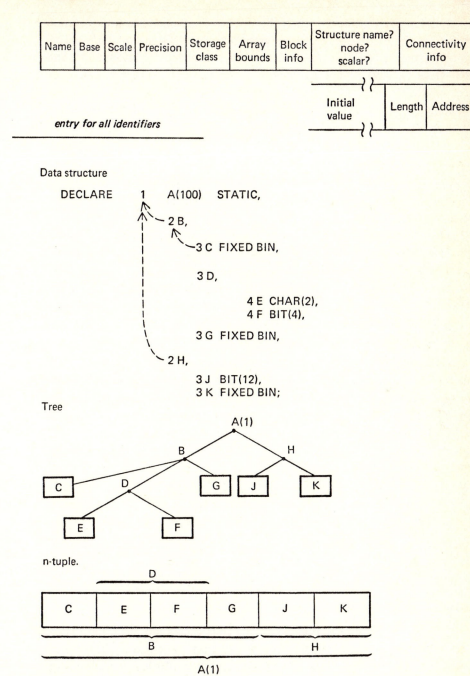

n-tuple.

FIGURE 8.30 Representation of a data structure

The lexical phase creates the entry by storing the name. The interpretation phase stores the base, scale, precision, array bounds, block information, indication of whether it is a structure, node, or scalar, connectivity information, and initial value (if any). Connectivity information consists of backward pointers indicating the "parent" of the substructure (see Fig. 8.30 dotted arrows). These pointers allow incomplete specification of references and permit us to replace references by uniform symbols. Storage assignment stores the length and address. The length is the amount of storage that this element and all the substructures or elements within it need.

2. Transform all references into uniform symbols. The interpretation phase creates a uniform symbol for structure references. The lexical phase has created entries in the identifier table for each identifier of the structure. The reference A.B.D.E is simply replaced by a uniform symbol pointing to E in the identifier table. To find the correct E, a search is made for all identifiers named E and successive pointers are traced back to check that the parent of this is D and the parent of D is B, and finally, that the parent of B is A. Similarly, the incomplete reference A.E would be verified and replaced by a uniform symbol indicating the correct version of E. A reference A.B, which denotes the scalars C,E,F,G, would be replaced by a uniform symbol pointing to the correct version of B.

3. Assign storage. The storage assignment phase must fill in the length and address entries in the identifier table. It also makes appropriate entries into the matrix to assure that storage is assigned and initialized. For our example structure of Figure 8.30 and for a 360-type machine where we can have a base register pointing to the base of the structure, we may lay out storage sequentially. For the structure that we have been using in our example, we may visualize storage as in Figure 8.31.

We place in the identifier table the length of all entries. In the case of a scalar this quantity is the length of the data element it represents (e.g., G of Fig. 8.30 has length = four bytes). For substructures the length is equal to all the scalars they denote (e.g., D of Fig. 8.30 length = three bytes). The length field is used by code generation to create proper code (e.g., A.B(1) = A.B(3) results in code to move a substructure). Thus steps 1 through 3 applied to our example would result in an identifier table as depicted in Figure 8.32. The reader should calculate the length and address himself.

4. Generate code and proper address. The code generation phase must either allocate the proper storage and initialize it or generate code that will allocate the storage at execution time. The use of data structures further complicates the generation of actual addresses (as opposed to symbolic ones). For example, the

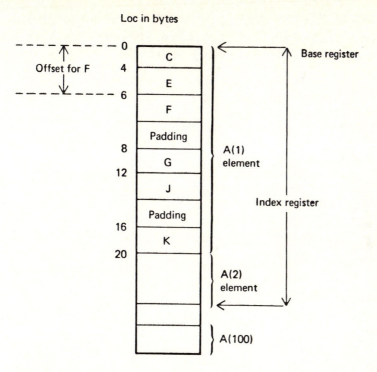

FIGURE 8.31 Storage assignment for an array

Index	Name	Base	Scale	Precision	Storage class	Array bounds	Block info	Indicator	Connectivity (index of parent)	Initial value	Length (bytes)	Address
1	A				STATIC	1,100		Structure	0	0	20	0
2	B							Substruc	1	0	11	0
3	C	BINARY	FIXED	31				Scalar	2	0	4	0
4	D							Substruc	2	0	3	4
5	E	CHAR	FIXED	2(char)				Scalar	4	0	2	4
6	F	BIT	FIXED	4				Scalar	4	0	1	6
7	G	BINARY	FIXED	31				Scalar	2	0	4	8
8	H							Substruc	1	0	6	12
9	J	BIT	FIXED	12				Scalar	8	0	2	12
10	K	BINARY	FIXED	31				Scalar	8	0	4	16

FIGURE 8.32 Identifier table entries for example of Figure 8.30

compiler cannot produce the instruction L 1,A.B.C(1); rather, it must generate L 1,4(8,9) where 4(8,9) denotes an actual address. For a reference like (load A.B.D.E.(5)), the code generation phase may produce:

   a. Code to load a base register with the base of structure A, (e.g., register 9).
   b. Code to load index register (e.g., register 8) with value of index that is equal to (5-1) x (length of structure).
   c. A load instruction with an offset equal to the value of address for E in the identifier table, a base register of the previous step a, an index register of the previous step b. (e.g., L 1,4(8,9).

The preceding three functions form the address of A(5).B.D.E. Note that in step b we generate code to calculate the index value rather than precomputing it at compile time. We do this to demonstrate the more general case where the index is a variable or expression, as, for example, in A.B.D.E.(DX+1), which can only be calculated at execution time.

8.3.2 Implementation

Here we briefly discuss some details of the implementations of steps 1 through 4.

Syntax and interpretation phases — first write a precise specification (e.g., BNF) of the syntax of a DECLARATION statement. Define action routines you think appropriate (e.g., ENTER enters array bounds, base, precision) and write reductions. Note that the interpretation phase inserts information into the identifier table in processing a declaration statement. When processing arithmetic statements that reference indexed variables, the interpretation phase must make matrix entries that will allow code generation to calculate the addresses, e.g., A.B.G(I) = 3 may result in a matrix

Operator	Operand 1	Operand 2
.ss	A.B.G	I
=	M1	3

that causes generation to produce code to compute the index and form the proper address of the code.

Lexical and storage assignment phases — as discussed above.

Code generation phase and assembly — There is no code associated with the declaration statements. However, there is code associated with accesses to elements that have been defined in the data structure. We have treated statement A = B by converting it into the matrix entry | = | A | B |. The storage assignment phase for simple scalars places their relative location with respect to the beginning of the area into the location field of their identifier table entry. The code generation phase for this simple assignment statement must formulate the addresses of B and A. These addresses consist of three parts: an offset, a base register, and an index register (which is not used here for scalars).

The offset may be set by looking up the entry for the identifier B in the identifier table. The base register number may be arbitrarily chosen; however, the code generation phase must produce code that loads that base register with the address of the beginning of the static storage area.

In the case of a reference to an indexed data structure, the address formation is slightly more complicated. Suppose we have the statement A.B.G(I)=3. The matrix for this statement is shown above. The macro .SS would cause code to be output that would calculate the *address* of A.B.G(I) and store this address into a temporary location associated with this particular matrix entry. To compute this address at execution time, the compiler must pass on the length of the structure A, and the location of G within A.

Again, addresses are composed of *three* components: an offset, contents of a base register, and contents of an index register. The offset is known at compilation time and may be generated then. However, the contents of the base and index registers must be calculated at execution time. On a machine like the 360 we may generate an instruction that loads a base register with the address of the beginning of this storage area. We may generate the appropriate arithmetic instruction to calculate the value of the distance from the beginning of the array to this particular element (e.g., (I-1) $\times$ (length of element A)). Code is created that loads this value into the index register. The macro = has as its two arguments the address of A.B.G(I) and the address of the literal 3. This is different from the definition of = of Part 2 where the arguments were addresses that contained the *value* of the operands.

8.4 RECURSION, CALL, AND RETURN STATEMENTS

Let us illustrate by example the key issue in compiling recursive procedures (those that call themselves). The example is of a PL/I routine that computes the factorial (see Section 4.3.3 for another example). We assume all storage used is static.

Let us compute N! where

$$N! = \begin{cases} N*(N\text{-}1) & \text{for } N > 0 \\ 1 & \text{for } N = 0 \end{cases}$$

Figure 8.33 depicts an algorithm for 3! that is incorrect. We include this to demonstrate the key issues in recursive procedures. The algorithm simply notes $N! = N*(N-1)!$ Thus, $3! = 3 * 2! = 3 * 2 * 1! = 3 * 2 * 1 * 0! = 3 * 2 * 1 * 1$. Thus, we may subtract one from N and call factorial again. If $N = 0$, then return.

The procedure of Figure 8.33 computes 3 factorial and leaves the results in ANS. Storage is assigned to N, ANS, TMP at the end of the program in the way described in part 2. Figure 8.34 depicts the values of these variables during the calls. Note that the program does not give the correct answer because TMP has the same value through all returns.

The reader should hand-simulate the program. He will note that on all returns $TMP = 1$, thus $ANS = 1$. One way to solve this problem is to make TMP a vector TMP(I) and index it. Each call sets $I = I+1$, thereby asserting a new TMP with each call. A return sets $I = I-1$, thus re-establishing the TMP associated with the previous call.

TMP (1)	First call
TMP (2)	Second call
TMP (3)	Third call
⋮	
TMP (i)	ith call

This scheme of storing variables is loosely called a stack, where setting $I = I+1$ (creating a new TMP) corresponds to *push down*, and returning ($I = I-1$) corresponds to *pop*. As we will see in the next section where we discuss data storage, it is possible to have a class of storage called automatic, which would automatically push and pop the stack on calls and returns.

We are not out of trouble yet, for this program presumably was called by some main program. The main program left its return address in some location known to the subroutine. When the factorial program calls itself, it leaves its return address in that same return location, thus wiping out the return address to the main program. When FACT calls itself again, the former return address would be lost and replaced by the new return address. Thus when it returned, it would only return to the address that was associated with the last call. To be specific, in the example above, we recall that the return address is left in register 14, the return statement was translated into the branch to register 14, and the call statement is translated into

```
L       15,FACT
BALR    14,15
```

In the first call register 14 contains the return address of the caller. The second

```
FACT:    PROCEDURE;
         DECLARE N FIXED BIN STATIC INITIAL (3);
         DECLARE (ANS,TMP) FIXED BIN STATIC;
         IF N = 0
              THEN ANS = 1 ;
              ELSE DO;
                   TMP = N;
                   N = N-1;
                   CALL FACT;
                   ANS = TMP * ANS;
                   END ;
         RETURN;
END;
```

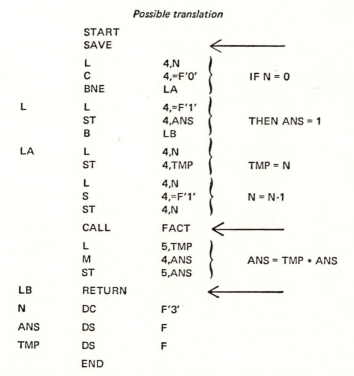

Possible translation

```
         START
         SAVE                      ⟵──────────

         L       4,N          )
         C       4,=F'0'      }      IF N = 0
         BNE     LA           )
L        L       4,=F'1'      )
         ST      4,ANS        }      THEN ANS = 1
         B       LB           )
LA       L       4,N          )
         ST      4,TMP        }      TMP = N
         L       4,N          )
         S       4,=F'1'      }      N = N-1
         ST      4,N          )
         CALL    FACT              ⟵──────────
         L       5,TMP        )
         M       4,ANS        }      ANS = TMP * ANS
         ST      5,ANS        )
LB       RETURN                    ⟵──────────
N        DC      F'3'
ANS      DS      F
TMP      DS      F
         END
```

FIGURE 8.33 Incorrect recursion program

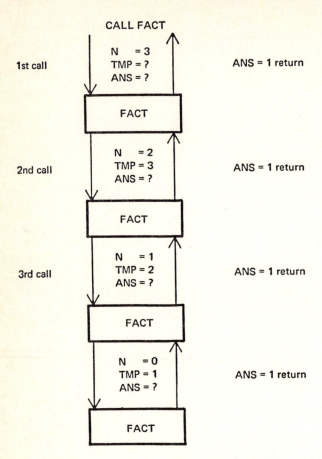

FIGURE 8.34 Computation of N! – incorrect algorithm

through last times it contains a return address in FACT. The question is, how do we get out of FACT? The answer is that we must save the contents of register 14 in a stack also, or in general, we must save the return address in a location that is associated with the call.

In many languages the stack manipulation is automated by the compiler. A portion of the stack is used for return addresses and another portion for automatic storage variables that may change values with each call. Efficiency dictates that all registers should be saved when a procedure is entered. Hence, we may have the following stack frame for the 360 (Fig. 8.35).

Calling another program would result in pushing down the stack by producing another frame containing the status of the machine and that of the variables associated with that particular call. The execution of a return statement would cause the "popping up" of a stack frame by returning the status of the machine to the conditions that prevailed before the call. Therefore, when entering a called procedure, we must execute a SAVE statement to store the machine status. The RETURN statement restores the status of the machine. A CALL statement must create a new stack frame.

A simple save, call, and return sequence that could be used in our example is depicted in Figure 8.36. This is an important item to understand, and the reader should simulate the sequences shown.

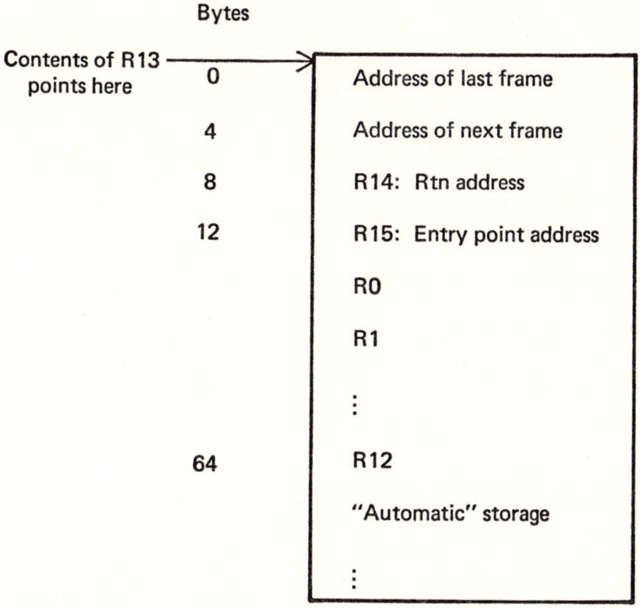

Bytes

Contents of R13 points here

0	Address of last frame
4	Address of next frame
8	R14: Rtn address
12	R15: Entry point address
	R0
	R1
	⋮
64	R12
	"Automatic" storage
	⋮

FIGURE 8.35 Stack frame

In processing recursions, then, the compiler must generate call, save, and return sequences to manipulate the stack. Note that if these sequences are standardized on a system, then PL/I programs may call FORTRAN programs, which in turn may call assembly language programs. Unfortunately, on most systems the compiler groups do not get together.

The SAVE, CALL, and RETURN sequences differ from machine to machine. In our discussion of dynamic linking loaders we will discuss calling sequences for the MULTICS systems on the HIS645.

SAVE	~	STM	14,12, 8(13)	Save all registers in present stack frame
		LR	2,13	Compute start of
		A	2, =F'	Compiler places the next frame
				length of frame
				(e.g., 68+length of
				automatic storage)
		ST	2,4(13)	Store address of next stack frame into byte 4 of this frame
		ST	13,0(2)	Store address of this frame in byte 0 of next frame
CALL	~	L	13,4(13)	Load address next frame
		L	15,PROC_ENTRY	Load address of called procedure
		BALR	14,15	Branch to called procedure and save return address in R14
RETURN	~	LM	14,12,8(13)	Restore registers from current frame
		L	13,0 (13)	Load address of old stack frame from byte 0 this stack frame
		BR	14	Branch to address in R14

FIGURE 8.36 Simple calling sequences

8.5 STORAGE CLASSES – USE

Today's computer user is starting to demand more flexible types of storage than those provided by FORTRAN, ALGOL, and COBOL. In particular, he would like to be able to allocate and free his storage as needed. While many people do not feel that PL/I is a good language, much of their criticism is levelled at its syntactical ambiguities. In the area of storage allocation, PL/I's powerful facilities are generally endorsed since they appear to fulfill the user's expanding requirements.

In this section we will discuss different types of storage allocation and their use. The next section presents their implementation. Because of their generality, we have chosen the types of storage PL/I offers the user; ALGOL 68 and many of the new languages provide somewhat similar facilities.

We will discuss the following types of storage:

1. Internal static
2. External static
3. Automatic
4. Internal controlled
5. External controlled
6. Based

8.5.1 Static Storage

Internal static is storage that is local to the program and is allocated prior to execution time. That is, at execution time this storage exists; it is reserved for all time, whether it is used or not, and the values remain intact throughout all calls.

As a note, internal static storage makes a procedure *impure* or *non-re-entrant.* A *pure* or *re-entrant* procedure is one that does not alter itself or contain data or any locations that are altered. We will discuss pure procedures later when we cover multiprocessing in Chapter 9.

External static storage is similar to internal in that it exists at all times; it is allocated before execution; and it exists whether or not it is used. However, it may be referenced by other procedures. It corresponds to FORTRAN's common.

There are two major reasons for using static storage: first, for storage containing values that should remain intact throughout all calls; second, it is usually the most efficient since the code generated for accesses to static storage is the simplest. A good example of where static storage is necessary would be in a program that is a random number generator. Usually, with each call the program uses the number last generated as a factor in producing the next "random number." Thus, the last number generated must exist throughout each call.

8.5.2 Automatic Storage

Automatic storage is internal in that it is local and may be referenced only in the procedure in which it is defined. The space for the storage is allocated when the procedure is activated. That is, space is allocated when the procedure is entered and is deallocated when the procedure is exited (this corresponds to a stack). There is no external automatic storage since it is meaningless to reference storage that may not exist.

The major uses for automatic storage are in conjunction with recursion, where we want the recursive variables to have values associated with each call. Thus a separate set of locations for the variables defined as automatic storage exists for each call. A return from a recursive procedure results in the restoring of the previous values to these variables. Another use of automatic storage is in promoting efficiency of memory usage. This can be demonstrated by a problem that plagued FORTRAN programmers: they always had to dimension an array used in a subroutine to fit the largest possible array that any calling program would want. When utilizing automatic storage, an array is allocated upon the call to the procedure. The size of the array for this particular call can be determined by passing the dimension of the array as an argument to the procedure. In this way only enough storage to fit the array would be allocated.

8.5.3 Internal Controlled Storage

Internal controlled storage allows the user to allocate a work space within a program. If storage is declared as controlled, then it does not exist at compilation time, nor does it exist at the activation of the procedure in which it was declared. Instead it is allocated at execution of an ALLOCATE statement. Controlled storage disappears when a FREE statement is executed. Each ALLOCATE gets a new copy of a specific variable and each FREE statement frees the most recent copy of the specified variable. Thus if a second ALLOCATE statement is executed before a FREE, the existing copy of the storage is pushed down in a stack. A FREE statement would free the storage on the top of the stack and pop up the previous copy. Internal controlled storage may only be referenced from the procedure in which it is defined.

8.5.4 External Controlled Storage

External controlled storage is different from internal controlled in that it can be referenced or freed by other procedures. Because of the flexibility of external controlled storage, the user is faced with problems analogous to those of the systems programmer concerned with locking and unlocking data bases. That is, it is possible with external controlled storage to have storage allocated by one procedure, freed by another, and then referenced unsuccessfully by a third.

8.5.5 Based Storage

Based storage is similar to controlled storage in that it is explicitly created and destroyed using ALLOCATE and FREE statements. Unlike controlled storage, however, there is no implied stacking and unstacking of copies of the storage. Each allocate statement that is executed causes a copy of the storage to be created. To permit references to a particular copy of based storage, a pointer to that storage is set by the ALLOCATE statement. To refer to or to free based storage, a pointer is used to indicate the copy that is being referenced.

8.6 IMPLEMENTATION

The compiler must perform the following for all storage classes: (1) assign address to all variables of that class; (2) assure that all storage gets allocated; and (3) assure that references to it are correct.

8.6.1 Static Storage

Storage that has been declared as static by the programmer is assigned by the compiler at compile time. The compiler outputs information to the loader to reserve this space at execution time. Typically, static storage is included in the text cards, just as if it were instructions.

Storage declared as external static is also allocated at compile time but in a separate segment from the procedure segment. All variables in external storage will be noted in the ESD cards produced. At this point, it is advisable that the reader review the section on loaders to refresh his memory as to the purpose of the TXT cards, ESD cards, and RLD cards that are used in a direct linking loading scheme. The allocation of the external storage as a separate segment is somewhat dependent upon the loading scheme used, but in general, the loader will load both the programs of a particular job and their external static segments. It checks to see if two external storage segments contain identical variables and makes sure that no storage is duplicated. For example, if A and B are declared to be external static in P1 and B to be external static in P2, these two programs would be compiled with two separate external segments, both containing the variable B. However, the loader would only create two locations, A and B. All references to the external static area would be made indirectly through a *"transfer vector"* (series of pointers) that points to all external static variables. This transfer vector is located in the internal static area of the program and is filled with the addresses of all external static variables by the loader. The segments outputted for a program with external static storage are depicted in Figure 8.37.

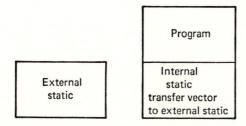

FIGURE 8.37 Storage methods for static

The transfer vector was placed in the internal static area, which is part of the program. This is the way it is done on a 360-type machine. However, in MULTICS, since (1) all procedures must be pure (not alter themselves) and (2) the same segment may have a different number within each user's address space, we cannot have the internal static area part of the main pure program. Therefore, the pointer to the external static in MULTICS is contained in a separate segment called a linkage segment.

8.6.2 Automatic Storage

Automatic storage is assigned when the procedure is activated during execution time. Therefore, the compiler must generate, for each procedure, a code called a *prologue*, which precedes the procedure's normal code and allocates storage that has been declared as automatic in the procedure. The generated code that appears in the beginning of the program is similar to the code associated with the SAVE macro used in recursion of a previous section. Thus, when a procedure that has automatic storage is entered, a stack frame is created (Fig. 8.38) that contains the status of all interrupts and registers and the values of all the automatic variables.

At each call a new stack frame is allocated. At tne corresponding return. that stack frame will be freed. A particular stack frame is specified by a *stack pointer*, which indicates the low order address of the frame. Automatic storage is accessed relative to the stack pointer of the current frame. When we enter a new procedure and wish to allocate, we simply move the stack pointer to a new frame. When we return from the procedure, we deallocate that storage by simply moving the pointer back to the stack frame associated with the calling program.

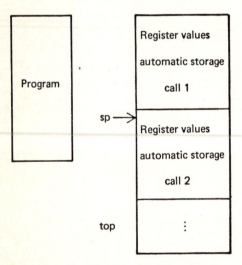

FIGURE 8.38 Storage method for automatic

8.6.3 Controlled and Based Storage

Controlled storage in PL/I may be implemented in a way similar to that used for automatic. The ALLOCATE statement is translated into a prologue that allocates the storage at execution time (usually by calls to the operating system). The FREE statement is translated into code that deallocates that storage.

To facilitate the task of "garbage collection" (collection of unused storage) we might not use a simple stack. We may employ a storage configuration called a *heap.* For example, if we had the following statements:

```
ALLOCATE A;
ALLOCATE B;
FREE A;
```

a portion of a heap associated with the control storage A may be followed by a portion of the heap associated with the control storage B, leaving a hole in the heap when A is freed. Thus we would be wasting that space. There are various free storage packages and allocation schemes whereby portions of these heaps will be moved, or storage is not allocated in sequence but by some other algorithm so that holes do not develop.

A free storage management system for controlled and based storage receives from the operating system a pool of available storage. It then disperses blocks of storage on demand by a call to a procedure ALLOC (length), which returns a pointer to an unused block with the specified length. Another procedure RET (length, pointer) is available to return the block of storage indicated by pointer to the pool. The compiler implements ALLOCATE and FREE statements by generating calls to the procedures ALLOC and RET with appropriate arguments. For internal control the pointer may be placed in internal static. For external control the pointer may be placed in external static so other procedures may reference it.

8.7 BLOCK STRUCTURE

Many modern languages, such as PL/I and ALGOL, allow the use of blocks and block structures. Block structure is a method for defining the scope of variables so that the user may use the same identifiers for different purposes. Blocks can be nested like DO statements of FORTRAN or THROUGH statements of MAD. Blocks define the scope of the definition of identifiers. For example, the scope of the identifiers in Figure 8.39 is depicted in Figure 8.40.

There are two problems that the compiler must handle with respect to block structures:

1. Several completely different variables with different declarations and at-

B1:   BEGIN;   DECLARE (V,W,X,Y) FIXED BIN(15) AUTOMATIC;

                          =

                       B2: BEGIN; DECLARE(Y,Z) CHAR(8) AUTOMATIC;

                            =

                              B3: BEGIN; DECLARE(Y,X) BIT(16) AUTOMATIC;
                                   Y = W;
                                   END;

                            =

                            END;
                       B4: BEGIN; DECLARE(W) FIXED DEC(4) AUTOMATIC;

                            =

                       END;

       END;

FIGURE 8.39 Block structure example

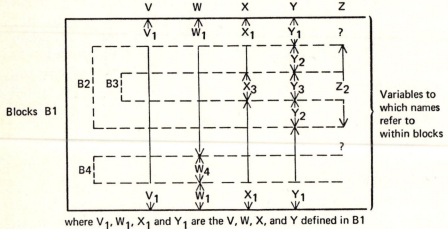

where V_1, W_1, X_1 and Y_1 are the V, W, X, and Y defined in B1

Y_2 and Z_2 are the Y and Z defined in B2

X_3 and Y_3 are the X and Y defined in B3

W_4 is the W defined in B4

? undefined

FIGURE 8.40 Scope of variables

tributes may be referred to by an identifier with the same name if they are
declared in different blocks. The compiler must determine which variable
a given identifier refers to. For example, in the statement Y=W of Figure
8.39, which Y is the programmer referencing — the one in B1, the one in
B2, or the one in B3?

2. The second problem associated with block structure is that automatic
storage defined in a block must be allocated when the block is entered and
released when the block is left. Block structure imposes no major additional
storage allocation problems with static or controlled storage.

8.7.1 Accessing Information for Block Structure

We first outline the problems and possible solutions associated with locating the
variable referred to by a given occurrence of an identifier. When the lexical phase
of a compiler finds an identifier, it must pass a uniform symbol on to subsequent
phases of the compiler. That uniform symbol points to an entry in the identifier
table. Which entry does it point to? Eventually, there may be two entries in the
identifier table associated with the same name of an identifier. For example, in
the preceding block structure, the identifier Y is defined in blocks B1, B2, and
B3. In B1 the identifier Y denotes a binary integer; in B2, a character string, and
in B3, a BIT string. The lexical phase cannot pass on a uniform symbol to different Ys since it knows nothing about declarations and blocks. Therefore, all
the lexical phase can do is enter names of variables into a name table.

A possible implementation would be to have the interpretation phase of the
compiler create new entries in the identifier table for the variables declared in
each block. It must also associate with each identifier the block in which it is
defined. Hence, when the variable is referenced, the interpretation phase searches
the identifier table for the identifier defined either in this block or in the closest
outer block, and then replaces the identifier with the proper uniform symbol.
Using our model we can outline briefly a way of implementing this feature. It is
desirable to separate the identifier table into two parts, one to name the identifier
and the other to define the identifier, as is shown in Figure 8.41 for the block
structure in Figure 8.39.

The lexical phase creates entries in the name table. When the interpretation
phase encounters a declaration statement in a block, it creates entries in the
identifier table. With each entry it sets a pointer pointing to the name of the
identifier in the name table. It places an indication of which block the identifier
is defined in. It also places an index to the identifier entry, which redefines this
same variable in another block. Thus when a reference is made to a variable
within a block, the interpretation phase must replace it by a uniform symbol. It

Identifier table

	Name table
1	V
2	W
3	X
4	Y
5	Z

	Pointers to name	Attributes	Index to next Def.	Block de-fined	Address
1	V_1		0	1	
2	W_1		9	1	
3	X_1		8	1	
4	Y_1		5	1	
5	Y_2		7	2	
6	Z_2		0	2	
7	Y_3		0	3	
8	X_3		0	3	
9	W_4		0	4	

FIGURE 8.41   Structure of identifier table for blocks

finds the correct entry in the identifier table by searching the identifier table for all occurrences of the variable, uses the block-defined information and the index to next definition to determine the correct uniform symbol.

There are other situations in which elements are declared without the use of declaration statements, for example, statement label constants.

L: /*is a declaration of a label */;

However, the declaration does not necessarily occur before the label has been used or referenced. The label is entered into the name table by the lexical phase. If the syntax phase notes there is no entry for the current block when the label occurs, we must force a new entry in the identifier table. If there is an entry for the current block and it is undefined, we define it as a label. If it is an entry for the current block that is defined, it is an error because we have a multiply defined label. References to a variable that has been defined within a block are depicted by a uniform symbol pointing to that element in the identifier table. If block structure is allowed, then we may have associated with the matrix entry the block number in which this identifier was declared. For the design presented here, the code generation phase would go to the entry in the identifier table to handle a reference. This entry would then point to the first block (this or another) in which the variable is defined, and noting which block this matrix entry appears in, it can then find the appropriate identifier to be referenced.

8.7.2 Storage Allocation for Block Structure

The second problem associated with block structure is the allocation of automatic storage that is defined within a block.

When block B1 is entered, all the variables defined in B1 must have storage allocated to them. The same is true for the variables within B2 and B3 when these blocks are entered. When B3 and then B2 are exited, storage must be released. Lastly, when B4 is entered, its storage must be created and when B4 and B1 are exited, their storage is freed. This is depicted in Figure 8.42.

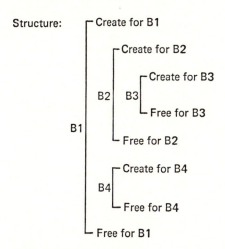

FIGURE 8.42 Successive allocations with block structure

The implementation of automatic storage and block structures could be treated in a similar way to that given in section 8.6.2 for automatic storage and subroutine calls, by creating a new stack frame. By analogy, whenever we enter a block we could create a stack frame that contains locations for all the variables in outer blocks plus locations for variables within this block. Entering a new block, we would create a new stack frame which contains all the variables in outer blocks (copying essentially the last stack frame) then include in the frame variables that are redefined in this block. Whenever we leave a block, we would simply delete the stack frames. However, we don't need the flexibility and generality required for procedure calls, because with block structure we have a well-defined pattern of the sequence in which blocks are entered and exited. In the case of procedures, we don't know which is going to call which first, or how the procedures are going to return. We may take advantage of the less flexible characteristic of block structure to implement a less general but slightly more efficient storage allocation feature. If the language allows only constants as dimensions of arrays, then we may use a simple allocation scheme for automatic storage as depicted in Figure 8.43.

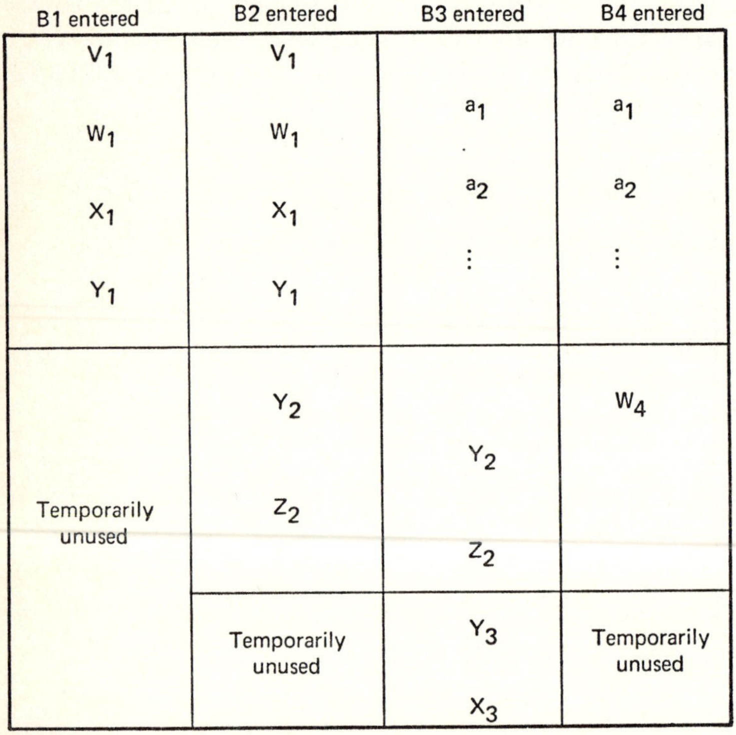

B1 entered	B2 entered	B3 entered	B4 entered
V_1	V_1	a_1	a_1
W_1	W_1		
X_1	X_1	a_2	a_2
Y_1	Y_1	$\vdots$	$\vdots$
	Y_2		W_4
		Y_2	
Temporarily unused	Z_2	Z_2	
	Temporarily unused	Y_3	Temporarily unused
		X_3	

FIGURE 8.43 Stack allocation for a program with block structure

When the block B1 is entered we will allocate the maximum storage for all the variables within it and its inner blocks. If all the dimensions are constant, we will know exactly how big this should be at compilation time. Therefore, code could be generated at the beginning of this program that would allocate the correct amount of storage at execution time. When the blocks B2 and B3 are entered, we will generate code that will use space within the area just allocated for B1 for all the variables within B2 and B3. When block B4 is entered, references to variables defined in it will occupy the same space as was previously used for variables defined within B2 and B3. When we exit from B1, we free all this storage.

If there was an array Z(N) defined in block B2 where N was computed in the outer block B1, then upon entering B2, we would have enough information to allocate space for Z. Before, whenever we entered the outermost block B1, the compiler assigned enough storage for B1 and all its inner blocks. It would simply use that storage over and over again, knowing that it had reserved the maximum that would ever be needed. However, in this case the dimension is unknown at compilation time and, in fact, unknown through the execution of the prologue of block B1 until the entrance to B2.

Languages that allow arrays with variable dimensions must use a different scheme for automatic storage, such as is depicted in Figure 8.44.

Figure 8.44 depicts a stack frame that was created when the procedure containing the block B1 was called. This call caused automatic storage defined in the block B1 to be allocated. Following this are storage pointers to the place for storage associated with blocks contained in B1. All of this is done by code that is generated by the compiler and is executed when the main procedure is called at execution time. The code allocates storage for B1 and sets up the display area.

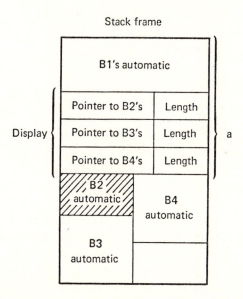

FIGURE 8.44 Use of display information to direct allocation for block structure

The code generated for B2 causes the pointer to its automatic storage area and the length of that area to be copied into the display area. The code generated when we entered the block B4 causes that storage to overlay the storage of B2 and B3 and the display to be altered accordingly.

For automatic storage it is necessary at execution time to have certain information about that storage, e.g., the size of an array must be determined before that array is allocated. If any variables are to be initialized, this must take place within that storage area. Therefore, along with all variables in automatic storage, we must have initialized variables and their values, sizes of arrays, etc., stored somewhere. It is the overhead associated with storing this information that makes automatic storage very costly. Information as to the size of the array, a pointer to the location of the array, and the dimensions of that array will be reserved in the static storage area. This information has been called an *array dope vector*. In addition, for any strings defined as automatic storage there is a corresponding *string dope vector*. There is a third type of dope vector that is used on the 360 implementation of PL/I called a *string array dope vector*, which is an array of dope vectors each of which points to a string array. In addition, any automatic variables that have been initialized by the programmer in his program must also be stored in the static storage area. When the automatic storage is assigned at execution time, these initialized values are copied into the newly created storage area. Thus it may take twice as much storage for automatic variables if they are initialized.

The operating system in which the compiled procedures are executed may assist greatly in the allocation of storage. As we will see in our discussion of the MULTICS system, segmentation greatly aids the allocation of storage.

8.8 NONLOCAL GO TO'S

PL/I allows label variables to be passed as arguments. Figure 8.45 contains an example of a nonlocal GO TO. We have three procedures, P1, P2, and P3 with a label variable defined in P1, which is passed as an argument to P2, which in turn passes the label on to the third procedure, P3. P3 contains a GO TO statement transferring to that label.

The PL/I language specifications state that a nonlocal GO TO which transfers to a procedure must restore the procedure to the state it was in when the label was set. Therefore, P1 must be restored to the same environment that occurred when the label variable LABZ was set to the label constant LAB. With each assignment of a label we must keep track of the location of the label and the particular stack frame associated with the procedure containing the assignment,

```
P1: PROC;
      IF  N = 3  THEN CALL P1;
      LABZ = LAB;
      CALL P2(LABZ);
LAB:  X = 1;
      END;
```

```
P2: PROC (LABX);

      ≡

      CALL  P3(LABX);
      END;
```

```
P3: PROC (LABY);

      ≡

      GO TO LABY;
      END;
```

FIGURE 8.45 Program with nonlocal go to's

so that we can *unwind* to that stack frame when a GO TO to that label is executed.

8.9 INTERRUPTS

An *interrupt* in PL/I is a means of specifying nonsequential flow of control. When a certain *condition* occurs, an interrupt is signaled. The programmer can specify what action is to take place when this happens by means of an ON statement, such as ON OVERFLOW X=Y. This action may be implemented as calls to the monitor system so that the system interrupt routine will execute the statement X=Y and then return to the interrupted program.

8.10 POINTERS

PL/I allows the use of pointers and pointer variables. A pointer is a means of qualifying a variable. For example, the statement P → A=4 indicates that the variable to which P points is set equal to 4. (There may be many As in the case of based storage. Which A is it? It is the A that P is pointing to. The implementation of such pointers means simply that the accessing explicitly uses this pointer information).

The code generated for access to a pointer-qualified variable will be preceded by code that loads the pointer into some base register. Then access to that storage uses the contents of the base register. For example, on a 360 the following code can be generated for all accesses

```
L     15,"Pointer"     /* load base register with pointer for storage */
L     AC, offset (15)  /* load accessed location into register AC */
```

where the second instruction loads the referenced variable into a register AC. The offset can be determined at compile time or in the case of indexing may be calculated at execution time.

As an observation, accesses to all classes of storage may be thought of as implicit pointer-qualified. For example, internal static storage may be considered as always having a pointer IS that points to the base of this storage. So if we declared A as being internal static, then we could make the statement

```
IS → A=4;
```

this is a statement which says A=4. Which A? The A that is in the internal static area.

Automatic storage may be thought of as having a default condition where its pointer qualifier is a stack pointer. The statement

```
SP → A=4
```

means the variable A is set equal to 4. Which A? The one that occurs in the stack frame. Continuing this analogy, if A was declared as controlled storage, the statement A=4 can be thought of as the default statement CP → A=4.

Thus, access to all storage classes may have the code above. Although for static storage the loader sets the value of "Pointer," for automatic and controlled storage, the free storage routines of the operating system set the value of the pointer.

For efficiency, if a storage class is accessed often, it may have its pointers placed in registers at execution time. For example, a register may always contain the stack pointer, pointing to automatic storage. Another register may contain the base of internal storage. In the case of based storage the user causes the pointer to that storage to be created, and the system saves that value.

8.11 SUMMARY

Our model is quite general. A compiler implemented this way could have its output code changed by simply modifying the code productions. The input language could be altered by changing the syntax reductions. In practical compilers some of this flexibility is foregone for reasons of efficiency. However, we feel that the design of such a compiler should follow the phases of our model; after implementation, some flexibility could be eliminated, e.g., by compiling syntax reductions and code productions.

We saw that the difficult problems associated with a compiler for modern languages are not in parsing arithmetic expressions, but rather in storage allocation and accessing.

The compiler itself and its output code must interact with the operating system, especially in compiling such features as conditions and storage classes where the operating system allocates and deallocates storage using various garbage collection schemes. The compiler must be aware of the operating system and generate calls and code to use the system's management routines.

QUESTIONS[1]

Part I

1. Draw a block diagram of the phases of a compiler and indicate the main function of each phase.

2. What is the essential difference between an interpreter and a translator? A compiler is described as a translator. Could any of its phases be described as interpreters? Which ones?

3. What is the difference between a phase and a pass; syntax analysis and semantic interpretation; a token and a uniform symbol? Give examples in your explanation.

4. What are the advantages and disadvantages to performing the assembly of the compiled program in the compiler rather than using the standard system assembler?

5. What is the purpose of the uniform symbol? Can uniform symbols be avoided? If so, what are the gains and losses?

6. The phases are not clear-cut sections operated sequentially; they interact with each other. The lexical, syntactic, and interpretation phases, for instance, are quite interlocked. What are some reasons for not replacing the three with a single "matrix-generation" phase?

7. Which phases use machine-independent data bases?

8. Is it always worthwhile to optimize a program?

Part II

9. Explain precisely the difference between the use of productions and the use of reductions.

10. We have emphasized the design of a compiler as a series of modular "plug-in" units. Such a design permits the isolation of language and machine-dependent and independent features. For the data bases listed below, check off the appropriate attributes. Note: a data base is considered to be machine- or language-independent only if both its structure and contents are.

---

[1]A † denotes that the question is a machine problem.

	Created table	Permanent table	Lang. dep.	Mach. dep.	Lang. indep.	Mach. indep.
Terminal table						
Identifier table						
Literal table						
Reductions						
Uniform symbols						
Matrix						
Matrix operators						
Code productions						
Action routines						

11. Suppose you had a compiler for PL/I running on the IBM 360 and you wanted it to produce code for the HIS 645. If you assume that the compiler is designed according to our model, what changes would be required? Remember that the compiler will still be running on the IBM 360.

12. What phases add to or modify the matrix, and what does each do? What phases reference the matrix without modifying it?

13. What information must be in the identifier table so that the code generation phase can generate code for the statement

    x=A.B.C(50)

14. What is wrong with the following set of reductions: (it can be assumed that reduction 3 appears further down in the table)?

    ```
        /// * /
    1 : ⟨idn⟩ /''/ */2
        ⟨op⟩ //S1/ 1
    2 : /procbgn/ */3
    
        ⋮
    ```

15. Give an example of a "permanent" table and an example of a "created" table.

16. There are many ways of describing languages. What is the basic difference between a specification via canonic systems, a specification via a set of reductions, and a specification via BNF?

17. Describe the matrix entry for a DCL statement; for a PROCEDURE statement.

18. The book contains several examples of code generation patterns (macros) for the add ("+") operation. These patterns are increasingly complex and reflect levels of optimization. Your problem is to present a code generation pattern for the binary subtract ("-") operation. The credit you receive will depend on the level of optimization you attempt but it is

better to do some method well than to partially present a more sophisticated method. Assume you are to generate code for the IBM 360.

    a. List assumptions as to what information you have access to, e.g., con-
tents of registers.

    b. Draw a flowchart representing the algorithm for code generation for a
subtract generator.

    c. Define the "-" macro in IBM 360 macro language.

    d. Describe where the output is left on completion of the generated code.

19.   Give three examples of machine-dependent optimization. State where
these types of optimization are performed in the compiler and explain the
tradeoffs of optimizing there rather than at some earlier or later time.

20.   In what phase is the elimination of common subexpressions performed?
Why?

21.   There are many different forms of optimization and each form contributes
a small amount to the finalized code. Some of the forms are more common than others and it is useful for you to be able to recognize their
occurrence by type. In the table below each column is labelled with a type
of optimization and each row corresponds to a PL/I statement.

    a. Note in the table in each column where the optimization for that
column can be applied to the statement. Note that more than one
optimization may apply.

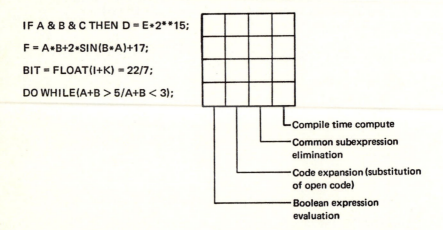

IF A & B & C THEN D = E*2**15;

F = A*B+2*SIN(B*A)+17;

BIT = FLOAT(I+K) = 22/7;

DO WHILE(A+B > 5/A+B < 3);

— Compile time compute

— Common subexpression
elimination

— Code expansion (substitution
of open code)

— Boolean expression
evaluation

    b. In which phase would each of the above types of optimization be
performed and why?

22.   *Elimination of subexpressions* — It is quite easy to observe visually that
-(A-B) and B-A are identical. Yet it is not included by the algorithm
section 8.2.4.2. Modify it to include this special case.

23. Assuming A,B,C have this declaration, FIX BIN, the statement

    A = B + C;

would appear in the matrix as

```
   i)   +   B  C
 i+1)   =   A  T
                i
```

and generate code such as

```
    L        0,B
    A        0,C
   [ST       0,T ]
              i
   [L        0,T ]
              i
    ST       0,A
```

(bracketed instructions might be eliminated by use of code optimization).

However, most modern compilers are able to utilize several different data types with the same logical operators.

For example, for the declarations:

```
DCL     (A1,B1,C1)  FIXED BINARY;
DCL     (A2,B2,C2)  FLOAT BINARY;
DCL     (A3,B3,C3)  FIXED DECIMAL;
```

the following similar-looking statements would generate very different code (non-optimized):

A1=B1+C1;		A2=B2+C2;		A3=B3+C3;	
L	0,B1	LE	0,B2	MVC	TEMP,B3
A	0,C1	AE	0,C2	AP	TEMP,C3
ST	0,T$_i$	STE	0,T$_i$	MVC	T$_i$,TEMP
L	0,T$_i$	LE	0,T$_i$	MVC	TEMP,T$_i$
ST	0,A1	STE	0,A2	MVC	A3,TEMP

a. What modifications would you make to the reductions of MINI-PL/I (Fig. 8.17) in order to handle the new arithmetic types described above? If none are needed, state why.

b. What modification to the action routines (Fig. 8.18) would you make to handle the arithmetic described above? If none, state why.

c. Would you need to modify the operations used in the matrix? Why?

d. Would you need to modify the code generation phase and its macro definitions? Be specific about any recoding you would make to the programs in this phase.

e. Assume that "mixed mode" expressions, that is, those in which the operands are not of the same data type, are to be allowed in the compiler. Suggest modifications, in addition to those you made above, that are needed to implement this feature.

24. Use the reductions and action routines of Figures 8.17 and 8.18. You are to act as the lexical phase, syntax phase, interpretation phase, and code generation phase of a compiler. You are to compile each of the following programs:

```
1)   BEGIN: PROCEDURE (A,B);
     DECLARE (A,B) FIXED BINARY (15) STATIC;
     A = 10;
     B = A;
     END;

2)   MIT: PROCEDURE (JOHN, STU, BILL);
     DECLARE   (JOHN, STU) FIXED BINARY (31)
                STATIC, BILL FIXED BINARY (15)
                STATIC;
     JOHN = STU * BILL;
     STU = JOHN - BILL * 10;
     RETURN (STU);
     END;
```

a. Give the contents of IDN and LIT tables after the lexical phase, after interpretation, and after storage assignment.
b. Write the contents of the stack immediately after END has been put into the stack.
c. Write the reductions which are interpreted in the order that they are interpreted.
d. Write the contents of the matrix after the interpretation phase.
e. Write the assembly language code that you think should be generated by the macros in the matrix.
f. Now modify the above reductions and action routines to accommodate the following:

Put in an error detection mechanism (call "error" if ++ or + * occur).

25. Consider the following FORTRAN statement

DO17I = 1,10,1   (a FORTRAN DO statement)

As any good FORTRAN programmer could tell you, there are actually three separate tokens (symbols) to the left of the equals sign. They are DO, 17, and I. They are perfectly distinguishable. Notice, however, that this is a legal FORTRAN assignment statement:

DO17I = 1

Therefore, not until the comma (or lack of comma) is found can these two statements be distinguished. In this latter case DO17I is a single token.

   a. What phases of the compiler would this apparent ambiguity affect and why?
   b. Can you suggest a method for overcoming the problem presented by the above two statements? Indicate how the affected phases would have to be changed.

26. It is possible to write a fast '1-pass' compiler in which the output of the action routines is actual machine numeric code, thus bypassing the need for the matrix and macro expansions. In terms of our compiler design, what are the major disadvantages to this scheme?

27. a. Flowchart an algorithm for parsing arithmetic statements with operators +, - . Use operator precedence (see problem 7.1).
   b. Implement (a) above using only reductions.
   c. Implement (a) above with a single PL/I routine.

28. †Implement an interpreter for reductions.

29. †Implement the action routines (Fig. 8.18) for MINI-PL/I.

30. †Instead of writing a code generator, implement an interpreter which is driven by a matrix. The matrix operators are those for the action routine of Figure 8.18, MINI-PL/I.

31. †Using

   a. The lexical program of problem 11 of Chapter 6
   b. The interpreter of problem 28 of this Chapter
   c. The action routines of problem 29 of this Chapter
   d. The interpreter of the matrix problem 30 of this Chapter

   implement a compiler for MINI-PL/I. Try compiling some sample PL/I programs.

Part III

32. What information about variables declared as automatic or controlled storage must be passed on to the executable program being compiled? This information is in the IDN table. Why must this information be passed on?

33. Is the use of automatic storage sufficient to eliminate the problem of recursion? (New allocation of all automatic variables is made every time the procedure is entered, and the latest allocation is freed only upon encountering a RETURN or END statement.) Why?

34. We have not discussed error handling in the text. We felt it would distract from the main theme and this allows us to ask the following. For each error, indicate what part or phase of the compiler you would modify to handle the error, why you chose that part, and suggest a possible repair action which would allow you to continue the error checking.

a. Check that all constant subscripts are within the range of legal subscripts.

b. Check the legality of identifiers, e.g., length, correct length, etc.

c. The IF statement of PL/I or ALGOL requires the keyword "THEN" to be present. How would you handle the case of an IF statement in which the keyword THEN was missing?

35. In this problem you will modify the PL/I subset of Figure 8.16, to include DO statements of the following forms:

   1)   DO { variable } = { exp1 } TO { exp2 } BY { exp3 } ;
   2)   DO;

a. First modify the BNF specifications of Figure 8.16 to include the new forms.

b. Modify reductions of Figure 8.17 to handle DO statements.

c. Now consider the permanent data bases (Fig. 8.13). Which require modification in order to implement the new statements? Which procedures will require change?

d. Be specific about phases 1, 2, and 3. If the lexical analyzer needs changing, specify how; if any new action routines are needed, be explicit as to their effects on all the data bases; etc. (Warning: DO-blocks are to be allowed.)

e. Repeat steps (a) through (d) for the "ADD-statement" defined as follows:

   ADD { var1 } , { var2 } , . . . , { var n } TO { variable p } ;

you may have any number of variables (at least one) appearing before the TO, all of which are to be added to the single variable appearing after the TO.

36. What types of declaration statements would result in assembled code?

37. The version of PL/I you are using may not support the use of based pointers as qualifiers, such as

   (P1 → A.B.NEXT) → A.B.C

a. What problems arise in implementation of this feature?

b. What modifications are necessary to overcome these problems?

38. Some of the more sophisticated features of languages are beyond the scope of the compiler alone. Discuss the compiler/operating system interface for:

a. Controlled/based storage

b. Conditions and signals

c. I/O

39. †,‡Implement a full PL/I compiler.

---

‡For the instructor who assigns all odd-numbered problems.

9

operating systems

As we noted in Chapter 1, there are numerous user viewpoints of an operating system. Some users view the system in terms of the utility functions it performs. Others are primarily concerned with the control languages used or the various facilities provided. From the viewpoint of systems programming, which is the orientation of this book, the structure and effectiveness of the operating system assume major importance. These factors are best discussed in terms of resource management, to which we now direct our attention.

In this chapter the description and capabilities of a general computer system, which were presented in Section 2.1, are explored in more detail. A discussion of I/O programming is included. There are four major resources that are controlled by the operating system: (1) memory, (2) processors, (3) devices, and (4) information, as noted in Figure 9.1.

It is the view of resource management that allows us to systematically study the design and implementation of various operating systems.

Resource	Examples	Example software to accomplish task
1. Memory	Core	Memory management, paging
2. Processors	CPUs, I/O channels	Traffic controller, scheduler
3. Devices	Tapes, drums, card punch	Spooling
4. Information	Segments (system, users, library segments)	File system, library, segment manager

FIGURE 9.1 System resources

A unified theory of resource management, and hence of operating systems, is just emerging. Within it the same theory and techniques are applied to the problems of managing the resources of memory, processors, devices, and information. The scheduling of memory presents the same problem as scheduling processors. Only recently have we acquired more hardware flexibility in scheduling memory, permitting us to partition it and allocate portions of it to users. Similar hardware flexibility for processors is not yet generally available; e.g., one cannot assign the arithmetic unit to one user and the logical processor to another.

PART 1

9.1 I/O PROGRAMMING: MULTIPLE PROCESSORS AND INTERRUPT MECHANISMS

In the preceding chapters we have been primarily concerned with the development of algorithms for various programming tools; in particular, assemblers, loaders, and compilers. For simplicity, we have been able to assume a sequential synchronous computer system and ignore many of the more "obscure" and complicating aspects of computer systems, such as I/O programming, I/O processors, multiple central processors, parallel computation, and asynchronous interrupts. Furthermore, we have largely avoided issues of system performance optimization and *throughput* (amount of "work" completed in a specific interval of time), except for a brief discussion of compiler optimization.

Fortunately, these omissions have little effect upon the relevance of the previous chapters because it is typical to localize all (or most) of the problems associated with asynchronous and parallel operation, as well as throughput optimization, into the operating system. In order to more fully understand and appreciate the following discussion of operating system resource allocation, it is necessary first to elaborate upon our earlier "simple" view of a computer system.

9.1.1 Evolution of Multiple Processor System

There are three basic components to a computer system: (1) the Central Processor Unit (CPU), (2) the main storage unit (memory), and (3) I/O devices (peripheral equipment). In the early systems, these components were interconnected as illustrated in Figure 9.2.

The central processor unit and memory essentially corresponded to the general machine structure presented in Chapter 2. In addition to ADD and SUBTRACT, there were such instructions as READ A CARD, PUNCH A CARD, and PRINT

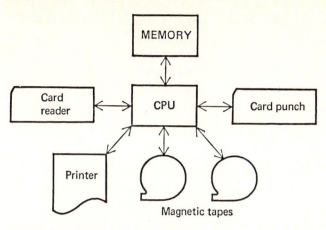

FIGURE 9.2 Early computer system

A LINE to operate the I/O devices one at a time. An ADD instruction might take 1 millisecond and a READ CARD instruction 500 milliseconds (100 cards per minute maximum speed) on an early computer.

As computer systems evolved, performance was upgraded by increasing speed and size. For example, memories with 1,000 words at 1 millisecond per access have been replaced by models with over 1 million words at less than one microsecond per access—a thousandfold increase in speed and size. In similar fashion CPUs have improved so that the typical instruction time is less than one microsecond.

Unfortunately, this evolution was not completely homogeneous. For example, conventional "high-speed" card readers and printers are limited to speeds of about 1,000 cards or lines per minute (50 milliseconds per card or line). Thus, the CPU could execute about 50,000 arithmetic instructions in the amount of time required for a single READ CARD instruction. Many of the other I/O devices, such as magnetic tapes, disks, and drums, are quite fast in comparison to the card reader, punch or printer, but they are still slow in relation to the CPU speeds.

The disparity in speeds between the I/O devices and the CPU-memory motivated the development of *I/O channels* or *I/O processors*, which are specialized processing units intended to operate the I/O devices. Since the I/O channels are simple, specialized, and need not be too fast, presumably they are much less expensive than a conventional CPU. Figure 9.3 depicts a computer system with several I/O channels. Because all input and output is executed via the channels, the CPU is free to perform its high-speed computations without wasting time "reading cards," for example. Furthermore, since it is possible to be operating several channels simultaneously, many card readers, punchers, and printers may function at the same time.

Although the basic idea remains the same, there are a great variety of I/O channels ranging from very simple processors to essentially fullblown central processor units. Some I/O channels connect only to a single device (i.e., need one channel for each I/O device), while others may be connected to several devices and operate them either one at a time (*selector channels*) or several at the same time (*multiplexer channels*).

The computer system shown in Figure 9.3 does not necessarily function efficiently without a considerable amount of effort. It is the function of the operating system to act as leader and to coordinate all the processors. In order for the reader to understand better the problems that the operating system must handle, we present in the following sections an example of I/O programming and the I/O interrupt mechanism.

9.1.2 I/O Programming

The central processing unit typically communicates with the I/O processor by means of specific instructions such as START I/O and HALT I/O. The I/O processor may observe the status of the central processing unit by inspecting a status register. Communication between the I/O channel and the CPU is usually performed by means of interrupts. An *interrupt* is a hardware facility that causes

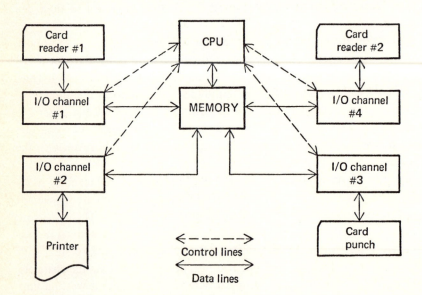

FIGURE 9.3 Computer system with I/O channels

the CPU to suspend execution, save its status, and transfer to a specific location. The transfer location specifies the address of a program that is intended to take action in response to the interrupt. The program that is executed as a result of an interrupt is called an *interrupt-handling* program.

The I/O processor interprets its own set of instructions. The programs written in these sets of instructions are known as I/O programs and their generation is loosely called *I/O programming*. Programmers do not usually write their own I/O programs but rather call a system supplied function that provides the I/O programs for them. The monitor system tailors the I/O programs to the particular needs of the user, and causes their execution.

We approach the I/O processor as we approached the CPU in Section 2.1.1; we answer the five basic questions that are asked when confronting a new machine or processor and we write some example I/O programs. I/O processors have not achieved the same standardization of instructions as central processing units. However, their functions can be generalized rapidly. We will take examples of I/O programming from the 370-type configuration. In the section on interrupt handling, we present a discussion of interrupt processing in a multiprocess system, specifically, with respect to the CPU and I/O channels.

9.1.3 I/O Processor Structure

Figure 9.4 depicts a system configuration exhibited on a 370-type computer.
Our five basic questions and answers about the 360-370 type I/O processor are:

A. Memory – What is the memory's basic unit, size, and addressing scheme?
The memory is the same one that the 360's central processing unit uses; basic memory unit is a byte, and the size is up to 2^{24} bytes. For addressing, the I/O channel uses a 24-bit absolute address.

B. Registers – How many registers are there? What is their size, function, and interrelationship?
The I/O channel has no explicit registers, but there is a program counter and data counter. Some I/O devices have internal registers similar to the internal CPU working registers used for instructions such as divide.

C. Data – What types of data can be handled by the processor? Primarily, logical data can be handled, e.g., a string of consecutive bytes from 1 to 2^{24} in length. Some I/O devices may include some types of code conversions on the data (e.g., code conversions from EBCDIC to BCD). The I/O processor also uses sense data pertaining to the state of an I/O device and may read and act on this type of data.

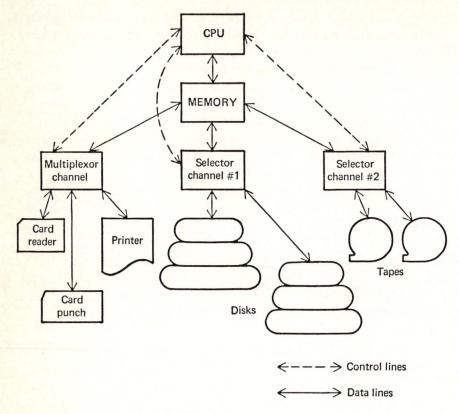

FIGURE 9.4 370 type system configuration

D. Instructions — What classes of instructions does the I/O processor interpret?
There are three basic groupings of I/O instructions (often called *commands*):

1. Data transfers: read, read backwards, write, sense (check on device status).
2. Device control: control (page eject, tape rewind, etc.)
3. Branching: transfers of controls within the channel program.

The channel fetches the channel instructions *(Channel Command Words — CCW)*
from memory and decodes them according to the following format.

OP CODE	Data address	Flag	Unused	Count
0 7 8	31 32	36 37	47 48	63

The OP codes consist of two to four operation bits and four to six modifier bits.
See Appendix A page 462 for listing of instructions.

The operation bits are standard while the modifier bits vary for each device.

The *data address* (bits 8-31) specifies the location of a byte in main storage. This is the beginning of the data field referenced by the instruction.

The *flags* further specialize the instruction. The five flags are:

1. The *chain data* flag (bit 32) denotes that the storage area designated by the next CCW is to be used with the current operation, once the initial data area is exhausted.
2. The *chain command* flag (bit 33) denotes that the next sequential CCW is to be executed on normal completion of the current operation.
3. The *suppress length indication flag* (bit 34) suppresses the indication to the program of an incorrect length indication.
4. The *skip* flag (bit 35) specifies suppression of transfer of information to storage.
5. *Programmed controlled interruption* flag (bit 36) causes the channel to generate an interruption condition when this CCW takes control of the channel.

The count field specifies the number of bytes in the storage area to be referenced by this CCW.

A group of multiple CCWs chained together is called a *channel program*. The CPU starts the channel executing instructions.

E. Special Features – Channels participate in the regular protection scheme of the 370 by associating a key with each I/O operation that is compared with the keys of the memory blocks referenced.

Channels are also an integral part of the 370 interruption structure. Both these points will be clarified in the following section on communication between the CPU and channel.

9.1.4 Examples of I/O Programs

EXAMPLE 1:

Let us write an I/O program that performs a "flush" function. This program is to read all cards in the card reader and ignore all information except that contained on the last one. The information on the last card is to be separated into two data fields, column 1 through 72 and column 73 through 80, and saved. This I/O function may be initiated when the CPU (executing in the executive system mode) detects an error in the current job. The operating system then simply wishes to read in the remaining cards to enable it to get onto the next job in the card reader, saving information on the last card for diagnostic purposes. Figure 9.5 contains three instructions coded in hexadecimal that will perform the flush task. These are the actual instructions as they might appear in memory.

Location   Instruction

OP CODE	Data address	Flag	Unused	Count

	Read			Data chain	
000600	02	000700	80	00	0048 (=72_{10})
				Continue	
000608	XX	000800	40	00	0008
000610	08	000600	XX	XX	XXXX
	Transfer				

000700   72 bytes for card data

000800   ___ 8 bytes for card sequence number

FIGURE 9.5 I/O program – flush

The I/O program in Figure 9.5 is assumed to start in location 600. The first channel command word has an OP code of 02, which is interpreted as READ. The instruction is to read 72 bytes of data from the card reader into locations 700 to 771. The flag field of 80 indicates that the rest of the data is to be handled by the next channel command word, which specifies that the last eight bytes of the card are to be read into locations 800 to 807. The flag of 40 indicates that the next channel command word is then to be executed.

The final channel command word is in location 610. The op code of 08 is interpreted by the I/O processor as a transfer to the CCW at location 600, as indicated in the data address field.

The I/O processor executing this program will read in the information on each card, continually overlaying into location 700 and location 800. After the last card is read, the I/O processor will try to execute the first instruction of the I/O program. Finding there are no more cards in the card reader, it will terminate and will indicate that fact to the CPU.

There are many other situations, such as searching for information on a magnetic disk, that involve I/O program loops. In general, most simple I/O programs do not have a loop.

EXAMPLE 2:

Let us write an I/O program that causes the printer to print a message, eject the page, and print a heading on top of the next page. Such an I/O program may be called at the termination of a user's job. The message we wish to print with this

I/O program is "END OF PAGE" and a message on the top of the next page is to be "TOP OF NEW PAGE." The program shown in Figure 9.6 accomplishes this.

The first I/O instruction is stored in the location starting at address 300; its op code is 01, which instructs the I/O processor to print a single line. The line to be printed is stored in location 400, as indicated in the address field, and consists of 11 characters.

The next instruction, at 308, has an op code of 8B, which results in the printer ejecting to the top of the next page. The last instruction, with an op code of 11, causes the 15 characters starting at location 500 to be printed. Further, the op code indicates that two lines are to be skipped after printing the header line.

Location	Instruction					Comments
	OP CODE	Data address	Flag	Unused	Count	
000 300	01	000 400	40	00	000B	Print line
000 308	8B	XXX XXX	40	00	XXXX	Skip page
000 310	11	000 500	00	00	000F	Print header line
⋮						
000 400	"END OF PAGE"					Data
⋮						
000 500	"TOP OF NEW PAGE"					

FIGURE 9.6 I/O print program

9.1.5 Communications between the CPU and the Channel

Now that we have seen how the channel itself works, we will examine how it communicates with the CPU. The purpose of having a channel is to free the CPU from controlling I/O operations that are often very time-consuming. The CPU and the channel are usually in a master-slave relationship. This means that the CPU tells the channel when to start and can command it to stop or change what it is doing. On the other hand, the channel cannot usually start any operation unless instructed by the CPU.

There are two classes of communication between the CPU and the channel.

1. I/O instructions initiated by the CPU (CPU to channel)
2. CPU interrupt initiated by the channel (channel to CPU)

I/O initiation instructions are executed by the CPU. This section will describe the relationship between I/O instructions of the CPU and the channel. The description of the I/O interrupts will be left for the next section.

All CPU I/O instructions have the following modified SI format:

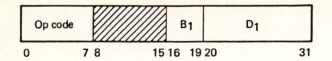

Op code	/////	B₁	D₁

0   7 8   15 16 19 20   31

The channel and device number are specified by the sum of the contents of register B_1, and the contents of the D_1 field. Bits 16-23 of the sum contain the channel address, while bits 24-31 contain the device on the channel.

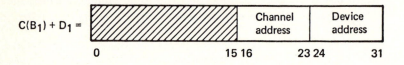

$C(B_1) + D_1 =$ ////////////// | Channel address | Device address |

0   15 16   23 24   31

There are four CPU I/O instructions: (Note: these are executed by the CPU).

1. START I/O — Two items are needed to start I/O: (a) channel and device number; and (b) beginning address of channel program. The START I/O instruction specifies channel and device number (e.g., SIO X^1 $00E^1$, where 0 is channel number 0, and 0E is device number 0E). Address $72\text{-}75_{16}$ in memory is the *Channel Address Word* (CAW), which specifies the start of the channel program; it is discussed below.
2. TEST I/O — The state of the addressed channel and device is indicated by setting the condition code (busy or not). The condition code can then be tested by the standard branch conditional instruction.
3. HALT I/O — Execution of the current I/O operation at the addressed I/O device and channel is terminated.
4. TEST CHANNEL — The condition code is set to indicate the state (busy or not) of the addressed channel.

The low addresses of memory (at least 0-128) are reserved for special purposes. Locations 64-71 are a doubleword, called the Channel Status Word (CSW), while locations 72-75 are a fullword called the Channel Address Word (CAW).

The Channel Status Word provides the detail status of an I/O device or the conditions under which an I/O operation has been terminated. The CSW may be set in the process of I/O operations and during execution of START I/O, HALT I/O, and TEST I/O. The format of the CSW is:

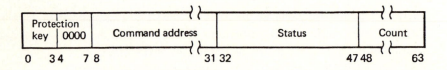

Protection key	0000	Command address	Status	Count

0   3 4   7 8   31 32   47 48   63

9.1.6 Interrupt Structure and Processing

Interrupt means to cause a transfer of control in response to signals that are asynchronous with respect to instruction execution. Typically, when such a signal is received, the processor (usually the CPU) replaces the contents of the instruction counter with a predetermined address after these contents and other program status information have been saved. Following the interrupt, the processor commences to execute an *interrupt routine.* The interrupt routine is a program that has been written to respond to the condition of the interrupt. For example, Figure 9.7 depicts the locus of an interrupted processor. At point 1 the processor was executing a program when the interrupt occurred, which forced the processor to transfer to the interrupt routine 2. At the termination of the interrupt routine the processor resumed processing of the original program at point 3.

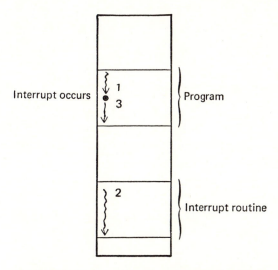

FIGURE 9.7 Locus of a process through an interrupt

The "state" or current condition of the CPU is stored in a doubleword register, called the *Program Status Word* (PSW). This corresponds to the CSW of the I/O processor. The PSW is used to control instruction sequencing and to hold and indicate the status of the system in relation to the program currently being executed. The active or controlling PSW is the "current" PSW. By storing the PSW during an interruption, the status of the CPU can be preserved for inspection or reloading. By loading a new PSW, or part of one, the state of the CPU can be changed.

The format of the PSW is as follows:

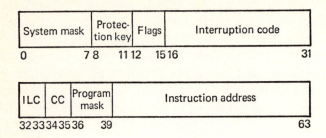

(See IBM manual, Principles of Operation, or Appendix A for an explanation of all the PSW fields.)

Bits in the PSW may be used to mask certain interruptions. When *masked*, I/O, external and machine check interruptions may be inhibited temporarily but kept pending. The program mask may cause 4 of the 15 program interruptions to be ignored. The other 11 program interruptions and the supervisor call interruption cannot be masked.

The programmer has at his disposal 11 status switching instructions; among these are: Load PSW (LPSW), Set Program Mask (SPM), Set System Mask (SSM), Supervisor Call (SVC), Set Storage Key (SSK) and Insert Storage Key (ISK).

These instructions to change, modify, and load the PSW are privileged instructions. A *privileged* instruction is one that a normal program cannot execute. It can only be executed by the operating system.

Together with the coding of the interruption handling routines, these instructions enable a programmer to uniquely and explicitly specify how the CPU is to react to any sequence of events. The complete details of interrupt processing, however, are beyond the scope of this chapter. What we are presenting here is a framework for the handling of simple I/O operations.

There are five classes of interrupts on the 370:

1. I/O
2. Programmer error
   a. Arithmetic
   b. Invalid instruction
   c. Storage protect
3. Supervisor call
4. External
   a. Timer
   b. Console interrupt button
   c. CPU to CPU interrupt
5. Machine Check — detection of machine failure error

Each of the five classes of interrupts, I/O, programmer error, supervisor call, external, and machine check, has associated with it two PSWs, called "old" and "new," stored in the memory of the computer. These are to be found in pre-determined main storage locations. When an interrupt occurs, the interrupt hardware mechanism stores the current PSW in the "old" position and loads the PSW from the "new" position. The CPU then starts executing instructions specified by the instruction address field of the current PSW, which corresponds to the new PSW. At the conclusion of the interrupt routine there may be an instruction to make the old PSW the current PSW. The system is restored to its previous status and the interrupted program continues. These special interrupt locations are depicted in Figure 9.8. (See also Appendix A page 455.)

Interrupt routines can access old PSWs to ascertain the condition that caused the interrupt. The old PSW contains an interrupt code and the location of the instruction being executed when the interrupt occurred.

An interrupt always takes place after one instruction is finished and before a new one is started. Most computer systems have a hardware mechanism called masking. *Masking* is a facility that temporarily prohibits the interruption of the CPU. Interruptions are taken only when the CPU is interruptable from the interrupt source. The system mask, program mask, and machine check mask are

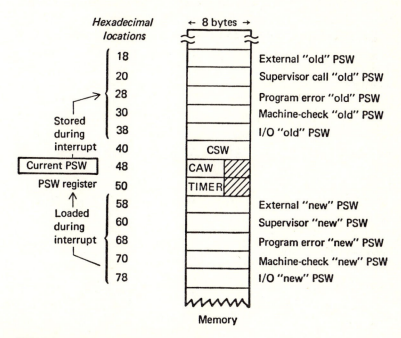

FIGURE 9.8 Special interrupt locations

mechanisms by which interrupts may be masked. For example, if while processing an interrupt another interrupt occurs, then an interrupt queue routine may be called. If, while executing the interrupt queue routine, another interrupt has occurred, then the interrupt queue routine would be called again, which may result in the loss of one of the interrupts. Therefore, for example, while the CPU is executing the interrupt queue routine, all other interrupts are masked.

9.1.7   Example of I/O Interrupt Processing (Fig. 9.9)

In the last three sections we have examined three portions of an I/O operation:

1. Execution of I/O commands by the channel.
2. Execution of I/O instructions by the CPU.
3. Communication of the channel with the CPU. This can be an interrupt, the storing of the CSW, or the setting of the CC.

To make the details more intelligible, we will now work through the complete life of a simple I/O operation. It is not necessary to discuss the remote possibilities in order to demonstrate the basic facilities for input/output.

This example consists of:

1. A main program that is executed by the CPU. The main program during its execution builds up 25 lines of data in an output buffer. Each line is 100 characters long. It then initiates an I/O instruction to cause the entire I/O buffer to be printed with 25 lines to the page, double-spaced.
2. Channel program. The channel prints out the information in the buffer in the manner described above.
3. An interrupt handler that processes the I/O interrupt occurring when the I/O channel completes the I/O program. The interrupt program is executed by the CPU.

This example is part of a program that is printing pages with headers on a 1403 printer, with channel and device address X'00E'. We will only examine the parts of core storage which are affected by the printing of the one page.

The programmer must provide the proper environment for his START I/O instruction by:

1. Writing a channel program
2. Providing data areas and constants
3. Filling in his buffer with contents of a page
4. Storing address of channel program in CAW
5. Getting into supervisor state (set bit in PSW)

Once these steps have been accomplished, the programmer may issue his START
I/O (SIO) instruction.

NOTE: We will use a new instruction format to write CCWs;

      CCW   opcode, address, flag, count

This is an assembler pseudo-op which creates a machine language CCW in core on
a doubleword boundary.

Step number	Contents	Hex address		Actual contents	Comments
		:			Device
10,13	I/O OLD PSW {	38		X'0000000E X X001500	Instruction address
8	CSW {	40		X'000021982C000000'	Command address
					Residual count = 0
2	CAW {	48		002000	Status
		:			
					Address of
11	I/O NEW PSW {	78		X'XXXXXXXXXX000500	I/O interruption
		:			Processing routine
12	INTERRUPT HANDLER {	500 : 600		I/O Interrupt handling routine	
Execution starts here	MAIN PROGRAM {	→ 842 : 1000		-Program which builds output buffer for next page	
1,2				-Store address of CCW No. 1 in CAW	
				SIO X'00E'	
3 9,14		1500		-Continue program, fill up next output buffer	
4	CHANNEL PROGRAM {	2000 CCW1	CCW	X'8B',*,X'40',0	(Skip to top of next page)
5		2008 CCW2	CCW	X'19',PAGEHDR,X'40',11	(Write and skip 3 lines)
6		2010 CCW3 :	CCW	X'11',LINE1,X'40',100 (23 more CCW's)	(Write and skip 2 lines)
7		2190 CCW27	CCW	X'11',LINE1+(24*100),0,100	
	DATA CONSTANT AREA {	2400 PAGEHDR :	DC	C'PAGE HEADER'	
		3000 LINE1	DS	25CL100 (25 lines to be printed)	
		39C4 LINE2	DS	25CL100 (Second buffer)	

FIGURE 9.9 Example program with I/O interrupt processing

The reader should follow steps 1 through 14 below:

CPU:

1. START I/O issued for device 00E. CPU checks status of channel, and device.
2. The CPU initiates the channel to examine CAW for address of channel program (which is 2000) and the channel starts executing program.
3. CPU resumes processing at location 1004, while channel starts executing CCW1 and appears busy to other I/O requests.

CHANNEL:

4. Channel decodes CCW1

      Bits 0-7 B'10001011'   —   Skip to channel 1 (top next page)
            32-35 B'0100'   —   Command chaining (go to next CCW op and data)

5. Channel decodes CCW2

      Bits 0-7 B'00011001'   —   Write, skip 3 after print
            8-31 X'002400'   —   Address of page header characters
            32-35 B'0100'   —   Command chain
            48-63 X'000B'   —   Print 11 characters

6. Channel decodes CCW3

      Bits 0-7 B'00010001'   —   Write, skip 2 lines after print
            8-31 X'003000'   —   Address of first data line
            32-35 B'0100'   —   Command chain
            48-63 X'0064'   —   Print 100 characters on line

               .
               .
               .

      CCW4 — CCW26 processed as in step 6

7. Channel decodes CCW No. 27

      Bits 0-7   B'00010001'   —   Write, skip 2
      Bits 8-31 X'003960'   —   Address of last line
      Bits 32-35 X'00'   —   This is the last I/O command referenced by channel
      Bits 48-63 X'0064'   —   Print 100 characters

8. Channel signals normal termination by generating a pending I/O interrupt and loading CSW with count, device unit, channel end conditions.
9. When mask bit for channel (0 bit of current PSW) = 0 and before execution of the next instruction (e.g., loc 1500) CPU accepts I/O interrupt (assume no others pending).

CPU:

10. Current PSW is stored at location 38 with the device address and the address of the next instruction to be executed.
11. Current PSW is replaced by new PSW from location 78 which gives control to I/O interrupt processing routine.
12. I/O interruption processing routine decides by examining the CSW that the operation terminated normally. This routine may signal a normal completion of an I/O operation to the original program in any predetermined manner.
13. The I/O interruption handling routine then returns control to the main program by reloading the current PSW from the old I/O PSW.
14. Program continues from location reached before interrupt occurred (loc 1500).

The channel is now ready for another page to be printed. If the programmer had two channel programs and two data areas, he could be preparing page 2 while page 1 is being printed. After completion of the first channel program (denoted by an interrupt), the main program would load the CAW and execute SIO for the second channel program. The main program may have to enter the wait state if the first channel program is not finished with its page. If the main program is in the wait state when the first channel program finishes (sends interrupt), the I/O handling routine would restore the old PSW (for the main program) with the state changed to active.

9.1.8 Multiple Processors

The channels or I/O processors on the IBM 360 and 370 are relatively simple in nature. In particular, they are unable to perform any conditional transfers (except for very special situations). For example, these channels would be unable to read cards one by one and stop (i.e. generate CPU interrupt) when a card with //JOB on it is read.

On some of the very large computer systems, such as the CDC 7600, I/O processors have evolved to the level of small central processors or minicomputers complete with arithmetic and conditional instructions. Furthermore, motivated by factors such as increased performance and reliability, computer manufacturers have produced some large systems that actually consist of several complete central processor units connected to a single memory. This type of generalized multiple processor system adds to the complexity that must be handled by the operating system.

PART 2

9.2 MEMORY MANAGEMENT

Memory management plays an important role in operating systems, and memory utilization has proved to be a major "bottleneck."

As noted in the previous section, optimal coordination of the multiple processors (e.g. CPUs and I/O channels) can be a complex task. In order to illustrate how memory management facilitates processor coordination and increased throughput, the concept of multiprogramming is introduced in this section. A more extensive discussion of multiprogramming will be found in the section on processor management.

In this section we present a broad, though not necessarily complete, spectrum of memory management schemes. These schemes will be presented going from simple to more complex, motivating each successive scheme by attempting to achieve increased throughput performance. Many of these techniques were not developed in the order we present them nor were their original philosophical motivations simply related to performance improvement. A detailed rendering of the history of these schemes is not particularly relevant.

The memory management schemes that are included in this section use a spectrum of hardwares:

1. Single contiguous allocation
2. Partitioned allocation
3. Relocatable partitioned allocation
4. Paged allocation
5. Demand paged allocation
6. Segmented allocation
7. Segmented-paged allocation

Each hardware capability allows us greater flexibility in the management of the resource of memory.

9.2.1 Single Contiguous Allocation

A single contiguous allocation scheme is depicted in Figure 9.10.

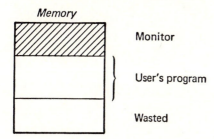

Memory

Monitor

User's program

Wasted

FIGURE 9.10 Simple batch monitor

The operating system (or resident monitor system) usually resides in either the upper or lower part of the core memory. A job is assigned all of core although it typically needs and uses only a small fraction. The job has complete control of the CPU until completion or until an error occurs. This is wasteful, especially in a system where the operator must perform manual actions such as loading a tape or card deck. Even in a system with I/O channels, the time in which the CPU remains idle while the I/O channel performs the input and output functions is appreciable.

The major problem with this type of system is that the resources are usually not managed in an efficient manner. There is not enough hardware flexibility to allow effective allocation of memory.

This type of allocation is often used for small, inexpensive computing systems. Despite its disadvantages, the simplicity of the contiguous allocation system is sufficiently appealing that some large computer installations have chosen to use it to minimize programming complexity.

9.2.2 Partitioned Allocation

To solve the problem of wasted time and wasted memory, the partitioned allocation scheme was introduced. It is based upon a partitioning of memory and is used on systems such as IBM's Operating System/360, MFT (Multiprogramming with a Fixed number of Tasks), and MVT (Multiprogramming with a Variable number of Tasks). An example of the memory allocation scheme is depicted in Figure 9.11. The memory is partitioned so that each job (or task) is allocated a separate contiguous section of core (Fig. 9.11a).

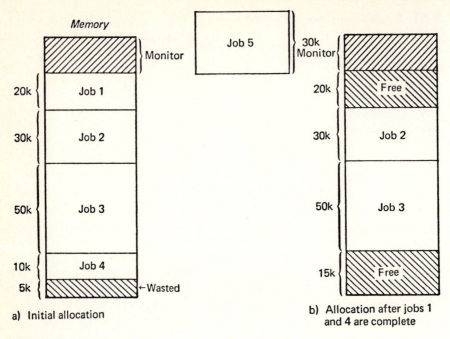

FIGURE 9.11 Partitioned memory

The increased performance of the partitioned operating system is based upon the technique of multiprogramming or multitasking. Multiprogramming, in the simplest sense, means to maintain two or more jobs concurrently in execution or states of execution. This is contrasted with the *serial processing* of the simple single allocation system in which only one job is run at a time.

In a typical multiprogrammed partitioned scheme, CPU time is allocated to each job on a time-slice priority basis. For a *time-slice* (a specific amount of time such as 100 ms) the operating system causes the processor to execute a program in its address space (partition) until one of the following four conditions occurs:

1. Job is completed
2. Error is detected
3. I/O is required
4. Job's current time-slice runs out

In each case the processor is then assigned to the job with the next highest priority. In the first two cases, the job can be purged from memory. In the last two, the job is only temporarily suspended; it is to be resumed.

The advantage of multiprogramming is the elimination or diminution of the wasted CPU idle time discussed earlier. For example, it may be possible to run two jobs that ordinarily would take one hour each so that they are both completed in about one hour in a multiprogramming system. This could happen if each job when run separately resulted in 50 percent CPU idle time due to I/O and manual operator intervention; if both balanced jobs were run at the same, the CPU could work on job 2 when job 1 required I/O, rather than idling (and vice versa).

In a random selection of jobs, it is unlikely that the jobs will be exactly balanced. Increasing the number of jobs being executed decreases the likelihood of all the jobs requiring I/O at the same time and increases the throughput. For contemporary job mixes, about five simultaneous jobs may be sufficient to result in CPU utilization of about 90 percent.

These anticipated throughput increases are not without tradeoffs. A multiprogramming system is usually more expensive than a simple single allocation for the following reasons:

1. Special *protection mechanisms* are required to prevent one job from unintentionally disrupting another. This may not be needed in a single allocation system since a job could only destroy itself or the monitor.
2. Additional core storage is required due to a more complex operating system and in order to fit enough jobs into core so as to fully utilize a multiprogramming system.

The major problem with a partitioned memory allocation scheme is fragmentation. Fragmentation is the development of unusable "holes" or "fragments" in memory. This can be seen in Figure 9.11. In this example the address space of job 1 occupies 20K of core; Job 2, 30K of core; job 3, 50K of core; job 4, 10K of core; and 5K of unused core. ("K" denotes 1,000 bytes of storage.) If there is a fifth job waiting to be processed whose programs require 30K of core, it must wait for a continuous block of 30K of storage before it can start. Let us assume that as time passes, job 1 is completed, freeing 20K of core, and job 4 is completed, thus freeing an additional 15K of core. We then have a total of 35K words of unused storage. However, there is not 30K of continuous core; therefore, job 5 still cannot be started. In this type of partition scheme we see that fragments of unused core often develop.

Thus, for example, a computer configuration and mix of jobs that might be expected to result in four or five jobs being multiprogrammed (as in part a of Fig. 9.11) may become degraded so that only two or three jobs are being multiprogrammed (as in part b) of Fig. 9.11). In this situation, CPU utilization and throughput decrease.

The problem of fragmentation may be solved in several ways. We will discuss two of these: relocatable partitions and paging.

9.2.3 Relocatable Partitioned Allocation

Let us consider three possible approaches to fragmentation:

1. Do nothing and be content with wasted memory and lower CPU utilization.
2. Increase the amount of core memory until there is sufficient multiprogramming to reach a higher CPU utilization.
3. Provide processor hardware facilities to help attack the cause of fragmentation.

The first two alternatives result in a substantial waste of memory, and in present-day computer systems memory often represents one-third of the total system cost. Therefore, it is not surprising that several attempts have been made to solve fragmentation by using reasonably economical processor features.

The scheme of relocatable partitions is one of the solutions to the fragmentation problem and is depicted in Figure 9.12.

In this example there are again four jobs in memory (Fig. 9.12a). When fragmentation prevents a new job from being loaded, the jobs remaining in the

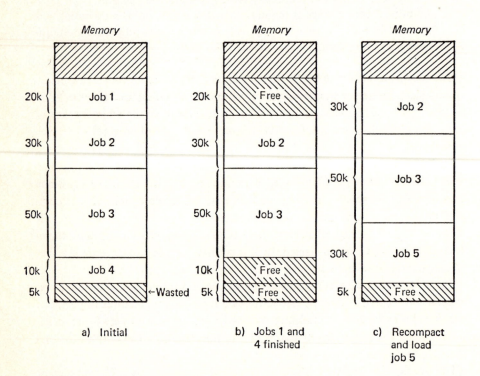

FIGURE 9.12 Relocatable partitioned memory

memory can be compacted by relocating them upwards. For example, when job 1 and job 4 are finished (Fig. 9.12b), jobs 2 and 3 are moved so that job 5 can be fitted into the contiguous area formed (Fig. 9.12c).

The partitions cannot be relocated efficiently without special hardware facilities. Once loaded, a program takes "root" much like a planted seed. The "root" generally develops due to address-dependent components of the program such as:

1. Memory referencing instructions
2. Parameter lists
3. Data structures

that use "address pointers." Therefore, in general, merely moving the contents of a partition will not insure that the program will function correctly in its new location unless all address-dependent components are suitably modified. Unfortunately, most modern computers do not have provisions to differentiate between data and addresses (such as data in "black" and addresses in "red"); therefore, there is no way for the monitor to know exactly which words must be altered. There are software techniques and conventions that could be used, but these are either very inefficient or restrictive (see references, Chapter 10).

There is a possible solution to the problem; that is, reload and start from the beginning every program to be relocated. Besides being extremely expensive, this restart may not be feasible if the program is already in the midst of updating and changing a master tape, or has performed some other irreversible action.

A "relativity" mechanism is needed that makes a program independent of its physical core memory location. This would be much like the physics of relativity whereby a person in a closed "ideal" boxcar cannot tell in which direction the train is moving or even whether it is stopped. A simple mechanism that serves this purpose is a *relocation register* whose contents are automatically added to every address that is used to reference memory. The relocation register may be considered an extra "hidden" index register that is automatically used for every memory reference instruction.

In the example of Figure 9.13, the contents of a single job's address space (left) is separated from the physical memory layout (right). Before relocation it is obvious that the instruction LOAD 2105 (LOAD from location 2105 to accumulator)[1] located at location 2100 will load 00047 into the computer's accumulator. After relocation the program starts at location 1000 instead of 2000 although all the instructions remain unchanged. Since the program has been moved to 1000 from 2000, the hardware relocation register is set by the monitor

---

[1] In these examples we will assume a simple single-address word-oriented computer.

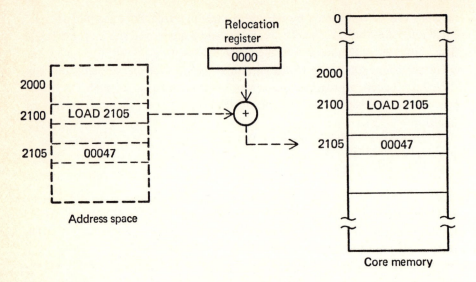

a) Before relocation

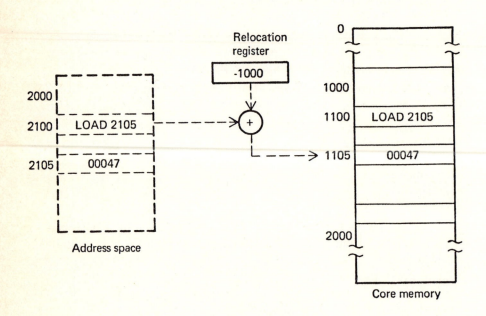

b) After relocation

FIGURE 9.13 Use of relocation register

to $1000 - 2000 = -1000$. Thus, when the instruction LOAD 2105 is encountered, rather than loading the accumulator from physical core location 2105, the contents of location $2105 - 1000 = 1105$ will be loaded, thus accessing the value 00047 as intended. The important point to note is that nothing within the program is aware of its actual physical core memory location; in the following example, every LOAD, ADD, BRANCH, etc. will behave as if the program were loaded at location 2000, even if it has been physically moved to location 1000.

Since their specific physical memory location is irrelevant in a computer system with a relocation register, all programs are usually treated as if they were loaded at location 0. In this way the contents of these relocation registers are always positive.

Although the mechanism of relocation is quite simple, it has significant conceptual implications. As shown in the preceding example, the job's address space (name space) is independent of the program's physical core memory location. This conceptual independence will be the basis of the more complex memory allocation schemes presented later.

There are two major problems with this scheme. First is the overhead of relocation: when a job ends, the system may have to relocate all the other jobs in order to recompact. Between the partition scheme and the relocation partitioned scheme there is the tradeoff between CPU time (recompact, overhead in the relocatable partition scheme) and wasted memory (fragmentation, in the partition scheme) that must be weighed. The Honeywell 635 computer system, for example, uses the mechanism of relocatable partitions. The second problem is that there is still a small amount of core wasted (see Fig. 9.12a).

9.2.4 Paged Allocation

Paging is another solution to the problem of fragmentation. A paging scheme is used in several contemporary computers such as the XDS 940. Consider the example depicted in Figure 9.14.

In the diagram, the job's address space is considered to be subdivided into 1000 byte units, called *pages*. As in the relocatable partitions scheme, the user is not aware of this subdivision because it has no apparent effect upon his address space. The physical memory also is subdivided into 1000 byte units, called *blocks*. The pages and blocks may be considered as the two parts of a set of plugs; that is, any page can be "plugged" into any block. As in the relocatable partitions scheme, it is necessary to provide a mechanism to allow the hardware to perform the mapping from user address space to physical memory. For this purpose, there is a separate register for each page; they are often called *page maps* or *page*

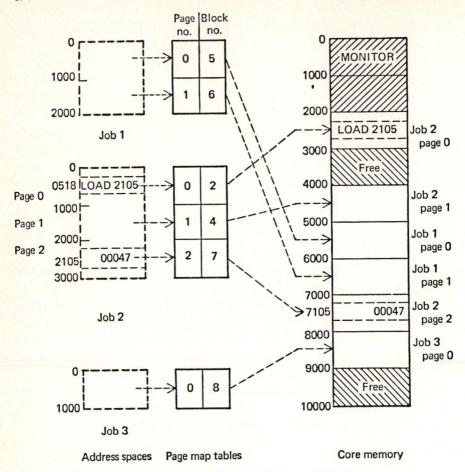

FIGURE 9.14 Paging scheme of memory allocation

map tables. These registers may either be special hardware registers or a reserved section of core memory. Note the page map tables are much smaller in size than the address spaces. In Figure 9.14 their sizes are not drawn proportionally. For example, Job 2's address space is 3000 locations where the page map table may be only 6 locations.

Since each page may be separately relocated, there is no need for a job's partition to be completely contiguous in core memory; only locations in a single page must be contiguous. Obviously, the choice of page size has a substantial effect upon the utility of this scheme. If the page size is too large, it becomes comparable to the size of the job's partition and, essentially, becomes a relocatable partitions scheme. If the page size is too small, it is necessary to have many page map registers, which greatly increases the cost of the computer system. As a result of these and other tradeoffs, many paging systems use a page size of about 4000 bytes.

In the example system of Figure 9.14, the address space of job 1 is divided into two pages; job 2 is divided into three pages; and job 3 consists of one page. There is a page table for each job, and in it is the associated page number and a location of that page in physical memory (block number). There is a mapping that must take place with each address. That is, each address in the job's address space can be transformed into an address in physical memory.

The LOAD 2105 instruction shown at location 0518 in the address space is actually located at location 518 within page 0. Likewise, the data word 00047 located at 2105 is considered to be at location 105 within page 2. The page table maps from address space page numbers to physical memory block numbers. Thus, the LOAD instruction is actually located at physical location 2518 (location 518 within block 2) since the page table shows that page 0 is stored in block 2. The hardware may achieve this mapping by taking the leftmost digit of an address, using that as an index to the page table, and then replacing that leftmost digit with the value of that index in the page table. Depending upon the actual details of the hardware implementation, the CPU mechanism required to perform the address mapping may decrease the computer's speed slightly.

The paging system scheme solves the fragmentation problem without the need to rearrange partitions after a job terminates. For example, in Figure 9.13 there are 2000 bytes of unused core memory, but they are not contiguous. If there were a fourth job, whose address space were less than 2000 words, we could rearrange core to produce a 2000-word contiguous partition. But rather than rearrange core, we could divide the address space of job 4 into two pages and place one at core location 3000 and the other at 9000. By setting the page map table for job 4 as shown below, it will appear as if its address space were contiguous.

Page	Block
0	3
1	9

Page map table of user **4**

There are several major problems with paging. The first is the overhead associated with each address transformation. Another problem is the extra core or extra registers needed for the page tables. Since a job may not be a multiple of 1000 bytes long, a portion of the last page will be wasted. This is called *page breakage.* On the average, there is half a page wasted for each job. This can be serious if there are a large number of small jobs.

There are three further disadvantages. First, as in relocatable partitions, there will still be wasted core if there is sufficient space for some, but not all of an additional job's pages. Second, in this type of paging scheme, all the pages of a particular job must be in core before that program can be executed. And third, a considerable amount of hardware support is needed.

9.2.5 Demand Paged Allocation

Demand paging is a memory allocation scheme that fulfills the programmer's ultimate dream, an infinite amount of memory (almost). Demand paging schemes are used on the IBM 360 Model 67, Honeywell 645, and RCA 3 and 7.

A *virtual memory* is another name for the address space in which a job operates under demand paging. A virtual memory in principle may be larger than the available core. The memory allocation scheme of demand paging may be exemplified by Figure 9.15.

In Figure 9.15 the job's address space consists of 10,000 bytes of programs and data and assumes that we only have 3,000 bytes of memory available. This 10,000-byte program can be run on the 3000-byte machine by means of demand paging. The page table (Fig. 9.15) has several fields for each page entry: page number, block number (the location in core), status (whether in core or out of core), and some judgement indication that will be explained later.

An allocation algorithm (software) may initially place three pages of the program into core; let us assume the first three pages. Presumably, the job starts executing in one of these pages. If within page 0 there is a transfer instruction to location 9005, the hardware mechanism would then use the 9 as an index to the page table; it would check the status of that page and note that it is not in core (i.e., not "OK"). It would then *demand* that page 9 be brought into core. The software would search secondary storage for page 9 and load it, overlaying (i.e., replacing) one of the other three pages. The decision as to which page gets overlaid is the motivation for the judgement bit field. The ideal situation is to overlay the page used most infrequently. In most programs the execution of the program is not uniformly distributed over the entire address space, but rather there are local areas in which the processor spends a higher percentage of time. It is desirable to keep only highly-used pages in core. There are many *paging algorithms* for keeping track of which page should remain in core and which page should not. One such paging algorithm may be to simply keep a count of the accesses to that page in the judgement field. The page that should be overlaid would be the one with the fewest number of accesses to that page. The judgement field must

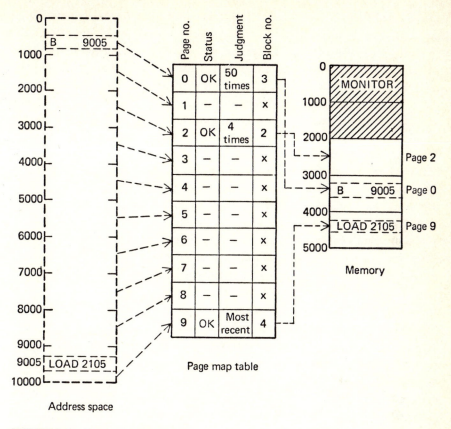

FIGURE 9.15 Demand paging scheme

be reset periodically because naturally the page with the fewest number of accesses will also be the page that was most recently brought into core; it should not necessarily be overlaid.

In most practical demand paging systems only part of the "demand" handling is done by the hardware. When the hardware finds that the status of a page is "not in core" (not OK), it stops processing and automatically generates an interrupt to the monitor; this is often called a *processor interrupt* or *page interrupt*. The monitor then actually performs the action of accessing secondary storage and acquiring the needed page. Furthermore, while the page is being brought into core, the monitor may multiprogram other jobs as in the previously described paging system.

In addition to providing the programming advantage of an apparently very large memory, demand paging aids system throughput in several ways. Studies have indicated that only a portion of a job's address space is actually used. This makes considerable sense if you consider error routines — which are often not used in any particular run — or tables that are only partly filled due to the data used for the run. This does not mean that these parts of the program are unnecessary; it merely implies that it is better not to load these parts unless they are actually used in a particular run. Some studies have shown that up to 25 percent of a typical program's address space is not used during any particular run. Thus, demand paging may allow the system to multiprogram 25 percent more users without any substantial additional effort.

Furthermore, many parts of a program are only used once, such as the initialization routines, the sequential phases of many programs (e.g., the subroutines of a compiler), etc. This characteristic is very dependent upon the nature of the particular program, but it is quite common to find that much less than 50 percent of a program's entire address space is actually needed over any small interval of time; the portion that is used during a given interval is called the *working set* (these concepts are discussed in the references, Chapter 10, in considerable detail).

By choosing sufficiently small intervals of time, demand paging can be very valuable in "time-sharing" systems which attempt to run dozens of programs simultaneously. As stated earlier in this chapter, multiprogramming with five or six jobs is usually sufficient to come close to reaching optimal throughput. Time-sharing dozens of jobs actually tends to decrease throughput, although there are other factors, such as response time, which may be enhanced. Of course, if too many programs are being time-shared, as may happen when using demand paging in a system with insufficient core memory (or poor paging judgement algorithms), pages may be read into core, replaced, and then read back in continually, resulting in very low throughput (under these circumstances throughput has been known to drop below 1 percent). In this extreme case, the system is said to be *thrashing*. Due to the importance of demand paging systems and the complexity of the thrashing problem, considerable research has been done to develop algorithms that minimize or eliminate the possibility of thrashing (see references, Chapter 10). Demand paging also suffers from most of the other disadvantages discussed in the preceding section on paging.

9.2.6 Segmented Allocation

Segmentation is both a memory and an information management scheme. We focus first on its memory management aspects. In Section 9.5 we return and focus on the information aspects. It should now be noted that although the relocatable partitions, paging, and demand paging operating systems exploit the notion of independence between the job's address space and physical core memory, the programmer still views the address space exactly as if it were a simple linear physical core memory. We ask ourselves the question: "How would a programmer *like* his address space to appear?" and then attempt to implement this apparent address space using techniques similar to the relocation and paging mechanisms.

A *segment* is a grouping of information that is treated as an entity. This may be one program or many programs, a single data base or multiple data bases. In a segmentated environment the programmer conceives of his address space as two-dimensional and addressed by two components: the name of a segment and an offset within that segment. Each segment has its own access rights associated with it. Segmentation facilitates the implementation of dynamic linking. At the time of the execution of a call statement, the loading mechanism finds the program, loads it into core, and binds that calling program to its caller during execution; thus there is no overhead incurred if the program is never actually called.

Figure 9.16 illustrates how a programmer might view a segmented address space. Each segment appears as a separate distinct linear memory of individual size (i.e., segments need not be the same size). Let us assume that ALPHA and BETA are segments that contain executable programs whereas DATA is a segment that contains only data. In a two-dimensional segmented system, every instruction must express an address reference in two parts: a segment name and

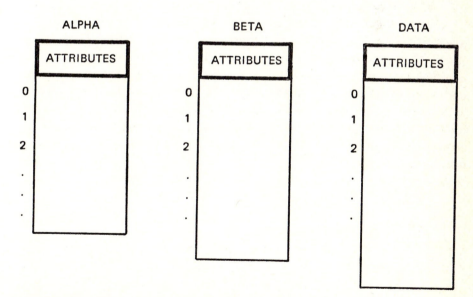

FIGURE 9.16 Segmented address space as seen by user

an offset (location) within that segment. For example, representative assembly language statements might be

```
LOAD          (DATA) I 25        Load word from location 25 of seg-
                                 ment DATA
TRANSFER      (BETA) I 7         Transfer to location 7 within segment
                                 BETA
```

The symbol I separates the segment and offset designations of an address.

In practical implementations of segmented address space systems, several techniques are used to simplify the hardware and programming. Generally, segments are referenced by number, not by name, just as conventional assembly language programs refer to locations symbolically, even though the machine instructions use numeric addresses. Thus, the symbolic instruction

```
TRANSFER      (BETA) I LOOP + 2
```

must be executed as

```
0500  3 I 26
```

if BETA were segment number 3 and LOOP were location 24 within BETA and 0500 were the machine language code for the TRANSFER instruction. Mechanisms such as index registers, base registers, and indirect addressing are often available, as on conventional computers, to assist addressing.

From the programmer's point of view, there are several advantages to a segmented address space. Specific attributes for access rights, such as read-only, write-only, execute-only, can be associated with each segment. Words within a segment that is specified as execute-only cannot be read or written. Thus, if ALPHA were specified as execute-only, the hardware would not permit instructions such as

```
LOAD          (ALPHA) I 22
```

or

```
STORE         (ALPHA) I 12
```

but would allow

TRANSFER   〈ALPHA〉 I 0

This prevents the accidental destruction of a program and insures the privacy of "proprietary" subroutines that may have a usage charge. Likewise, segments that are read-only can be used for the storage of data that must be protected against accidental or malicious alteration.

Implicit in the notion of arbitrary length segments is that the programmer need not specify the maximum length of the segment in advance (note: as an implementation constraint, arbitrary length does not imply infinity since the segment offset field in the instructions must be a finite number of bits). Thus, segments are a very convenient way to organize tables and matrices of unpredictable sizes. The instruction

STORE   〈DATA〉 I 1500

would cause the size of segment DATA to extend to location 1500 if it were not already that large.

In addition to the programming convenience provided by segmented address spaces, there are definite advantages to the resource management of the operating system. The operating system is, of course, able to use the segment attributes and automatic segment size expansion to assist its functions. But significant throughput advantages can be further derived from dynamic binding and sharing.

In the previous systems it was assumed that all the job's subroutines had been linked together into a linear address space by software relocation of the individual subroutines prior to the start of execution. This process, called *linkage editing, binding,* or sometimes *relocation loading* and discussed in Chapter 5, contributes to the time required to complete a job. In many cases this process takes as much time as the compilation and execution of the job. In a segmented system it is not necessary to relocate the addresses within a subroutine segment. It is only necessary to convert symbolic references between segments to numeric segment numbers. By virtue of the presence of a hardware-detected indication in each intersegment reference instruction to differentiate between unlinked references (in form of character string) as generated by the compiler and actual linked segment numbers, the binding will be performed only when an instruction is encountered that requires the linkage. This is called *dynamic binding,* or *dynamic linking* and *dynamic loading.* A program ALPHA[2] such as

```
          .
          .
          .

ALPHA|0201        LOAD           ⟨DATA⟩ |5


ALPHA|0500        TRANSFER       ⟨BETA⟩ |0
          .
```

will activate the binding process when the instruction LOAD ⟨DATA⟩ | 5 is encountered and will be changed to

```
          .
          .
          .

ALPHA|0201        LOAD                  4 |5
          .
          .
          .

ALPHA|0500        TRANSFER       ⟨BETA⟩ |0
```

if the segment DATA is (or has been) assigned segment number 4 by the dynamic binding component of the operating system.

If the instruction TRANSFER ⟨BETA⟩ |0 is not activated due to conditionals or premature termination, it is not bound and BETA may not even be loaded. In large complex programs, such as an information retrieval system or even a compiler, many of the "optional" subroutines may not be needed during any particular execution. Thus, it is possible to save considerable time and increase throughput by only binding subroutines that actually need to be bound. Although there are software techniques for performing dynamic linking without segmentation hardware, they are usually inefficient or overly restrictive.

The major impact of the previous memory management schemes was derived from their ability to increase the throughput by means of multiprogramming as many jobs as possible. Segmentation offers an additional technique to increase multiprogramming by *sharing.*

---

[2]Placing the address in the instruction makes ALPHA an impure procedure that places certain limitations on sharing, which is discussed in the section on information management.

Figure 9.17 illustrates a simple multiprogramming environment with two jobs. Each job has four segments in its address space, but both require the same system library SIN subroutine. In most other systems, each user would get a separate copy of the SIN routine bound into his address space. If the SIN routine is *shareable,* it is not necessary to have two separate copies of it.

It is common for programmers to write programs that are *serially reusable.* A serially reusable routine is one which can be used many times by reinitializing itself for each usage. A routine is made reusable by appropriate initialization procedures each time it is called so that values left from previous calls are not used. Some routines, such as *random number generators* which are intended to return different values each time they are called, deliberately violate this condition. To be effectively shared in a multiprogramming system, routines must be *concurrently reusable;* these are also called *re-entrant* or *pure* routines (a routine which does not alter itself).

Serially reusable routines could be shared if their execution on behalf of one job is always completed before they are used by another. This can be accomplished by means of queues and interlocks, but such techniques are sufficiently complex and inefficient that most systems using sharing require re-entrant routines.

A re-entrant routine permits multiple calls and executions before prior executions are complete. Unconstrained re-enterability requires read-only code; a pure

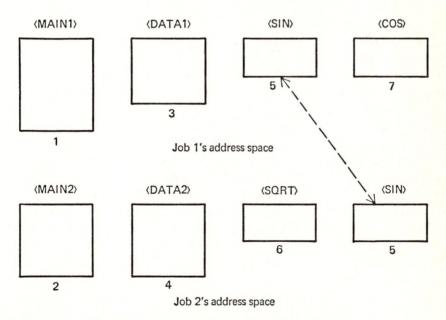

FIGURE 9.17 Sharing in a multi-programmed segmented environment

procedure operates only on variables in registers or in separate data segments associated with the job; it never stores or alters itself. The example demonstrating dynamic linking was not pure since it required altering the load instruction. There are other dynamic linking techniques that accomplish the same thing but do not affect the "purity."

Thus, in Figure 9.17 both jobs can share a single copy of the SIN routine if it is a pure procedure using DATA1 and DATA2 respectively for variable data storage. This can be accomplished by keeping the appropriate data segment number in an index or base register.

In addition to library routines, there are many system elements conducive to sharing. The various system facilities, such as file system and input/output routines, may be shared. Programmers may share each other's routines and/or data segments. Finally, entire systems such as a PL/I compiler or a BASIC interpretive language processor may be shared. Thus, for example, 10 jobs may be compiling PL/I programs at the same time. The PL/I compiler may require a 100,000-byte program segment plus a 10,000-byte data segment for the various tables and variables used during compilation. The total memory required for the 10 jobs would be $10 \times (100,000 + 10,000) = 1,100,000$ bytes. By sharing a single copy of the PL/I compiler segment and using separate copies of the data segment, the actual memory required can be reduced to $100,000 + 10 \times 10,000 = 200,000$ bytes (an 82% reduction).

Up to this point we have assumed that it was possible to produce physically segmented memories. Since practical memories are linear, it is necessary to use a *segment map* to convert the job's apparently disjointed segmented address space into a linear memory, much as the page map was used to convert the user's apparently linear address space into discontiguous pages and blocks. Figure 9.18 illustrates such a segment map.

Each individual segment is allocated as a contiguous portion of physical memory. In this example, the hardware segment map mechanism automatically translates a segmented address into a physical address by using the segment number as an index into the segment map, and then adding the segment offset to the segment base address to get the physical memory address. The segment map also contains a field for each segment that specifies its current length; attempts to use a segment offset that goes beyond the segment is automatically detected by the hardware and then processed by the monitor by means of an interrupt.

Although some computer systems, such as the Burroughs 5500, use a segmentation system as described above, there are two major drawbacks. First, since the words of each segment must be contiguous, fragmentation can be a major problem, especially if segments are allowed to dynamically grow. Second, the size of the total address space is limited by the size of physical memory. In a sense, the

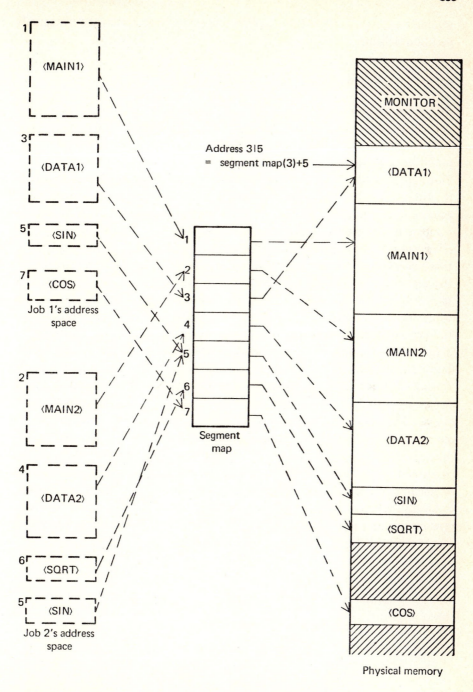

FIGURE 9.18 Mapping of segmented address space to physical memory

segmented system has the same memory allocation problems as the relocatable partitions scheme.

9.2.7 Segmented-Paged Allocation

An appealing idea would be to combine the best features of the previously presented techniques. Segmentation can be used to facilitate sharing and protection; paging can be used to resolve the fragmentation and recompacting problems; and demand paging eliminates the restriction on address space size. This approach has been taken on several advanced computer systems, such as the IBM System/360 Model 67 and HIS 645. Figure 9.19 illustrates a segmented address system using a separate page table for each segment. The reader should compare this diagram with Figure 9.18.

We will return to segmentation in Section 9.5 and explore its role in information management, but several points are worth noting here. Due to the size of the segment table and page tables, they are typically stored in core memory rather than hardware registers. Thus, the hardware processing of an instruction could require up to three accesses to memory to load a data word (one access to the segment table, one to the corresponding page table, and then a third to the actual data location). Techniques such as small high-speed associative memory buffers have been very effective at reducing the number of memory accesses required by "remembering" frequently used segments and pages; this approach is used on both the IBM System/360 Model 67 and the HIS 645 computers.

Even with associative memory buffers, however, there is a degradation of computer speed due to the multi-level addressing; usually this degradation can be kept below 10 percent but may vary significantly due to program characteristics and the effectiveness of the associative memory buffers. Of course, the segmentation and paging hardware increases the cost of the computing system.

Clearly, a considerable amount of sophistication is required in the operating system memory management to utilize the full capabilities of the segmented-paged scheme.

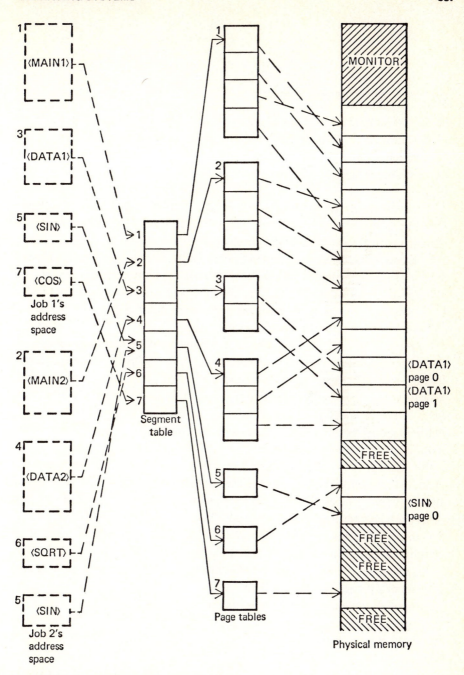

FIGURE 9.19 Segmented system using paging

PART 3

9.3 PROCESSOR MANAGEMENT

Multiprogramming must be employed to attain the increased throughput claimed in the previous sections on multiple processors and memory management. In this section we present specific mechanisms associated with multiprogramming and multiprocessing. The discussion is applicable to a wide range of computer systems.

The requirement to share subroutines and control asynchronous activities, including interrupts, presents complex problems. The following specific terminology is useful in describing these mechanisms.

A *process* is basically a program in execution. In a simple case, a single process may be associated with a single user's job. We use the term address space synonymously with name space, which consists of those addresses that may be generated by a process. The memory space or physical memory consists of the set of addresses that correspond to memory locations.

A *processor* is a hardware device that is capable of executing a sequence of instructions. Another view of a process is that it is the "path" of the processor through an address space while executing a job. Thus, at various times, a process may be in the operating system, user program, or shared program. *Multiprogramming* is the interleaved execution of two or more processes by a processor. *Multiprocessing* is the simultaneous execution of two or more processes by a multiple processor computer system.

The basic problem of processor management is to allocate processors to processes in a manner that minimizes the overhead. A process may be in one of three states: running, blocked, or ready. A process is *running* when its instruction sequence is being executed by a processor. A process is *blocked* when it is waiting for an event to occur before continuing execution. A process is *ready* if all conditions are satisfied for the process to be in the running state and it is waiting for a processor. A process is suspended whenever it is blocked or ready. A "state" diagram of a process is shown in Figure 9.20.

In general, there are fewer processors than processes (e.g., typically only one processor); therefore, the processors must be rationed. The list of processes in the ready state, called the *ready list*, would all be running if there were enough processors to go around.

Since the transition from running to blocked is usually determined by external factors (e.g., the speed of the I/O channel and I/O devices), these transitions are for the most part out of the control of the operating system. Thus the problem of processor management can be rephrased as follows:

1. Keep track of the status of each process;
2. Select processes from the ready-list to be run;
3. Suspend a running process when it runs out of allotted time; and
4. Coordinate interprocess communication.

The component of the operating system that performs these tasks has been called the *traffic controller* by Saltzer (references, Chapter 10); it is convenient to isolate the part of the traffic controller that actually selects processes to be run (task 2), calling it the *scheduler.* The traffic controller has (1) the mechanism to take care of changing the status of a process; and (2) a scheduler to help it allocate the processor to the processes in a manner that results in minimum overhead and fair treatment to all of the users.

9.3.1 Scheduler

The scheduler is needed to ration the scarce resource of processor time to the various ready processes desiring to consume it. The scheduler performs two functions: (1) it selects which ready process is to be run next, and (2) it specifies the *time-slice* (maximum amount of processor time that is to be assigned at a time). When a process exceeds its assigned time-slice, a timer-interrupt occurs, and the process temporarily reverts back to the ready status as is illustrated in Figure 9.20.

In general, whenever a running process is suspended, either to the blocked or the ready state, a process from the ready list is elevated to running status and it is assigned the use of the free processor. There are two common ways of ac-

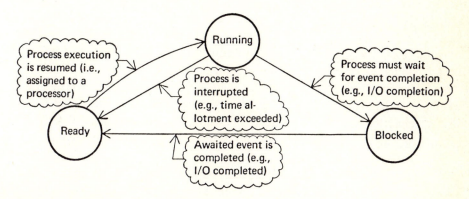

FIGURE 9.20 State transitions for a process

complishing the mechanics of scheduling. Both ways involve a list of processes in a ready state *(ready list)*. One way is to have the list ordered by the scheduler each time a process is placed in the ready list. Thus when a processor is free, the scheduler simply takes the first process in the list and places it in the running state. The other way is to place processes in the ready list in a random order. When a processor becomes free, the scheduler scans the entire list and decides which process is to be placed in the running state.

Depending upon the scheduling strategy being used and the objectives of the system, one of these scheduling mechanisms may be easier or more appropriate than the other.

When there is more than one process in the ready list, the scheduler must depend on a scheduling policy to determine which process should be chosen to run. This is often accomplished by assigning different priority levels to processes.

The policy and priorities are dictated by such factors as:

1. Bought. By paying a higher rate, the user "buys" a higher priority that in general means quicker throughput for his job, a technocratic version of tipping the head waiter for a better table.

2. Required. By decree users may be assigned priorities in order of importance, such as for a job needed to prevent a nuclear reactor from imminent explosion or, more commonly, to help a project that is a week overdue.

3. Deserved. In some cases it is advantageous for the system itself to assign priorities. For instance, it may automatically assign high priorities to short jobs. Another example would be for the system to designate priorities so as to achieve a balanced load, such as one job with heavy input/output requirements *(I/O bound)* and one job with very little input/output *(CPU bound)* running concurrently. If all jobs are at one extreme, either the I/O channel will be overworked and the CPU idle, or vice versa. Thus it is advantageous for maximum throughput for the system to assign priorities so as to maintain the proper mix and balanced load. Similarly, the system may desire to increase the priority of a job that is tying up resources (such as previously scheduled tape drives) so as to complete the job and release these resources for other use.

As in almost any rationing situation, there is considerable controversy over what are "equitable," "efficient," or "economical" policies. The reader may wish to consult some of the references (Chapter 10) for additional details of scheduling policy; a considerable amount of computer "folklore" has developed in this area.

It is quite convenient to represent much of the scheduling policy in the form of a state transition diagram. A more sophisticated scheduling algorithm than that of Figure 9.20 is represented in Figure 9.21. Here we have subdivided the states of *ready* and *blocked* to further control allocation of processors.

This scheduling algorithm is a simplification of a *desired* policy that might be used in a timesharing operating system with a paging memory management. In particular, note that the blocked processes are divided into three groups (blocked for terminal I/O, blocked for disk or tape I/O, and blocked for paging I/O), and the ready processes are divided into three groups (CPU bound, high-priority I/O bound, and medium-priority I/O bound.) The scheduling policy is to select a process from the high-priority ready list; if there is none, a process is selected from the medium-priority ready list. A low-priority process is only run if there are no higher priority processes.

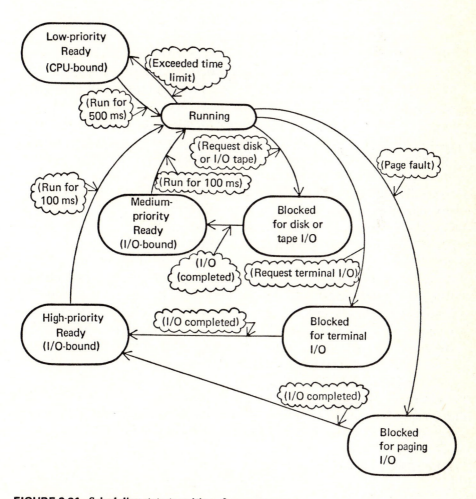

FIGURE 9.21 Scheduling state transitions for a process

There are many subjective policies implemented in this algorithm. For example, if a process runs for more than 100 ms (about 100,000 instructions) without requesting I/O, it is temporarily considered to be CPU bound. In order to keep the I/O channels and devices busy, I/O bound processes are always run before a CPU bound process. If all I/O bound processes are blocked, then a CPU bound process is given a chance at the processor and is allowed to run five times as long (500ms) before being stopped unless it becomes blocked by an I/O request. The reader should examine Figure 9.21 and identify other subjective policies that underlie the algorithm as well as the shortcomings of these sample policies.

9.3.2 Traffic Controller

The tasks of the traffic controller are to keep track of the status of each process, suspend and resume processes, and coordinate interprocess communication.

In order to resume a suspended process, the traffic controller must save a "snapshot" of the process's state, called a *state-word,* at the time that it was blocked. The process state word includes the contents of registers, the instruction address, condition codes, etc. The traffic controller may be called explicitly, for example, by the I/O request, or implicitly by interrupts, such as an I/O completion interrupt, a timer interrupt, or a page fault interrupt. A process may also go into the blocked state when it requests from the operating system a resource that is presently unavailable, such as more memory space or use of a tape drive; at a later time when that resource becomes available, the traffic controller places the previously-blocked process into the ready list. It is essential that all state transitions be handled by the traffic controller; otherwise, chaos is likely to develop or processes will become "lost."

There may be several processes in operation which need to communicate with each other under program control. That is, a process may wish to place another process in a ready state or in a blocked state. If this is permitted, the traffic controller must be able to accept calls that send another process into the blocked state. Similarly, the traffic controller must accept calls from a process wishing to communicate to a blocked process that some conditions have been met and thus it can be activated. This facility can usually be accomplished by the traffic controller and is known as *interprocess communication.*

Associated with processor allocation and interprocess communication are two problems of synchronizing processors and processes, race and "deadly embrace." These situations are further discussed in the following section.

9.3.3 Race Condition

A *race* condition occurs when the scheduling of two processes is so critical that the various orders of scheduling them result in different computation. Race conditions result from the explicit or implicit sharing of data or resources among two or more processes. Figure 9.22 illustrates a simple form of a race.

In Figure 9.22 we assume that two processes are being run (multiprogrammed). Each process occasionally requests to print a line on the single printer. Depending upon the scheduling of processes 1 and 2, all of the printout of process 1 may precede or follow the printout of process 2. But most likely, the printout of each process will be interspersed on the printed paper.

One solution to this predicament is to require that a process explicitly *request* use of the shared resource (the printer in this case) prior to using it. When all use of the resource is completed, (e.g., all printout completed), the resource may then be released by the process. The operations *request* and *release* are usually part of the operating system facilities that are handled by the traffic controller. If a process "requests" a resource that is already in use, the process automatically becomes blocked. When the resource becomes available as a result of a later "release," the blocked process may be assigned the resource and made ready.

This technique of coordinating processes is often called *interlocking* or *synchronizing*. The operations of request and release have historically been known as *P* and *V*.

Note that cooperation is important to the successful use of interlocking. If a process "forgets" to release an allocated resource, that resource will never again be available for use by any other process. In practice, the operating system usually releases all resources allocated to a process when the process terminates. Alternate solutions to the printer problem are discussed in the device management section.

9.3.4 Stalemates

A *stalemate* is a situation in which two processes are unknowingly waiting on resources that are unavailable.

The operations of request and release do not completely eliminate all race conditions; in fact, they may result in fatal races known as stalemates or more exotically *deadly embraces*. Consider the two processes depicted in Figure 9.23.

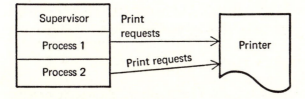

FIGURE 9.22 Simple race condition

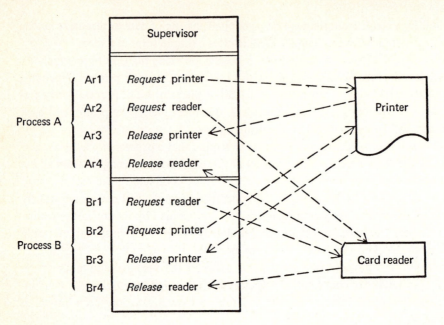

FIGURE 9.23 Stalemate situation

Processes A and B are sharing use of the printer and card reader by means of the request and release operations. Due to the independent scheduling of the processes, the request and release operations may be interspersed in several different orders such as:

(1)   Ar1, Ar2, Ar3, Ar4, Br1, Br2, Br3, Br4
(2)   Br1, Br2, Br3, Br4, Ar1, Ar2, Ar3, Ar4
(3)   Ar1, Ar2, Br1, Ar3, Ar4, Br2, Br3, Br4

The reader should observe that these sequences are reasonable and perform correctly. Note that in number 3 process B is temporarily blocked by Br1 until process A issues Ar4.

Let us consider a sequence that starts with Ar1 (request printer for process A) and Br1 (request reader for process B). What happens next? If Ar2 (request reader for process A) occurs, process A must be blocked because the reader is already in use by process B. Then when Br2 (request for printer for process B) occurs, process B must also be blocked because the printer is in use by process A. We are confronted with a stalemate. Both processes A and B are blocked, each waiting for the other to release a needed resource.

The problem of stalemate can occur in many different ways in a multiprogramming system. Unfortunately, there are presently no simple *and* efficient techniques for overcoming this problem. Probably the simplest technique is to request all the resources to be needed at the same time even if they are not really needed until much later in the processing; but this is clearly not an efficient solution. Considerable research is being performed in this area.

9.3.5 Multiprocessor Systems

In order to enhance throughput, additional processors have been added to some systems. In early multiprocessor systems the additional processors had specialized functions, e.g., I/O channels. Multiprocessing systems further evolved to the concept of one large CPU and several peripheral processors (CDC 6600). These may perform quite sophisticated tasks, e.g., running a display. A third type of multiprocessing is exhibited by the HIS 645 system, where there can be more than one CPU, each of equal power. A fourth and most general type is the computer network, where many different computers are connected, often at great distances.

Figure 9.24 illustrates the manner in which multiple processors may be used for multiprogramming. Usually we visualize several separate processes as being in memory. In actuality, a process is often paged so that only part of it is in

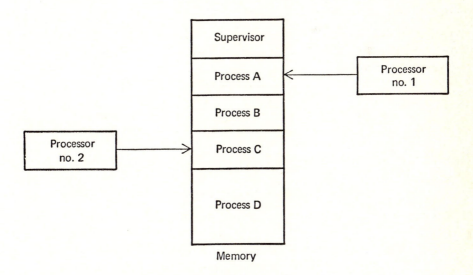

Processor no. 1 working on process A
Processor no. 2 working on process C

FIGURE 9.24 Multi-programming with multi-processors

memory at one time; this allows the number of processes active in the system to be very large. A processor is assigned to a task and operates on it until it is blocked. When a task is blocked, the processor selects another task and continues processing. After the blocking condition has been satisfied, a processor will eventually be assigned to the process; it need not be the same physical processor as before.

Process blocking can occur on a uniprocessor as well as multiprocessor system. In Figure 9.25 we see a uniprocessor multiprogramming system. Processes A and D both require the use of a tape drive. Let us assume that there is only one tape drive available, and process A requests it first. The drive is assigned to pro-

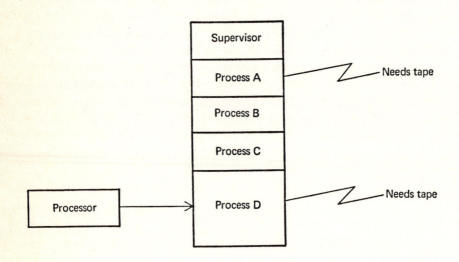

If both processes A and D need a tape drive and there

is only one drive available, one process is assigned

the drive (for example, A) and the other process

(process D) is blocked. Operation continues with

processes A, B, and C as normal. When process A is

completed, the tape drive can then be reassigned and

D can commence again.

Note: The processor never stops, merely "logical" change.

FIGURE 9.25   Single-processor interlock

cess A. Later, when process D requests a tape drive, it must be blocked until process A releases the tape drive.

Being blocked is an attribute of the process, not the processor. It means that the processor will switch only among processes A, B, and C, and ignore process D. Usually process D will tie up a portion of memory, but in some systems it can be "rolled out" or "paged out" of memory onto secondary storage. Thus the blocking of process D has only a logical effect that results in a redistribution of resources; the resources need not be wasted.

In general, a multiprocessor system performs in the same way as the uniprocessor systems. There are a few special techniques that are used to coordinate the processors. One such technique is called *software processor lockout,* which coordinates the use of data bases by the multiple processors. We discuss this technique here, first presenting possible software conflicts with a single processor, Figure 9.26, then a two-processor system (Fig. 9.27) and then a solution (Fig. 9.28).

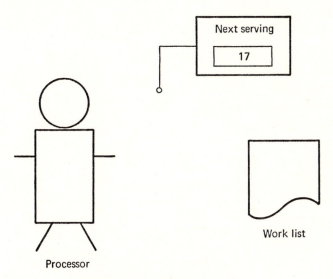

When current process completed or postponed:

    1. Find current process in work list

    2. Mark it "complete" or "postponed"

    3. Note "next serving" number (17)

    4. Find process 17 in work list

    5. Make note of process to be done

    6. Pull lever to advance "next serving" number (18)

FIGURE 9.26 Scheduling (single processor)

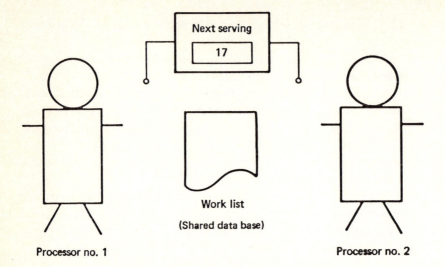

Processor no. 1   Processor no. 2

Consider both processors complete process at same time:

1. Processor 1 finds its current process in work list

2. Processor 2 finds its current process in work list

3. Processor 1 marks its current process

4. Processor 2 marks its current process

5. Processor 1 notes "next serving" (17)

6. Processor 2 notes "next serving" (17)

7. Processor 1 finds process 17 in work list and notes it

8. Processor 2 finds process 17 in work list and notes it

9. Processor 1 pulls lever to advance "next serving" (18)

10. Processor 2 pulls lever to advance "next serving" (19)

Now both processors are simultaneously working on the same process
and process 18 has been skipped.

FIGURE 9.27 Scheduling (multiprocessors)

There is a crucial system data base that lists all the processes and their current
status. This list is called the job queue, task queue, ready list or work list. When
a process becomes blocked, its entry in the ready list is found and its status is
stored. The next process to be serviced is determined. In our example we will
assume a simple round-robin selection. The selected process is examined, its status
is restored by reloading active registers, etc., and indication is left of the next
process to be serviced later.

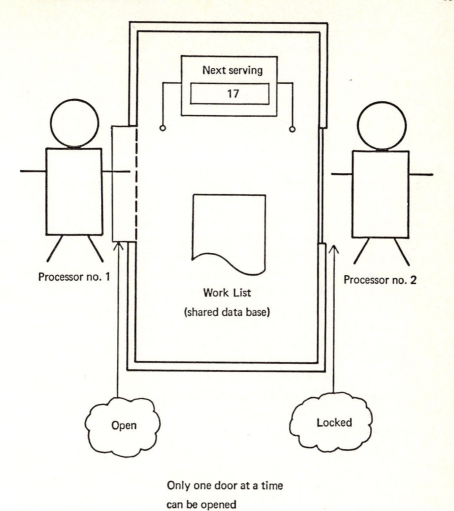

Next serving

17

Processor no. 1

Processor no. 2

Work List

(shared data base)

Open

Locked

Only one door at a time
can be opened

FIGURE 9.28 Scheduling (multiprocessors with lockout)

The above scheme works fine for a single processor, but runs into trouble for multiple processors as shown in Figure 9.27.

Assume that two processes, each on a separate processor, get blocked at approximately the same time. After saving the status of the current processes, each processor determines the next process to be served. Since both processors use the same algorithm independently, they will choose the same process. Furthermore, in readjusting the selection criterion, it is possible to upset the work list, for example bypassing a process as illustrated in Figure 9.27.

This problem is the direct result of multiple processors processing common data bases asynchronously. There are usually many other data bases in an operating system, such as the memory allocation map, the page allocation map, the I/O list, etc.

In order to resolve this problem, the processors that usually operate independently must be synchronized with regard to access to these common data bases. Figure 9.28 illustrates the logical process.

Before accessing the data base, a processor checks a specific "lock bit" — if it is not set, the data base is not in use, and the processor may set the bit and commence operation on the data base. When it has completed its function, the processor resets the bit. If a second processor requires access to the data base in the interim, it will find the "lock bit" set and must wait until the "lock" is removed. Under this condition, the second processor is said to have undergone *software processor lockout* and has been temporarily idled. This can happen to a second, third, fourth, or any number of processors at a time.

Recall that blocking was a phenomenon of a process and it was possible for the supervisor to reallocate the resources and switch the processor to another process without stopping. Software processor lockout essentially occurs within the supervisor, and without risking conflicts with other processors, there is nothing the processor is allowed to do except stop. Thus a physical resource, processors, is actually idled by software lockout.

Analyzing the effect of software processor lockout on the performance of a multiprocessor system is a very complex problem. Due to the extensive dynamics of such a system, only actual running can accurately measure the effect; but it is possible to produce analytical probabilistic models that can approximate the situation.

The detailed implementation and full implications of the issues of processor management are beyond the scope of this book. The reader may wish to consult the references in Chapter 10 for additional discussions of these topics.

PART 4

9.4 DEVICE MANAGEMENT

A contemporary computer system may include a wide assortment of "input/output" devices, more formally called *peripheral devices,* such as printers, card readers, magnetic tape units, magnetic disks and drums. A large installation may devote over half the system cost to peripherals. Therefore, it is desirable to use these devices in the most efficient manner.

9.4.1 Device Characteristics

Almost anything imaginable can be, and probably has been, used as a peripheral device to a computer. These devices range from steel mills to laser beams, from radars to mechanical potato pickers, and from thermometers to space ships. Fortunately, most computer installations utilize only a relatively small set of peripheral devices.

Peripheral devices can be generally categorized into two major groups: (1) input or output devices, and (2) storage devices. An *input device* is one by which the computer "senses" or "feels" the outside world. These may be mechanisms such as thermometers or radars, but more conventionally, are devices to read punched cards, punched paper tape, or messages typed on typewriter-like terminals. An *output device* is one by which the computer "affects" or "controls" the outside world. These may be mechanisms such as a temperature control knob or a radar direction control; but more commonly are devices to punch holes in cards, punch holes in paper tape, print letters and numbers on paper, and control the typing of typewriter-like terminals. These input and output devices have been discussed in considerable detail in section 9.1 along with examples of actual I/O programming.

A *storage device* is a mechanism by which the computer may store information, a procedure commonly called *writing,* such that this information may be retrieved at a later time *(reading).* Conceptually, a storage device is analogous to human storage devices, such as pieces of paper, pencils, and erasers.

It is useful to differentiate between two types of storage devices: serial access and direct access. A *serial access* storage device can be characterized as one that relies on a strict physically-sequential positioning and accessing of information. Access to an arbitrary stored item requires a "linear search," so that such an access requires as much time as reading half of all the information stored. A

Magnetic Tape Unit (MTU), is the most common example of a serial access storage device. The MTU is based upon the same principles as the audio tape deck or tape cassette, but rather than storing music or voices, binary information, generally bytes, is stored. A typical serial access device is depicted in Figure 9.29.

Information is usually stored as groups of bytes, called *records*, rather than single bytes. In general, a record can be of arbitrary length, such as from 1 to 32,768 bytes long. In Figure 9.29 all the records are four bytes long. Records may be viewed as being analogous to "spoken words" on a standard audio tape deck. Each record can be identified by its physical position on the tape; the first record is 1, the second record is 2, etc. The current record counter of Figure 9.29 serves the same function as the "time" or "number of feet" meter of audio tape decks. If the tape is positioned at its beginning (i.e., completely rewound), and we wish to read record number 101, it is necessary to skip over all intervening records (e.g., 1, 2, . . ., 99, 100) in order to reach record number 101. Contemporary magnetic tape units can store up to 1,600 bytes in one inch of tape and can move the tape at speeds up to 200 inches per second. Even at this speed it would take about one minute to get to the middle record of a standard 2,400 foot tape starting from the beginning. Serial access storage devices are normally used for applications that only require sequential accessing, such as the intermediate file copies produced by pass 1 of the assembler (Chapter 3) and the loader (Chapter 5).

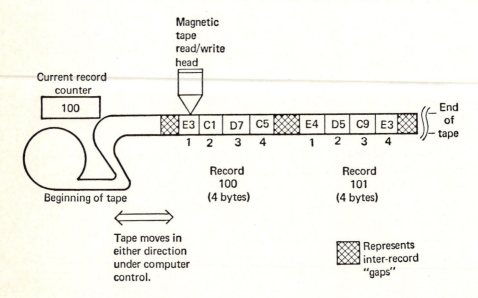

FIGURE 9.29 Serial access storage device

A *Direct Access*, or *Random Access, Storage Device* (DASD), can be characterized as one that does not require a strict physically-sequential accessing of information. The main storage memory of the computer system is an example of a direct access storage device; any byte of memory can be accessed directly without waiting to "skip" over any bytes. In general, most contemporary direct access peripheral storage devices are a compromise between being truly direct access (e.g., core memory) and being serial access (e.g., magnetic tape unit). Figure 9.30 depicts a direct access storage device similar to a magnetic drum.

A magnetic drum can be simplistically viewed as several adjacent strips of magnetic tape wrapped around a drum so that the ends of each tape strip join. Each tape strip, called a *track*, has a separate read/write head. The drum continuously revolves at high speed so that the records repeatedly pass under the read/write heads (e.g., record 1, record 2, . . ., then record 1 again, record 2, . . ., etc.). Each individual record is identified by a track number and then a record number. For example, record (2,1) is X'C4C9E2D2', and record (5,1) is X'D1D6C8D5' in Figure 9.30. Magnetic drums spin very quickly and have several hundred read/write heads; thus a random access to read or write can be accomplished in 5 or 10 milliseconds in contrast to the minute required for

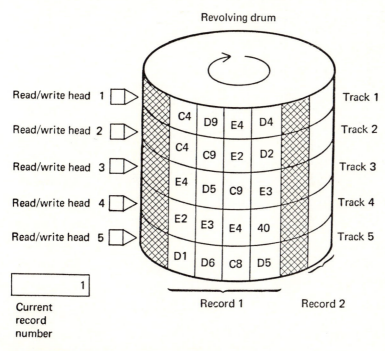

FIGURE 9.30 Drum – type direct access storage device

random access to a record on a full magnetic tape.

There are many different direct access storage devices. The magnetic disk is very similar to the magnetic drum but is based upon the use of a flat disk with a series of concentric circles, one for each read/write head. This is analogous to a phonograph disk (disc). Since read/write heads are expensive, some devices do not have a unique head for each track. Instead, the heads are physically moved from track to track; such units are called moving arm or moving head DASD.

In order to identify a particular record stored on the moving arm DASD shown in Figure 9.31, it is necessary to specify the arm position, track number, and record number. Notice that arm position is based upon radial movement whereas record number is based upon circumferential movement. The moving arm disk-type DASDs have 10 to 50 tracks, 200 to 400 arm positions and are capable of storing over 100,000,000 bytes of data.

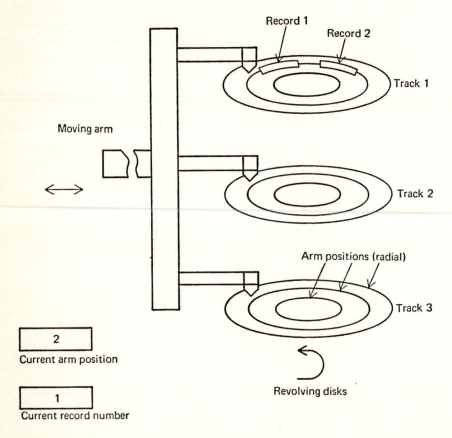

FIGURE 9.31 Moving arm disk-type direct access storage device

9.4.2 Device Management Techniques

In a simple batch monitor system device allocation is very inefficient, in that only one job is run at a time and any devices, usually the majority of devices, not used by that particular job are idle. A multiprogramming system utilizes the sum of the devices required by all active jobs. An obvious objective of such a system is to maximize usage of all the peripheral devices and maintain an effective throughput. In a sense, the various concurrent jobs are allocated resources from the pool of peripheral devices. This allocation is typically of two forms: dedicated and shared access.

DEDICATED

Certain devices, such as card readers, magnetic tapes, and printers, by their very nature can only be used in a serial, one-at-a-time manner. It is generally considered disadvantageous, for example, to have printed output for three jobs randomly interspersed on the paper. These devices must, in general, be dedicated to one job at a time.

A straightforward allocation strategy is to assign, or *dedicate* such devices to jobs and only start a job if the device is available. This complicates the multiprogramming and priority scheduling. There are certain obvious bottleneck areas. For example, almost every job produces some printed output, thereby requiring use of a printer. But if a system only has two printers, a simple dedicated device allocation would result in limiting multiprogramming to two jobs or less — which is very inefficient. A common solution to this bottleneck is *SPOOLING* (*S*imultaneous *P*eripheral *O*perations *On-L*ine) whereby all job output intended to be printed is saved either in memory, or more reasonably, on a direct access device (e.g., drum or disk) until the job is completed. The saved output is then printed at high speed rather than intermittently spread over the entire duration of the job. As long as the total printed output requirements of all jobs can be handled by the printers, all of the saved output will eventually be printed. An analogous strategy is also used for card reader input; that is, a job's card input is read at high speed by the operating system and saved on a direct access device before the job even begins.

SHARED ACCESS

Certain peripherals, such as direct access devices (e.g., magnetic drums, disks, and data cells) can be used concurrently by more than one job. Information stored on a direct access device is directly accessible, much like the locations of memory; thus there is very little mutual interference when various jobs access different locations on the device.

There are two problems associated with the use of shared access devices that must be handled by the operating system. Although there is very little interference caused by multiple jobs sharing access to the device, there can be only one access occurring at a time (i.e., only one read or write per device can be serviced at once). Depending upon the device, an access may take from a small fraction of a second to several seconds. Thus if two or more jobs wish to access the same device simultaneously, the operating system must act like a traffic policeman. In fact, this function is often called *I/O traffic control.* The effectiveness of the operating system in directing I/O traffic, which is usually of considerable volume in a large system, has a substantial effect on multiprogramming efficiency and throughput performance. Even dedicated devices contribute to the traffic control problem since the I/O channels (I/O computers) have capacity limitations that may require scheduling if there is very high usage (e.g., it is usually not possible to handle the information transfer if every tape, disk, and drum is active simultaneously). The specific details of I/O traffic control will not be further discussed here since they are very dependent upon device characteristics and CPU peculiarities.

The second problem with shared access devices is the need for protection from accidental or malicious access to one job's area by another job. This protection is usually accomplished by a combination of hardware and software facilities. In addition to memory protection mechanisms discussed in the previous sections, computers designed for multiprogramming usually have two modes of operation called master/slave (also called supervisor/problem or privileged/nonprivileged). When operating in *nonprivileged mode,* certain instructions, such as for input/output and protection setting, are considered illegal and cause control to be transferred to the operating system. The operating system operates in *privileged mode* and can use any of the computer's instructions. Thus all input/output can be initiated only by the operating system. The validity of each I/O request is checked by the operating system, occasionally with the assistance of the I/O hardware.

PART 5

9.5 INFORMATION MANAGEMENT

The most important function of an operating system is the effective management of information. We frequently use the expression "information processing system" to refer to a computer system. The operating system itself is an example of an information resource; it is used by every job. The modules of the operating system dealing with the management of information are often called the *file system*.

The file system is intended to provide convenient management of information so the programmer is freed from the problems related to the allocation of space for his information, as well as other physical problems, such as storage format and I/O accessing. Thus the programmer need only deal in terms of the logical structure and operations performed on his information. File systems may also offer the ability to share information among users and protect information from unauthorized access.

We will deal with file systems on the systems programmer level not on the applications level. It is useful to distinguish between file systems, data management systems, and data base systems.

1. A file system is concerned with the logical organization of information. The file system deals with collections of unstructured and uninterpreted information at the operating systems level. Each separately identified collection of information is called a *file*.

2. A data management system is a file system that performs some structuring of information, for example, the common indexed sequential file organization. Most programmers operate at this level of information management.

3. A data base system is a file system concerned with the structure and interpretations of data items, e.g., airline reservations systems where a user may ask "How many people on flight 904?" Most end users operate at this level of information management.

A *file* is a collection of related information units *(records)* treated as a unit. A record is itself a collection of related data elements treated as a unit. For example, in an inventory control application, one line of an invoice is a data item, a complete invoice is a record, and the complete set of such records is a file.

9.5.1 Development of File Systems

PRE-FILE SYSTEM ERA

In the earlier, simpler days of data processing, no information was permanently stored within the computer system. Each programmer was responsible for bringing all necessary information (e.g., compilers, subroutines, data, etc.) to the computer and, likewise, manually storing any information produced by the system that was to be used again at a later date. For example, a programmer wishing to compile, load, and execute a FORTRAN program would use separate card decks for the FORTRAN compiler, assembler, and loaders. A computation center might classify these card decks by different colors and place them in different locations in the room. The classification of these various information items (or files) of a system was the ancestor of modern file systems.

EARLY FILE SYSTEMS (SYSTEM TAPES)

Most of the early batch operating systems, such as the IBM 7094 FORTRAN Monitor System (FMS), developed a limited file system capability that was contained on what was usually termed the "system tape." Various systems programs, such as the compilers and loaders, were stored on magnetic tape (or magnetic disks). The programmer merely needed to supply control cards, such as * FORTRAN or * LOAD, and the operating system would retrieve the necessary program from the system tape. These routines were stored on the system tape in core image form and the operating system knew the precise absolute location on the system tape of each of them.

LIBRARY FILE SYSTEMS

Eventually, it became desirable to have frequently used application programs (e.g., payroll program, sort/merge package, etc.) permanently stored in the computer system to further reduce manual card handling. Since it was not considered convenient to rewrite the operating system every time a program was to be added or deleted from the "system tape," a more general mechanism was needed. This necessitated the introduction of a program, usually called the *librarian,* which kept track of the allocation of space on one or more *library tapes* (which might include the system tape). The librarian would add or delete programs to the library as requested and maintain an *index directory* that recorded the location of each stored program.

When the operating system processed a control card that requested the execution of a specific program it would turn to the librarian's index directory to find the location of the program.

GENERALIZED FILE SYSTEMS

The librarian provided an adequate solution to the problem of management and storage of programs; however, it usually provided no assistance in the handling of the other form of information – data files. Data files range in variety from payroll and employment files to census data, from tables of scientific data to copies of source programs. In a generalized file system the programmer is able to store this information in a simple and easy way. Furthermore, he can access and alter it at a later time.

9.5.2 Structure of a General File System

A general reference that the file system must handle is

READ file (D) from loc [F] into loc [M] for [n] locations

where D is the name of the file and F and M are locations within the file and memory, respectively. Files may be logically organized in various ways. The most common file organizations are *sequential records* and *direct access records*. In a sequential organization it is assumed that every record in the file will be processed one after the other in a sequential manner. In a direct access organization it is assumed that only certain records in the file will be processed and that the accessing will not necessarily be sequential.

GENERAL FILE SYSTEM MODEL

We can functionally divide the file system into seven logical phases: (1) accessing methods; (2) logical file system; (3) basic file system; (4) file organization strategy; (5) allocation system strategy; (6) device strategy; and (7) I/O control system. Figure 9.32 depicts the general file system model. For example, a programmer makes a read request with the symbolic name of the file to be read. The logical file system accepts the symbolic name and finds the corresponding numeric file identifier. The basic file system takes the numeric file identifier and obtains a file descriptor. The file organization strategy module uses the file descriptor to determine the physical address. The device strategy module produces the physical I/O commands to access the information (as was discussed in section 9.4), and the I/O control system schedules the execution of the physical file commands. This model that we use to study and design file systems was conceived at M.I.T.[3] by Stuart Madnick.

9.5.3 Example of a File System

Let us assume that a file named ALPHA is stored on a drum. ALPHA consists of 11 records, where each is 250 bytes long. Figure 9.33 depicts a drum-type device

---

[3] "Design Strategies for File Systems", Stuart Madnick, MAC-TR-78, M.I.T., Cambridge, Mass., Oct. 1970.

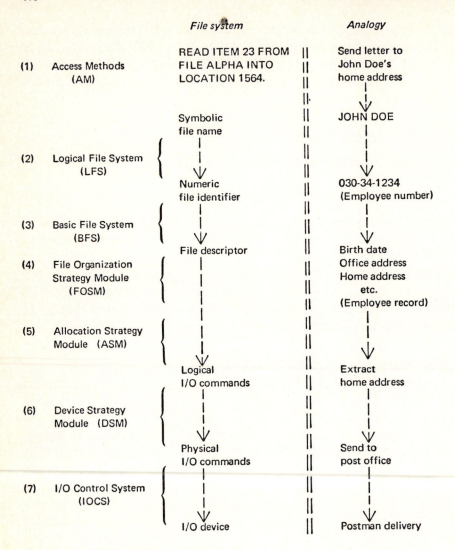

FIGURE 9.32 Model of file system

with 1,000-byte-long physical records, which we will call *blocks* to minimize confusion with the file's logical records. For graphical convenience we have "flattened" the drum (see Fig. 9.30 for another view of a magnetic drum storage device).

In Figure 9.33 we have assigned each physical block a unique number. Since the blocks are 1,000 bytes long, we can store four 250-byte logical records in each block. Let us assume that the 11 records of file ALPHA have been stored in

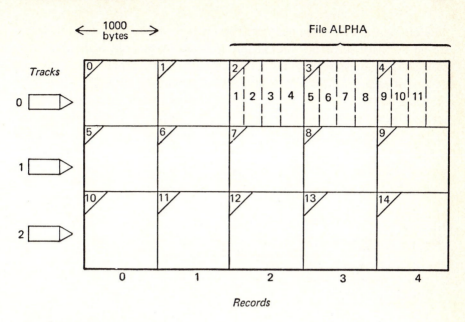

FIGURE 9.33 Physical file storage

physical blocks 2, 3, and 4 as shown in the diagram; we will refer to these as ALPHA's *logical blocks* 0, 1, and 2. In this example, logical blocks and logical records have been allocated contiguously.

SAMPLE REQUEST

The programmer wishing to access the file may write the PL/I-like statement:

    READ FILE(ALPHA) RECORD(6) SIZE(250) LOCATION(BUFF)

to read the sixth of the 250-byte logical records from file ALPHA and copy it into main storage at location BUFF. The compiler would translate this READ statement into the appropriate subroutine calls to the file system.

Let us consider the actions that must be performed by a simple file system in order to satisfy the above request:

1. The physical location of file ALPHA must be determined.
2. The physical block containing record 6 must be determined.
3. The physical block must be read from the drum into a buffer in main storage.
4. Record 6 must be extracted from the block buffer and moved to location BUFF.

Before we can even attempt to perform the first action, it should be clear that we do not have sufficient information. How do we find out where ALPHA is stored? There must be a table that specifies the name, length, and beginning address of each file. This table is often called the *file directory* or *Volume Table of Contents* (VTOC). This latter name comes from viewing the storage device medium as a "container of information" and thus a *volume*. The distinction between a storage device and a volume becomes important when removable volumes (e.g., disk pack, tape reel, etc.) are used. These can be disconnected from one storage device and later connected to another storage device (of the same type) on possibly a different computer system.

Entry	Name	Length	Location
1	BETA	900	6
2	ALPHA	2750	2
3	GAMMA	2000	7

FIGURE 9.34 Volume Table Of Contents (VTOC)

Figure 9.34 illustrates a VTOC. The length may be represented in various ways. We will use the number of bytes occupied by the contents of the file. Thus ALPHA's length is 2750 bytes (11 records times 250 bytes) and its logical block 0 is actually physical block 2.

We can now proceed with the processing of the READ request as itemized in Figure 9.35.

1. The VTOC is searched to find the entry for ALPHA (entry no. 2).
2. The record's logical byte address is computed as (record number -1) x (record size), which is (6-1) x (250) = 1250.
3. Logical byte address 1250 corresponds to byte 250 within logical block 1.
4. Since we know from VTOC that logical block 0 = physical block 2, then logical block 1 = physical block 3.
5. Using I/O routines as described in section 9.1, physical block 3 is read into a 1000-byte buffer area.
6. From step 3 above, we know that logical record 6 starts at byte 250. Thus we move bytes 250-499 from buffer to location BUFF. This completes the READ request processing.

FIGURE 9.35 Steps required to process READ request

OPERATIONAL CONSIDERATIONS

There are several operational considerations even in this simple file system:

1. How are the VTOC entries created and filled in?
2. Where is the VTOC stored?
3. Is it necessary to search the entire VTOC for every request?

We will answer these questions in order and develop a series of file systems, each more flexible than the last. In a system such as IBM's Disk Operating System/360 (DOS/360), the programmer must keep track of available storage space and maintain the VTOC by control cards similar to:

```
CREATE  ALPHA,LENGTH=2750,LOCATION=2
        and
DELETE  BETA
```

The CREATE command adds a new entry to the VTOC and the DELETE command removes an entry from the VTOC.

If the VTOC is kept in main memory all the time, significant core may be used in storing this table, which may be quite large. We would like to treat the VTOC as a file and place it on the storage device. The user's files may be easily transferred to another system by transferring the volume (e.g., tape reel, disk pack, etc.) which contains these files as well as the VTOC.

If the VTOC is stored in the file system, then the latter must load and search the VTOC blocks when accessing files. It may take a substantial amount of time to search the VTOC, especially if it is not stored in main memory. Although the VTOC may be quite large, with thousands of entries, usually only a few files at a time are ever used. If we copy the VTOC entries for files that are currently in use into main memory, the subsequent search times can be substantially reduced. Most file systems have two special requests, OPEN, to copy a specific VTOC entry into main memory, and CLOSE, to indicate the VTOC entry is no longer needed in main memory. Likewise, we talk about a file being *open* or *closed* depending upon the current location of its VTOC entry.

9.5.4 Features of a General File System

Although the simple file system presented above is adequate for some applications, it lacks many desirable features such as:

1. Minimal I/O operations
2. Unrestricted flexibility between logical record size and physical block size
3. Automatic allocation of file space
4. Dynamic allocation of file space
5. Flexible *file naming* facilities (e.g., links, aliases, subdirectories, etc.)

MINIMAL I/O OPERATIONS

According to the algorithm presented in Figure 9.35, if file ALPHA were to be processed sequentially, it would require 11 I/O operations (each operation reading one physical block) to access the 11 logical records. Since the entire file only occupies three physical blocks, we may suspect that there are ways to reduce the number of I/O operations by eliminating redundant operations.

The number of I/O operations can be reduced by using techniques very similar to the compiler's machine-dependent code optimization techniques discussed in Chapter 8.2.6.2. For each I/O read operation a physical block is copied into a buffer in main memory. If we keep track of which physical block is presently in the buffer, we can modify step 5 of the algorithm (Fig. 9.35) to test whether or not the desired block has already been read. If the block is already in the buffer, the I/O read operation may be skipped. In the case of file ALPHA, the request for record 1 will cause physical block 2 to be copied into the buffer. The subsequent requests for records 2, 3, and 4 will operate upon the buffer without need for any additional I/O operation. The request for record 5 will then cause physical block 3 to be copied into the buffer, etc. In this way the entire file ALPHA can be processed sequentially with only 3 I/O operations instead of 11.

This technique is often called *file buffering* and there are numerous variations and alternatives. For example, there may be separate buffers assigned to each opened file, or only one buffer, to be used by all files. Furthermore, to minimize the detrimental effects of random accessing, as opposed to sequential accessing, and to allow certain I/O overlapping, it may be desirable to assign multiple buffers to a single file (whence comes the term *double buffering*). The considerations involved in effective buffering strategies are very similar to those relating to the page replacement algorithms discussed under *Demand Paging* in Section 9.2.5.

INDEPENDENCE OF LOGICAL RECORD SIZE AND PHYSICAL BLOCK SIZE

In the simple system we postulated, a physical record can hold some integral number of logical records, with no space left over. There are, unfortunately, application situations in which the programmer desires to process logical records of lengths such as 13 (not a factor of block length) or 2,415 bytes (larger than one physical block). There are various ways to overcome some of these difficulties. For example, by using 20-byte logical records, which are really 13-byte records with 7 bytes of wasted space, we can effectively store fifty 13-byte logical records in the 1000-byte blocks (albeit inefficiently).

Many storage devices allow a certain amount of flexibility in the format of the individual tracks. For example, some permit the programmer to change the track format from five 1000-byte blocks (Fig. 9.33) to fifteen 300-byte blocks or three 2000-byte blocks. This format change is usually not linear since there is a certain amount of extra space that must be used for every block no matter how long it is.

The solutions presented above involve some manual or explicit action by the programmer. It should be a rather simple task for the reader to revise the six-step procedure presented in Figure 9.35 so that logical records can straddle physical blocks and even extend over several blocks. This point is mentioned because there are so many existing file systems that do not include this capability.

AUTOMATIC ALLOCATION OF FILE SPACE

The manual allocation of file space, as necessitated by the LOCATION field of the CREATE control card, is quite inconvenient. First, it forces the programmer to manually keep track of space. This may be a very cumbersome task when using a typical storage device with 10,000 to 100,000 blocks or more. Second, since there are usually many programmers using the same storage device, it is necessary to keep track of everyone else's files as well if a programmer is to know what spaces are available. Finally, the following control cards:

```
CREATE ALPHA, LENGTH = 2750, LOCATION = 2
CREATE BETA,  LENGTH =  900, LOCATION = 3
```

which cause files ALPHA and BETA to overlap, would not be flagged as errors in many simple file systems; although this might be desirable under some strange circumstances, it is usually indicative of an error in manual allocation.

For the above reasons, it is very desirable for the programmer to merely specify

```
CREATE ALPHA, LENGTH = 2750
```

and let the file system allocate the necessary space. Generally, the programmer has no interest in the specific location.

There are numerous techniques by which the system can keep track of space. One simple way is to maintain "dummy" or "free" VTOC entries, one for each contiguous area of blocks that are not assigned (free). Then, to satisfy the request for three blocks for ALPHA, the file system looks for a free VTOC entry that specifies an area three blocks long. If there is no area of exactly this length, a free area of greater length is chosen and split into two pieces. One piece, three blocks long, is allocated to ALPHA; the remainder is allocated as a free area. Figure 9.36 illustrates this process for the control cards:

CREATE ALPHA, LENGTH = 2750
CREATE BETA, LENGTH = 900

Entry	Name	Length	Location
1	VTOC	2000	0
2	Free	(3000)	2
3	GAMMA	2000	5
4	Free	(9000)	7
5	. . .		
6	. . .		

Entry	Name	Length	Location
1	VTOC	2000	0
2	ALPHA	2750	2
3	GAMMA	2000	5
4	BETA	900	7
5	Free	(8000)	8
6	. . .		

(a) Before CREATES are processed   (b) After CREATES are processed

FIGURE 9.36 Automatic file space allocation

There must be an entry in the VTOC for the VTOC itself to indicate where it is stored and how much space it requires. Thus it may be possible for a program to read or write the records of the VTOC using the exact same steps as for any other file. The IBM Operating System/360 (OS/360), for example, uses techneques similar to the automatic file allocation mechanism described above.

DYNAMIC ALLOCATION OF FILE SPACE
Although the automatic file allocation mechanism simplifies the programmer's tasks, some problems remain. Contiguous allocation of file space can result in a phenomenon similar to fragmentation (see section 9.2). For example, in Figure 9.36a there is a total of 12,000 bytes of free space (a 3,000-byte and 9,000-byte free area), yet it would not be possible to create a single file 10,500 bytes in size. Some systems, such as IBM's 1130 Disk Monitor System, overcome this problem by actually moving files around (e.g., move file GAMMA of Fig. 9.36 from blocks 5 and 6 to blocks 2 and 3) so that all free space is contiguous. Unfortunately, this recompaction can be a very time-consuming operation and thus not an adequate solution.

In many cases, for example those of the copy files for the assembler and loader, it is impossible to predict in advance the amount of file space needed since that depends upon the input data (e.g., on the number of source or object cards). If the programmer "guesses" too large a size, file space is wasted; if he "guesses" too small a size, the program probably will not run correctly.

One solution to both of the above problems is dynamic noncontiguous file space allocation. This means that space may be added to a file's size dynamically during program execution and the physical blocks allocated need not be contiguous. There are various techniques that may be used; one popular approach utilizes file maps as illustrated in Figure 9.37.

In dynamic noncontiguous file space allocation, the VTOC has the same form as in Figures 9.34 and 9.36, but the location field is used to specify the physical block address of the corresponding file map. The file map contains the correspondence between logical block numbers and physical block numbers for the file. For example, the file map for the file ALPHA is stored in physical block 4. The three blocks assigned to file ALPHA are blocks 3, 7, and 8. Typically, a file map is copied into main memory along with the VTOC entry when the corresponding file is opened. This noncontiguous allocation merely requires a simple change to READ request processing step 4 (Fig. 9.35) such that physical block number = file map (logical block number).

Entries in the file map that are not filled in indicate that the corresponding

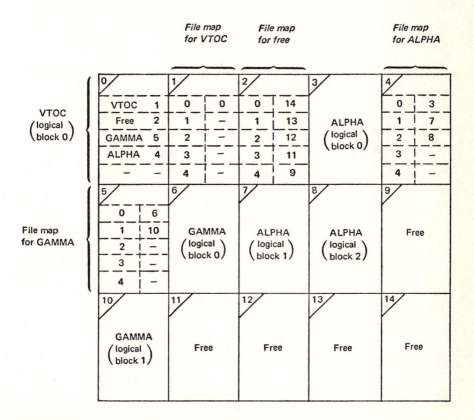

FIGURE 9.37 Example of file map organization

physical blocks have not been allocated. To use this dynamic allocation scheme, the control card need only specify the file name (e.g., CREATE ALPHA). This will cause a VTOC entry to be set up and a block for the file map to be allocated and initialized; no other blocks will be allocated at this time. During execution, if a WRITE request references a record for which a physical block has not been allocated (e.g., WRITE FILE(ALPHA) RECORD(14)), a block is removed from the "free" file map (e.g., block 9) and assigned to file ALPHA by placing it in ALPHA's file map. The VTOC entry is then revised to indicate the new lengths of the two files. Conversely, when a file is deleted, its blocks are added to the "free" file map.

The file map organization eliminates the need for contiguous file space allocation and allows for dynamic allocation during execution. The reader should notice a similarity between this file map mechanism and the page map technique presented in Section 9.2.4. This similarity will be discussed later in this chapter.

FLEXIBLE FILE NAMING

The symbolic file name is a very convenient way for a programmer to remember and refer to his files, but there are several shortcomings to the VTOC scheme presented. If we assume that there are many users creating and using files, it is possible that two different programmers may accidently choose the same name for a file (e.g., ALPHA). Thus, when one of them uses the control cards:

```
DELETE  ALPHA  /* delete my old copy */
CREATE  ALPHA  /* create a new copy */
```

he may be deleting the other programmer's file ALPHA. Likewise, the READ and WRITE requests will use the same file for both programmers. There are numerous solutions to this problem, such as an installation "clearing house" for names, similar to the Automobile License Bureau. Such a scheme, though adequate, is far from ideal.

In a more generalized system there are circumstances when two different programmers should be permitted to use the same name for two different files. On the other hand, it is sometimes desirable for two programmers to use two different names in referring to the same file. This latter case could occur if the name of the file had not been decided upon between the two programmers until after the programs had been completely written. Similarly, a single programmer may find it convenient to refer to one of his files by more than one name (this facility is often called using *alias* file names).

We will briefly present a scheme for developing a flexible file-naming capability. Let us assume that all files are merely assigned numbers instead of symbol names.

VTOC

Entry	Length	Location	
1	500	1	(This is really VTOC file)
2	3000	2	(This is really "free" file)
3	2000	5	(This is really GAMMA file)
4	2750	4	(This is really ALPHA file)
5	900	9	(This is really BETA file)
	...	...	

FIGURE 9.38 VTOC without symbolic names

Figure 9.38 depicts this situation.

The VTOC shown in Figure 9.38 is very similar to the VTOC of Figure 9.36 except that the symbolic name field has been omitted. We can refer to any file by its VTOC entry number (e.g., entry number 4 is really file ALPHA).

Now that we have simplified the system, we are ready to reinstate the symbolic naming ability, but in a new way. We introduce *directory* files, which are just like regular data files but are used to establish a correspondence between symbolic names and VTOC entry numbers. To eliminate or at least minimize naming conflicts, each programmer or programmer group can be assigned a separate directory. Thus there is a need for a *master directory* or *root directory* that specifies the VTOC entry for each programmer's private directory.

Figure 9.39 illustrates the details of a simple hierarchical file structure. The first two entries of the VTOC are for the VTOC itself and the "free" file, respectively. The third VTOC entry is always assigned to the master directory file; for all practical purposes this is just like any other file with a file map, VTOC entry, etc.

The master directory file has an entry for each programmer which indicates his directory (e.g., JOHN's directory is defined by VTOC entry 8). Each programmer's directory has the list of files accessible to him and the corresponding VTOC entry. JOHN has two files, ALPHA and BETA, whereas STUART has four files, ALPHA, BETA, GAMMA, and DELTA.

Notice that both programmers' file BETA is really the same; this is often called a *linked file*. On the other hand, JOHN's file ALPHA is not the same as STUART's file ALPHA. There are several other flexibilities illustrated in this example; STUART's files ALPHA and DELTA are really the same file. Finally, STUART's file named GAMMA is the same as JOHN's file ALPHA. The reader

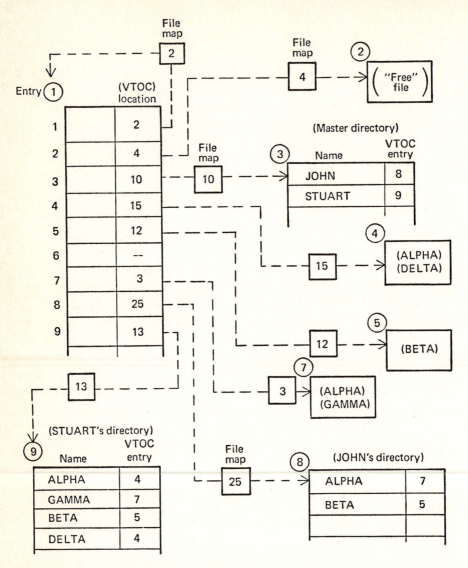

FIGURE 9.39 Detailed hierarchical file structure

should confirm these observations by studying the figure carefully.

A hierarchical file structure such as described above is often diagrammed as a tree structure as demonstrated in Figure 9.40. Several file systems allow the programmer to create multi-level subsidiary directories, sometimes called private libraries, so that the structure may become several levels deep.

MASTER DIRECTORY (ROOT)

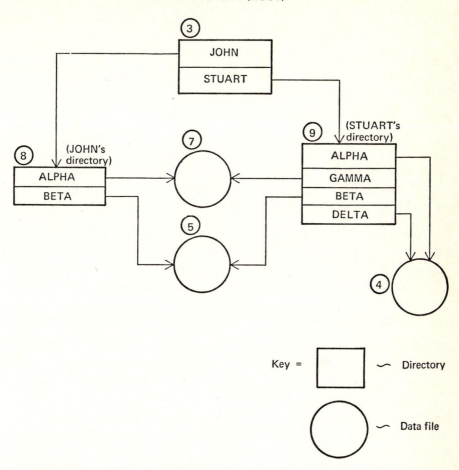

FIGURE 9.40 Abstract hierarchical file structure

9.5.5 General File System Model Revisited

In Section 9.5.3 we started out with a very simple file system design. As we progressed through Section 9.5.4 this simple design gained considerable complexity. (It is important to realize that increased complexity and flexibility do not necessarily impose an unwieldy overhead burden: in many ways the sophisticated file system may perform much more efficiently than the unoptimized simple system.)

We now wish to consider the complete organizational structure of the general file system (as introduced in Section 9.5.2) as it applies to the processing of a request (originally presented in Fig. 9.35). We will divide the processing into seven steps or phases:

1. ACCESS METHOD (AM)

The logical record number is converted to a logical byte address within the file. Control then passes to the Logical File System.

2. LOGICAL FILE SYSTEM (LFS)

The symbolic file name is converted to its corresponding VTOC entry number. This may involve searching through the master directory and subsidiary directories if the name is not in the Active Name Table (ANT). (Since these directories are just like regular files, the LFS can use the Basic File System described below to read through the directories.) Control then passes to the Basic File System.

3. BASIC FILE SYSTEM (BFS)

The VTOC entry number is used to determine if the file is already open with an entry in the Active File Table (AFT). If not, the VTOC entry is copied into the AFT. (Since the VTOC is just like a regular file, the BFS can use the File Organization Strategy Module described below to read the VTOC entry).

Control then passes to the File Organization Strategy Module.

4. FILE ORGANIZATION STRATEGY MODULE (FOSM)

The logical byte address is converted to a logical block number and offset. Using the file map, the logical block number is translated to a physical block number.

If the desired block is already contained in a buffer, the logical record is returned to the caller. If the desired block is not in a buffer, the Device Strategy Module is called to read the physical block and then the logical record is returned to the caller.

If this were a WRITE request, and the corresponding physical block had not been assigned, the Allocation Strategy Module would be called to assign a block.

5. ALLOCATION STRATEGY MODULE (ASM)

A "free" physical block is removed from the "free" file and placed in the file map of the designated file.

Control returns to the caller.

6. DEVICE STRATEGY MODULE (DSM)

The physical block number is converted to the address format needed by the device (e.g., cylinder number, track number, physical record number). Appropriate I/O commands are set up.

Control then passes to the Input/Output Control System.

7. INPUT/OUTPUT CONTROL SYSTEM (IOCS)

The IOCS schedules the use of the I/O channels, initiates the I/O commands, and processes the interrupts.

When the I/O has been completed, control returns to the caller.

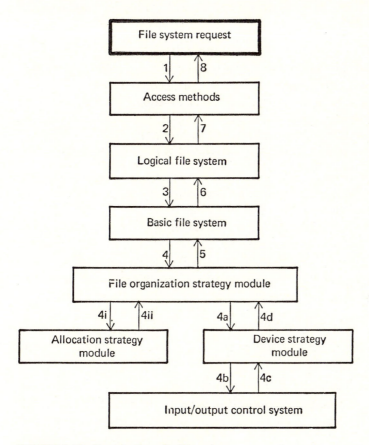

FIGURE 9.41 Organization of a file system

Figure 9.41 illustrates this organization of a file system and traces the calls and returns that might occur in processing a request. Although the particular details presented in the previous sections (e.g., format of VTOC, file maps, etc.) may vary significantly from system to system, the basic structure of Figure 9.41 underlies most contemporary file systems.

9.5.6 Segmentation

Segmentation (with paging), as presented in Section 9.2, is applicable to information management as well as memory management. There are many aspects of the generalized file system that are also characteristic of a segmented memory system:

1. The notions of file and segment both involve the logical organization of information.
2. Both files and segments may have arbitrary size and may grow in size dynamically.
3. Files and segments require two-dimensional addressing (e.g., interchange file name and logical bytes or segment name and offset).
4. The Volume Table of Contents (VTOC) functionally corresponds to a descriptor segment.
5. The file map functionally corresponds to a page map.
6. The memory buffers functionally correspond to memory blocks/pages.

This comparison could be extended but the similarities are sufficiently clear. The information management aspects of segmentation may be utilized in two ways: (1) as a separate mechanism from the file system, or (2) integrated into the file system so that there is a single-segmentation file-system mechanism. This latter approach has been taken in the MULTICS system implemented on the HIS-645 computer system. In this section we will review concepts of segmentation and illustrate how they may be used to accomplish information management.

INFORMATION MANAGEMENT

Objectives of a segmented environment The objectives of a segmented environment include the following.

1. To allow physically *shared procedures.* For example, if a square root routine is used by two processes it is wasteful and possibly undesirable if two separate copies of the routine exist. We wish to allow only one copy to be made and to separate the data that is impure since the data values get changed during the execution of the program and may be different for each user.
2. To allow *dynamic linking.* This permits the programmer to defer linkage to programs until it is necessary to execute them. Furthermore, it is not necessary to explicitly name the called segment until execution time.
3. To allow a segment to be *invariant under the recompilation* of other segments. That is, if a segment 'A' references a variable x in segment 'B,' if B is subsequently recompiled such that x is located differently within that

segment it should not be necessary for the calling segment A to also be recompiled.

4. To allow *controlled access*. Segmentation must be implemented so that segments may be protected and logically shared. These may be conflicting requirements, but they are demanded by users of modern systems.

5. To allow *dynamically growing segments*. Segmentation should provide the user with the ability to have segments dynamically grow and shrink.

6. To provide a *two-dimensional address space*. The program addresses its address space by two operands, a name of a segment, and an offset within the segment. The address space may be visualized as consisting of a number of segments each of which can grow and shrink independently as depicted in Figure 9.42.

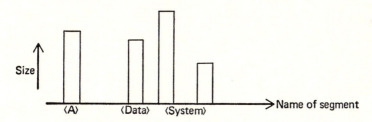

FIGURE 9.42 A two-dimensional address space

The implications of the preceding objectives are described below.

Objective number 1 (shared procedures) implies that we have a separate impure linkage segment, which is not shared, associated with each pure procedure segment, which is shared. The linkage segment contains all external references of the procedure segment.

Objective number 2 (dynamic linking) means that binding external references cannot be done until execution time.

Objective number 3 (segments invariant under recompilation of other segments) will imply that we have another segment associated with every procedure segment, namely, a symbol table.

We will see that the protection scheme associated with the implementation we have chosen for segmentation permits objectives 4, 5, and 6 to fall out naturally.

IMPLEMENTATION

The hardware of a segmented computer system interprets an address reference as a segment number and offset, $\langle S,x \rangle$. In Figure 9.43 the reference $\langle S,x \rangle$ is converted to actual core address by the hardware. The hardware uses S as an index

Entry in descriptor for segment S

1. Name = S

2. Length = N

3. Accessing information

4. Location = L

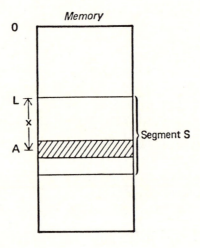

(S,x)→ hardware index to descriptor segment → ⟨d,x⟩ → hardware → A=L+x

FIGURE 9.43 Hardware address in a segmented computer

into a table (the descriptor segment) to get the location L of the segment. The hardware adds the offset x to L and obtains the address.

The implementation of the segmentation that we are about to discuss is similar to that implemented in the HIS-645 computer on the MULTICS system, a joint M.I.T., Honeywell, and Bell Labs project.

Let us assume we have a segmentation environment of the type depicted in Figure 9.44. The address space is defined by the descriptor segment, which contains information about all segments of the job. The Descriptor Base Register (DBR) must be set to point to the descriptor segment. Since the linkage and stack segments are referenced often, we usually assign registers pointing to these segments.

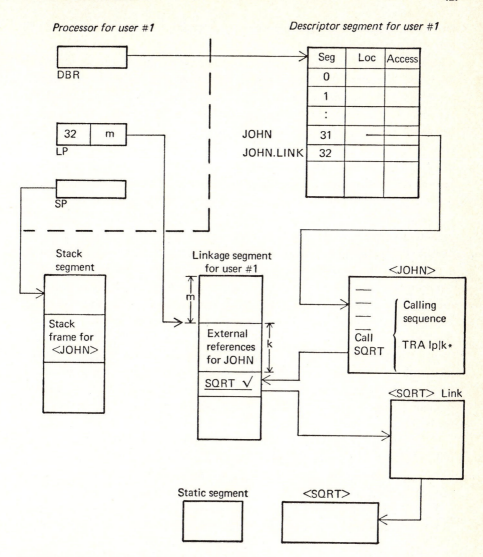

FIGURE 9.44 Segmented address space for user #1

When a job is being executed, the DBR is pointing to its descriptor segment. If a new job is to be processed, then the DBR must point to this job's descriptor segment. Segment number is used as an index in the descriptor segment, which contains the location of the segment. The offset is added to that location. The MULTICS system is implemented on a paged memory location scheme, so that the descriptor segment does not point to the location of the segment in the core but to the page tables. Since paging is not necessary for segmentation, we will ignore its *paging* aspects.

We will use the example of Figure 9.44 to develop a mechanism for segmentation. Let us assume that we have a procedure segment named JOHN. JOHN's source code consists of a statement CALL SQRT. A compiler would translate a call statement into a calling sequence (see section on recursion in Chapter 8) terminating in a transfer statement. Let us focus on the transfer address of this statement.

It might appear that a simple transfer to the SQRT routine is all that is required. However, objective number 2 (dynamic linking) dictates that the compiler cannot generate a transfer directly to the square root routine, because this routine may not be in core at execution time. Execution therefore must transfer to a supervisor that would load the square root routine at the time that this statement is executed. Alternatively, then, it might appear that the compiler could generate a transfer to the supervisor: the supervisor finds and loads the SQRT routine, replacing the address of the transfer statement with that of the square root routine, and re-executes the transfer statement. However, this will not work. It fails because it would make JOHN an impure procedure (objective number 1 — sharing). Consequently, if a second job were then to execute the transfer statement, it might transfer to the wrong SQRT routine. For example, the first job may wish to transfer to a SQRT routine in the system library, while the second may wish to transfer to its own SQRT routine. Yet because of requirement number 1 that we share procedures, JOHN may be the same physical procedure for both jobs.

Therefore, the compiler does not generate a transfer to the supervisor, but an indirect transfer to the linkage segment associated with JOHN. A separate copy of the linkage segment associated with JOHN is provided for each user. The linkage segment is used so often that we have a register (Lp) pointing to it.

Thus the compiler generates a transfer statement TRA Lp/K*. The star indicates indirect address, which means we transfer to the address contained in the location referenced. Lp denotes the linkage register. K is a number that is computed by the compiler and is associated with the routine square root; if the square root is the first routine called in the segment JOHN, K would be 1. The compiler then would generate a linkage segment, insert in first location the word SQRT (actually a pointer to the word SQRT), and set a fault-bit on in the location.

When the transfer to this location in the linkage section occurs at execution time, the hardware detects the fault-bit as an interrupt, causing a transfer to the execution routines.

Let us return now and start from the beginning. The code associated with the

CALL SQRT is the calling sequence (saving all the registers and updating stack pointers) and ends in a transfer statement. The transfer branches indirectly through the linkage register, which consists of a two-dimensional address — a segment number (32) and an offset (m). Hardware uses the 32 as an index in the segment table and finds the location of a linkage segment. It then adds m to that address to obtain the address of the particular linkage segment section associated with JOHN. The hardware adds K to that address thus obtaining the memory location in the linkage section associated with square root. The hardware, on referencing this location, notes that the fault-bit is on. The fault-bit causes execution to transfer to the executive system; the executive system at this time must find the segment SQRT in the file system.

Specifically, when a missing segment fault occurs, execution is passed to a segment fault handler which stores the proper segment attributes in the appropriate descriptor segment. It sets the segment fault-bit off in the linkage segment. The segment fault handler corresponds to the basic file system on our model. In searching for the segment SQRT it would consult a table of segments that are in core, to see if the segment has already been loaded. If not referenced in the table, SQRT is then loaded. Once the segment is in core, the segment fault handler places into the descriptor segment its segment number, its location, and its access rights with respect to job number 1. If the segment square root were loaded into a different job segment, it could have different access bits. The segment fault handler then would replace the segment fault-bit with the address of the linkage segment of SQRT.

It cannot replace the segment fault-bit with the address of SQRT for Lp still points to the linkage section of JOHN. We must change Lp to point to the linkage section of SQRT since we may encounter a further call in SQRT, say CALL TANGENT. This tangent would be compiled into a similar calling sequence and lastly into a transfer statement TRA Lp/K*. If this statement were executed it would transfer through the linkage segment associated with JOHN. Therefore, before we get into SQRT we must change the linkage register Lp to point to the linkage segment section associated with square root. Hence, when transferring from JOHN we could transfer through JOHN's linkage segments into the linkage segment of SQRT. This could contain code causing the loading of the Lp register pointing to the linkage segment of SQRT, and also code transferring into the SQRT routine.

It is beyond the intention of this book to dwell on the particular details of the implementation of segmentation. Let us say further that protection on a segment basis is assured since the hardware must examine the descriptor segment with each core reference. One may add "protection bits" in the descriptor segment table.

Schemes similar to that outlined above may be devised for multiprocessing systems.

9.5.7 MULTICS File System and the General Model

Figure 9.45 depicts the correspondence between the MULTICS segmentation hardware and the general model of our file system. The command used to activate the file system in Figure 9.45 is a command to store something in an externally defined segment. In MULTICS this generates the code "store indirectly through some linkage section." Here we have combined paging with segmentation.

There is overhead associated with segmentation. For every normal access to a data item in memory, the hardware must make an access to the descriptor segment and then into the hardware location. (In actuality, it accesses sequentially the descriptor segment, the page table, and the location.) This overhead may be reduced by the use of associative memories and by binding several segments together, thus avoiding external references. The binding would be done with segments that were executed often and that were fully debugged. In general, segmentation offers many advantages and is a concept that will exist in many computer systems of the future.

9.6 SUMMARY

In this chapter we have discussed various aspects of operating systems and the design of some of the modules of operating systems. We have focused on the aspects of the operating system that interacted closely with the system components we have presented in this book. We took a resource allocation point of view which allowed us to discuss in a somewhat uniform manner the broad range of functions from memory allocation to processor allocation, device allocation, and information allocation. We have not given the detailed design of many of these modules; however, we have tried to make the reader aware of the options that he has available to him. The model of the states of a processor is applicable to a broad class of systems. The user is encouraged to apply it to a small real-time system as well as the large system presented in this book. Similarly, the model of the file system given may be applied to a wide variety of file systems, both in designing and studying them.

Throughout our discussion of resource management we have stressed the systems role in management of these resources. This raises the question of whether the user himself can manage his own resources as well as the operating system

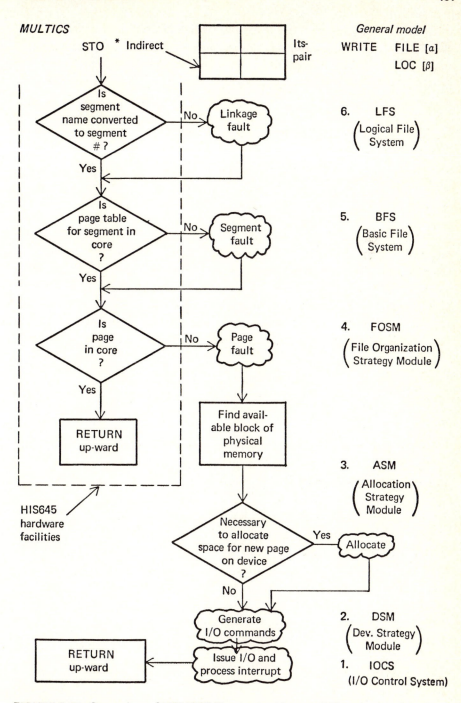

FIGURE 9.45 Comparison of MULTICS file system with general file system model

does. The operating system is able to optimize with knowledge of the intermediate status of the entire multiprogramming system and dynamically make decisions that result in total efficiency. For example, in a multiprogramming system, total system strategy seldom corresponds to optimum strategy for a single job if it were running alone.

QUESTIONS[4]

Part I

1. a. What is a channel?
    b. Why do channels exist?
    c. What are the functions of the channel status and program status words? How are they similar? What role do they play in communication between the channel and the CPU?
    d. Can the channel tell the CPU when and why it has finished an I/O operation? How?

2. Consider a small computer with no I/O channels, but with instructions such as "WRITE CHARACTER," "OUTPUT I/O COMMAND," "TEST I/O STATUS," etc. Only 1 character at a time can be written on a device such as a teletype, at a rate of 10 characters a second, and the I/O is done by the processor itself. What is the importance of interrupts from the device to such a system?

3. *Assume that the I/O channel program starting at location 1600_{16} below is being executed by a 1403 printer. You are to trace the I/O program and describe what is printed (use Appendix A page 462, 463).

Location				
1600	8B 000000	40	00	0000
1608	09 001638	40	00	000A
1610	11 001638	40	00	000A
1618	11 001642	80	00	000B
1620	00 001700	40	00	0004
1628	09 001638	40	00	000A
1630	89 001638	00	00	000A
1638	5C 5C5C5C	5C	5C	5C5C
1640	5C 5CD1D6	C2	40	D5E4
1648	D4 C2C5D9	40	00	0000
. . .				
1700	F6 F2F5F1	00	00	0000

4. In Figure 9.9 locations 38, 40, 48, and 78 are important. Who changes them (I/O channel program, user program)? Why? When are they changed?

5. Programming the I/O channel is similar to programming the CPU in machine language. To ease the process of writing CPU programs, assembly languages were invented. In Chapter 3 we discussed the design of assemblers.

    a. Can one invent an "assembly language" for the I/O machine instructions?

---

[4] An * denotes that the question may require the use of IBM 360 manuals.

    b. Define an I/O assembly language for the IBM 360, that is, give mnemonics for each instruction.

    c. What modifications to the basic assembler in Chapter 3 are necessary to process this language?

    d. IBM has chosen to use system macros to handle the I/O rather than have the user write "I/O assembly language" programs. What are the merits of this approach over those of the assembler?

6. An instruction such as "A 1,1317" will result (on the 360) in an interrupt because it does not address a full word boundary. Write an interrupt routine for the 360 which would receive and perhaps correct such an addressing error, that is, make the 360 behave like the 370 which can operate on data that is not aligned.

Part II

7. State which of the following data bases of a compiler and assembler may be pure and which may not (pure means not modify itself). Use one or two sentences in your explanation.

    a. Symbol table
    b. Reductions
    c. Code
    d. Macro table
    e. Op-code table
    f. Matrix

8. With respect to operating-systems memory management, what is the problem of fragmentation, and how can it be solved?

9. a. List three differences between a page and a segment.
    b. Is it possible to have paging without segmentation and vice versa?

10. Define a pure procedure and give two advantages of using one.

11. In designing a system, the tendency of the overzealous systems analyst may be to apply the most sophisticated memory management techniques he can think of. Under what conditions might implementation of advanced techniques become useless or even regressive in terms of increased system performance?

12. The section on memory management gave several computer architectural configurations that allowed more flexibility in management of the memory resource.

    Explain the flexibility that the following memory hardware configurations provide and give examples of memory allocation schemes. List advantages and disadvantages in comparison with the other systems.

    a. Single contiguous allocation
    b. Relocatable partitioned allocation
    c. Simple paging
    d. Segmentation with demand paging

13. a. Define the user's address space.
    b. What is its correspondence to core in

    1) Single contiguous allocation
    2) Relocatable partitioned allocation
    3) Segmentation with demand paging

Part III

14. Why can processors be assigned arbitrarily to a process in a multiprocessed system, rather than requiring a one-to-one correspondence between processor and process?

15. In addition to the states of Ready, Running, and Blocked, we introduce another state, *Stopped*, which may be important in a large system. In a large environment, a user may be inactive (e.g., a terminal user who is thinking of what to do next) and it is desirable to free his core space. The Stopped state indicates that the user is currently on secondary storage, but may at any time resume processing, so he is still known to the scheduler. Another reason for being in the Stopped state is that the user may have very low priority and may be *rolled out* of core to make room for a higher priority user. In this case he is ready to run but since he is not in core, he is not in the Ready state.

    a. Draw a state transition diagram for the four states described above. Show the reasons for the transitions in your diagram. As an example of a transition diagram, consider the following state diagram for your daily actions. Your diagram should be similar to Figure 9.20.

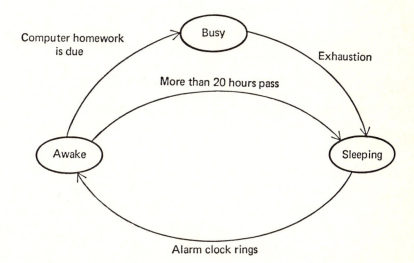

b. You are aware that core memory is expensive and is limited in size as opposed to secondary memory which can theoretically grow indefinitely. Assuming that paging is available, we see that it is not necessary to load the entire program in order to run it. A page-fault handler could retrieve the missing pages from a secondary storage device (drum, disks) on a needed basis. The time involved in such an operation is small compared to other I/O apparatus; therefore, this suggests splitting one of the states into two states. Which one? Why? Let *page-wait* be the new state, the old name being used for the other half of the split state. Redraw the state-transition diagram. Specify explicitly the transitions. What are the advantages of identifying this new state?

c. A real-time process is one which must perform an action in real time. That is, it has a very critical time period in which to perform its action and if the action is not completed in that time the process is worthless. For example, controlling a reactor requires a quick response to prevent blowing up the reactor or allowing it to shut down. Therefore, a real time process is given a very high priority which allows it to preempt the system whenever it is "awakened." What additional changes, if any, must be made to the diagram for real-time processes.

d. There are many types of I/O devices which could be on the system. For example, an output message could be directed to a tape for later printing or to a teletype for an on-line response. Do you see any reasons for splitting some state into two states **TTY** and **TAPE**. Which one? Why? Redraw the state diagram.

16. Distinguish between races and stalemate. How do they arise, and what can be done to prevent or handle them?

17. When, if ever, is communication between processors useful?

Part IV

18. What is spooling? Is it feasible for all types of I/O?

19. Describe the function of the I/O traffic controller.

20. Give an example of an application that is well-suited to use of a serial-access device. Give an example of an application that requires the use of a direct-access device. Explain each answer briefly.

Part V

21. What is the purpose of the OPEN and CLOSE commands? Why do they improve system efficiency?

22. Why is a segmented, paged environment conducive to file management?

23. You are developing a file system for a very simple computer. Its only I/O operations transfer a character into or out of the accumulator. A second register EXT specifies the I/O device address in the left-hand half-word, and the address (if any) of the place to put the character on the

specified I/O device is in the right-hand halfword. An example I/O instruction is

Read (into accululator)   (from device specified by EXT)

a. Is it possible to develop a file system, for this computer, like that given in section 9.5? Explain your answer.
b. What modules of the system would be most effected by the above I/O transmission system? Assume that in other respects the machine is like a 360 with only two registers.
c. Outline how such a file system might process the request

WRITE FILE (TAPE) FROM (CARD)

where TAPE is a symbolic name of a tape file and CARD is an 80-character record. Indicate what module must perform what action.

24. a. Machine problems in Chapter 4 were examples of *serially reusable programs*. What does this phrase mean? Appraise critically the similarities and differences between "serially reusable programs" and "pure procedures."
b. Is segmentation and/or paging essential to the operation of time-sharing systems? Explain your answer.
c. What part does segmentation play in making dynamic storage allocation possible?
d. How does segmentation facilitate protection?

25. The list below contains typical hardware/software modules used by an operating system. Examine these carefully and answer the questions following the list.

File system
Job scheduler
File of unique file descriptions
File of unique file identifiers
Drum
Disk
Line printers
Console typewriter
Store module (core)
Extended store modules (plastic cards)
Card reader
Descriptor Base Register (DBR)
Linkage Pointer (LP)
Argument Pointer (AP)
Stack Pointer (SP)
Tape
Relocation register
Procedure Base Register (PBR)
I/O channel

a. Which of the modules would you classify as (1) primary storage (2) secondary storage?

In each of the following you must point out why each module is necessary and how it dovetails with the other modules. It is recommended that you draw a block diagram.

b. Which modules are essential for (1) segmentation; (2) paging?
c. Which modules are necessary for the implementation of dynamic linking?
d. Which modules are used in loading user programs into core?
e. Which of the above modules would need to be considered in the design of the following file system functions:

   1) Access Methods (AM)
   2) Logical File System (LFS)
   3) Basic File System (BFS)
   4) File Organization Strategy Module (FOSM)
   5) Device Strategy Module (DSM)
   6) Allocation Strategy Module (ASM)
   7) Input Output Control System (IOCS)

26. Why is it necessary to have the linkage for a procedure segment located in a separate segment (the linkage segment)?

27. How is the linkage segment for a procedure addressed and how is that address established when the procedure is called?

28. Consider a file system state as illustrated in Figure 9.37. Identify the steps required to satisfy the following READ requests. (Your answer should be in a form similar to Figure 9.35. You may ignore the use of OPEN and CLOSE.)

    a. READ FILE (ALPHA) RECORD (4) SIZE (55) LOCATION (BUFF);
    b. READ FILE (ALPHA) RECORD (19) SIZE (55) LOCATION (BUFF);

29. a. What hardware features of the HIS 645 and the IBM 360 are useful in implementing pure procedures?
    b. Is segmentation a good solution for the problem of protection? Why?

30. a. As we noted in the DLL, there are at least two distinct processes to loading a program. There is linking which resolves external references and the process of placing the program physically into core. In what order are these processes performed in MULTICS? Is the second process performed immediately after the first (as is the case in the DLL)? Why?
    b. Would an assembler for a segmented system like MULTICS have to produce RLD cards? Explain your answer. Assume MULTICS has address constants similar to the IBM 360.
    c. Recall that in MULTICS a file and a segment refer to the same concept, namely, a logical unit of information or more explicitly, an ordered collection of words. A particular instance of a segment (file) will consist of three parts: the segment body, a name, and a descriptor created by the MULTICS system. What is the purpose of this descriptor word?

For example, what kinds of information are located in the descriptor word and how are they used in MULTICS?

31. Figure 9.44 depicts a dynamic linking scheme. A process was executing procedure JOHN when it encountered the code equivalent to a CALL to procedure SQRT.

  a. What procedure (e.g., loader, linker, traffic controller, JOHN, JOHN's linkage segment, SQRT, etc.) sets the value of m?
  b. Who sets the contents of LP?
  c. Who sets the value of k?
  d. Why is it necessary to transfer to the linkage segment of SQRT and not directly to SQRT?

32. Under the two-dimensional addressing scheme used on the HIS 645 it is possible to "remap" all of name space simply by changing the contents of the DBR.

All references to segment k are found by checking the contents of the C(DBR)+k location for the base core address of the segment. If the contents of the DBR are changed, C(DBR)+k will be different and a different location will be examined for the base address of segment k.

There are several methods (hardware and/or software) for implementing a two-dimensional addressing scheme without use of a DBR. One method is to have a set of registers, each of which contains the address of the corresponding segment. Discuss the advantages and disadvantages of such a system compared with the one used on the HIS 645.

In the MULTICS system it is possible to contain the descriptor segments for several users in core at the same time, loading the DBR with the appropriate descriptor segment base address when a particular user is running. In one implementation, the procedure which switches among users (SWAP_DBR) has the same *segment number* in everybody's name space (that is, the offset within the descriptor segment of the core address of the procedure is the same for everybody: $k_A = k_B$). It is then possible to switch users by executing a single instruction — the one that changes the contents of the DBR.

Discuss the complications introduced if the switching procedure (SWAP_DBR) has a different segment number for each user.

33. The Humble Time-Sharing Co. (HTS) is a small struggling time-sharing service bureau handling about fifty simultaneous remote users (jobs). HTS uses the standard Bonanza I Real-Time Multiprogramming Time-Sharing Universal Operating System (with paging and segmentation). After hiring Frank Fasttalker as head salesman, HTS now has one hundred simultaneous users and is having trouble maintaining adequate throughput. Harry Moredough, HTS's computer agent, has suggested four changes to improve throughput:

  a. Buy more main memory.
  b. Purchase the new and faster Model 2 CPU.

    c. Replace their old Elephant Model A drums with the new and faster Pachyderm B drums.

    d. Switch to the Bonanza II operating system with improved information management features.

For each of these suggestions describe circumstances (job mix, environment, e.g., CPU bound) where (1) the change will have significant results, and (2) the change will result in very little improvement.

34. Problems 4 and 5 of Chapter 1 asked you essentially to flowchart OS 360; for this mission (should you decide to accept) you are to implement OS 360.

10

bibliography and suggestions
for further reading

It is impossible in a one-volume text to cover all aspects of computer systems. We list here related books and articles. References are grouped by subjects, and the sections follow the sequence in which the material appears in the text.

GENERAL

Gear, C. William: *Computer Organization and Programming*, McGraw-Hill, New York, 1969.

Hartman, Philip H., and David H. Owens: *How To Write Software Specifications; Proceedings, 1967 Fall Joint Computer Conference,*[*] pp. 779-790.

Knuth, Donald E.: *The Art of Computer Programming*, Addison-Wesley, Reading, Mass. (seven volumes, two already published).

Rosen, Saul: *Programming Systems and Languages*, McGraw-Hill, New York, 1967.

Wegner, Peter: *Programming Languages, Information Structure and Machine Organization*, McGraw-Hill, New York, 1968.

MACHINE STRUCTURE, ASSEMBLY LANGUAGE, 360-370

We list some pertinent IBM Manuals. The reader may wish to pursue different machine architectures, ones that allow parallel processing, more flexible allocation of parts of processors, stack machines, buffer memories, or associative memories. One important area that we have not covered is micro programming.

---

[*]Communications of the ACM, Fall Joint Computer Conference, and Spring Joint Computer Conference will be abbreviated respectively as CACM, FJCC, and SJCC throughout this chapter. Correspondingly, JACM refers to the Journal of the Association of Computing Machinery, AFIP refers to American Federation of Information Processing.

Germain, Clarence B.: *Programming the IBM 360,* Prentice-Hall, Englewood
    Cliffs, N.J., 1967.
IBM System/360 Principles of Operation, Form No. A22-6821-7.
*A Programmers' Introduction to the IBM System/360 Architecture, Instructions,
    and Assembler Language,* C20-1646-4.
IBM System/360 Operating System Assembler Language, C28-6514-6.

ASSEMBLERS

The text by Corbató, et al., is an excellent introduction. See also Wegner in the
General section of this bibliography.

Batson, Alan: "The Organization of Symbol Tables," *CACM,* vol. 8, No. 2,
    February, 1965, pp. 111-112.
Corbató, F.J., J.W. Poduska, and J.H. Saltzer: *Advanced Computer Program-
    ming,* MIT Press, Cambridge, Mass., 1963.

TABLE MANAGEMENT

We have discussed basic techniques. The references develop other algorithms.
An important subject that we have not treated is list representation and processing. LISP is a list-processing language.

Madnick, Stuart: "String Processing Techniques"; *CACM,* vol. 10, no. 7, July
    1967, pp. 420-424.

Searching and Sorting

CACM, vol. 6, no. 5, May, 1963, ACM Sort Symposium. The whole issue is on
    sorting. Especially good articles are.
    Gotlieb, C.C.: "Sorting on Computers."
    Hibbard, Thomas N.: "An Empirical Study of Minimal Storage Sorting."
    Hall, Michael H.: "A Method of Comparing the Time Requirements of
        Sorting Methods."
Buchholz, Werner: "File Organization and Addressing," *IBM Systems Journal,*
    vol. 2, June 1963, pp. 86-111.
Hamming, R.W.: *Numerical Methods for Scientists and Engineers,* McGraw-Hill,
    New York, 1962.
Iverson, Kenneth E.: *A Programming Language,* Wiley, New York, 1962.
Knuth, op. cit. (General section).

Address Calculation and Hashing

Flores, I.: "Computer Time for Address Calculation Sorting," *JACM*, 7, 1960, pp. 389-409.

Heising, W.P.: "Note on Random Addressing Techniques," *IBM Systems Journal*, vol. 2, June 1963, pp. 112-116.

Johnson, L.R.: "An Indirect Chaining Method for Addressing on Secondary Storage Keys," *CACM*, vol. 4, no. 5, May 1961, pp. 218-222.

Maurer, W.D.: "An Improved Hash Code for Scatter Storage," *CACM*, vol. 11, no. 1, Jan. 1968, pp. 35-38.

Morris, Robert: "Scatter Storage Techniques," *CACM*, vol. 11, no. 1, January 1968, pp. 38-44.

Peterson, W.W.: "Addressing for Random Access Storage," *IBM Journal of Research and Development*, vol. 1, no. 2, pp. 130-146, April 1957.

Schay, G. Jr. and W.G. Spruth: "Analysis of a File Addressing Method, *CACM*, vol. 5, no. 8, August 1962, pp. 459-462.

Comparative Sorts

Grassner, Betty Jane: "Sorting by Replacement Selection," *CACM*, vol. 10, no. 2, February 1967.

Shell, D.L.: "A High Speed Sorting Procedure," *CACM*, vol. 2, no. 1, January 1959, pp. 30-32.

Distributive Sorts

MacLaren, Donald M.: "Internal Sorting by Radix Plus Shifting," *JACM*, vol. 13, no. 3, July 1966, pp. 404-411.

Binary Searching and Tree Sorts

Arora, S.R. and W.T. Dent: "Randomized Binary Search Technique," *CACM*, vol. 12, no. 2, February 1969, pp. 77-80.

Clampett, H.A., Jr.: "Randomized Binary Searching with Tree Structures," *CACM*, vol. 7, no. 3, March 1964, pp. 163-165.

Patt, Yale N.: "Variable Length Tree Structures Having Minimum Average Search Time," *CACM*, vol. 12, no. 2, February 1969, pp. 72-76.

Sussenguth, E.H., Jr.: "Use of Tree Structures for Processing Files," *CACM*, vol. 6, no. 5, May 1963, pp. 272-279.

MACRO INSTRUCTION PROCESSORS

We have presented a traditional macro processor. One may view a macro processor generally as a text editor. The reader may wish to examine the various text editors – "line editors," "context editors," "QED-type editors," TRAC.

Of particular interest are the articles by Halpern and Kent. Chapters 2 and 3 of Wegner's text treat macros well. The paper by Dijkstra treats recursion Rosenbloom's book contains a good annotated bibliography on mathematical logic.

Brown, P.J.: "The ML/I Macro Processor," *CACM*, vol. 10, no. 10, 1967, pp. 618-623.

Dijkstra, E.W.: "Recursive Programming," in Rosen, Saul (ed): *Programming Systems and Languages*, McGraw-Hill, New York, 1967.

Farber, D.J.: R.E. Griswold, and I.P. Polonsky: "SNOBOL, A String Manipulation Language," *JACM*, vol. 11, no. 2, 1964, pp. 21-30.

Graham, M.L., and P.Z. Ingerman: "A Universal Assembly Mapping Language," *Proceedings, ACM 20th National Conference*, 1965, pp. 409-421.

Greenwald, I.D.: "A Technique for Handling Macro Instructions," *CACM*, vol. 2, no. 11, 1959, pp. 21-22.

Halpern, M.: "XPOP: A Meta Language Without Metaphysics," *Proceedings, AFIPS, 1964 FJCC*, pp. 57-68.

Kent, William: "Assembler – Language Macroprogramming," *Computing Surveys*, vol. 1, no. 4, 1969, pp. 183-196. (See also Dorn's "Editor's Preview" to the article.)

Maurer, Ward Douglas: "The Compiled Macro Assembler," *Proceedings, AFIPS, 1969 SJCC*, pp. 89-93.

McIlroy, M.D.: "Macro Instruction Extensions of Compiler Language," *CACM*, vol. 3, no. 4, 1960, pp. 214-220.

Mooers, C.N.: "TRAC, A Procedure Describing Language for the Reactive Typewriter," *CACM*, vol. 9, no. 3, 1966, pp. 215-219

Rosenbloom, P.: *The Elements of Mathematical Logic*, Dover Publications, 1950.

Strachey, C.: "A General Purpose Macrogenerator," *Computer Journal*, vol. 8, no. 3, 1965, pp. 225-241.

LOADERS

McCarthy, John, Fernando J. Corbató and Marjorie M. Daggett: "The Linking Segment Subprogram Language and Linking Loader," *CACM*, vol. 6, no. 7, June, 1963, pp. 391-395.

McGee, W.C.: "On Dynamic Program Relocation," *IBM Systems Journal*, vol. 4, no. 3, 1965, pp. 184-199.

PROGRAMMING LANGUAGES

Some readers may wish to investigate the existence of other language features than those we present; this would allow them to make comparisons and to become aware of the fundamental differences. A partial list includes: LISP (a list processing language), SNOBOL (a symbol manipulation language), AMBIT (a two-dimensional language), BCPL (a typeless language), GPL (an extensible language), and APL (an interactive language).

IBM System 360 PL/I Reference Manual, Form No. C28-8201-0.

Corbató, F.J.: "PL/I As a Tool for Systems Programming"; DATAMATION vol. 15, no. 5, May 1969, pp. 68-76.

Iverson, Kenneth E.: *A Programming Language,* Wiley, 1962.

McCarthy, J. et al.: *LISP 1.5 Programmer's Manual,* M.I.T. Press, Cambridge, Mass., 1962.

Rosen, op. cit. (General section).

Sammet, Jean E.: *Programming Languages: History and Fundamentals,* Prentice-Hall, Englewood Cliffs, N.J., 1969.

FORMAL SYSTEMS AND AUTOMATA

This is an extremely broad area, but one that is only tangential to our focus in this book. Rosenbloom (see the Macro Instruction Processors section) presents a good annotated bibliography in logic; Curry and Feys present a more detailed approach to formal systems. We have not touched on the related field of automata theory. For an introduction to this, see Ginzburg or Minsky. Some interesting research areas are complexity of translators and languages, automatic generation of compilers, theory of unsolvability, and machine structural analysis and design.

Newell's review of Minsky and Papert's *Perceptrons* is well worth reading. Newell discusses the aims, approaches, and methods of computer science.

Birkhoff, G., and T. Bartee, *Modern Applied Algebra,* McGraw-Hill, New York, 1967.

Burstall, R.M.: "Proving Properties of Programs by Structural Induction", *Computer Journal,* vol. 12, no. 1, February 1969, pp. 41-48.

Curry, H.B., and R. Feys: *Combinatory Logic,* North Holland Publishing Co., Amsterdam, 1958.

Davis, Martin: *Computability and Unsolvability,* McGraw-Hill, New York, 1958.

Floyd, Robert W.: "On the Non-existence of a Phrase-structure Grammer for ALGOL 60", *CACM* vol. 5, no. 9, 1962, pp. 483-484.

Ginsburg, Seymour: *The Mathematical Theory of Context-Free Languages,* McGraw-Hill, New York, 1966.

Ginzburg, Abraham: *Algebraic Theory of Automata,* Academic Press, New York, 1968.

Hopcroft, John E., and Jeffrey D. Ullman: *Formal Languages and Their Relation to Automata,* Addison-Wesley, Reading, Mass., 1969.

Minsky, Marvin: *Computation — Finite and Infinite Machines,* Prentice-Hall, Englewood Cliffs, N. J., 1967.

Minsky, Marvin, and Seymour Papert: *Perceptrons, An Introduction to Computational Geometry,* M.I.T. Press, Cambridge, Mass., 1969.

Newell, Allen: "A Step Toward the Understanding of Information Processes", *Science,* 165:3895, p. 780.

Post, Emil L.: "Absolutely Unsolvable Problems and Relatively Undecidable Propositions — Account of an Anticipation", in Martin Davis, *The Undecidable.* Raven Press, Hewlett, New York, 1965.

Post, Emil L.: "Formal Reductions of the General Combinatorial Decision Problem", *American Journal of Mathematics,* 65, 1943, pp. 197-215.

Rogers, Hartley Jr.: *Theory of Recursive Functions and Effective Computability,* McGraw-Hill, New York, 1967.

Smullyan, Raymond M.: "Theory of Formal Systems", *Annals of Mathematics Studies,* no. 47, Princeton University Press, Princeton, N. J., 1961.

CANONIC SYSTEMS

To date this approach to language definition has not been deeply explored. Minsky presents a relevant discussion of Post systems and Smullyan presents formal mathematical properties of similar systems. See also Post's papers in Davis' *The Undecidable* in the Formal Systems and Automata section.

Alsop, Joseph W.: "A Canonic Translator", Project Mac Technical Report Mac-Tr-46, M.I.T., Cambridge, Mass., 1967.

Donovan, John J., and Henry F. Ledgard: "A Formal System for the Specification of Syntax and Translation of Computer Languages", *Proceedings, AFIPS* 1967 *FJCC,* pp. 553-569.

Haggerty, Joseph P.: *Complexity Measures for Language Recognition by Canonic Systems,* S.M. Thesis, M.I.T., Cambridge, Mass., 1969.

COMPILERS AND COMPILING

ALGOL was in many ways the precursor to PL/I and is the subject of much of the earlier literature. A good bibliography of the current work in translator-writing systems appears in Feldman and Gries. Some readers may use our model as a basis for case studies of compilers for the languages mentioned above under PROGRAMMING LANGUAGES. Readers may also wish to consider the generality of the model.

We have presented two classes of optimization, machine-dependent and machine-independent, and some techniques. Another class of optimization is "heuristic": the compiler adjusts itself to produce optimal code for its environment. The reader may wish to pursue this area as research.

Arden, Bruce W., Bernard A. Galler, and Robert M. Graham: "The MAD Definition Facility", *CACM*, vol. 12, no. 8, August 2, 1969, pp. 432-439.

Bell, James R.: "A New Method for Determining Linear Precedence Functions for Precedence Grammars", *CACM*, vol. 12, no. 10, October, 1969, pp. 567-569.

Breuer, Melvin A.: "Generation of Optimal Code for Expressions Via Factorization", *CACM*, vol. 12, no. 6, June, 1969, pp. 333-340.

Dijkstra, E.W.: "Recursive Programming", in Rosen, *Programming Systems and Languages*, McGraw-Hill, New York, 1967, pp. 221-227.

Feldman, J. and D. Gries, "Translator Writing Systems" *CACM*, vol. 11, no. 2, February, 1968.

Finkelstein, Mark: "A Compiler Optimization Technique", *Computer Journal*, vol. 2, no. 1, May 1968, pp. 22-25.

Freiburghouse, R.A.: "The MULTICS PL/I Compiler", *Proceedings, AFIPS, 1969, FJCC*, pp. 187-199.

Gear, C.W.: "High-speed Compilation of Efficient Object Code", *CACM*, vol. 8, no. 8, August 1965, pp. 483-488.

Gries, D., M. Paul and H.R. Wiehle: "Some Techniques Used in the Alcor Illinois 7090", *CACM*, vol. 8, no. 8, August 1965.

Hopgood, F.R.A.: *Compiling Techniques*, American Elsevier Publishing Co., Inc., New York, 1969.

Ingerman, Peter Z.: *A Syntax-Oriented Translator*, Academic Press, New York, 1966

Jensen, Jorn: "Generation of Machine Code in ALGOL Compilers", *BIT*, vol. 5, no. 4, 1965, pp. 235-245.

Kanner, H., P. Kosinski, and S.L. Robinson: "The Structure of Yet Another ALGOL Compiler", *CACM*, vol. 8, no. 7, July 1965, p. 427.

Lowry, Edward S., and C.W. Medlock: "Object Code Optimization", *CACM*, vol. 12, no. 1, January 1969, pp. 13-22.

Nievergelt, J.: "On the Automatic Simplification of Computer Programs", *CACM*, vol. 8, no. 6, June 1965, pp. 366-370.

Perlis, Alan J.: "Procedural Languages". *Proceedings, 2nd Congress Information Systems Science*, pp. 189-210.

Randell, B. and L.J. Russell: *ALGOL 60 Implementation*, Academic Press, New York, 1964.

Randell, B., and L.J. Russell: "Single-Scan Techniques for the Translation of Arithmetic Expressions in ALGOL 60", *JACM*, vol. 11, no. 2, April 1964, pp. 159.

OPERATING SYSTEMS

The references treat many aspects of system design. There is, of course, an important overlap between considerations of system design and of machine structure. The May 1968 CACM (vol. 11, no. 9) is devoted to operating systems. For an introduction, see the Wilkes and Needham (Computer Journal) articles. See also Rosen in the General section.

We present a view of operating systems as resource managers. As a research area òne may develop a general theory and mathematics that are applicable to the management of the four resources of a computer system: memory, processors, devices, and information.

Arden, B.W., B.A. Galler, T.C. O'Brien and F.H. Westervelt: "Programming and Addressing Structure in a Time-Sharing Environment", *JACM*, vol. 13, no. 1, January 1966, pp. 1-16.

Bright, Herbert S.: "A Philco Multiprocessing System", *Proceedings, AFIPS 1964 FJCC*, Part II, pp. 97-141.

Clayton, B.B., E.K. Dorff and R.E. Fagen: "An Operating System and Programming Systems for the 6600", *Proceedings, AFIPS 1964 FJCC*, Part II, pp. 41-57.

Coffman, E.G., Jr., and L. Kleinrock: "Computer Scheduling Methods and Their Countermeasures", *Proceedings, AFIPS 1968 SJCC*, pp. 11-21.

Coffman, E.G., Jr. and R.R. Muntz: "Models of Pure Time-Sharing Disciplines for Resource Allocation", *Proceedings, ACM 24th National Conference*, pp. 217-228.

Connors, Thomas L., and Donald E. Walker, (eds.): "Software Concerns in Advanced Information Systems", in *Information System Science and Technology*, Thompson Book Co., Washington, D.C., 1967, pp. 395-398.

Corbato, F.J. and V.A. Vyssotsky: "Introduction and Overview of the MULTICS System, *Proceedings, AFIPS 1965 FJCC*, pp. 185-196.

Daley, Robert C., and Jack B. Dennis: "Virtual Memory, Processes, and Sharing in MULTICS", *CACM*, vol. 11, no. 5, May 1968, pp. 306-312.

Denning, Peter J.: "Thrashing: Its Causes and Prevention", *Proceedings, AFIPS 1968 FJCC*, Part I, pp. 915-922.

Denning, Peter J.: "The Working Set Model for Program Behavior", *CACM*, vol. 11, no. 5, May 1968, pp. 323-333.

Dennis, Jack B.: "Segmentation and the Design of Multiprogrammed Computer Systems", *JACM*, vol. 12, no. 4, October 1965, pp. 589-602.

Dijkstra, Edsger W.: "The Structure of the 'THE' Multiprogramming System", *CACM*, vol. 11, no. 5, May 1968, pp. 341-346.

Gibson, Charles T.: "Time-sharing in the IBM System/360 Model 67". *Proceedings, AFIPS, 1966 SJCC*, pp. 61-78.

Glaser, E.L., J.F. Couleur and G.A. Oliver: "System Design of a Computer for Time-Sharing Applications", *Proceedings, AFIPS, 1968 FJCC*, Part I, pp. 197-202.

Graham, Robert M.: "Protection in an Information Processing Utility", *CACM*, vol. 11, no. 5, May 1968, pp. 365-369.

Hellerman, H.: "Some Principles of Time-sharing Scheduler Strategies", *IBM Systems Journal*, vol. 8, no. 2, 1969, pp. 94-117.

Kinslow, H.A.: "The Time-Sharing Monitor System", *Proceedings, AFIPS, 1964 FJCC*, pp. 443-454.

Kleinrock, L.: "Time-Shared Systems: A Theoretical Treatment", *Journal of the ACM*, vol. 14, no. 2, April 1967, pp. 242-261.

Lampson, Butler W.: "A Scheduling Philosophy for Multiprocessing Systems", *CACM*, vol. 11, no. 5, May 1968, pp. 347-360.

Madnick, Stuart, "Multiprocessor Software Lockout", *Proceedings, 1968 ACM National Conference*, pp. 19-24.

Mendelson, Myron J., and A.W. England: "The SDS SIGMA 7: A Real-Time Time-Sharing Computer", *Proceedings, AFIPS 1966 FJCC*, pp. 51-64.

Oppenheimer, G. and N. Weizer: "Resource Management for a Medium Scale Time-Sharing Operating System", *CACM*, vol. 11, no. 5, May 1968, pp. 313-322.

Randell, B. and C.J. Kuehner: "Dynamic Storage Allocation Systems", *CACM*, vol. 11, no. 5, May 1968, pp. 297-306.

Randell, B.: "A Note on Storage Fragmentation and Program Segmentation", *CACM*, vol. 12, no. 7, July 1969, pp. 365-369, 372.

Rosin, Robert F.: "Supervisory and Monitor Systems", *Computing Surveys*, vol. 1, no. 1, March 1969, pp. 37-54.

Sackman, H.: "Time-Sharing Versus Batch Processing: The Experimental Evidence", *Proceedings, AFIPS 1968 SJCC*, vol. 1, no. 10.

Saltzer, J.H.: "Traffic Control in a Multiplexed Computer System", MAC-TR-30 Thesis, Project MAC, Cambridge, Mass. July 1966.

Tonik, Albert B.: "Development of Executive Routines, Both Hardware and Software", *Proceedings, AFIPS, 1967 FJCC*, pp. 395-408.

Vyssotsky, V.A., F.J. Corbató and R.M. Graham: "Structure of the MULTICS Supervisor", *Proceedings, AFIPS, 1965 FJCC*, Part I, pp. 203-212.

Wichmann, B.A.: "A Modular Operating System", *Proceedings, IFIP Congress 1968*, Software 2, Booklet C. pp. 48-54.

Wilkes, M.V.: "The Design of Multiple-Access Computer Systems (Part 1)", *Computer Journal*, vol. 10, no. 1, May 1967, pp. 1-9.

Wilkes, M.V. and R.M. Needham: "The Design of Multiple-Access Computer Systems (Part 2)", *Computer Journal*, vol. 10, no. 4, February 1958, pp. 315-320.

Wilkes, M.V.: "A Model for Core Space Allocation in a Time-Sharing System", *Proceedings, AFIPS, 1969, SJCC*, pp. 265-271.

Wilkes, M.V.: *Time-Sharing Computer Systems*, American Elsevier Publishing Company, New York, 1968.

Witt, Bernard I.: "M65MP: An Experiment in OS/360 Multiprocessing", *Proceedings, ACM 23rd National Conference*, 1968, pp. 691-703.

Wood, Thomas C.: "A Generalized Supervisor for a Time-Shared Operating System", *Proceedings, AFIPS, 1967 FJCC*, pp. 209-214.

PROTECTION AND PROCESS COMMUNICATION

de Bruijn, N.G.: "Additional Comments on a Problem in Concurrent Programming Control", Letter to the Editor, *CACM*, vol. 10, no. 3, March 1967, pp. 137-138.

Corbató, F.J., and J.H. Saltzer: "Some Considerations of Supervisor Program Design for Multiplexed Computer Systems", *Proceedings, IFIP Congress* 1968, Invited Papers, pp. 66-71.

Dijkstra, E.W.: "Solution of a Problem in Concurrent Programming Control", *CACM*, vol. 8, no. 9, September 1969, p. 569.

Habermann, A.N.: "Prevention of System Deadlocks", *CACM*, vol. 12, no. 7, July 1969, pp. 373-377, 385.

Knuth, Donald E.: "Additional Comments on a Problem in Concurrent Programming Control", Letter to the Editor, *CACM*, vol. 9, no. 5, May 1966. pp. 321-322.

Lampson, B.W.: "Dynamic Protection Structures", *Proceedings, 1969 FJCC*, pp. 27-28.

Ossanna, J.F., L.E. Mikus and S.D. Dunten: "Communications and Input/Output Switching in a Multiplex Computing System", *Proceedings, AFIPS, 1965 FJCC*, Part 1, pp. 231-241.

Randell, B. and C.J. Kuehner: "Dynamic Storage Allocation Systems", *CACM*, vol. 11, no. 5, May 1965, pp. 297-306.

FILE SYSTEMS

Chapin, Ned: "A Comparison of File Organization Techniques", *Proceedings, ACM 24th National Conference*, pp. 273-283.

Daley, R.C. and P.G. Neumann: "A General-Purpose File System for Secondary Storage", *Proceedings, 1965 FJCC*, Part 1, pp. 213-229.

Madnick, Stuart E. and Joseph W. Alsop: "A Modular Approach to File System Design", *Proceedings, AFIPS 1969 SJCC*, vol. 1, no. 13.

Madnick, Stuart E.: "Design Strategies for File System", MIT Project MAC report TR78, Cambridge, Mass., Oct. 1970.

Sundeen, Donald H.: "General Purpose Software", *Datamation*, vol. 14, no. 1, January 1968, pp. 22-27.

Weingarten, Allen: "The Analytical Design of Real-Time Disk Systems", *Proceedings, IFIP Congress* 1968, Hardware 1, Booklet D, pp. 131-137.

Wilkes, M.V.: "A Programmer's Utility Filing System", *Computer Journal*, vol. 7, no. 3, October 1964, pp. 180-184.

appendix a

$\mathbf{IBM}^{\circledR}$ System 360
Reference Data Card*

*Reprinted by permission of International Business Machines Corporation.

IBM System/360 Reference Data

MACHINE INSTRUCTIONS

NAME	MNEMONIC	OP CODE	FORMAT	OPERANDS
Add (c)	AR	1A	RR	R1,R2
Add (c)	A	5A	RX	R1,D2(X2,B2)
Add Decimal (c,d)	AP	FA	SS	D1(L1,B1),D2(L2,B2)
Add Halfword (c)	AH	4A	RX	R1,D2(X2,B2)
Add Logical (c)	ALR	1E	RR	R1,R2
Add Logical (c)	AL	5E	RX	R1,D2(X2,B2)
AND (c)	NR	14	RR	R1,R2
AND (c)	N	54	RX	R1,D2(X2,B2)
AND (c)	NI	94	SI	D1(B1),I2
AND (c)	NC	D4	SS	D1(L,B1),D2(B2)
Branch and Link	BALR	05	RR	R1,R2
Branch and Link	BAL	45	RX	R1,D2(X2,B2)
Branch and Store (e)	BASR	0D	RR	R1,R2
Branch and Store (e)	BAS	4D	RX	R1,D2(X2,B2)
Branch on Condition	BCR	07	RR	M1,R2
Branch on Condition	BC	47	RX	M1,D2(X2,B2)
Branch on Count	BCTR	06	RR	R1,R2
Branch on Count	BCT	46	RX	R1,D2(X2,B2)
Branch on Index High	BXH	86	RS	R1,R3,D2(B2)
Branch on Index Low or Equal	BXLE	87	RS	R1,R3,D2(B2)
Compare (c)	CR	19	RR	R1,R2
Compare (c)	C	59	RX	R1,D2(X2,B2)
Compare Decimal (c,d)	CP	F9	SS	D1(L1,B1),D2(L2,B2)
Compare Halfword (c)	CH	49	RX	R1,D2(X2,B2)
Compare Logical (c)	CLR	15	RR	R1,R2
Compare Logical (c)	CL	55	RX	R1,D2(X2,B2)
Compare Logical (c)	CLC	D5	SS	D1(L,B1),D2(B2)
Compare Logical (c)	CLI	95	SI	D1(B1),I2
Convert to Binary	CVB	4F	RX	R1,D2(X2,B2)
Convert to Decimal	CVD	4E	RX	R1,D2(X2,B2)
Diagnose (p)		83	SI	
Divide	DR	1D	RR	R1,R2
Divide	D	5D	RX	R1,D2(X2,B2)
Divide Decimal (d)	DP	FD	SS	D1(L1,B1),D2(L2,B2)
Edit (c,d)	ED	DE	SS	D1(L,B1),D2(B2)
Edit and Mark (c,d)	EDMK	DF	SS	D1(L,B1),D2(B2)
Exclusive OR (c)	XR	17	RR	R1,R2
Exclusive OR (c)	X	57	RX	R1,D2(X2,B2)
Exclusive OR (c)	XI	97	SI	D1(B1),I2
Exclusive OR (c)	XC	D7	SS	D1(L,B1),D2(B2)
Execute	EX	44	RX	R1,D2(X2,B2)
Halt I/O (c,p)	HIO	9E	SI	D1(B1)
Insert Character	IC	43	RX	R1,D2(X2,B2)
Insert Storage Key (a,p)	ISK	09	RR	R1,R2
Load	LR	18	RR	R1,R2
Load	L	58	RX	R1,D2(X2,B2)
Load Address	LA	41	RX	R1,D2(X2,B2)
Load and Test (c)	LTR	12	RR	R1,R2
Load Complement (c)	LCR	13	RR	R1,R2
Load Halfword	LH	48	RX	R1,D2(X2,B2)
Load Multiple	LM	98	RS	R1,R3,D2(B2)
Load Multiple Control (e,p)	LMC	B8	RS	R1,R3,D2(B2)
Load Negative (c)	LNR	11	RR	R1,R2
Load Positive (c)	LPR	10	RR	R1,R2
Load PSW (n,p)	LPSW	82	SI	D1(B1)
Load Real Address (c,e,p)	LRA	B1	RX	R1,D2(X2,B2)
Move	MVI	92	SI	D1(B1),I2
Move	MVC	D2	SS	D1(L,B1),D2(B2)
Move Numerics	MVN	D1	SS	D1(L,B1),D2(B2)
Move with Offset	MVO	F1	SS	D1(L1,B1),D2(L2,B2)
Move Zones	MVZ	D3	SS	D1(L,B1),D2(B2)
Multiply	MR	1C	RR	R1,R2
Multiply	M	5C	RX	R1,D2(X2,B2)
Multiply Decimal (d)	MP	FC	SS	D1(L1,B1),D2(L2,B2)
Multiply Halfword	MH	4C	RX	R1,D2(X2,B2)
OR (c)	OR	16	RR	R1,R2
OR (c)	O	56	RX	R1,D2(X2,B2)
OR (c)	OI	96	SI	D1(B1),I2

②

OR (c)	OC	D6	SS	D1(L,B1),D2(B2)
Pack	PACK	F2	SS	D1(L1,B1),D2(L2,B2)
Read Direct (b,p)	RDD	85	SI	D1(B1),I2
Set Program Mask (n)	SPM	04	RR	R1
Set Storage Key (a,p)	SSK	08	RR	R1,R2
Set System Mask (p)	SSM	80	SI	D1(B1)
Shift Left Double (c)	SLDA	8F	RS	R1,D2(B2)
Shift Left Double Logical	SLDL	8D	RS	R1,D2(B2)
Shift Left Single (c)	SLA	8B	RS	R1,D2(B2)
Shift Left Single Logical	SLL	89	RS	R1,D2(B2)
Shift Right Double (c)	SRDA	8E	RS	R1,D2(B2)
Shift Right Double Logical	SRDL	8C	RS	R1,D2(B2)
Shift Right Single (c)	SRA	8A	RS	R1,D2(B2)
Shift Right Single Logical	SRL	88	RS	R1,D2(B2)
Start I/O (c,p)	SIO	9C	SI	D1(B1)
Store	ST	50	RX	R1,D2(X2,B2)
Store Character	STC	42	RX	R1,D2(X2,B2)
Store Halfword	STH	40	RX	R1,D2(X2,B2)
Store Multiple	STM	90	RS	R1,R3,D2(B2)
Store Multiple Control (e,p)	STMC	B0	RS	R1,R3,D2(B2)
Subtract (c)	SR	1B	RR	R1,R2
Subtract (c)	S	5B	RX	R1,D2(X2,B2)
Subtract Decimal (c,d)	SP	FB	SS	D1(L1,B1),D2(L2,B2)
Subtract Halfword (c)	SH	4B	RX	R1,D2(X2,B2)
Subtract Logical (c)	SLR	1F	RR	R1,R2
Subtract Logical (c)	SL	5F	RX	R1,D2(X2,B2)
Supervisor Call	SVC	0A	RR	I
Test and Set (c)	TS	93	SI	D1(B1)
Test Channel (c,p)	TCH	9F	SI	D1(B1)
Test I/O (c,p)	TIO	9D	SI	D1(B1)
Test under Mask (c)	TM	91	SI	D1(B1),I2
Translate	TR	DC	SS	D1(L,B1),D2(B2)
Translate and Test (c)	TRT	DD	SS	D1(L,B1),D2(B2)
Unpack	UNPK	F3	SS	D1(L1,B1),D2(L2,B2)
Write Direct (b,p)	WRD	84	SI	D1(B1),I2
Zero and Add (c,d)	ZAP	F8	SS	D1(L1,B1),D2(L2,B2)

NOTES FOR PANELS 1-3

a. Protection feature   d. Decimal feature   code is loaded
b. Direct control feature   e. Model 67   p. Privileged instruction
c. Condition code is set   n. New condition   x. Extended precision
                                                              floating point feature

MACHINE FORMATS

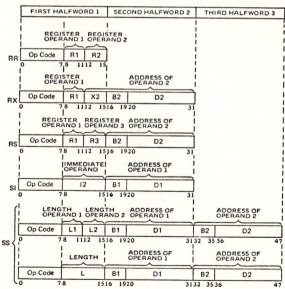

③

FLOATING-POINT FEATURE INSTRUCTIONS

Add Normalized, Extended (c,x)	AXR	36	RR	R1,R2
Add Normalized, Long (c)	ADR	2A	RR	R1,R2
Add Normalized, Long (c)	AD	6A	RX	R1,D2(X2,B2)
Add Normalized, Short (c)	AER	3A	RR	R1,R2
Add Normalized, Short (c)	AE	7A	RX	R1,D2(X2,B2)
Add Unnormalized, Long (c)	AWR	2E	RR	R1,R2
Add Unnormalized, Long (c)	AW	6E	RX	R1,D2(X2,B2)
Add Unnormalized, Short (c)	AUR	3E	RR	R1,R2
Add Unnormalized, Short (c)	AU	7E	RX	R1,D2(X2,B2)
Compare, Long (c)	CDR	29	RR	R1,R2
Compare, Long (c)	CD	69	RX	R1,D2(X2,B2)
Compare, Short (c)	CER	39	RR	R1,R2
Compare, Short (c)	CE	79	RX	R1,D2(X2,B2)
Divide, Long	DDR	2D	RR	R1,R2
Divide, Long	DD	6D	RX	R1,D2(X2,B2)
Divide, Short	DER	3D	RR	R1,R2
Divide, Short	DE	7D	RX	R1,D2(X2,B2)
Halve, Long	HDR	24	RR	R1,R2
Halve, Short	HER	34	RR	R1,R2
Load and Test, Long (c)	LTDR	22	RR	R1,R2
Load and Test, Short (c)	LTER	32	RR	R1,R2
Load Complement, Long (c)	LCDR	23	RR	R1,R2
Load Complement, Short (c)	LCER	33	RR	R1,R2
Load, Long	LDR	28	RR	R1,R2
Load, Long	LD	68	RX	R1,D2(X2,B2)
Load Negative, Long (c)	LNDR	21	RR	R1,R2
Load Negative, Short (c)	LNER	31	RR	R1,R2
Load Positive, Long (c)	LPDR	20	RR	R1,R2
Load Positive, Short (c)	LPER	30	RR	R1,R2
Load Rounded, Extended to Long (x)	LRDR	25	RR	R1,R2
Load Rounded, Long to Short (x)	LRER	35	RR	R1,R2
Load, Short	LER	38	RR	R1,R2
Load, Short	LE	78	RX	R1,D2(X2,B2)
Multiply, Extended (x)	MXR	26	RR	R1,R2
Multiply, Long	MDR	2C	RR	R1,R2
Multiply, Long	MD	6C	RX	R1,D2(X2,B2)
Multiply, Long/Extended (x)	MXDR	27	RR	R1,R2
Multiply, Long/Extended (x)	MXD	67	RX	R1,D2(X2,B2)
Multiply, Short	MER	3C	RR	R1,R2
Multiply, Short	ME	7C	RX	R1,D2(X2,B2)
Store, Long	STD	60	RX	R1,D2(X2,B2)
Store, Short	STE	70	RX	R1,D2(X2,B2)
Subtract Normalized, Extended (c,x)	SXR	37	RR	R1,R2
Subtract Normalized, Long (c)	SDR	2B	RR	R1,R2
Subtract Normalized, Long (c)	SD	6B	RX	R1,D2(X2,B2)
Subtract Normalized, Short (c)	SER	3B	RR	R1,R2
Subtract Normalized, Short (c)	SE	7B	RX	R1,D2(X2,B2)
Subtract Unnormalized, Long (c)	SWR	2F	RR	R1,R2
Subtract Unnormalized, Long (c)	SW	6F	RX	R1,D2(X2,B2)
Subtract Unnormalized, Short (c)	SUR	3F	RR	R1,R2
Subtract Unnormalized, Short (c)	SU	7F	RX	R1,D2(X2,B2)

SUMMARY OF CONSTANTS

TYPE	IMPLIED LENGTH, BYTES	ALIGNMENT	FORMAT	TRUNCA- TION/ PADDING
C	–	byte	characters	right
X	–	byte	hexadecimal digits	left
B	–	byte	binary digits	left
F	4	word	fixed-point binary	left
H	2	halfword	fixed-point binary	left
E	4	word	short floating-point	right
D	8	doubleword	long floating-point	right
L	16	doubleword	extended floating-point	right
P	–	byte	packed decimal	left
Z	–	byte	zoned decimal	left
A	4	word	value of address	left
Y	2	halfword	value of address	left
S	2	halfword	address in base-displacement form	–
V	4	word	externally defined address value	left
Q*	4	word	symbol naming a DXD or DSECT	left

*OS only

④

EXTENDED MNEMONIC INSTRUCTION CODES

GENERAL

Extended Code		Machine Instruction		Meaning
B	D2(X2,B2)	BC 15,	D2(X2,B2)	Branch Unconditionally
BR	R2	BCR 15,	R2	Branch Unconditionally
NOP	D2(X2,B2)	BC 0,	D2(X2,B2)	No Operation
NOPR	R2	BCR 0,	R2	No Operation (RR)

AFTER COMPARE INSTRUCTIONS (A:B)

BH	D2(X2,B2)	BC 2,	D2(X2,B2)	Branch on A High
BL	D2(X2,B2)	BC 4,	D2(X2,B2)	Branch on A Low
BE	D2(X2,B2)	BC 8,	D2(X2,B2)	Branch on Equal B
BNH	D2(X2,B2)	BC 13,	D2(X2,B2)	Branch on A Not High
BNL	D2(X2,B2)	BC 11,	D2(X2,B2)	Branch on A Not Low
BNE	D2(X2,B2)	BC 7,	D2(X2,B2)	Branch on A Not Equal **B**

AFTER ARITHMETIC INSTRUCTIONS

BO	D2(X2,B2)	BC 1,	D2(X2,B2)	Branch on Overflow
BP	D2(X2,B2)	BC 2,	D2(X2,B2)	Branch on Plus
BM	D2(X2,B2)	BC 4,	D2(X2,B2)	Branch on Minus
BZ	D2(X2,B2)	BC 8,	D2(X2,B2)	Branch on Zero
BNP	D2(X2,B2)	BC 13,	D2(X2,B2)	Branch on Not Plus
BNM	D2(X2,B2)	BC 11,	D2(X2,B2)	Branch on Not Minus
BNZ	D2(X2,B2)	BC 7,	D2(X2,B2)	Branch on Not Zero

AFTER TEST UNDER MASK INSTRUCTIONS

BO	D2(X2,B2)	BC 1,	D2(X2,B2)	Branch if Ones
BM	D2(X2,B2)	BC 4,	D2(X2,B2)	Branch if Mixed
BZ	D2(X2,B2)	BC 8,	D2(X2,B2)	Branch if Zeros
BNO	D2(X2,B2)	BC 14,	D2(X2,B2)	Branch if Not Ones

CNOP ALIGNMENT

Double Word							
Word				Word			
Half Word		Half Word		Half Word		Half Word	
Byte	Byte	Byte	Byte	Byte	Byte	Byte	Byte
0,4		2,4		0,4		2,4	
0,8		2,8		4,8		6,8	

EDIT AND EDMK PATTERN CHARACTERS (in hex)

20–digit selector	40–blank	5C--asterisk
21–start of significance	4B--period	6B--comma
22–field separator	5B--dollar sign	C3D9--CR

PERMANENT STORAGE ASSIGNMENTS

ADDRESS			
DEC	HEX	LENGTH	PURPOSE
0	0	double word	Initial program loading PSW
8	8	double word	Initial program loading CCW1
16	10	double word	Initial program loading CCW2
24	18	double word	External old PSW
32	20	double word	Supervisor Call old PSW
40	28	double word	Program old PSW
48	30	double word	Machine-check old PSW
56	38	double word	Input/output old PSW
64	40	double word	Channel status word
72	48	word	Channel address word
76	4C	word	Unused
80	50	word	Timer (uses bytes 50, 51 & 52)
84	54	word	Unused
88	58	double word	External new PSW
96	60	double word	Supervisor Call new PSW
104	68	double word	Program new PSW
112	70	double word	Machine-check new PSW
120	78	double word	Input/output new PSW
128	80	(1)	Diagnostic scan-out area

(1) The size of the diagnostic scan-out area depends on the particular model and I/O channels; for models 30 through 75, maximum size is 256 bytes.

(5)

CONDITION CODES

Condition Code Setting	0	1	2	3
Mask Bit Position	8	4	2	1

FLOATING-POINT ARITHMETIC

Add Normalized S/L/E	zero	$<$zero	$>$zero	--
Add Unnormalized S/L	zero	$<$zero	$>$zero	--
Compare S/L (A:B)	equal	A low	A high	--
Load and Test S/L	zero	$<$zero	$>$zero	--
Load Complement S/L	zero	$<$zero	$>$zero	--
Load Negative S/L	zero	$<$zero	--	--
Load Positive S/L	zero	-	$>$zero	--
Subtract Normalized S/L/E	zero	$<$zero	$>$zero	--
Subtract Unnormalized S/L	zero	$<$zero	$>$zero	--

FIXED-POINT AND DECIMAL ARITHMETIC

Add H/F/Dec.	zero	$<$zero	$>$zero	overflow
Add Logical	zero, no carry	not zero, no carry	zero, carry	not zero, carry
Compare H/F/Dec. (A:B)	equal	A low	A high	--
Load and Test	zero	$<$zero	$>$zero	--
Load Complement	zero	$<$zero	$>$zero	overflow
Load Negative	zero	$<$zero	--	--
Load Positive	zero	-	$>$zero	overflow
Shift Left Single/Double	zero	$<$zero	$>$zero	overflow
Shift Right Single/Double	zero	$<$zero	$>$zero	-
Subtract H/F/Dec.	zero	$<$zero	$>$zero	overflow
Subtract Logical	--	not zero, no carry	zero, carry	not zero, carry
Zero and Add	zero	$<$zero	$>$zero	overflow

LOGICAL OPERATIONS

AND	zero	not zero	--	--
Compare Logical (A:B)	equal	A low	A high	-
Edit	zero	$<$zero	$>$zero	--
Edit and Mark	zero	$<$zero	$>$zero	--
Exclusive OR	zero	not zero	--	--
OR	zero	not zero	--	--
Test under Mask	zero	mixed	--	one
Translate and Test	zero	incomplete	complete	--

INPUT/OUTPUT OPERATIONS

Halt I/O	interruption pending	CSW stored	halted	not oper
Start I/O	started	CSW stored	busy	not oper
Test I/O	available	CSW stored	busy	not oper
Test Channel	available	interruption pending	burst mode	not oper

MISC. OPERATIONS

Test and Set	zero	one	--	--
Load Real Address (Mod. 67)	successful	segment unavailable	page unavailable	--

PROGRAM STATUS WORD

System Mask*	Key	AMWP*	Interruption Code
0 7	8 11	12 15	16 23 24 31

ILC	CC	Program Mask*	Instruction Address
32 34	34 35	36 39	40 47 48 55 56 63
33 35			

0 Multiplexer channel mask
1 Selector channel 1 mask
2 Selector channel 2 mask
3 Selector channel 3 mask
4 Selector channel 4 mask
5 Selector channel 5 mask
6 Selector channel 6 mask
7 External mask
12 ASCII-8 mode (A)

13 Machine check mask (M)
14 Wait state (W)
15 Problem state (P)
32-33 Instruction length code (ILC)
34-35 Condition code (CC)
36 Fixed-point overflow mask
37 Decimal overflow mask
38 Exponent underflow mask
39 Significance mask

*A one-bit equals on, and permits an interrupt.

⑥

CODES FOR PROGRAM INTERRUPTION

Interruption Code		Program Interruption Cause	Interruption Code		Program Interruption Cause
Dec	Hex		Dec	Hex	
1	0001	Operation	10	000A	Decimal overflow
2	0002	Privileged operation	11	000B	Decimal divide
3	0003	Execute	12	000C	Exponent overflow
4	0004	Protection	13	000D	Exponent underflow
5	0005	Addressing	14	000E	Significance
6	0006	Specification	15	000F	Floating-point divide
7	0007	Data	16*	0010	Segment translation
8	0008	Fixed-point overflow	17*	0011	Page translation
9	0009	Fixed-point divide			

*Model 67

HEXADECIMAL AND DECIMAL CONVERSION

From hex: locate each hex digit in its corresponding column position and note the decimal equivalents. Add these to obtain the decimal value.

From decimal: (1) locate the largest decimal value in the table that will fit into the decimal number to be converted, and (2) note its hex equivalent and hex column position. (3) Find the decimal remainder. Repeat the process on this and subsequent remainders.

HEXADECIMAL COLUMNS											
6		5		4		3		2		1	
HEX	= DEC	HEX	= DEC	HEX	= DEC	HEX	= DEC	HEX	= DEC	HEX	= DEC
0	0	0	0	0	0	0	0	0	0	0	0
1	1,048,576	1	65,536	1	4,096	1	256	1	16	1	1
2	2,097,152	2	131,072	2	8,192	2	512	2	32	2	2
3	3,145,728	3	196,608	3	12,288	3	768	3	48	3	3
4	4,194,304	4	262,144	4	16,384	4	1,024	4	64	4	4
5	5,242,880	5	327,680	5	20,480	5	1,280	5	80	5	5
6	6,291,456	6	393,216	6	24,576	6	1,536	6	96	6	6
7	7,340,032	7	458,752	7	28,672	7	1,792	7	112	7	7
8	8,388,608	8	524,288	8	32,768	8	2,048	8	128	8	8
9	9,437,184	9	589,824	9	36,864	9	2,304	9	144	9	9
A	10,485,760	A	655,360	A	40,960	A	2,560	A	160	A	10
B	11,534,336	B	720,896	B	45,056	B	2,816	B	176	B	11
C	12,582,912	C	786,432	C	49,152	C	3,072	C	192	C	12
D	13,631,488	D	851,968	D	53,248	D	3,328	D	208	D	13
E	14,680,064	E	917,504	E	57,344	E	3,584	E	224	E	14
F	15,728,640	F	983,040	F	61,440	F	3,840	F	240	F	15
0 1 2 3	4 5 6 7			0 1 2 3	4 5 6 7			0 1 2 3	4 5 6 7		
BYTE				BYTE				BYTE			

BINARY CONVERSION

Dec	= Hex	= Binary
0	0	0000
1	1	0001
2	2	0010
3	3	0011
4	4	0100
5	5	0101
6	6	0110
7	7	0111
8	8	1000
9	9	1001
10	A	1010
11	B	1011
12	C	1100
13	D	1101
14	E	1110
15	F	1111
16	10	0001 0000

POWERS OF 16 TABLE

16^n	n
1	0
16	1
256	2
4 096	3
65 536	4
1 048 576	5
16 777 216	6
268 435 456	7
4 294 967 296	8
68 719 476 736	9
1 099 511 627 776	10
17 592 186 044 416	11
281 474 976 710 656	12
4 503 599 627 370 496	13
72 057 594 037 927 936	14
1 152 921 504 606 846 976	15

Comments about this card may be sent to the Technical Publications Dept. at the White Plains address below. All comments and suggestions become the property of IBM.

IBM

International Business Machines Corporation
Data Processing Division
1133 Westchester Ave., White Plains, N.Y. 10604
(U.S.A. only)

IBM World Trade Corporation
821 United Nations Plaza,
New York, New York 10017
(International)

Printed in U.S.A. GX20-1703-8

⑦

Decimal	Hexadecimal	Instruction Mnemonic (RR Format)	Graphic & Control Symbols BCDIC / EBCDIC	7-Track Tape BCDIC	Punched Card Code	System/360 8-bit Code
0	00		NUL		12-0-1-8-9	0000 0000
1	01		SOH		12-1-9	0000 0001
2	02		STX		12-2-9	0000 0010
3	03		ETX		12-3-9	0000 0011
4	04	SPM	PF		12-4-9	0000 0100
5	05	BALR	HT		12-5-9	0000 0101
6	06	BCTR	LC		12-6-9	0000 0110
7	07	BCR	DEL		12-7-9	0000 0111
8	08	SSK			12-8-9	0000 1000
9	09	ISK			12-1-8-9	0000 1001
10	0A	SVC	SMM		12-2-8-9	0000 1010
11	0B		VT		12-3-8-9	0000 1011
12	0C		FF		12-4-8-9	0000 1100
13	0D	BASR (4)	CR		12-5-8-9	0000 1101
14	0E		SO		12-6-8-9	0000 1110
15	0F		SI		12-7-8-9	0000 1111
16	10	LPR	DLE		12-11-1-8-9	0001 0000
17	11	LNR	DC1		11-1-9	0001 0001
18	12	LTR	DC2		11-2-9	0001 0010
19	13	LCR	TM		11-3-9	0001 0011
20	14	NR	RES		11-4-9	0001 0100
21	15	CLR	NL		11-5-9	0001 0101
22	16	OR	BS		11-6-9	0001 0110
23	17	XR	IL		11-7-9	0001 0111
24	18	LR	CAN		11-8-9	0001 1000
25	19	CR	EM		11-1-8-9	0001 1001
26	1A	AR	CC		11-2-8-9	0001 1010
27	1B	SR	CU1		11-3-8-9	0001 1011
28	1C	MR	IFS		11-4-8-9	0001 1100
29	1D	DR	IGS		11-5-8-9	0001 1101
30	1E	ALR	IRS		11-6-8-9	0001 1110
31	1F	SLR	IUS		11-7-8-9	0001 1111
32	20	LPDR	DS		11-0-1-8-9	0010 0000
33	21	LNDR	SOS		0-1-9	0010 0001
34	22	LTDR	FS		0-2-9	0010 0010
35	23	LCDR			0-3-9	0010 0011
36	24	HDR	BYP		0-4-9	0010 0100
37	25	LRDR	LF		0-5-9	0010 0101
38	26	MXR	ETB		0-6-9	0010 0110
39	27	MXDR	ESC		0-7-9	0010 0111
40	28	LDR			0-8-9	0010 1000
41	29	CDR			0-1-8-9	0010 1001
42	2A	ADR	SM		0-2-8-9	0010 1010
43	2B	SDR	CU2		0-3-8-9	0010 1011
44	2C	MDR			0-4-8-9	0010 1100
45	2D	DDR	ENQ		0-5-8-9	0010 1101
46	2E	AWR	ACK		0-6-8-9	0010 1110
47	2F	SWR	BEL		0-7-8-9	0010 1111
48	30	LPER			12-11-0-1-8-9	0011 0000
49	31	LNER			1-9	0011 0001
50	32	LTER	SYN		2-9	0011 0010
51	33	LCER			3-9	0011 0011
52	34	HER	PN		4-9	0011 0100
53	35	LRER	RS		5-9	0011 0101
54	36	AXR	UC		6-9	0011 0110
55	37	SXR	EOT		7-9	0011 0111
56	38	LER			8-9	0011 1000
57	39	CER			1-8-9	0011 1001
58	3A	AER			2-8-9	0011 1010
59	3B	SER	CU3		3-8-9	0011 1011
60	3C	MER	DC4		4-8-9	0011 1100
61	3D	DER	NAK		5-8-9	0011 1101
62	3E	AUR			6-8-9	0011 1110
63	3F	SUR	SUB		7-8-9	0011 1111

NOTES FOR PANELS 7 – 10

1. Add C (check bit) for odd or even parity as needed, except as noted
2. For even parity use CA
3. Decimal feature
4. Model 67
5. EBCDIC code required for graphics) + (= and '

RR FORMAT

Decimal	Hexadecimal	Instruction Mnemonic (RX Format)	Graphic & Control Symbols BCDIC	Graphic & Control Symbols EBCDIC	7-Track Tape BCDIC (1)	Punched Card Code	System/360 8-bit Code
64	40	STH		SP	(2)	no punches	0100 0000
65	41	LA				12-0-1-9	0100 0001
66	42	STC				12-0-2-9	0100 0010
67	43	IC				12-0-3-9	0100 0011
68	44	EX				12-0-4-9	0100 0100
69	45	BAL				12-0-5-9	0100 0101
70	46	BCT				12-0-6-9	0100 0110
71	47	BC				12-0-7-9	0100 0111
72	48	LH				12-0-8-9	0100 1000
73	49	CH				12-1-8	0100 1001
74	4A	AH	•	¢		12-2-8	0100 1010
75	4B	SH	•	.	B A 8 21	12-3-8	0100 1011
76	4C	MH	⊓)(5)	<	B A 84	12-4-8	0100 1100
77	4D	BAS (4)	[	(	B A 84 1	12-5-8	0100 1101
78	4E	CVD	<	+	B A 8 4 2	12-6-8	0100 1110
79	4F	CVB	⊞	l	B A 8421	12-7-8	0100 1111
80	50	ST	& + (5)	&	B A	12	0101 0000
81	51					12-11-1-9	0101 0001
82	52					12-11-2-9	0101 0010
83	53					12-11-3-9	0101 0011
84	54	N				12-11-4-9	0101 0100
85	55	CL				12-11-5-9	0101 0101
86	56	O				12-11-6-9	0101 0110
87	57	X				12-11-7-9	0101 0111
88	58	L				12-11-8-9	0101 1000
89	59	C				11-1-8	0101 1001
90	5A	A		!		11-2-8	0101 1010
91	5B	S	$	$	B 8 21	11-3-8	0101 1011
92	5C	M	•	*	B 84	11-4-8	0101 1100
93	5D	D	]	)	B 84 1	11-5-8	0101 1101
94	5E	AL	;	;	B 842	11-6-8	0101 1110
95	5F	SL	Δ	¬	B 8421	11-7-8	0101 1111
96	60	STD	-	-	B	11	0110 0000
97	61		/	/	A 1	0-1	0110 0001
98	62					11-0-2-9	0110 0010
99	63					11-0-3-9	0110 0011
100	64					11-0-4-9	0110 0100
101	65					11-0-5-9	0110 0101
102	66					11-0-6-9	0110 0110
103	67	MXD				11-0-7-9	0110 0111
104	68	LD				11-0-8-9	0110 1000
105	69	CD				0-1-8	0110 1001
106	6A	AD				12-11	0110 1010
107	6B	SD	,	,	A 8 21	0-3-8	0110 1011
108	6C	MD	% ((5)	%	A 84	0-4-8	0110 1100
109	6D	DD	⅄	_	A 84 1	0-5-8	0110 1101
110	6E	AW	\	>	A 842	0-6-8	0110 1110
111	6F	SW	⧻	?	A 8421	0-7-8	0110 1111
112	70	STE				12-11-0	0111 0000
113	71					12-11-0-1-9	0111 0001
114	72					12-11-0-2-9	0111 0010
115	73					12-11-0-3-9	0111 0011
116	74					12-11-0-4-9	0111 0100
117	75					12-11-0-5-9	0111 0101
118	76					12-11-0-6-9	0111 0110
119	77					12-11-0-7-9	0111 0111
120	78	LE				12-11-0-8-9	0111 1000
121	79	CE				1-8	0111 1001
122	7A	AE	ƀ	:	A	2-8	0111 1010
123	7B	SE	# -(5)	#	8 21	3-8	0111 1011
124	7C	ME	@ ' (5)	@	84	4-8	0111 1100
125	7D	DE	:	'	84 1	5-8	0111 1101
126	7E	AU	>	=	842	6-8	0111 1110
127	7F	SU	√	"	8421	7-8	0111 1111

RX FORMAT

Op Code	R₁	X₂	B₂	D₂

0   78   1112 1516 1920   31

R1, D2 (X2, B2) or R1, S2 (X2)
R1, D2 (0, B2) or R1, S2

Decimal	Hexadecimal	Instruction Mnemonic (Var.Formats)	Graphic & Control Symbols BCDIC	EBCDIC	7-Track Tape BCDIC	Punched Card Code	System/360 8-bit Code
128	80	SSM				12-0-1-8	1000 0000
129	81			a		12-0-1	1000 0001
130	82	LPSW		b		12-0-2	1000 0010
131	83	(Diagnose)		c		12-0-3	1000 0011
132	84	WRD		d		12-0-4	1000 0100
133	85	RDD		e		12-0-5	1000 0101
134	86	BXH		f		12-0-6	1000 0110
135	87	BXLE		g		12-0-7	1000 0111
136	88	SRL		h		12-0-8	1000 1000
137	89	SLL		i		12-0-9	1000 1001
138	8A	SRA				12-0-2-8	1000 1010
139	8B	SLA				12-0-3-8	1000 1011
140	8C	SRDL				12-0-4-8	1000 1100
141	8D	SLDL				12-0-5-8	1000 1101
142	8E	SRDA				12-0-6-8	1000 1110
143	8F	SLDA				12-0-7-8	1000 1111
144	90	STM				12-11-1-8	1001 0000
145	91	TM		j		12-11-1	1001 0001
146	92	MVI		k		12-11-2	1001 0010
147	93	TS		l		12-11-3	1001 0011
148	94	NI		m		12-11-4	1001 0100
149	95	CLI		n		12-11-5	1001 0101
150	96	OI		o		12-11-6	1001 0110
151	97	XI		p		12-11-7	1001 0111
152	98	LM		q		12-11-8	1001 1000
153	99			r		12-11-9	1001 1001
154	9A					12-11-2-8	1001 1010
155	9B					12-11-3-8	1001 1011
156	9C	SIO				12-11-4-8	1001 1100
157	9D	TIO				12-11-5-8	1001 1101
158	9E	HIO				12-11-6-8	1001 1110
159	9F	TCH				12-11-7-8	1001 1111
160	A0					11-0-1-8	1010 0000
161	A1					11-0-1	1010 0001
162	A2			s		11-0-2	1010 0010
163	A3			t		11-0-3	1010 0011
164	A4			u		11-0-4	1010 0100
165	A5			v		11-0-5	1010 0101
166	A6			w		11-0-6	1010 0110
167	A7			x		11-0-7	1010 0111
168	A8			y		11-0-8	1010 1000
169	A9			z		11-0-9	1010 1001
170	AA					11-0-2-8	1010 1010
171	AB					11-0-3-8	1010 1011
172	AC					11-0-4-8	1010 1100
173	AD					11-0-5-8	1010 1101
174	AE					11-0-6-8	1010 1110
175	AF					11-0-7-8	1010 1111
176	B0	STMC (4)				12-11-0-1-8	1011 0000
177	B1	LRA (4)				12-11-0-1	1011 0001
178	B2					12-11-0-2	1011 0010
179	B3					12-11-0-3	1011 0011
180	B4					12-11-0-4	1011 0100
181	B5					12-11-0-5	1011 0101
182	B6					12-11-0-6	1011 0110
183	B7					12-11-0-7	1011 0111
184	B8	LMC (4)				12-11-0-8	1011 1000
185	B9					12-11-0-9	1011 1001
186	BA					12-11-0-2-8	1011 1010
187	BB					12-11-0-3-8	1011 1011
188	BC					12-11-0-4-8	1011 1100
189	BD					12-11-0-5-8	1011 1101
190	BE					12-11-0-6-8	1011 1110
191	BF					12-11-0-7-8	1011 1111

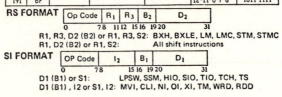

RS FORMAT

| Op Code | R₁ | R₃ | B₂ | D₂ |

0   78   11 12   15 16   19 20   31

R1, R3, D2 (B2) or R1, R3, S2: BXH, BXLE, LM, LMC, STM, STMC
R1, D2 (B2) or R1, S2: All shift instructions

SI FORMAT

| OP Code | I₂ | B₁ | D₁ |

0   78   15 16   19 20   31

D1 (B1) or S1: LPSW, SSM, HIO, SIO, TIO, TCH, TS
D1 (B1) , I2 or S1, I2: MVI, CLI, NI, OI, XI, TM, WRD, RDD

Decimal	Hexadecimal	Instruction Mnemonic (SS Format)	Graphic & Control Symbols BCDIC	Graphic & Control Symbols EBCDIC	7-Track Tape BCDIC (1)	Punched Card Code	System/360 8-bit Code
192	C0		?		B A 8 2	12-0	1100 0000
193	C1		A	A	B A 1	12-1	1100 0001
194	C2		B	B	B A 2	12-2	1100 0010
195	C3		C	C	B A 2 1	12-3	1100 0011
196	C4		D	D	B A 4	12-4	1100 0100
197	C5		E	E	B A 4 1	12-5	1100 0101
198	C6		F	F	B A 4 2	12-6	1100 0110
199	C7		G	G	B A 4 2 1	12-7	1100 0111
200	C8		H	H	B A 8	12-8	1100 1000
201	C9		I	I	B A 8 1	12-9	1100 1001
202	CA					12-0-2-8-9	1100 1010
203	CB					12-0-3-8-9	1100 1011
204	CC					12-0-4-8-9	1100 1100
205	CD					12-0-5-8-9	1100 1101
206	CE					12-0-6-8-9	1100 1110
207	CF					12-0-7-8-9	1100 1111
208	D0	MVN	!		B 8 2	11-0	1101 0000
209	D1	MVC	J	J	B 1	11-1	1101 0001
210	D2	MVZ	K	K	B 2	11-2	1101 0010
211	D3		L	L	B 2 1	11-3	1101 0011
212	D4	NC	M	M	B 4	11-4	1101 0100
213	D5	CLC	N	N	B 4 1	11-5	1101 0101
214	D6	OC	O	O	B 4 2	11-6	1101 0110
215	D7	XC	P	P	B 4 2 1	11-7	1101 0111
216	D8		Q	Q	B 8	11-8	1101 1000
217	D9		R	R	B 8 1	11-9	1101 1001
218	DA					12-11-2-8-9	1101 1010
219	DB					12-11-3-8-9	1101 1011
220	DC	TR				12-11-4-8-9	1101 1100
221	DD	TRT				12-11-5-8-9	1101 1101
222	DE	ED (3)				12-11-6-8-9	1101 1110
223	DF	EDMK (3)				12-11-7-8-9	1101 1111
224	E0		+		A 8 2	0-2-8	1110 0000
225	E1					11-0-1-9	1110 0001
226	E2		S	S	A 2	0-2	1110 0010
227	E3		T	T	A 2 1	0-3	1110 0011
228	E4		U	U	A 4	0-4	1110 0100
229	E5		V	V	A 4 1	0-5	1110 0101
230	E6		W	W	A 4 2	0-6	1110 0110
231	E7		X	X	A 4 2 1	0-7	1110 0111
232	E8		Y	Y	A 8	0-8	1110 1000
233	E9		Z	Z	A 8 1	0-9	1110 1001
234	EA					11-0-2-8-9	1110 1010
235	EB					11-0-3-8-9	1110 1011
236	EC					11-0-4-8-9	1110 1100
237	ED					11-0-5-8-9	1110 1101
238	EE					11-0-6-8-9	1110 1110
239	EF					11-0-7-8-9	1110 1111
240	F0		0	0	8 2	0	1111 0000
241	F1	MVO	1	1	1	1	1111 0001
242	F2	PACK	2	2	2	2	1111 0010
243	F3	UNPK	3	3	2 1	3	1111 0011
244	F4		4	4	4	4	1111 0100
245	F5		5	5	4 1	5	1111 0101
246	F6		6	6	4 2	6	1111 0110
247	F7		7	7	4 2 1	7	1111 0111
248	F8	ZAP (3)	8	8	8	8	1111 1000
249	F9	CP (3)	9	9	8 1	9	1111 1001
250	FA	AP (3)				12-11-0-2-8-9	1111 1010
251	FB	SP (3)				12-11-0-3-8-9	1111 1011
252	FC	MP (3)				12-11-0-4-8-9	1111 1100
253	FD	DP (3)				12-11-0-5-8-9	1111 1101
254	FE					12-11-0-6-8-9	1111 1110
255	FF					12-11-0-7-8-9	1111 1111

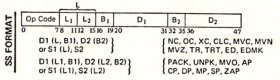

SS FORMAT

| L | | | | | | | |

| Op Code | L₁ | L₂ | B₁ | D₁ | B₂ | D₂ |

0   7 8   11 12   15 16   19 20   31 32   35 36   47

D1 (L, B1), D2 (B2) } { NC, OC, XC, CLC, MVC, MVN
or S1 (L); S2   } { MVZ, TR, TRT, ED, EDMK

D1 (L1, B1), D2 (L2, B2) } { PACK, UNPK, MVO, AP
or S1 (L1); S2 (L2)   } { CP, DP, MP, SP, ZAP

⑪

CHANNEL ADDRESS WORD

Key	0000	Command Address
0 3	4 7	8 15 16 23 24 31

CHANNEL COMMAND WORD

Command Code	Data Address
0 7	8 15 16 23 24 31

Flags	000	/////////	Byte Count
32 36	37 39	40 47 48	55 56 63

CD   Bit 32 (80) causes use of address portion of next CCW
CC   Bit 33 (40) causes use of command code and data address of next CCW
SLI   Bit 34 (20) causes suppression of possible incorrect length indication
SKIP Bit 35 (10) suppresses transfer of information to main storage
PCI   Bit 36 (08) causes an interruption as Program Control Interrupt

CHANNEL STATUS WORD

Key	0000	Command Address
0 3	4 7	8 15 16 23 24 31

Status	Byte Count
32 39 40	47 48 55 56 63

32 (8000) Attention	40 (0080) Program-controlled interruption
33 (4000) Status modifier	41 (0040) Incorrect length
34 (2000) Control unit end	42 (0020) Program check
35 (1000) Busy	43 (0010) Protection check
36 (0800) Channel end	44 (0008) Channel data check
37 (0400) Device end	45 (0004) Channel control check
38 (0200) Unit check	46 (0002) Interface control check
39 (0100) Unit exception	47 (0001) Chaining check

Byte Count: bits 48-63 form the residual count for the last CCW used.

DASD CHANNEL COMMAND CODES (see GA26-5988 and GA26-3599)

Command for CCW		Count	M-T Off Hex	M-T Off Dec	M-T On Hex	M-T On Dec
Control	No Op	Not Zero	03	03		
	Seek	6	07	07		
	Seek Cylinder	6	0B	11		
	Seek Head	6	1B	27		
	Set File Mask	1	1F	31		
	Space Count	Not Zero	0F	15		
	Transfer in Channel	X	X8			
	Recalibrate (Note 1)	Not Zero	13	19		
	Restore (2321 only)	X	17	23		
Sense	Sense I/O	6	04	04		
Switching	Release Device } (Note 2)	Not Zero	94	148		
	Reserve Device	Not Zero	B4	180		
Search†	Home Address EQ	4 (usually)	39	57	B9	185
	Identifier EQ	5 (usually)	31	49	B1	177
	Identifier HI	5 (usually)	51	81	D1	209
	Identifier EQ or HI	5 (usually)	71	131	F1	241
	Key EQ	1 to 255	29	41	A9	169
	Key HI	1 to 255	49	73	C9	201
	Key EQ or HI	1 to 255	69	105	E9	233
	Key & Data EQ		2D	45	AD	173
	Key & Data HI		4D	77	CD	205
	Key & Data EQ or HI		6D	109	ED	237
Continue Scan	Search EQ		25	37	A5	165
	Search HI	(Note 3)	45	69	C5	197
	Search HI or EQ		65	101	E5	229
	Set Status Modifier*		35	53	B5	181
	Set Status Modifier*		75	117	F5	245
	No Status Modifier		55	85	D5	213
Read†	Home Address	5	1A	26	9A	154
	Count	8	12	18	92	146
	Record R0		16	22	96	150
	Data	Number	06	06	86	134
	Key & Data	of bytes	0E	14	8E	142
	Count, Key & Data	transferred	1E	30	9E	158
	IPL		02	02		
Write	Home Address	5 (usually)	19	25		
	Record R0	8+KL+DL of R0	15	21		
	Count, Key & Data	8+KL+DL	1D	29		
	Special Count, Key & Data	8+KL+DL	01	01		
	Data	DL	05	05		
	Key & Data	KL+DL	0D	13		
	Erase	8+KL+DL	11	17		

X = not significant
Note 1. For 2311 or 2314 only.
Note 2. Two-channel switch required except for a 2314/2844 combination.
Note 3. Include mask bytes in search

argument; these commands are a special feature on 2841.
*Sense byte determines command used.
†M-T On = M-T Off except during Search and Read, bit 0 = 1 in M-T On.

CHANNEL COMMAND CODES

⑫

Device	Command for CCW	0	1	2	3	4	5	6	7	Hex	Dec
1052	Read Inquiry BCD	0	0	0	0	1	0	1	0	0A	10
	Read Reader 2 BCD	0	0	0	0	0	0	1	0	02	02
	Write BCD, Auto Carriage Return	0	0	0	0	1	0	0	1	09	09
	Write BCD, No Auto Carriage Return	0	0	0	0	0	0	0	1	01	01
	No Op	0	0	0	0	0	0	1	1	03	03
	Sense	0	0	0	0	1	0	0	0	04	04
	Alarm	0	0	0	0	1	0	1	1	0B	11

Device	Command for CCW		0	1	2	3	4	5	6	7
2540	Read, Feed, Select Stacker SS	Type AA	S	S	D	0	0	0	1	0
	Read	Type AB	1	1	D	0	0	0	1	0
	Read, Feed (1400 compatability mode only)		1	1	D	1	0	0	1	0
	Feed, Select Stacker SS	Type BA	S	S	1	0	0	0	1	1
	PFR Punch, Feed, Select Stacker SS	Type BA	S	S	D	1	0	0	0	1
	Punch, Feed, Select Stacker SS	Type BB	S	S	D	0	0	0	0	1

SS	Stacker	D	Data Mode
00	R1	0	EBCDIC
01	R2	1	Column Binary
10	RP3		

1442·N1

	M	M	M	M		Read	M	M	M	0	0	0	1	0
Read	0	0	X		Eject and SS1	Write	M	M	M	0	0	0	0	1
Read	1	0	X		Eject and SS1	Control	M	M	0	0	0	0	1	1
Read	0	1	X		Eject and SS2	No Op	0	0	0	0	0	0	1	1
Read	1	1	X		Eject and SS2	Sense	0	0	M	M	0	1	0	0
Write	0	0	X		SS1									
Write	1	0	X		Eject and SS1									
Write	0	1	X		SS2	X = 0 means EBCDIC mode								
Write	1	1	X		Eject and SS2	X = 1 means Column Binary Mode								
Control	1	0			Eject and SS1									
Control	0	1			SS2									
Control	1	1			Eject and SS2									
Sense				1	1 Punch diagnostic									
Sense			0	1	1 Read diagnostic									

Device	Command for CCW	0	1	2	3	4	5	6	7	Hex	Dec
1403 or 1443	Write, No Space	0	0	0	0	0	0	0	1	01	01
	Write, Space 1 After Print	0	0	0	0	1	0	0	1	09	09
	Write, Space 2 After Print	0	0	0	1	0	0	0	1	11	17
	Write, Space 3 After Print	0	0	0	1	1	0	0	1	19	25
	Write, Skip To Channel N After Print	1	C	H	A	N	0	0	1		
	Diagnostic Read (1403)	0	0	0	0	0	0	1	0	02	02
	Diagnostic Read (1443)	0	0	0	0	0	1	1	0	06	06
	Sense	0	0	0	0	1	0	0	0	04	04

Device	Command for CCW	0	1	2	3	4	5	6	7	Hex	Dec
Carriage Control	Space 1 Line Immediately	0	0	0	0	1	0	1	1	0B	11
	Space 2 Line Immediately	0	0	0	1	0	0	1	1	13	19
	Space 3 Line Immediately	0	0	0	1	1	0	1	1	1B	27
	Skip To Channel N Immediately	1	C	H	A	N	0	1	1		
	No Op	0	0	0	0	0	0	1	1	03	03

C	H	A	N	Channel		C	H	A	N	Channel
0	0	0	1	1		0	1	1	1	7
0	0	1	0	2		1	0	0	0	8
0	0	1	1	3		1	0	0	1	9
0	1	0	0	4		1	0	1	0	10
0	1	0	1	5		1	0	1	1	11
0	1	1	0	6		1	1	0	0	12

Device	Command for CCW	0	1	2	3	4	5	6	7	Hex	Dec
UCS	Allow buffer loading	1	1	1	0	1	0	1	1	EB	235
	Load buffer (no folding)	1	1	1	1	1	0	1	1	FB	251
	Load buffer (folding)	1	1	1	1	0	0	1	1	F3	243
	Block data check latch	0	1	1	1	0	0	1	1	73	115
	Reset block data check latch	0	1	1	1	1	0	1	1	7B	123

Device	Command for CCW	0	1	2	3	4	5	6	7	Hex	Dec
2400 Tape*	Read Backward (Overrides Data Converter On)	0	0	0	0	1	1	0	0	0C	12
	Sense	0	0	0	0	0	1	0	0	04	04
	Write	N N N	0	0	0	0	0	0	0	1	01	01
		0 0 0	1600 bpi P.E. **									
	Read	0 0 1	800 bpi NRZI	0	0	0	0	0	0	1	0	02	02
				0	0	C	C	C	1	1	1		
	Control		D	D	M	M	M	0	1	1		
			1	1	N	N	N	0	1	1		

C	C	C	Control Codes	Hex	Dec		D	D	7 Track Density		Set Density	Set Odd Parity	Set Even Parity	Data Converter On	Data Converter Off	Translator On	Translator Off	Request TIE (Track in Error)
0	0	0	REW	7	7		0	0	200									
0	0	1	RUN	0F	15		0	1	556	7 Track								
0	1	0	ERG	17	23		1	0	800**									
0	1	1	WTM	1F	31		1	1	***									
1	0	0	BSR	27	39													
1	0	1	BSF	2F	47		M	M	M (Mode Modifiers)									
1	1	0	FSR	37	55		0	0	0 No Op		—	—	—	—	—	—	—	
1	1	1	FSF	3F	63		0	0	1 Not Used									

*9 track op. forces 800 BPI and odd parity; also, it overrides 7 track but does not reset 7 track. Load/Sys Reset forces 7 track to 800 BPI, odd parity, data converter on, translator off.

** Reset condition

*** Set 9 Track mode, Models 4-6

	D	D			Set Density	Set Odd Parity	Set Even Parity	Data Converter On	Data Converter Off	Translator On	Translator Off	Request TIE
0	1	0	Reset Condition		X	X		X			X	
0	1	1	Nine-track only									X
1	0	0			X		X		X		X	
1	0	1			X		X		X	X		
1	1	0	Reset Condition		X	X		X			X	
1	1	1			X	X		X		X	X	

appendix b

linkage conventions

1. SAVING AND RESTORING REGISTER CONTENTS

According to the conventions established for the IBM System/360, when every program and/or subroutine returns control to the program that called it, the contents of general registers 2 through 14 must be the same as when the routine was entered. Therefore, it is standard programming practice to save the values contained in the general registers as soon as a routine is entered, and then restore those values prior to returning control. Thus, as control is passed from the operating system to a problem program and to subprograms, the contents of the registers are preserved at each stage.

The following general registers have specifically assigned roles when performing program linkages:

Register 15 — Entry point in the called program
(may contain a return code on return)
Register 14 — Return location in the calling program
Register 13 — Address of a save area where the called program can save the general registers
Registers 0 — Optional facility to pass parameters (register 1 usually contains
and 1   the address of a list of addresses; each address specifies a parameter)

2. SAVE AREA

Whenever control is transferred to a subprogram, the calling program, by convention, must provide a "save area" to the called program for storing the general registers. Register 13, the "save area register," must be loaded with the address of a save area before any calling sequence is executed. The save areas are linked or chained together as control is progressively transferred to lower-level programs. Register contents can then be restored as control is returned to the higher-level programs. The save area occupies 18 fullwords, must be aligned on a fullword boundary, and has the following standard format (Fig. B.1).

Word	Displacement	Contents
1	0	Indicator used only for PL/I programs
2	4	Address of save area in calling program (previous)
3	8	Address of save area in called program (next)
4	12	Return address (register 14)
5	16	Entry point (register 15)
6	20	Register 0
7	24	Register 1
8	28	Register 2
9	32	Register 3
10	36	Register 4
11	40	Register 5
12	44	Register 6
13	48	Register 7
14	52	Register 8
15	56	Register 9
16	60	Register 10
17	64	Register 11
18	68	Register 12

FIGURE B.1 Contents of first 18 words of save area

3. STANDARD SYSTEM LINKAGE

The entry linkage requires four functions:

1. Storing the contents of registers 14, 15, and 0 through 12 in the save area pointed to by register 13.
2. Establishing a base register.
3. Loading the address of a save area into register 13.
4. Storing addresses to chain save areas.

At completion, return linkage requires:

1. Restoring address of calling program's save area in register 13.
2. Restoring registers 14, 15, and 0 to 12, and return.

The coding sequence that follows illustrates standard linkage requirements on entry and exit from assembly language programs:

```
EXAMPLE    START
           USING      *,15
           STM        14,12,12(13)     Save registers
           LR         11,13            Copy SAVEAREA address
           LA         13,SAVEAREA      Get new SAVEAREA address
           ST         13,8(0,11)       Put address of SAVEAREA in
                                          calling program
           ST         11,4(0,13)       Put address of calling program
                                          SAVEAREA in our SAVEAREA
           .
           .
           .
           L          13,4(0,13)       Restore original SAVEAREA
                                          address
           LM         14,12,12(13)     Restore registers
           BR         14               Return to caller
SAVEAREA   DS         18F
           END
```

Note: The lowest level subroutine, a subroutine that calls no other subroutines, can use an abbreviated sequence since it need not establish a new save area:

```
EXAMPLE    START
           USING      *,15
           STM        14,12,12(13) save registers
           .
           .
           .
           LM         14,12,12(13) restore registers
           BR         14
           END
```

4. SAMPLE PROGRAM LINKAGE

To illustrate the complete process of subroutine linkage, the simple FORTRAN subroutines below have been translated into corresponding assembly language using standard linkage conventions.

```
//     EXEC     FORTRAN
       INTEGER   I,J,SUM
       DO    100      I = 1, 25
       DO    100      J = 1, 50
       CALL      ADD(SUM,I,J)
100    CONTINUE
       END

//     EXEC     FORTRAN
       SUBROUTINE  ADD (X,Y,Z)
       INTEGER      X,Y,Z
       X = Y + Z
       RETURN
       END
```

Assembly language equivalent of "MAIN"

```
MAIN    START
        USING       *,15
        STM         14,12,12(13)
        LR          11,13
        LA          13,SAVE
        ST          13,8(0,11)
        ST          11,4(0,13)
        DROP        15
        BALR        10,0
        USING       *,10
IC      EQU         4
JC      EQU         5
IR      EQU         6
JR      EQU         7
        L           IC,=F'25'
        L           IR,=F'1'
ILOOP   L           JC,=F'50'
        L           JR,=F'1'
JLOOP   ST          IR,I
        ST          JR,J
        LA          1,ARGS
        L           15,=V(ADD)
        BALR        14,15
        A           JR,=F'1'
        BCT         JC,JLOOP
        A           IR,=F'1'
        BCT         IC,ILOOP
        L           13,4(0,13)
        LM          14,12,12(13)
        BR          14
SUM     DS          F
J       DS          F
I       DS          F
ARGS    DC          A(SUM,I,J)
SAVE    DS          18F
        END
```

At entry to ADD, the parameters are passed as diagrammed below:

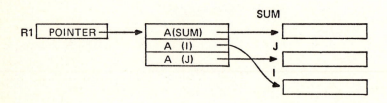

Assembly language equivalent of "ADD"

```
ADD    START
       STM        14,12,12(13)
       BALR       BASE,0
       USING      *,BASE
AC     EQU        8
ADDR   EQU        9
BASE   EQU        10
       L          ADDR,4(0,1)
       L          AC,0(0,ADDR)      AC   ←    I
       L          ADDR,8(0,1)
       A          AC,0(0,ADDR)      AC   ←    AC + J
       L          ADDR,0(0,1)
       ST         AC,0(0,ADDR)      SUM  ←    AC
       LM         14,12,12(13)
       BR         14
       END
```

Note that the MAIN program obeys the same conventions as subroutines. The MAIN program actually is a subroutine of the operating system.

5. IMPLEMENTATION OF ARGUMENT HANDLING

As we have noted in Chapter 8, in most high level languages there is a prologue that initializes the subroutine. Amongst the tasks of the prologue is the handling of parameters that are passed. On the 360, in particular, as shown above, parameters are passed by a special register (e.g., R1), which points to a list of addresses. The called program may wish to access these parameters in several different ways. We will briefly describe these ways.

1. The called program may essentially indirect through the parameter register (R1) to get the address of appropriate parameters. This technique has the advantage of no overhead for the prologue, i.e., the register 1 contains all necessary information. But it has two disadvantages:
   a) The pointer register, R1, must not be altered.
   b) Every access may have to do an indirection. Note that this is the technique we have used in the above FORTRAN program (e.g., L ADDR, 4 (0, 1) then L AC, 0 (0, ADDR) to get I).
2. The prologue may copy the argument list (the list of addresses) into some stack or storage area used by the called program. Now the pointer register, R1, is free, but we still have the disadvantage of accessing through an indirection, and now the prologue has a small overhead. This technique is normally used by the IBM PL/I (F) version 5 compiler.

3. The prologue may copy the actual values of argument variables into some storage area associated with the called program. The advantage of this is that the pointer register is free and no indirection is needed for accessing. However, the disadvantage is that more overhead is required in the prologue and it may be necessary to recopy the values of the arguments on the return. This technique was assumed in compilation of the MINI-PL/I of Figure 8.1.

Programming languages in general may specify three policies for argument passing, which require different implementations.

1. "Call by location" (also called "call by address" or "call by reference"): language specifies that the item passed is the address of the argument, (e.g., FORTRAN example above) which can be implemented using either technique 1 or 2 above.

2. "Call by value": language specifies that the item passed is the value of the arguments, which can be implemented using technique 3.

3. "Call by name": language specifies that each time an argument is used, its current value is recomputed, as ALGOL 60 specifies.

Note the PL/I (F) version 5 compiler, when compiling the MINI-PL/I program used as our example for Chapter 8 (Figure 8.1), will give a warning error message. We have stated in the PROCEDURE statement that RATE, START, FINISH are arguments passed to this program. Yet in the next statement we have declared storage for them in this program.

This is not consistent with a "call by location" strategy, but it does simplify the compilation of the example program for our demonstration purposes.

index

(Numbers in boldface indicate pages containing
the main discussion of a particular entry.)